CAVALRYMAN OUT OF THE WEST

General William C. Brown, from a photograph by Pach Bros., New York.

CAVALRYMAN OUT OF THE WEST

Life of General William Carey Brown

by

GEORGE FRANCIS BRIMLOW

THE CAXTON PRINTERS, LTD.
CALDWELL, IDAHO
1944

Printed, lithographed, and bound in the United States of America by
The CAXTON PRINTERS, Ltd.
Caldwell, Idaho
59984

To
My Mother, Agnes Willetts Brimlow
Sisters, Mary and Frances
Brother, Morgan

and

Francis (Cotton-Top),
boy of sunny Tennessee, who became
a contributor of immeasurable joy.

Author's Preface

I NEVER met General Brown face to face. I wanted to chat with him. Fate decreed otherwise. Yet one does not have to meet a man to know him, to rely upon him, to call him a friend.

By letter, I introduced myself to the veteran Cavalryman of Denver in November of 1934, seeking his counsel in preparation of a Master of Arts thesis on the Bannock Indian War of 1878. From that time forward we corresponded frequently. He, as well as Dr. Robert Carlton Clark of the University of Oregon, my scholarly adviser, realized there was a paucity of accurate material for my writing task. In manuscripts and documents placed at my disposal, I faced an abundance of discrepancies. Essential, therefore, were data which General Brown sent to me, data on which I could rely for an impartial story approaching the goal of accuracy.

After I had completed my thesis, General Brown and Dr. Clark encouraged me to revise and elaborate upon it for publication as a case study. The book was not long off the press when both men relinquished earthly tasks.

Meanwhile, General Brown had told me much about others, but little of himself. He had given assent to none who desired to write the story of his life. I urged him to send me material dealing with highlights of his career. This he did, at the same time expressing his desire to do an autobiography that would be more accurate than boastful.

Two months before Brown's death on May 8, 1939,

Colonel James Boyd wrote me in regard to the General, of whose estate he was named executor:

"I do know that there has been nothing in his actions in the past that he would not care to have published if they are correct and I am sure that, from what he has told me of you, he has sufficient respect for your passion for facts that you have ascertained the truth of your statements. . . . . I trust that at some future time you will be able to write a book on his career, which he will never be able to do."

I answered soon thereafter that I planned to come to Denver in June to interview the General. Mrs. Ora McDaniel, a friend, relayed the contents of my letter to the dying campaigner in the third-story apartment of his home. She sent me his last penciled message, in two feebly written sentences, without punctuation:

Reply
    Unable to converse but could answer questions if alive
    Am very low & liable to go at any time
                               W C Brown

When in June I climbed stairs and entered the General's den, a treasure house of history, I found it as he had left it, meticulous, inviting. Immediately I felt at home. Humbly, I realized I had a task to perform, a labor of love.

So I have written of a man who lived courageously, unselfishly, without enmity, unaware of his own enduring stature.

To individuals as well as institutions I offer acknowledgments for loyal assistance and encouragement in the writing of this book. Especially do I owe a debt of gratitude to Colonel Boyd for his sanction of the work, his placing in my hands of necessary documentary material, and his confidence in its fashioning. Colonel John G. Knauer, Medical Corps, has shown hearty appreciation in giving research aid, advice, and criticism. Cheerful and prompt

assistance came from General Charles D. Rhodes and
Captain William L. Kost, tireless officials of the Association of Graduates of the United States Military Academy.
Letters of General George Van Horn Moseley conveyed
valuable reminiscences. Colonel R. Ernest Dupuy, Chief
of News Division, Bureau of Public Relations, War Department, kindly granted permission to quote from his
Where They Have Trod. It is a book which, like Colonel
W. A. Ganoe's *History of the United States Army*, goes far
beyond animated reference.

In no small measure was personal co-operation given by
Dr. P. M. Hamer, Chief of Division of Reference of The
National Archives, by his assistants, by the staffs of the
Historical Section, Army War College, and by the Library
of Congress. Resources at their disposal provided rich ma-
terial for study and use.

Among authorities in fields of history, who responded
unhesitantly to requests for verification of documentary
sources, Dr. Paul C. Phillips, head of the History Department, University of Montana, gave erudite opinion. Dr.
Percy S. Fritz, History Department, University of Colorado, generously yielded of his time and talent to the reading of the manuscript and in strengthening its revision.
Stimulating was the cordiality of Dr. Dan E. Clark, head
of the History Department, University of Oregon, and
members of his staff.

For essential information thanks are returned particular-
ly to Mrs. M. B. Nash and Mr. J. A. Harrington of the Ida-
ho Historical Society; to Librarian Nellie B. Pipes and Mr.
James J. Donegan of the Oregon Historical Society; to the
Public Library, La Grande, Ore.; the Nevada State
Library; the University of Tennessee and Tennessee State
Libraries; to the editors of *Winners of the West*, St. Joseph,
Mo.; to the Herald Publishing Company, St. Peter, Minn.;
and to George T. Mayer of Highland Falls, N. Y., for use
of his father's unpublished diary of the Bannock War.

To Velma Ardell Young is extended appreciation for her interest in numerous tasks.

The gracious helpfulness rendered by Florence J. Parisot and Nettie R. Logan in completion of this work cannot be fully measured in mention accorded here.

GEORGE FRANCIS BRIMLOW.

Blue River, Oregon.

Foreword

TO BUT few officers of our army has been accorded the
privilege of leading the usefully industrious, constructive military life experienced by William Carey Brown
throughout his more than eighty years of service to his
country. From early boyhood until finally incapacitated
physically after army retirement, his was a temperament
and nature that brooked no idleness, physical or mental,
and which chafed at inactivity.

Some half dozen classes at the United States Military
Academy, which included names of many who later distinguished themselves in battle operations, remember
"Lieutenant W. C. Brown, Adjutant" best by what they
were wont to call his "pernicious activity"; reporting
cadets for minor irregularities, in which task he was deemed
indefatigable. However, Major General Kuhn, of distinguished military record, and at one time a cadet during
Brown's tour as Adjutant at the Academy, remembered
him "as a most faithful, conscientious, and hard-working
officer."

For his was a mentality continually on the alert to improve existing conditions. His studies led him to prepare
and publish many articles on professional subjects, and, in
his later years, to devote much time and effort to research
work in American history, with especially valuable results
in locating and mapping accurately the sites of many Indian battlefields which, through the years, had been well-
nigh forgotten or obliterated by the march of civilization.

The more notable of General Brown's published writings

were: "Aluminum and Its Alloys for Military Equipment"
(1896); "Equipment for Officers in the Field" (1893);
"The Military Academy and Education of Officers"
(1895); "Reorganization and Graded Retirement for
Cavalry" (1896); "The Diary of a Captain, Kept in
the Santiago Campaign" (1898); "The Carbine versus the
Rifle" (1899); "Experimental Firing with the U. S. Magazine Rifle, Model 1903" (1905); "Rifle Practice in Australia" (1907); "Australian Horses for the Philippines"
(1907); "Notes on Cavalry Equipment" (1907); "The
Cavalry Pack" (1908); "Notes of a Trip Through Java
and India" (1909); "Report on the Mobilization of the
National Guard" (1916); "History of the Sheepeater
Campaign in Idaho, 1879" (1926); and "Old Traverse des
Sioux" (1929).

From "Small Town Schoolboy" to Brigadier General in
our democratic army, Brown ever made rich use of his
opportunities; and exemplified in a high degree the motto
of the Military Academy—devotion to "Duty, Honor, and
Country."

CHARLES DUDLEY RHODES,
Major General, U. S. Army, Retired

Washington, D. C.
September 1, 1942

Contents

Illustrations

CAVALRYMAN OUT OF THE WEST

CHAPTER I

In Youth

THE blood of frontiersman and soldier flowed with tidal power in the veins of William Carey Brown's progenitors. The great-great-great-grandfather, George Brown, was a tiller of virgin soil at Cambridge, Pennsylvania, in 1752. William Brown, great-great-grandfather, went to battle with the Pennsylvania Militia against Indians, and he fought with Washington's troops at Yorktown. Pioneers, too, were great-grandparents, George and Alice (Hardesty) Brown, and grandparents, William and Mary Magdalene (Young) Brown.

From the resolute Cope family of Philadelphia came Edith Piersol, great-grandmother. Religiously, the Piersols clung to the Quaker faith. The Browns were Scotch dissenters of Irish lineage. Their names came to the forefront in Ohio, in political arenas, in churches, and in schools. An uncle, P. Y. Brown, gained prestige in Negley, and the Reverend W. K. Brown was to serve as president of Cincinnati Wesleyan College.

William Carey Brown's parents were Garretson Addison and Sue (Carey) Brown, the former born in December, 1829, and the latter in September, 1832. At the age of twenty-four, Garretson confessed his love for Sue Carey. But land in eastern Ohio, where they lived, was advancing in price. People were moving westward to the Mississippi River and beyond, building a new empire. So in 1853 the young ambitious suitor journeyed to Minnesota to "spy out the land." Quickly, he envisioned new opportunities. He returned to Ohio and on March 8, 1854, married the girl who was prepared to leave her people.

That year the couple had a long boat trip down the Ohio River, then up the Mississippi. The last leg of the journey, from Shakopee to Traverse des Sioux (Crossing of the Sioux), was by oxcart. The bridegroom, industrious and thrifty, had some money to invest. Between the time of arrival and 1857, when he entered the livestock business, the husband operated The Northwest Emporium, a mercantile establishment. He became postmaster for a brief period, and from 1859 to 1868 served as judge of probate, Nicollet County. The county was named for the intrepid Jean N. Nicollet, who explored the region in 1838 with John C. Frémont, famed "Pathmarker of the West."

There is no settlement of Traverse des Sioux in this day, but before and for some time after the arrival of the white man in the country of the Dakotas, its location was one of importance. "Oiyuwega," or "Crossing," was the name given by the Indians to this place where an ancient trail led from the forests of eastern Minnesota to cross the Minnesota River. Here, where a convenient fording was possible, a trading post had been erected in the last half of the eighteenth century, a forerunner of others.

In 1846, white men found the young but wise Chief Red Iron heading the Sisseton village at Traverse des Sioux. A year previously, this chief and his brother, displaying signs of progress, had each built a log cabin, barn, and storehouse for products harvested from a few cultivated acres of land.

By midyear of 1850 the first steamer had paddled its way to the crossing. Three years later, the last train of the famed Red River carts, made entirely of wood and rawhide, stopped there to transfer pemmican and furs to flatboats which floated down to St. Louis. This trade soon was shifted direct to St. Paul. The village of 1850, with three white mission buildings and Indian tents and lodges, was not long in adding others to its thirty residents on the prairie which sloped gently back from the river's edge.

In July, 1851, under a sheltering bower of foliage at Traverse des Sioux, a few federal commissioners and other white men negotiated successfully an all-important treaty with Red Iron and powerful fellow chieftains. As a result of the agreement, the Sioux ceded to the whites some 24,-000,000 acres of rich agricultural lands, comprising more than half the area of Minnesota, along with large slices of Iowa and South Dakota. Encamped upon the ridges encircling the place of treaty at the time of its signing were 7,500 interested Indians. There they witnessed the first step in their withdrawal to reservations.

Present at the historical event was a man whom William Brown was to meet many years later in Baltimore. Frank Barnwell Mayer, artist, had come with the Treaty Commission to sketch the colorful scenes and personages. His work, when rediscovered, would prove of high value.

By the time the treaty was confirmed on July 31, 1853, Traverse des Sioux had registered a healthy growth. In 1852 it had gained a post office, half a dozen stores, a church, and more residences. The next year came new warehouses, the erection of sawmills near by, and an influx of settlers and businessmen, making for a population of 200. A newspaper, which thrived only for a few months, was welcomed in September, 1857, and when 1858 rolled around, 300 persons made their homes in the village.

William, the first of four children, arrived at the Brown home December 19, 1854. He was the second white boy to be born in Nicollet County. His only brother, Frankie, came into the world October 8, 1857.

Then dissolution befell the town of their birth at the river's slippery banks. On October 12, 1858, an election fight over the location of the county seat, between Traverse des Sioux and its newly prosperous neighbor, St. Peter, was won by people favoring the latter townsite. Soon the majority of citizens at the crossing transferred themselves and their buildings to St. Peter.

William was an indifferent tot of four years when the exodus began, but as he grew up in his father's spacious and well-built frame house in the vicinity, he had reason never to forget the period of transition. Deer and bear roamed through wooded patches across the river. Wild buffalo grazed on the prairies north of Fort Ridgely. Indians, gaining subsistence by the chase, and the gathering of wild fruits and roots, drifted back and forth until established at their agencies.

Fast transportation was to be had on the St. Paul stages, reeling a tri-weekly schedule in 1857. In the summertime stern- and side-wheel steamboats wooed popularity. Some bore family names, like the *Mollie Mohler* or *Frank Steele;* others those of animals, the graceful *Antelope* or ferocious *Tiger.* The Brown boy counted four or five of them on the the river at a single time. Flat-bottom barges, fifty to sixty feet long, and ten to twelve feet wide, also furnished carriage. Manned by a crew of a dozen men, oars were employed, but propelling was done principally with long poles wielded by men who walked on "running boards" on each side of the barge. The poles had pads at the upper end to fit the shoulder, thus lending a cushion to heavy pushing.

Among early residents of Traverse des Sioux threaded Edward Eggleston, who later would achieve fame as the author of *The Hoosier Schoolmaster.* The Minnesota village provided the setting for his book *Mysteries of Metropolisville.* Eggleston, coming from Indiana, bowed his way into Traverse as a Methodist clergyman in 1856. To supplement his meager salary as a preacher, he made and sold soap, and engaged in farming, surveying, and photography. Fellow citizens, displaying proper appreciation of his ministerial efforts, bought a suit of clothes and presented it to him at an old-fashioned "donation party." Eggleston, recognized among the Minnesotans as a spell-binding evangelist, attracted large and well-mixed crowds to his revival services. During his sojourn at Traverse he married Miss McGraw.

As a barefoot boy, William herded sheep on the un-fenced prairie, side-stepping sandburs which were the bane of all shoeless youngsters. And at the crossing of the Minnesota River, when in dry season the water came up only to his armpits, he learned to swim with other lads.

His father owned a hayfield of twenty-eight acres in the big bend of the river near Traverse, and William cocked the hay, cut with scythes. In that section, mowing ma-chines had just begun to appear. Wild grapes, plums, cherries, and berries could be gathered in satisfying quan-tities. Flocks of wild passenger pigeons often darkened the skies. So many of them came to rest in a tree near Brown's hayfield that they broke down the branches. When the boy came to be an elderly man his lament before Minnesota's pioneers was, "Not one of these birds is now left except as stuffed specimens in museums." In the fall months, ducks and geese flew in noisy convoy, and prairie chickens mingled with domestic poultry in the barnyard.

Like many women of the frontier, William's mother possessed strong character, which was revealed startlingly in a particular instance. While walking along a dusty street, Mrs. Brown suddenly came face to face with Chief Red Iron, who, at the moment, had assumed a belligerent attitude. He lifted a rifle and took aim. The woman's gaze met his with such a fiery glow that the Indian lowered his weapon and resumed his stalking up the street. He had merely wished to satisfy himself on the point of feminine fortitude.

Mrs. Brown gave birth to her first daughter, Mary Grace, on August 2, 1859, and on November 26, 1861, the family welcomed the arrival of a second baby girl, Helen Mary. Soon brothers William and Frankie were "playing injun" for their benefit, innocently unaware of a more realistic drama in the offing.

There came the vivid tragedy which centered in the attack of vengeful Sioux upon New Ulm in August, 1862. This outbreak, when massacre and pillaging reddened the day, was imprinted indelibly on the minds of the Browns and their neighbors. Because of many military forces being drawn into the Civil War and the suddenness with which the uprising came, small regular army units sought assistance from local guardsmen. People hurriedly deserted their homes and farms to seek a haven in the nearest settlement. St. Peter cared for refugees, including the Brown family.

William, eight years old, acted as male head of his household, looking to his mother for needed encouragement. His father was in the East on a business trip, when a man came to borrow a saddle while giving alarm of the outbreak to the people. Mr. Alexander G. Huggins, missionary, rescued Mrs. Brown and her children.

For two weeks they remained in an old stone granary twelve feet square, sharing it with two women neighbors. Close by was the camp of volunteer troops, and William had utmost confidence in their ability to offer fullest protection. He reminded them, however, that he too could shoot straight enough to down a redskin, if he only had a rifle.

The outbreak, climaxed by the hanging of thirty-eight death-dealing red men, was written in bloodshed and chaos. White families, driven from their homes, besieged and overcrowded in places of defense, suffered severely from food shortage and other deprivations.

Yet punishment of guilty warriors did not tame all the hostiles. The next year, a small party of war-bent Indians stole down the river. They murdered a few whites, then hid in thick stands of timber. Paleface volunteers got on their trail so rapidly the scare faded overnight. Fear, how-

ever, was easily resurrected because of the massacre of
1862. Some frantic preparations were made. William
Brown watched a minister of the gospel and others mould-
ing bullets by lamplight, while the women kept on a red-
hot stove huge wash boilers full of steaming water. They
were ready to fill large dippers and hurl the contents at any
red men who lacked timidity. Men and boys, women and
girls, slept crowded on floors of separate rooms in order to
be near alert defenders. William came to envy well-
equipped soldiers who had good guns and who pursued a
career that led often to action.

That young Brown was cut out to be a soldier is disclosed in the story told by Mrs. Jennie Pettijohn Tyler, a
neighbor, in *Old Traverse des Sioux*.

"Who was it said 'The boy is father to the man'? One
long ago day, when sandburs were ripe, a lanky boy was
seen coming over the hill from his home west of Traverse.
The observer was another lad, on his father's buckskin
pony, herding sheep. Riding up to the footman, he inquired, boylike, his destination, his errand, and so forth,
and on learning that the chap was going to Gus Stempel's
store, after ammunition to go hunting, the rider said, 'Tell
you what I'll do, you give me a couple of charges of powder
and shot, and I'll give you a ride down there, and back this
far, on Selim.' The bargain was carried out to the entire
satisfaction of both parties thereto. The lanky boy shall be
nameless, but the boy who was storing up ammunition and
was going to have a gun 'some day' is .... William C.
Brown. ....."

It is not of record that the parents Brown were "set
against" William's becoming a soldier. They probably
liked the idea, for their admonishments emphasized worth
in a combination of discipline and thorough book-learning.
And as staunch members of the Presbyterian Church they
looked askance at any lagging behind the spiritual and
moral principles of Calvinism. No so strongly theocratic

were they, however, that they would permit inflexibility of judgment on the wayward. Strangers on the frontier were good until proved bad, and sinners often tasted mercy.

One "Reverend Brown," introducing himself in clerical garb as a Presbyterian preacher from Ohio, arrived in Traverse by way of St. Paul and Mankato. He took up a claim near the townsite of St. Peter, and delivered a series of sermons in Traverse. He railed thunderously against ungodliness. The Brown family listened dutifully. Then one night storekeeper Brown lost a barrel of flour. A team of horses disappeared from the community at the same time. Horse stealing had become too much the "usual" thing, and a search was begun.

The stolen team was found, but left hidden so the thief might be seized when he would appear to feed the animals. The watchers caught the Reverend Brown. In the house of the "preacher," storekeeper Brown found his barrel of flour, and other citizens recovered things they had missed. But the thief was permitted to return to St. Paul, without trial. The citizenry concluded that the preaching benefits outweighed the singular sin.

Later, in exchange for sums paid by three different parties, the banished man handed over three deeds to his claim. Upon his immediate exit, it was learned he was the ringleader of a group of thieves. A sheriff chased him down, only to have him escape permanently from custody.

Even as neighbors of Traverse shared their joys with one another so did they suffer together. Hard winters and scarcity of conveniences they faced with stern reality. Diphtheria, measles, scarlet fever, and smallpox invaded the ranks of young and old in virtually every household. Families exchanged help as need fell due. Little heed was paid quarantine except, probably, when smallpox struck. The winter of 1865 bit deeply. One family, in a fortnight, parted with three children. Frankie Brown, a victim of smallpox, was claimed by death October 21. The loss of his eight-year-old brother brought piercing grief to William. Slowly, he turned to his schoolmates for a compensating measure of companionship.

A school had been opened in Traverse as early as 1855. William entered it in the winter term of 1862-63. The frame building had served as a church for a Baptist congregation, since melting away. For a few years, however, the students shifted to a room on the upper floor of a large brick store. Some time after 1864, the frame structure was moved to a more favorable site and given a face lifting.

So competent were the repairmen that the schoolhouse was to continue as a hall of learning down through generations. William sat in a new seat and, when called upon, wrote on a wooden blackboard that was long enough to accommodate several others without too much jostling. The teacher, Samuel Warner Bennett, had a long tenure there. He ruled from a desk on the platform where preachers had formerly punctuated sermons with pounding fists on the pulpit. William found Bennett "a rigid disciplinarian and most successful teacher." Traverse School was "a name to conjure by," chiefly because of "the occasional spelling bouts with other schools in the vicinity, as well as in declamation." Proudly, Brown boasted that "our school was never 'spelled down.'"

Drill in fundamentals carried William safely through his high school days at St. Peter from 1871 to 1873. He entered spiritedly into athletic contests with the boys, but no time was frittered away with "puppy love." Neither is there evidence to show that he was ever to have a serious love affair. To his father, mother, and sisters he was to remain devoted until each should be lost by death. Never, seemingly, did he entertain thoughts of marrying. In his last year of high school, the youth looked forward eagerly to the examination necessary for admittance to the United States Military Academy.

Before spring breezes melted snow off the prairies in

Minnesota in 1873, William's parents and sisters moved to Colorado. Garretson Brown, incited by prospects similar to those which drew him and his bride to Traverse, established himself in Denver. That cattle and mining center, pulsating with quickened life of the new West, became the family's final choice for residence. The father labored steadily, while sometimes failing to measure correctly the depth of prospects. The mother, ever visioning her children receiving full bounty of education, guarded the budget.

One of six candidates for West Point from the Second Congressional District of Minnesota, William took the competitive examination at Shakopee on May 14. The examining board, Professor C. W. G. Hyde and the Reverend William R. Powell of Shakopee, and Captain John H. Brown, Willmar, knew the papers of applicants by number instead of by name. The class average was 7.86. Applicant Brown's grade, 8.90, stood highest, and he received the coveted appointment from Congressman H. B. Strait.

The appointee lost no time in telegraphing the good news to his father, then answered a letter from Representative Strait concerning the matter of filling out the warrant to be sent to West Point. Congratulations and some expense money came from Denver on the twenty-third. And that same day triumphant William bought a diary, to be carefully kept with those for every succeeding year of his army career.

At the month's end, the impatient youth boarded a train for his first trip to the East. The start was none too auspicious. A tunnel cave-in held up the train in Wisconsin eight hours. For want of better accommodations, the cadet-to-be slept overnight in the barroom of a Camp Douglas hotel. Before reaching Pittsburgh he stopped off to visit Uncle P. Y. Brown. Other relatives, including

Uncle Samuel Read and his wife Margaret, saw to it that William "had a very pleasant time."

The journey scarcely was resumed when the locomotive jumped the track, but scheduled connections were made at Pittsburgh for Philadelphia and New York City. The husky youth from the prairies of Minnesota swallowed hard as he took in the immensity of Manhattan. He rushed from the train to the pier and in midafternoon leaped to the deck of the West Point-bound steamer, *Mary Powell*.

It was June 4. Two days previously, the conditional appointment as a cadet by the President of the United States had been signed by Secretary of War, William Worth Belknap. The appointee was to report in person "at once" to the Superintendent of the Academy. Further examinations and reports of "personal, military, and moral deportment" would determine delivery of the warrant of appointment to the seeker.

CHAPTER II

A Plebe at West Point

WILLIAM BROWN, pacing the deck of the *Mary Powell,* exulted in the chance to stretch his legs. A cool, clean breeze swept away any lingering odors of smoky cities and stuffy railway cars. When the white vessel sliced the river opposite Stony Point, the youth recalled the tragedy which had occurred there September 16, 1871. From the same Hudson flyer on a down-river trip, Dennis Hart Mahan, Sr., had leaped or fallen overboard. The death of West Point's notable professor had meant a great loss to his government, the army, and the academic world.

Landing before the towers of West Point was early enough to permit the Minnesotan his first view of evening parade by the Cadet Corps. He spent the night at Cozzens' West Point Hotel. Memory went back to a May day in 1866, when the aged General Winfield Scott, after returning to the United States Military Academy, had died in a hotel room. How many others had stopped here!

But immediate problems jerked the boy out of his reverie. Before turning out the gas light, he reread the circular on cadetship issued by the War Department. Succinctly, it listed entrance qualifications and physical disqualifications. It also provided information on residence and courses to be pursued in the four-year schooling.

He who had "served in any capacity in the military or naval service of the so-called Confederate States during the late rebellion" could not hope to become a cadet at the Military Academy. Yet this carrying on of a war, ended some years before, was getting stale. Soon, Brown knew, the son of the North would welcome the son of the South on an equal basis of loyalty to one flag, to one country. As it stood, any officer or enlisted man who had for not less than a year served in the Union Army in the Civil War was eligible for appointment till he became twenty-four years old. Other appointees, upon entrance, had to be over seventeen and under twenty-two.

Once admitted, the cadet received yearly pay of five hundred dollars and one ration daily—enough support if economy became the watchword.

A cadet was required to bring with him:

2 pairs of ankle-boots; 6 pairs of white gloves; 7 shirts and 12 collars; 6 pairs winter socks, same number summer socks; 4 pairs summer drawers, 3 pairs for winter; 6 pocket handkerchiefs; 6 towels; 1 clothes-bag (ticking); 1 clothes-brush, hair-brush, tooth-brush, comb; 2 pillow-cases; 2 pairs sheets; 1 pair blankets; 1 quilted bed-cover; 1 trunk.

To be bought by each cadet at "regulated prices" at West point were:

1 gray cloth coatee; 1 gray cloth riding jacket; 1 regulation great-coat; 2 pairs of gray cloth pantaloons, for winter; 6 pairs of drilling pantaloons for summer; 1 fatigue-jacket for encampment; 1 black dress cap; 1 forage cap; 1 black stock; 2 sets of white belts; 1 mattress; 1 pillow; 1 chair; 1 tumbler; 1 account book; . . . .

Further, each cadet "will unite with his room-mate in purchasing for their common use, one looking-glass, one wash-stand, one wash-basin, one pail, and one broom, and shall be required to have one table, of the pattern that may be prescribed by the Superintendent."

Already William had practiced economy, observing the regulation of carrying no money with him beyond traveling costs. Parents were advised to send to the Academy's treasurer the amount needed by the son "for his necessary expenses until he is admitted, and for his clothes, &c., thereafter." Upon admittance, the outlay for uniform and incidentals totaled $88.79.

"If, upon arrival," the circular stated discreetly, the cadet "has the necessary sum to his credit on the books of the Treasurer, he will start with many advantages, in a pecuniary point of view, over those whose means are more limited, and who must, if they arrive, as many do, totally unprovided in this way, go in debt on the credit of their pay—a burden from which it requires many months to free themselves; while, if any accident compel them to leave the Academy, they must of necessity be in a destitute condition."

Permission from the superintendent had to be gained if a cadet were to receive money or supplies from parents or any other person.

The academic period extended from September 1 until the closing days of June. Classes took thorough examinations for proficiency ratings of their members in January and June, those found deficient in courses or deportment being dropped unless the grave Academic Board thought it best to extend grace.

In July and August the encampment was held. The cadet then received practical training, freed from the book-boring that went with the classrooms.

The entering student found a signpost in reading the final warning of the circular:

VI. A sound body and constitution, a fixed degree of preparation, good natural capacity, an aptitude for study, industrious habits, perseverance, an obedient and orderly disposition, and a correct moral deportment are such essential qualifications that candidates knowingly deficient in any of these respects should not, as many do, subject themselves and their friends to the chances of future mortification and disappointment, by accepting appointment to the Academy and entering upon a career which they cannot successfully pursue.

After a night of sound slumber, William reported early at the Adjutant's office. He received mail from home and instructions from the Adjutant and the office of the cadet barracks, stood the test of his first squad drill, and passed the physical examination. Two days later, he wrestled grammar, geography, and history. On his first Sunday at West Point, he attended the chapel services and found time to write his mother and an uncle. He was "getting along pretty well."

The First Class—Fourth Year—graduated the next "June Week." On the eighth, inspired William wrote in his diary: "In the evening there was a Mortar Drill. The shells went up high in the air and then came down to the mark. Then came the fireworks which were the best that I had ever seen. Especially the balls from mortars which exploded sending forth a multitude of beautifully colored balls. Went to Cadets prayer meeting."

The diarist thereafter attended Wednesday evening prayer meetings and Sunday chapel services regularly. Regular, too, were the letters sent to Denver. His home training had instilled the desire for spiritual guidance, though dogmatism was left out in the cold. Habits of smoking or drinking of liquor, of vulgarity or profanity were unnecessary. Physical fitness and mental alertness spelled something, but to be a "reformer" just was too much of a sepulchral idea.

On Thursday, the plebe, relieved from squad drill, was fitted out, from new cap to clean slate. The cadets staged their sham battle before President Grant, class of 1843, and General Sherman, '40. With awe, Plebe Brown saw the Sherman graduation ball.

Next morning, the cadets drew up in front of the library, erected in 1841, and standing, vine-clothed, on the same site today. Colonel Thomas H. Ruger, '54, superintendent from 1871 to 1876, revealed his pride in the Corps. And so did Colonel Emory Upton who, succeeding Henry M. Black in 1870, was to be the stirring Commandant of Cadets to midway of 1875. Secretary of War Belknap, and Sherman delivered addresses, after which the graduates received their diplomas from the hands of the nation's President. Grant, wrote diarist Brown, "is a very small man and his face somewhat wrinkled. He has the appearance of a very quiet man."

The band thrilled the assemblage with "Yankee Doodle." Graduates exchanged farewells in the mess hall with those left to carry on. The second cadet from St. Peter, Minnesota, whom Brown succeeded, would become known as Colonel John August Lundeen. The two struck up a trading deal. In exchange for some wearing apparel, Brown gave Lundeen his satchel and the promise of a few dollars in cash.

Squad drill chiseled rough edges off the plebes. For smiling in ranks at parade, William stood extra time at attention in the office. On the twenty-first, a Saturday, the plebes rolled up their bedding and moved into camp. At noon, after the pitching of tents, white gloves contrasting with the blackened boots of marchers, they were led formally into tent rows by the band. In the Sunday morning parade, William got "skinned" (reprimanded) for his dirty shirt and pants. Within two days he lost his tentmate, W. H. Williams, who was granted a leave of absence to visit a sick grandmother in Illinois.

Double step and double time around the plain left the plebe with aching hip joints. Gradually, however, setting-up exercises ironed out the kinks. And swimming in the Hudson River was a boon.

On the last day of June, William took his oath before the Adjutant. Admitted with pay July 1, his stay was contingent on an examination before the Academic Board the following January. On the same day, William returned from Illinois, and Brown obtained his first army gun. The rear portion of the barrel was scoured so vigorously the bronze came off. He got a new gun, while drawing eight pairs of white pants, two white jackets, and a shell jacket.

From the celebration of the Fourth, with fireworks, until the eleventh of August, Plebe Brown found himself on the "jump" in camp so continuously that he had no time left for diary entries. "The Rules of W. P.," he scratched, "are like the laws of the Medes & Persians which change not."

Confined to the hospital on August 12 because of a sore throat, he enjoyed the first sleep he had had in a bed for two months. Four days later he returned to active duty, sorely irked to discover that another plebe had removed the barrel, trigger guard, and bayonet from his gun. He faced more drilling, instruction in artillery, and guard duty.

Soon some September men began reporting. On Sunday, the twenty-fourth, William heard for the first time, a sermon by the Reverend John Forsyth, successor to Chaplain John W. French, who had died in the summer of 1871.

With the end of the month came the return of the furlough men, amid great rejoicing, prior to reporting to the Commandant. While hundreds of visitors looked on, the encamped battalion struck tents and moved back to barracks. William made his initial appearance at dress parade in front of the superintendent's quarters. And, the diarist noted, twenty-one of the fifty-four September men were rejected, but "the rejected ones" did not seem to be "unhappy."

Upon division of classes into sections, William was put in the second section. The division stemmed from the reorganization in 1817 by the farseeing Colonel Sylvanus Thayer, "Father of the Military Academy." Individualized instruction for each student, with opportunity for the brighter men to go beyond basic requirements, was an objective attained far ahead of similar patterns to be adopted by civilian institutions. Eagerly the cadet from Minnesota widened his knowledge of the background of his school.

The Academy, founded in 1802, traced its flow of utility from the spring that bubbled ceaselessly with the spirit of service under the superintendency of the bachelor, Thayer,

1817-33. Alumnus of Dartmouth and West Point, officer in the War of 1812, Thayer's brilliancy and strength of character had drawn him close to that able soldier-engineer of the United States Government's early defense force, General Joseph G. Swift, superintendent of the Academy from 1805 to 1812. Swift recognized the worth of study in Europe by Thayer of Napoleonic tactics and French technological methods as exemplified in fortifications.

Sharing progress with the Academy for a quarter of a century had been the West Point Foundry at Cold Spring, across the Hudson. Established by Gouverneur Kemble, Swift, and two residents of Orange County, it not only turned out cannon for the country's defense, but, in its heyday, had been the source of things made of iron for a large section of the East. A West Point cadet of the 1820's, Robert P. Parrott, who became a teacher of mathematics and philosophy at the Academy, later superintended the foundry. His rifled cannon gave the North many victories.

Great had been the need at West Point for energizing, and Thayer vowed to recognize meritorious service after the shortsighted Alden ("Old Pewt") Partridge, cross-grained dispenser of partiality, was relieved in 1817. He had been acting as superintendent for two hectic years. The scientific educational impulse America possessed from 1820 to 1870 came, in no small degree, from the Military Academy and its graduates, who taught and wrote texts there and in other halls of learning. The school for soldiers became, also, a school for leaders in civil pursuits. Within bounds, struggling with or against conflicting congressional or executive dictates, the plant, curriculum, and staff of the national military institution registered a steady growth.

West Pointers in Brown's day could trace Thayer's tutelage in its most lustrous aspects through Dennis Hart Mahan and Peter Smith Michie, students and instructors of their Alma Mater. Mahan had become full professor of civil and military engineering at the beginning of the year

1832. He wrote and used his notes on specialized subjects. Before his death in 1871—preceding the venerable Thayer's demise by only one year—Mahan had become an outstanding authority on military history and principles. Through his son, Alfred Thayer Mahan, who entered the Naval Academy at Annapolis in 1856, the world came to realize the power of command of the seas.

Michie, a plebe at West Point in 1859, had won notable acclaim as an engineer in the Union Army. In 1867 he became Mahan's chief assistant, and by 1871 occupied the chair of natural and experimental philosophy. His training in mathematics and engineering had been practical. Therefore his students, when dealing with principles, above all learned the urgency of self-control and adjustment to necessity. Michie, like Mahan, wrote texts and followed avidly the national educational trends. Before his death, many soldiers would drink from his hands of the glass passed on by Sylvanus Thayer, the contents labeled "Duty, Honor, Country."

Also furnishing light for the marching Corps in the seventies were other sturdy teachers, including mathematician Albert E. Church, whose death in 1878 ended a career of forty-eight years at West Point; Julius B. Wheeler and Oswald H. Ernst, in engineering; George L. Andrews, professor of French.

Commandant Upton instructed in artillery, infantry, and cavalry tactics, his imprint on the corps being unmistakably permanent. He had graduated at West Point in 1861, early displaying a manner of forthright expression with a high degree of scholarship. In the Civil War he had served with distinction in the Union's artillery, infantry, and cavalry, rising to the rank of brevet major general. Severely wounded at Opequon (Winchester, Virginia), he had proved himself, as in other battles, to be master over fearful strain.

In 1867, after being called back to service at West Point,

Upton had witnessed adoption of his system of infantry tactics. In that year appeared his first published book, *A New System of Infantry Tactics, Double and Single Rank, Adapted to American Topography and Improved Firearms*. Outstanding officer-writer on the history of militarism as well as tactics, his *The Armies of Asia and Europe* came forth in 1878.

Brown, like the majority of cadets, admired the Commandant in spite of his being a strict disciplinarian. Deeply religious, he was known to say his prayers nightly. On the field or in the classroom, his face, tapering rather sharply from forehead to chin, invariably delineated decisiveness and absorption in matters of gravity.

Ruger, as superintendent, was bent on keeping deportment and studies on a high plane. He had graduated No. 3 in the class of 1854, and, like Upton, had been brevetted major general before the Civil War ended. Later, he had served as colonel of the Regular Army's Thirty-third Infantry.

In spite of circumstances dictated by the times, the Academy of the Seventies was "looking up" while clinging to a deal of tradition. The white belts had been introduced by Partridge in 1814. Two years later had come the first issue of "Cadet Gray," similar to the uniform worn by Brown and his successors. Regulation overcoats had appeared in 1828. Equipment as well as accouterment was stamped with historicalness. Connected with the superintendency of Major Richard Delafield, 1856-61, had been Captain George B. McClellan, class of '46. His efforts had produced the McClellan saddle; good enough for several generations.

A hall, in which riding could display its excellent quality, had replaced, in 1855, a flimsy building recalled by some army commanders of the Civil War.

The current was swifter in the educational setup. Early in Thayer's regime, the academic staff had taken quarters in conformity with seniority. Thayer, in 1819, moved into new quarters, the same building occupied by successive superintendents. A cadet stood on merit alone; untrained and undisciplined militia had proved detrimental in the War of 1812. The honor system, its roots in Thayer, flourished and bore fruit. The bond of truth and sincerity among cadets grew stronger with each graduation. After Partridge had gone down the Hudson, the Corps learned the futility of presenting petitions of grievances to the superintendent.

Thayer had installed the cadet salary system to thwart social discrimination. Cadets, left without money in their pockets, drew from the stipulated account by check. If checks were written too often or for too large an amount, the writer had to wait until he accrued further credit. There was no staying on for the cadet who could not complete the courses in the time allotted. When Thayer put the Academy on a twelve-month basis, furloughs for a designated period replaced extended vacations.

It was not until 1870, however, that written entrance examinations had superseded the oral recital. Under the superintendency of Robert E. Lee, 1852-55, the course had been extended to five years to permit its enlargement. Later it had been reduced to four, tried at five again, then re-established at four.

In 1819, the Attorney General of the United States had handed down a ruling, the import of which strengthened the Military Academy immeasurably. West Point's Corps was adjudged a part of the country's land forces, subject, therefore, "to the rules and articles of war, and to trial by courts-martial,"* as ordered by Congress. Thus, shortly thereafter, Thayer had been able to use pressure on the unfit through the simple resignation procedure.

Blackboard instruction in classrooms as given in earliest

---

* Colonel R. Ernest Dupuy, *Where They Have Trod*, Frederick A. Stokes Company, New York, 1940, p. 152.

days remained indispensable; also the grading of cadets as employed by Thayer, the marks running from a 3.0 for perfect recitation down to 0.0 for absolute failure. The precise drill, summer camp, and marches had been on Thayer's program, along with the system of graduation Brown was to taste.

In languages taught, emphasis was on English and French. English, however, had been wiped off in 1867 and did not reappear as a study until 1877, the year of Brown's departure from the classrooms. Thayer, unsuccessfully, had tried to find time for Latin and Greek in the curriculum. Spanish had been unavailable till 1856. A Law Department, first presided over by Major Asa Bird Gardiner, enticed cadets for the first time in 1874.

Enmeshed as Cadet Brown may have been in the course set for him, by no means did he bend irrevocably to docility. Nor was that expected of him. Without initiative, a soldier could not advance far in his career. And if a man never complained, his lot might not be bettered. An overdose of complacency was not good for the rank and file of troops. Where there were grumbles there was spirit; and spirit there had to be to generate a spark. All this William Brown argued with his classmates.

Class after class at West Point "ran it" off the reservation to places where the hedge of conviviality was not trimmed too closely. No sooner had Thayer annexed the property on which was situated Gridley's Tavern, at the south edge of the reservation, than Benny Havens' place filled the need of merrymakers.

Benny moved a couple of times before establishing himself in "The House by the River," east of the site on which now stands the Highland Falls post office. There, from 1843 to the middle of the seventies, the run-outs sought food and drink from Benny and his wife. The lusty Brown found the Dutchwoman's cooking alone worth any risk. He learned that Edgar Allan Poe discovered in genial Benny

a better course than that which he dropped at the
Academy. And, while visiting Havens, those who went on
to graduate or to become generals, owed protection to the
ingenuity of Benny.

Hazing, for many years, seemed to be an essential in-
gredient in the academic dish. The plebes of the fifties had
defied its heaped-up portions because of the sectional dif-
ferences of opinion which presaged the internal strife to
come. Upper classmen became inquisitors, but newcomers
could rely on a bayonet which pricked. Various forms of
hazing, as in other educational institutions of the country,
were to continue at West Point until the dawn of the
twentieth century.

In building and keeping West Point's tradition, William
Brown was eager to share. So with pride he would watch its
growth, comparing it with the growth of a certain tree.

In 1833, a farmer of the hills beyond Butternut Falls had
set out an elm sapling as a tribute to his departing friend,
Slyvanus Thayer. The tree, with branches ever reaching
outward, still stood in 1873. It would still be standing
after Brown no longer was able to seek its shade.

CHAPTER III

The Course Is Run

FROM First Year, Fourth Class, to Fourth Year, First Class, the trail led upward—winding, but sure. It was far to the summit above the clouds. Four departments at the beginning did not loom so large, but they were enough.

Mathematics—Algebra, Geometry and Trigonometry.
French Language—Books on Grammar and Verbs, Tabular System, Essays and Dictionary.
Tactics of Artillery and Infantry—Practical Instruction in Schools of the Soldier, Company, and Battalion. Practical Instruction in Artillery.
Use of Small Arms—Instruction in Fencing and Bayonet Exercise.

William had his severest struggles with "math" and French. The second week of September was decidedly discouraging: "Weather very cool & the quarters are rather uncomfortable in the mornings on account of the cold. We have 7 or 8 pages a day in both Algebra & French. It is *awful* hard. I made almost a complete failure in both today." Again: "Recited Algebra tolerable well but made a complete failure in French. I expect to go home in January."

Nevertheless, there were better recitations on better days. The instructor in algebra had his battles also, what with being too inebriated at times to hear the sections through. "They call him 'Old Whiskey' here," wrote William. On perilous occasions, Professor Church took over and steadied all forces.

The plodder's lack of money and his never-failing hunger for sweets, which the ration did not provide, wrinkled his brow and stomach. It was an event when roommate Williams treated him to cake, pie, and candy at the confectioner's, or when each member of the battalion had two peaches or oyster soup for dinner. Clothes needed repairing, and the sisters in Denver received requisitions for needles and thread. Their brother rewarded them with his own diagram of West Point, and the promise of photos of himself in the uniform he was not certain of wearing after December.

In quarters, at drill, or in the classroom, regulations demanded wariness. The lid of the candle box must be kept closed. There were "skins' (demerits) for boots not blacked well for parade, for powder touched off in rooms, for shuffling about in ranks at guard mounting, for tardiness at reveille at six of a frosty morning. Apples found in the room, along with dirt in the vicinity of steam coils, wore on the inspector's patience. No abuses of telephone privileges could be reported, however, for at West Point installation of telephones did not come until 1887.

In the handling of a gun and in artillery drill and firing, William made his greatest strides toward the goal he had in mind. Impressive were battalion skirmish drills and sham battles, when the smoke could hardly be seen through. General Sherman and the Secretary of War dropped in on October 2, 1873, for a review. And just as William leaped happily to the Gatling battery and his first lesson in fencing, he met with transfer from the second to the eighth section in "math." He started "boning" (digging) more diligently in algebra. It paid. Grades in that subject, as well as in French, took a turn for the better. Yet the "fesses" (slips) and "raggings" (barking) still caused worry, and now and then the "boner" got "bugled" (challenged).

October was well advanced when the Minnesotan strolled down Flirtation Walk to gather chestnuts. Then came the cold rains. The cadets did double time marching to breakfast. Meanwhile, William had found his way to the Dutchwoman's, leaving his watch there to have it taken to Cold Spring for repairing. Soon overcoats became necessary at dress parade and at inspection line-up. The first snowstorm of the season left a heavy fall of flakes. The boy from the North chuckled over the curious fact that Cadet J. B. Walker of Florida "never saw snow before."

Thanksgiving arrived, and the mess hall provided the best meal that Cadet Brown's eyes had rested on since entering the Academy. Plenty of turkey for everybody, including some guests from the Seventh New York Regiment. Any expansion of the waistline was brought back to normal by a climb to the top of Crow's Nest.

That the mess had its bad moments could not be denied. Within a fortnight there was complaining of a "lousy" breakfast: bad batter, soggy rolls, and poor coffee. Then, for a Sunday: "We had chicken slumgudgeon for dinner today and Mr. Hewitt found a chicken crop in it and it didn't go down worth a cent. It was taken to the Officer in charge and he simply said to 'take it out.' "

A joyful notation was made when buckwheat cakes hit the spot, and a happier one when a number of First Class men got skinned for their shaggy sidewhiskers.

The Fourth Class missed out completely on yuletide leaves. But on Christmas Eve there was freedom from quarters until sounding of "Taps." The Christmas dinner vied with the one for Thanksgiving. In the holiday's spare hours, William boned hard on his "math." Between "Tattoo" and "Taps" he shared with another homesick comrade the leftover turkey brought up from the mess hall.

The boning went on at a terrific pace during the last days of December. So much so that after marching to church at route step in a deep snow, William spent the rest of a cold Sabbath pouncing on irregular French verbs.

In the first week of January, 1874, the Fourth Class faced the august Academic Board in the Library, and other classes were examined by committees. Tremulously, William "fessed" only to the extent that he felt he had not been "found." When he learned that he had passed safely, his rejoicing was dampened by the resignation of Williams and his departure for New York City. Others, too, had gone down the river before and after the last-ditch fight. William wrote scantily of successive roommates in the diaries which were packed with entries until 1876.

He made satisfactory headway after the January examinations had been conquered. He guarded against demerits and kept an economic eye on the little fund he had to spend. On March 7, Secretary of War Belknap signed the document that was his to cherish.

Know ye, That the PRESIDENT has been pleased to appoint William C. Brown a CADET of the UNITED STATES MILITARY ACADEMY, to rank as such from the first day of July, 1873. . . . .

The determined youth became a yearling on the twentieth day of May. With self-satisfaction and gloating, he scanned the plebes as they began reporting. Williams came back with restored hope, to take another walk with his buddy. It was hazing time. Once more groups of haughty classmen were "hived" and "skinned" for interfering with new cadets.

When results of the examination for a hundred were read out at dinner, thirty-seven of them learned their careers at West Point had died in bud. Four Negroes were among those who had reported, and all were "found." After their departure, a yearling from Georgia, Henry Ossian Flipper, felt the warmth of admiration of his fellows. In Brown's class, he was, in 1877, to become the first Negro cadet to graduate from the Military Academy.

The end of the academic year again brought the strain of examinations and the excitement of graduation. On the last day of May, two British officers in uniforms weighted with lace inspected the battalion and barracks. The desire of one of them to learn how the bedding was piled fuddled a friend of William's. The cadet upset the bedding, and out rolled a pair of roller skates, a mirror, and a broomstick!

When Secretary and Mrs. Belknap arrived, the Third Classmen fired the Napoleons in a fifteen-gun salute, and the band serenaded at the hotel. The same salute boomed upon the appearance of the Board of Visitors, who reviewed the cadets. White pants were resumed. Invitations for the hop came out. Billy Williams treated Bill Brown to a feast at the Dutchwoman's. Bill, in a letter to sister Grace, elaborated on his strolling around Flirtation Walk. Commandant Upton expressed high satisfaction with what he termed "the best battalion drill" he had been able to stage. Then a murmur of regret supplanted, for the moment, happy whisperings. The Secretary of War left suddenly for Iowa where his son had died.

Cavalry and mortar drills, alumni dinner and ball, fireworks, skirmishing and sham battle, the going and coming of the racing *Mary Powell,* and hundreds of visitors, all vied for attention with examinations and leave-taking. On the second Sunday in June, William, for want of a seat, sat in the choir loft to hear Doctor Forsyth's farewell sermon to the graduates. And for supper that evening, he tasted the first strawberries set before him in two years.

The graduates, in farewell parade, marched out in the rear rank with sidearms, then up to the line officers, where each shook hands with the Commandant. They cheered as the companies passed in quick time. After the address at the Library, they accepted their diplomas, and marched to the front of the barracks to hear orders read. Handshaking and last words came at the dinner hour. Again the country received its quota of future generals.

All tests vanquished, the battalion went into another summer camp. There were drenching rains, and William's spare time called for touching up the gun that gathered rust. His marksmanship varied. At target practice, he snuffed out the candle flame two out of five shots, but shooting in the riding hall was something else. He needed more tutelage.

His checkbook now showed him to be out of debt in the amount of $14.92. This called for celebration. The economizer "took a bath and went to the Dutchwoman's." His weight of 145 pounds could be increased without risk. He saw his first balloon, its faltering over West Point disrupting a trip to the library.

In August, a swim was doubly valued because of the finding of immense huckleberry patches. Sometimes as many as two dishes of blackberries appeared on each table at suppertime. To make the evenings less drab, dances were held, guest singers and other entertainers invited. The cadets staged impromptu celebrations, costume acts, and muscular feats. Midshipmen from the Naval Academy visited as supper guests. A talented singer, Miss Kellogg, accompanied by General Sherman in his "cits" (civilian clothes), appeared in the mess hall, and a thousand candles illuminated the tent camp for a few festive hours.

The night before the tents were struck, return of the furlough men called for a final fair-weather fling. "A big hop," which somehow developed into "a big drunk," led to inevitable chastisement. Reveille at half an hour before six o'clock in the morning was an afterthought.

The Corps began to settle down to the grind of classrooms. The sixth of September, a Sunday, William checked as a red-letter day in his diary. Accompanying Colonel Upton in inspection on the plain was none other than General Alexander McD. McCook. In West Point tradition there was the recalling of the night of April 21, 1861, when cadets had serenaded the member of the Class of '52. Lieutenant McCook had been called to the colors to march with and against former members of the Corps.

To push on through Second Year, Third Class, William found it needful to broaden his studies. Progression in mathematics included, also, surveying and calculus. There were more entanglements in French, plus wanderings in Spanish. The flanker pounced on drawing, with its penmanship, topography, and related essentials. And added to instructions in infantry and artillery were those of cavalry. Tactics in cavalry—that would put him on the back of a horse again.

He waited for the chance to ride the "Empress," the best horse in the stable for cadets. But on a late September day, an unwary cadet rode the Empress into a tree. So stunned was the prize mount it was decreed that she be shot. The order went into effect the day before Brigadier General John Pope reviewed the cadet battalion on the plain.

Luckily, William prevailed on his roommate to keep their living quarters meticulous. One day, Colonel Upton came along the hallway with his brother-in-law and sister, Mr. and Mrs. Baird. The Colonel stepped into Brown's room ahead of his kinsfolk, complimented the boys on the good order of things, and asked them to button up their coats. Thereupon he invited the guests to enter, introducing them pleasantly to the stiffly bowing cadets.

Artillery drill was no boy's play; often it led to casualties. The trail of a gun fell on one of William's toes, and the injury spelled incapacitation for several days. But the victim enjoyed the rest. Delightfully, he injected frankness into a diary entry: " 'Wheatoned it' again on drill with my big toe. A sore toe is a mighty handy thing just now."

Painfully, he became a better student of "math" and French. When, from time to time, a recitation was given unfalteringly, the diarist had an apt expression for it. With great pressure on the pen point, he wrote: "The Gen. Standing up today."

Occasionally the cadets turned out for fire-fighting practice. On a chilly November evening, William scribbled:

"Firing drill this P. M. from 4:05 to 5:05. We had a fire started in the engine and went down near old Tony's house at a double time and squirted at an old tree for a while, a lot of cadets hived all the apples on a couple of trees near by. We then came back at a double time, squirted a little while in the area, then put the machine up. We wore shell jackets."

Ofttimes ladders were hoisted against the barracks' walls and drill was held with buckets filled with water. If an officer turned his back, orderlies received drenchings. Too many spilled buckets lowered the supply in the reservoir, and Saturday baths were postponed until Sunday.

His second Christmas away from home meant a dull day to William. He was disconsolate in spite of release from quarters, in spite of a dinner table weighted with a change of victuals. He boned part of the day and cut supper, as did many of his fellows. Those who had leaves would come back in high glee. That was irony.

The year 1875 rode in on a near-zero wind. While it howled around stone walls, cadets dragged beds up to heaters and crammed on verbs and nouns and equations from Church's never-failing notes. Tactics came easier. The Franco-Prussian War still remained a live subject. It had caused a swing from stressed Napoleonic strategy and matériel to the plans executed by the soldiers of Bismarck. The youth from Minnesota was a bit bewildered by some of the problems, but at the term's end he won his fight to keep up with the average student of the class.

While in midwinter the mercury plunged to several degrees below zero, William's confidence and enthusiasm shot upward. He took his studies in better stride, widened his circle of friends, and reveled in incidents that enlivened dragging hours. Dogs, regardless of official frowns, were encouraged to stay around quarters. On a cold night after "Taps," a dog fight in a division led to a steely inquiry the next morning. But room orderlies, as usual, were a poor prime for the pump of information.

Boastful backers of the winning dog posted a sign on the door of the gymnasium. A reward of five dollars was offered for the return of a missing dog. A few days later came the climax to the disturbance. The cadets, at reveille, froze in smiles as they glanced at the railing in the rear of the engine house. Tied thereon was a stuffed pup with an appended placard:

> I am the dog with shaggy tail
> Who awoke the night with my mournful wail
> I once was *lost* but now I'm *found*
> And here behold me safe & sound.

Commandant Upton lost no time in finding scent. The trail led to Company B. In that unit, at the noon hour, an order was published. Should any more "strange noises" be heard, or any more placards be posted, the edict read, an all-night guard would be kept over certain quarters. Fighting dogs became scarcer.

William now began to acquire the proficiency in horseback riding which was to make him an outstanding cavalryman. He had straddled the back of a mount ever since his earliest recollection of wide prairies, and in the riding hall and on the paths at West Point fellow cadets and instructors took notice. Properly, he mounted and dismounted at a walk, galloped with raised legs, used watering bridles while in saddle without stirrups. Then came cross stirrups and raising of legs; the "unsaddle" and riding bareback; mounting and dismounting at gallop and trot; unbridling and marching in a column of fours. No matter if the hospital beckoned a youth who was thrown, stepped on, or kicked. As the intricacies of riding and cavalry tactics grew in number, William mastered them all.

He preferred riding to skating, the latter indulged in by large groups on the plain or river. On intensely cold days of February and March, the gas ran low. Then the cadets seized a good excuse for a round of visits. On some floors the lights faded out entirely, but the commissary limited its issue of candles to one pound for each room. Drill was suspended until the snow was cleared away. Formations continued, however, and William got skinned for a turned-up coat collar. A friend, who thought the weather a fine answer for not attending church, received half a dozen extra duties and confinement of twenty days to the limits of the area.

The faculty noticed that marks slid upward during the winter term. Too, there were fewer expenses. In debt for some months, William calculated jubilantly in mid-March that the checkbooks showed him to be $10.71 out of the red.

He took cognizance of the opening of furlough accounts. His "fessing" in Spanish and "math" tapered off. In the Drawing Academy, presided over by Professor Charles W. Larned, he obtained one of the best seats in the statuary room. His gaze centered upon "a very fine picture" drawn by William Tecumseh Sherman on May 1, 1838.

The sketching cadets did not lack spirit. At the beginning they threw slices of bread at a bent-over student, talked, idled, trifled, and broke plates and tumblers. Chewers of tobacco spat on plaster casts. After the culprits were reported, and all men in the statuary room confined for two days, the Drawing Academy became a saner place.

On the first of April, reveille was pushed up to 5:30 A. M., and to 5:00 the next month. Infantry drills commenced in the area between four-fifteen and five-twenty in the afternoon, sometimes followed by company drill on the cavalry plain. Again there was artillery drill, undress and dress parade, with emphasis on the *dress*. Fifty years later, Brown was to remark before a meeting of reserve officers in Denver:

I know of nothing which more aptly illustrates the changes which have taken place in the last half century than a short paragraph taken from Dufour's *Strategy and Tactics*—translated from the French as we had few American military books in those days—and which I studied when a cadet. The paragraph reads:

"If the combat is foreseen the troops should fight in full uniform. This mark of politeness is due to a respectable enemy, and troops who are trying to appear to the best advantage will usually do the best in the engagement."

Our uniform of that day was quite in keeping with this idea—a helmet with brilliant yellow plume and abundant gold lace with other like adornments contributed to a spectacle which people would go miles to see.

Commandants, like superintendents, gave of their capabilities to the Corps and then were shifted to other fields. On May 6, an order was read that Upton would be relieved the first of July. Lieutenant Colonel Thomas Hewson Neill, Sixth Cavalry, who had distinguished himself at Malvern Hill, Chancellorsville, and Spottsylvania, was to replace him.

Guest preachers, some highly inspiring and some not, lent aid to the chaplain. William, finding the Reverend Doctor Ormiston, of New York City, worthy of praise, wrote: "His sermon was one of the best I have ever heard and was very much liked by the Corps. Nearly half of the Corps went to hear his address to the Prayer Meeting which was excellent."

Diary entries became fewer as June Week of 1875 approached, to be followed by the usual encampment. Yet, in late May it was of sufficient importance to mention that mess-hall attendants began setting out a glass of milk for each cadet at breakfast and supper.

Assuredly, William kept up diaries for the next two years. But they have not come to light. Summarized later, however, on the last few pages of the 1873-75 record are marks of his four-year course and listing of demerits.

In the Third Year, Second Class, he waded further into drawing, tactics of artillery, cavalry, and infantry. First steps were taken in natural and experimental philosophy, embracing mechanics, acoustics, optics, and astronomy. Also picked up, were chemistry and practical military engineering, the latter consisting chiefly of instruction in signaling and telegraphy. William maintained his position halfway in class standings.

The Class of '76 graduated with forty-eight men. Among them were two soldiers who would become exceedingly well known beyond their country's borders—William Crozier, ranking fifth, and Hugh L. Scott, many numbers below. Three days after the diplomas were given out, the dashing Custer and his Seventh Cavalrymen pointed their mounts to the Little Big Horn and death. Before long, Scott would be making a diplomatic study of the red men, mastering their sign language, hailed as a great and just mediator.

In September of the same year, Major General John M. Schofield was appointed superintendent of the Military Academy. Of dignified bearing, he came with a record of frontier fighting and soldierly achievement seldom equaled. William Brown gained in him a magnanimous counselor.

A deal of counsel proved essential as the Fourth Year, First Class, program unfolded. No snap was the Department of Military and Civil Engineering and Science of War, providing study of Mahan's thorough works. In practical military engineering and tactics of artillery, cavalry, and infantry there was more of the usable; likewise in ordnance and gunnery. Mineralogy and geology provided depths to explore, but of more immediate interest were ethics and law, with emphasis on international military aspects and courts-martial procedure.

The scholastic sickle needed a keen edge. William took the final year cautiously, never swinging in so narrow an arc that any subject stood neglected. He carried six demerits into the last six months but wiped them off before graduation. Eighteen was his standing in discipline for the four years. In general merit he ranked Number 41 in a line-up of seventy-six graduates. Hunter Liggett, the future army commander, would hold the same number in a departing class of sixty-seven cadets in 1879.

George Washington McCrary had become Secretary of War in March, 1877, and he gave Brown's class his blessing. William M. Black led the group. He and four others—Walter L. Fisk, William B. Gordon, David Price, Jr., and Montroe P. Thorington—earned early special duty consideration. Leaves of absence until the thirtieth of September, following, were granted the remainder. Flipper, Negro graduate, was transferred to the Second Cavalry as a second lieutenant.

Newly commissioned officers, whom Brown soon would meet again in their first Indian campaign, included Oscar J. Brown, Francis J. Patten, and Jacob G. Galbraith.

And there was Charles B. Gatewood, who would prove to his superiors that Geronimo could be taken and warring Apaches dispersed. Others, like many graduates before them, were to become leaders in various professions.

The First Classmen of 1877 had the distinction of contributing the last stanza of "Benny Havens, Oh!" the song West Pointers have never forgotten. It was on May 29, 1877, that Benny died.

On November 8 of the same year, a caisson carried the body of Sylvanus Thayer to reinterment at the Point. All cadets of the Corps, marching on, participated in the military rites.

William Brown, however, had left the banks of the Hudson.

CHAPTER IV

A Cavalryman's Initiation

THE day after he dropped his cadetship, Brown stepped forth as an additional second lieutenant, Second Cavalry. Headquarters of the regiment, Colonel Innis N. Palmer commanding, were at Fort Sanders, Wyoming Territory. Leave of absence for the graduate, with rank entitling him to a yearly reward of $1,500 in pay and emoluments, seemed fair enough. He went home to Denver.

On July 18, special orders from headquarters of the Department of the Platte, General George Crook commanding, promoted the vacationer to a second lieutenancy in the First Cavalry, as of July 3. To this regiment he would cling for a quarter of a century; the regiment from which Robert E. Lee had resigned his commission as colonel to stand with Virginia. The promotion was occasioned by the death of Lieutenant S. M. Rains, who, with a small party of troopers, had been slain by Nez Perce warriors. The Nez Perces, under Chiefs Looking Glass and Joseph, then were being pursued eastward across Idaho Territory by troops led by Brigadier General Oliver Otis Howard, commander of the Department of the Columbia.

For some time after the Civil War, advancement came slowly to the Regular-Army man. In Indian fighting was to be gained rich experience. Much of theory learned at West Point had to be shorn in the field. Brown, anxious to join his new regiment, appealed to the Adjutant General's Office at Washington to have his leave shortened, to resume it at a later date. Regulations were regulations, and his request was denied.

He chafed at the delay in his first call out of Denver.

It was not until the first week of December that he obtained transportation at the depot in Cheyenne, Wyoming, en route to Fort Walla Walla, Washington Territory. The sleeping-car company furnished him with a double berth from Ogden to Kelton, Utah. This was rosy in comparison with the 550 miles he must ride by stage for five days and nights to complete his journey.

On December 16 he joined Company L, First Cavalry, at Fort Walla Walla. Colonel Cuvier Grover commanded the post and regiment. Out along the tossing waters of the mighty Columbia—the old river Oregon—the youth stood ready to embark upon his career. About two months previously the great Chief Joseph of the Nez Perces had surrendered to General Howard and Colonel Nelson A. Miles in the ice-crusted Bear Paw Mountains of northern Montana.

When Lieutenant Brown assumed the role of a hard-riding cavalryman at Walla Walla, his fellows found few rough spots in his make-up. Of trim and athletic build, the young officer boasted a swarthy but smooth complexion, with the thick dark hair of his head brushed back from a half-visible line on the left side. From under heavy dark eyebrows the straightforward gleam of blue eyes commanded ready attention. His eyes were his forte; eyes of a medal-winning marksman. Shielding a slightly prominent nose was a lip-length mustache, the hair curling slightly at the ends. An abbreviated goatee squared itself off below the underlip. His facial adornments were assets that a well-poised soldier of the time felt need of displaying.

Although the Lieutenant leaned toward the rigid disciplinarian, his spirit of camaraderie and his love for action must yield him constant loyalty, respect, and friendship from soldiers of all ranks. Alert for the needs of his men, he could overlook much of the "belly-aching" common to regulars tiring of routine. He resolved to ask no one to undertake a task unless he might share the risk. Above all, there would be little patience with the shirker. Sheer doggedness meant more than flashing adventure.

As a signal officer, he performed regular garrison duty until the spring of 1878. In May he reported with seventy-eight pack mules at Fort Lapwai, District of the Clearwater, in Idaho, and turned over the animals with full equipment to Captain W. H. Winters, Company E, First Cavalry. His return to Walla Walla coincided with fresh Indian flares on the frontier.

The powder of war became ignited when on May 30 three white herders of Big Camas Prairie, southern Idaho, were attacked suddenly by Indians posing as traders. For a long time Bannock leaders from Fort Hall had been warning white men to remove cattle and hogs from the camas ground which had been promised the red men in the treaty of 1868. The Bannocks no longer found fruitful the treks made to the plains for buffalo.

Buffalo Horn, though small in stature, was chief of the Bannocks, who generally ranged fairly tall. He had been a leading scout for the white soldiers in previous campaigns, but had become disgruntled while pursuing the Nez Perces in 1877. Ostensibly, he looked upon the new outbreak as a challenge, for he quickly led the malcontents on to their course of plundering.

Desire for revolt had been stirred up among many bands of Indians, numbering between 1,500 and 2,000. They had an abundance of horses, but lacked adequate preparation and organization. The actual number of warriors, poorly supplied with arms and ammunition, did not exceed seven or eight hundred. Attempts made immediately after the outbreak by the military commander at Fort Hall, within the westernmost limits of the Department of the Platte, in sending Indian messengers to persuade Buffalo Horn to halt all violence met with failure. In the confusion of field maneuvers, runners were stopped by volunteer troops who misunderstood their errand. Their friendly mission was looked at askance and they were sent back.

In the heart of arid eastern Oregon, Agent W. V. Rinehart reported that the aggregate number of Indians belonging to Malheur Reservation for Paiutes at the time of the Bannock outbreak was 846. On June 1, 370 Malheur Indians sought and procured rations, but forty-six Bannocks accompanying them were denied. The Bannocks, an offshoot of the Shoshones, displayed friendliness toward the Paiutes, their less robust cousins, and sometimes there were intermarriages.

Sagacious Chief Egan, veteran war chief of the Paiutes, divided his issue of rations with the visitors after making a plea that they be fed. The next day runners brought word to them that the Bannocks had started on the warpath in Idaho. The Malheur Indians, harboring various grievances, fully deserted their reservation the first week of June.

Late in the night of May 30, a telegrapher for the Associated Press at Boise City, Capital of Idaho Territory, tapped out to the nation's newspapers the message that troops of the First United States Cavalry under Captain (Brevet Colonel) Reuben Frank Bernard were leaving Fort Boise, near by, to quell the uprising on Camas Prairie. Bernard, well seasoned by campaigns against Apaches, Snakes, and Modocs, nevertheless met surprise in the vast scope of ensuing hostilities. Not since the flinging of red forces against Custer had so many Indians forsaken the way of peace.

Brief orders had come from General Howard, who, at home with his family in Portland, Oregon, had been handed a telegram apprising him of the critical eruption. The Commander of the Columbia Department, staunch advocate of an admixture of military and Christian principles, had lost his right arm early in the Civil War, and at its close stood sixth ranking general in the Union's Army. He had reason to fear another Indian war after the disastrous

Nez Perce campaign of 1877. But the trouble, he thought, would emanate from Chief Moses and unappeased bands on the Upper Columbia rather than from those who wandered to the south along the Snake River and its tributaries.

Further orders sent out from departmental headquarters in Vancouver, Washington, within the next few days started other troop movements. Captain David Perry's Company F, First Cavalry, to be commanded by Lieutenant Peter S. Bomus, left Fort Walla Walla with Company L on June 3. Fresh in memory was the sanguinary misfortune that had befallen Perry at White Bird Canyon the previous year. Company L's officers for 1878 were Captain Stephen G. Whipple, First Lieutenant E. H. Shelton, and Lieutenant Brown. At the time his command took the field, however, Brown was under orders to proceed to Fort Lapwai again. On June 4, Colonel Grover started for Boise City, to direct his regiment's operations in the campaign.

Troops of infantry and artillery from Forts Vancouver, Canby, Stevens, and Townsend went up the Columbia River by boat to Umatilla Landing in eastern Oregon, then marched and rode in wagons on the overland stage road. Subsequently, other troops from the Departments of Arizona and California (including Nevada) followed the same routes after arrival by ship from San Francisco. A few trudged across country from Utah and Nevada.

There was reason for a deal of confusion once the soldiers encountered dim and rugged trails. At times Howard became no less puzzled because of the lack of maps of the sparsely settled mountains and baked sage lands than did his immediate superior, Major General Irvin McDowell, of Bull Run fame, and commander of the Military Division of the Pacific. Division Headquarters were at the presidio of San Francisco.

On June 9, after more Indian depredations, Howard arrived at Walla Walla. There he consulted Colonel Frank Wheaton of the Second Infantry and commander of the

Clearwater District. Wheaton was advised to remain in his district with restricted forces, and three days later Howard took personal field command at Fort Boise.

By this time the hostiles, who had been camped for a month in the lava beds between Big Camas Prairie and the Snake River, had advanced hurriedly westward to join other malcontents, principally the Paiutes of Malheur Reservation. They had raided King Hill Station and Glenns Ferry before crossing the Snake on a ferryboat. And, on their way to the Bruneau Valley, they had left telltale bloodstains in the killing of three white men.

On June 5, Brown's previous orders were revoked and he was instructed to take charge of a detachment of eight or ten cavalrymen, to join their companies at Boise City or en route thereto. Two days later they rode out of the post. The Lieutenant reached Boise City on the sixteenth, but three more weeks slipped by before he could overtake his original command. Fast-changing events demanded hasty movement of troops.

With twenty-six mounted and armed volunteers, Captain J. B. Harper, on June 8, rode out from Silver City toward Battle Creek in Idaho, seven miles from South Mountain, a small mining village near the eastern boundary of Oregon. His force flushed sixty Bannocks led by Buffalo Horn, and dealt a stinging blow to hostile leadership. In the impetuous clash, the red chieftain, in his early thirties, fell victim to a bullet said to have been fired by Paiute Joe, raucous Indian scout. Hastily, the bronze warriors hid the body in a ravine.

In the near-by red men's camp lamentation was pro-
ged and loud. Indian women, in remorse for frustration,
ort their heavily braided black hair and, unstringing
lorful beads from wrists and neck, crunched them
ded bits. Some of the warriors lost hope even
re speedy vengeance. Many were forced to
ing in order to unite with several hundred

Paiute and other malcontents in Steens Mountains, eastern
Oregon, there to beg Chief Egan to lead them in a solid
front.

Egan, a dozen years the senior of Buffalo Horn, became
active war chief against his will. In his early days he had
had enough of fighting. The newer generation, however,
was eager for redress of grievances by force. They persuaded Egan to lead them. First, though, the chieftain
permitted a number of red and white friends to make
hasty escapes. Oits, Paiute medicine man, having long
pleaded for revenge against the whites' encroachments,
and noting how more than a few of his own race were
drifting away from faith in his practice, stirred up new
as well as old hatreds.

Though all Paiutes quit the Malheur Reservation at the
outbreak, some bands refused to join in the war. Followers
of Chief Winnemucca II were led away from the mountainous rendezvous in a ruse effected by Sarah and Mattie
Winnemucca, daughter and daughter-in-law of the aging
leader. They found refuge at Camp McDermitt in northern Nevada. Earlier, Chief Ochoco had led his band to the
vicinity of Camp Bidwell in northern California. The intelligent and daring Sarah and Mattie chose to accompany
Howard's troops as interpreters and guides throughout
the campaign.

The General's foremost desire, to keep the Bannocks
confined to southern Idaho, could not be met. Black-
bearded Captain Bernard had galloped across sage land to
Sheep Ranch, a telegraph station on the Winnemucca,
Nevada, stage road, and 110 miles southeast of Boise City.
Howard, joining him there on June 14, planned immediate
pursuit of the enemy into Oregon. Boise City became the
base for general field supplies.

On the sixteenth, Howard announced his first major
campaign plan. Three principal columns of troops were
assigned lines of advance, with employment of means of

communication and supply. The infantry and artillery companies in the field averaged about twenty men each, the cavalry forty. Military units of the Department of the Columbia got into full swing by the eighteenth. Howard sent a dispatch to General McDowell reporting that he had a total of 852 men under his command. More troops were sent to interior Oregon, the country demanding wide distribution of forces.

First to press the enemy across the expanse by the shortest route rode Bernard with four companies of the First Cavalry, designated as the left column. Colonel Orlando (Rube) Robbins, granitic campaigner from Idaho, and his twenty starchy scouts accompanied the unit. Captain Thomas McGregor with Company A, First Cavalry, received advice to leave Camp Harney, at the western edge of Malheur Reservation, and join Bernard at the first opportunity.

The center column, under Colonel Grover and consisting of three cavalry companies commanded by Major George B. Sanford, along with Company F, Second Infantry, was to march from Boise City by way of Keeney's Ferry on the Snake River. Further movements would depend upon the swaying of the pursuit.

Held in reserve were five companies of the Twelfth Infantry under Captain Harry C. Egbert, who made forced marches across the country from Cornucopia, Nevada. They comprised a controlling force around Silver City, at near-by Camp Lyon, and along the Winnemucca stage route. In deeper reserve stood two companies of the Fourth Artillery, led from Winnemucca to Camp McDermitt by Captain John Egan.

The remaining right column served as immediate reinforcement for Bernard. Although Major Joseph Stewart of the Fourth Artillery held command of the force, General Howard, who at forty-eight years of age could still push a mount with unalloyed assiduity, made arrangements to accompany it with his personal staff. Stewart had two companies of the Twenty-first Infantry. Acting as assistant inspector general was Major Edwin C. Mason, infantryman. Lieutenant E. W. Stone became chief commissary of subsistence, and Lieutenant Frederick H. E. Ebstein chief quartermaster in the field. Both were of the Twenty-first Infantry. On the general staff accompanying Howard closely as aides-de-camp were Lieutenants Melville C. Wilkinson and Charles E. S. Wood, also infantrymen. The group advanced first from Rinehart's Crossing of the Malheur River to Malheur Reservation.

Lieutenant Brown, on June 18, received orders from Howard to proceed with his detachment to Keeney's Ferry and there guard the subdepot. This done, a telegram from Aide-de-Camp Wood, dated at Malheur City, Oregon, June 21, was received via Boise City.

Leave Keeney Ferry at   Proceed at once with your Commissary's Stores and Pack Train and Wagons to Malheur Agency You will abandon no property unless it is necessary to do so on arriving at Agency Report to Lieut Stone Boise what Supplies and General Condition of things you find there You will form Sub-Depot at Malheur and act as Guard

The recent graduate of West Point began to wonder if, instead of fighting Indians, he was to continue as a prodder of mules and caretaker of supplies. Correctly, he surmised that battle lay ahead for his Troop L with Bernard's command.

Brown arrived at the agency the night of the twenty-fourth, to find the war gaining momentum. The previous day General Howard had posted a temporary guard at the agency and then left for Fort Harney. On the twenty-third, Bernard's battalion of cavalry, accompanied by scouts under Robbins, and a few Oregon ranchers, had attacked the hostiles at Silver Creek, forty-five miles west of Fort Harney. Taken by surprise in the morning hours, the warriors led by Egan nevertheless fought audaciously against the blue-coated troopers and the scouts who charged through the camp from either end of a grassy flat. Egan sustained two crippling wounds in a mounted duel with Robbins, but rallied his followers to a stand atop protecting bluffs.

The red men, behind hastily built breastworks of black lava rock, held off their attackers through the day and into the night. To succeed in their flight northward under cover of darkness, the Indians set fire to huge piles of sagebrush within their lines of defense. The soldiers, believing the fight would be resumed on the same spot at the dawn of another day, rested in preparation for the battle to be denied them. Three of their number had been killed and several wounded. Indian casualties, carefully screened, were difficult to ascertain.

Upon hearing of the attack, Howard ordered his reinforcements to hasten their advance. Others he distributed in a manner to cut off any retreat by the enemy. The Indians, as usual, stuck to the security of rugged country. They zigzagged northward to the John Day Valley, pillaged ranches, and fought off irate mounted volunteers from Canyon City, thriving mining town of Grant County. The military found it hard to overtake red men who were familiar with old trails and water courses, and who traveled exceedingly light with hundreds of ponies.

Meantime, Brown, assisted by agency employees, hastened the inventory of government property on the sprawling, tenantless reservation. With joy he dropped his task when he received orders to bring his supplies immediately to the advanced troops. By June 27 he was pacing, slapdash, the sixty miles to Fort Harney. It was the same distance by horseback trail from the post to Canyon City, but Brown, as a provisioner, trod seventy-five.

The wayworn Lieutenant arrived at Canyon City July 1. He left his pack train, guarded by eight cavalrymen, on the outskirts and, accompanied by an orderly, pushed into

Courtesy of Don Russell, Chicago, Ill.

Captain Reuben F. Bernard (brevet colonel), First Cavalry, in Bannock War of 1878. Photo taken at Walla Walla, Washington, probably in 1878.

town. There he learned of the latest fighting developments
—that Bernard, with Howard's reinforcements, was pursuing the Indians who "were then crossing the John Day
valley about ten miles below town and going north."

Brown, later recalling the venture in Canyon City,
wrote:

. . . . In fact, from the hills about town the smoke from burning houses
at various places down the valley could plainly be seen. Townspeople
were in tremendous excitement as an attack was feared. Advantage had
been taken of a cave or entrance to a mine where women and children
had taken refuge. I was questioning people, trying to size up the
situation and considering the feasibility of going down the valley with
my little command supplemented by such civilians as might volunteer
to go with me. . . . . While my inquiry was in progress a great shout
went up: "Here they come! Here they come! The Indians are coming
right down the road." Pandemonium had broken loose. Men were
yelling; dogs barking; women and children screaming; one woman
was running wildly down the street with her luxuriant tresses streaming
in the wind—women in those days didn't wear their hair bobbed!
Hurrying to where I could see the cause of the tumult, I discovered
that in my absence the chief packer had concluded to bring the train
on into town, either for safety or to get a glass of beer—perhaps both.
My train had been mistaken for an onslaught of the hostiles. . . . .

Near the mouth of the South Fork of the John Day, on
July 3, Brown appeared in a jumbled camp made by
Howard's troops. The pack mules relieved a situation which
had been jeopardized by slowly moving wagons, some
pulled by oxen. Shortly, the Lieutenant caught up with
Troop L. Tongue in cheek, he absorbed the kidding for
being a mule driver while missing out on the battalion's
fight at Silver Creek.

To keep the fun going, he told his fellow cavalrymen of
the rider of a war-bedecked pony who a few hours previously had galloped up to Howard and his staff shouting
that he was fleeing from white men who had shot at him.
The venerable General, after surveying the excited man's
mount with open amusement, advised removal of aboriginal
decorations. The man had tied to the mane and tail of his

horse a fulsome array of red rags, varicolored beads, and an assortment of feathers. He was, Brown commented, a newspaper reporter from Walla Walla with a curious appetency for Indian mementos.

As the hostiles continued their retreat toward the Columbia River their numbers swelled. Those who joined in depredations represented malcontents from bands of Columbia Indians, some Lemhis, Shoshones, Cayuse, and others. Few Umatillas became hostile, most of them discreetly remaining neutral.

Before daylight had vanished on the sixth, Howard and the cavalry made egress on the western fringe of Camas Meadows. With tall marsh grass and water near at hand, the prairie offered an ideal place to halt and again seek information. Soldiers wandering in the vicinity came upon the lifeless forms of two settlers. Blatting of sheep not far away led to further investigation. Some of the animals' forelegs had been whittled off, leaving dangling stumps. Bodies of others lay scattered over the snipped grass. Calloused red men had hastily wreaked havoc and departed.

Soon a scout rode into camp. Volunteers, he reported, had skirmished with a group of hostiles on the headwaters of Birch Creek, a considerable distance northeast of the prairie. It was understood that Captain C. B. Throckmorton's battalion of infantry and artillery, from Wheaton's force, had rushed to the aid of the white men.

Next day, Howard's command bore to the northwest and then back to the northeast while skirting irregular troughs and spurs of the mountains above the meadowland. In the evening it reached Pilot Rock, a small isolated hamlet raddled with pole corrals. From here, a short distance below the southern boundary of Umatilla Reservation, in a huge bend of Birch Creek, it was not many miles eastward to the fork of Stewart and McKay's creeks, or westward to the course of Butter Creek. The Blue Mountains,

which offered a ready haven to the Indians, raised themselves in a smoky haze as a barrier on the east. From all
reports, the hostiles' bivouac was near by, with the rolling
Columbia inviting a crossing into Washington Territory.

The Department Commander welcomed with unabashed
eagerness the arrival of Throckmorton's troops and Captain
Winter's company of the First Cavalry from Fort Lapwai.
Sarah Winnemucca expressed her opinion to the General
that his troops now were in front of the Indians, rather
than behind. And, therefore, most of the hostiles, aware
that the military was on the west side of the mountains,
would, if attacked successfully, take position in hills and
timber instead of attempting to rush northward.

While falling to evening mess, the officers received three
couriers who reported nearly fifteen hundred hostiles maneuvering in the hills fifteen miles away. Howard sent out
more scouts to observe the Indians' encampment, while his
troops gained a rest during the night. Wily scouts of the
red men, however, viewing the conjunction of soldiers and
the dispatching of lookouts, relayed word which caused
the main war party to shield itself from close observation.

Noise of camp subsided. Dew fell on hot trails and
parched grasses. Brown and his comrades sought serene
sleep at the sprawling feet of cool, silent mountains.

Under Fire of Bannocks and Paiutes

THE newborn light of July 8, 1878, bathed in red the
ridges' combs, and shadows streaked down rippling
slopes. Throckmorton's column of some sixty soldiers and a
sprinkling of volunteers moved along the sun-cracked stage
road to Butter Creek's pine-board post office. Howard,
accompanying Bernard's column of 280 cavalrymen, and
reinforced by Robbins' scouts and a Gatling gun, advanced
three miles toward Butter Creek's headwaters.

Two scouts dropped back to tell the General that the
main body of Indians was sheltered atop wooded hills three
miles distant and nearer the course of Butter Creek's
drainage area. Brown and his comrades, itching for action,
rebounded to the news with elation. It was to be the
Lieutenant's first fight, but just fray Number 100 for the
bristly Bernard—with the one-armed department head on
the ground to witness it.

Howard, whose career had been more closely twined
with artillery and infantry, readily saw this was a cavalryman's fight. His orders made it so.

Captain Bernard, unhesitantly, urged his men into a
quick trot over corrugated and brush-covered foothills.
At the head of the several troops rode Captains Winters,
Whipple, and Charles Bendire, and Lieutenants W. R.
Parnell, Frederick K. Ward, Bomus—and William Carey
Brown. Captain McGregor's company guarded the pack
train.

Throckmorton was too far away to be called back. And
still farther away was Captain Evan Miles's battalion of

the Twenty-first Infantry which had jogged northward with Howard from Silver Creek, now moving up from Camas Prairie.

Along the curving crest of a steep-banked hill, colorfully arrayed and painted bronzed riders sank their toes into the ribs of skittish ponies as they plunged back and forth. Blankets were whirled in the air and guns shaken in invidious challenge. Dismounted groups snaked along the ground, giving vent to highly pitched outcries interspersed with rhythmic chants as their bodies twisted in emphatic gesturing.

"Innnnnnng Haaaaaaa."*

The war whoop rolled like the approach of a thousand pounding hoofs on baked crust of earth.

"Innnnnnng Haaaaaaa. Innnnnnng Haaaaaaa."

It rose and fell like torrents of water tearing out roots from caving banks, then tumbling over cliffs onto rocks far below.

Oits, crunching his teeth, stationed himself well in front with a chosen group of subchiefs. Boldly he denounced those who would lean toward early flight.

Immediately behind his reckless, tufted warriors rode War Chief Egan, an arm in a willow sling. Fretfully, he bemoaned his incapacity. Doubtfully, he kept to himself the fears he entertained for his people who faced the onslaught of the whites. They should not be too anxious to taste lead.

Although the enemy appeared to be securely ensconced among huge jagged rocks rising above the steepest benches, the troopers advanced with scant trepidation. They seized advantage of several half-protecting, oblique approaches and, in the face of withering fire, charged with closed ranks. Some horses, seared and punctured with bullets fired aimlessly from above, pitched and reared in the

---

* The general war whoop of Pacific Northwest Indians, as set forth after searching inquiry by Robert J. Hendricks, in *Innnnnng Haaaaaa! A Triology in the Anabasis of the West*. (Privately printed, Salem, Oregon, 1937.)

climb. A few blue-clad soldiers, victims of the leaden spraying, tumbled from their saddles.

Bernard's cavalrymen dismounted to do better fighting. They pressed on with reins of bridles looped around the forearm, holding themselves steady in sharp ascent as they fired their carbines from hillsides and gullies. Horses, excitedly jerking at the bridle straps, their flesh twitching, were held taut for a chance to make a sudden charge. Officers shoved among heavy-breathing men who lent ear to crisp orders.

Brown, having twenty-four birthdays behind him, met with relish his first baptism of fire. His patience snapped when he discovered he could not use his revolver effectively. He seized a trooper's carbine. With trained eye, he fired again and again at the emboldened red warriors who tried to encircle the attackers. The ring was too far flung —a distance of 800 yards—and true aim fell short.

In the heat of combat, Sarah and Mattie Winnemucca joined the General when he took his stand at the belching Gatling gun. Under the hot pre-noon sun, they stood near the line of fire while bullets rasped the hard-baked earth and ricocheted from glistening rocks. In spite of her enthusiasm for the efficiency of the soldiery, Sarah voiced the hope that her own people would not become overzealous and suffer unnecessary losses. Irked she was, though, when above the whine of speeding lead she heard the defiant Preacher Oits hurl the taunt:

"Come on, you white dogs—what are you waiting there for?"

But of hand-to-hand fighting there was little. In less than an hour's feverish action the resisting warriors were dislodged from crested strongholds. The hostiles, abandoning 200 half-starved ponies, warily made a series of brief stands on elevations where dense patches of pine afforded the temporary protection. The pressing Cavalry, after successive gains with Robbins and the scouts, pushed their opposition four or five miles farther back into the mountains of indigo.

High noon brought a halt to Howard's fight at Birch Creek. Men and horses limped in weary clusters. The soldiers, knowing the hazards of the wilderness, called it a day. The Indian fighters retreated toward the Wallowa country, once the home of Nez Perce Chief Joseph, to unite with their women and children who had been shunted away from the scene of the encounter. Again their casualties were their own secret. Again Egan was assured of security, but his spirit as well as his body sought a chance for mending. Pluckily, however, he displayed nothing but an armor of courage before his fellows, advising them against uncertainties.

The troopers counted nearly twenty of their horses killed and five of their men seriously injured, a sergeant and four privates. One, Private Richard Smith, suffered a mortal wound. In the death watch of the night after battle, Sarah and Mattie rendered him what aid they could. General Howard, still "Havelock of the Army," comforted him with scriptural reading and prayer.

In the morning, the lad was buried in ground shaded by the verdant branches of a pine, sentinel in the vast reaches of russet grassland. Later, in the fall, the body was to be disinterred by charitable Odd Fellows and removed to Walla Walla.

Preparations made to forestall a crossing of the Columbia River by hostiles had been carried out successfully by Howard's scattered soldiers, aided by the services of Governor S. F. Chadwick of Oregon and Governor Elisha P. Ferry of Washington, with volunteers. On the day Howard was turning back the main body of the enemy at Birch Creek, two armed steamers inflicted telling damage on small parties of red men who attempted to cross the Columbia. A few gained the northern shore and, traveling toward Yakima City, murdered Lorenzo Perkins and his wife, settlers who were given no warning.

Most of the fleeing Bannocks and Paiutes, officers and scouts believed, would follow the Grande Ronde River to its junction with the Snake, whence the trek would continue into Idaho. Sarah, however, was convinced the main parties of Paiutes would turn southward in the Blue Mountains in striving to return to the Malheur country.

The General, to stop dividing groups from any direction, planned disposition of his increasing troops accordingly. He first sought telegraphic facilities on his way to Walla Walla, urging pursuit along the Grand Ronde and the guarding of trails in the region between the Snake and Salmon rivers of Idaho. Sarah and Mattie remained with Bernard's column, soon to receive orders to proceed to Lewiston, by way of Walla Walla, where supplies could be renewed.

Brown and his troopers camped at Fort Walla Walla for a day, on the twelfth. Howard had left that morning to take the boat for Lewiston, after instructing Lieutenant Colonel James W. Forsyth, First Cavalry, to take command of Bernard's force. Forsyth, lately arrived from General Phil Sheridan's headquarters in Chicago, wore an immaculate uniform. Yet he, who at the side of Sheridan had observed combat between French and Prussian forces, soon became one with those in tattered and dust-caked attire.

After a march of sixty-eight miles, Forsyth's cavalrymen halted on the morning of the fourteenth to pitch camp on Wild Horse Creek, Oregon. Their horses, fatigued by the pace, were to be given a day's rest and proper feeding. The supply of hay had been short and none too sustaining. A brief order, issued by Forsyth, read in part:

A Board of Survey will assemble at these Headquarters at 9 o'clock A. M. today, or as soon thereafter as practicable, for the purpose of fixing the price to be paid for the use of a Wheat field belonging to William Ferguson for grazing purposes for the stock of this command.

Brown and Captains Bernard and Winters were named as detail for the board.

The trio quickly appraised the value of the crop at $100. Then Brown committed a *faux pas*. He started to mount his horse to return to camp and there unsaddle it. No sooner did he have a foot in the stirrup than Bernard checked him gruffly.

"Lieutenant, your horse needs to eat. He needs rest. You will please unsaddle the animal here."

The young officer's acquired tan hid his blushing as he noted that Bernard and Winters at that moment were unsaddling their horses in order to set them loose in the wheat.

"Yes, sir. I did not understand correctly, sir."

Speedily, he dismounted, removed his own saddle and carried it back to camp. His admiration for Bernard doubled, and he never forgot the lesson. In his future years as a cavalry commander, he would demand of his men the sort of care their animals merited.

The direction of march from the Wild Horse camp soon was altered by fresh developments. The main body of the hostiles had turned back from hasty flight. On the thirteenth, Captain Evan Miles, with a mixed force of artillery, infantry, and volunteers, repulsed and scattered the red men near the Umatilla Indian Agency. Company K, First Cavalry, led by Bendire, which had joined Miles on the tenth, also knifed into the conflict. Retreat of the hostiles again was to the south and east.

Miles had won permanent recognition for his calm planning and keenly executed maneuvers. Here, too, a young second lieutenant of the cavalry displayed such conspicuous courage that to him came the brevet of higher rank. He was Robert P. P. Wainwright. His son, Jonathan M. Wainwright, would, as a lieutenant general, earn the highest praise for valiant and stubborn defense of the Bataan Peninsula against smothering Japanese invaders.

On the morning of the fifteenth, Forsyth tarried near Emigrant Springs in the Blue Mountains. There Brown peered into a gunnysack opened by unfeeling bearers. It contained the head of Chief Egan. Umatilla Indians under Umapine, hereditary chief of the Cayuses, had become overzealous in their desire to clear themselves before the whites. They had ambushed and killed several Bannock and Paiute warriors in council with Egan.

While troops under Major Sanford guarded the country to his left and rear, Forsyth pushed southward. With Troop I of Sanford's command rode Lieutenant Oscar J. Brown, West Point graduate of '77. Umatillas again had attacked the enemy and reported the direction of flight. The trail of the hostiles led into steep canyons, over high and rugged mountains, through a mesh of burnt and fallen timber.

Forsyth's troopers, with scouts and the inseparable Paiute women, Sarah and Mattie, came to the canyon of the North Fork of the John Day River on the morning of the twentieth. Here, not far from the settlement of Independence, or Mound City, they sighted the Bannock-Paiute rear guard. Bernard, leading his Troop G, displayed anxiety to chalk up fight Number 101 for himself. Lieutenant Brown, facing his second battle, felt more like a seasoned fighter. He had no heavy beard, but the hair of his head draped over the back of his collar, and he could boast a wavy mustache and a rough square of whiskers almost hiding his chin.

The battalion of four mounted troops and eight scouts slid down a precipitous 1200-foot trail, then spent an hour and a half in gaining the summit of the opposite side. A few pack animals lost their footing on the steep walls and fell backward into the gorge's rocky bottom. The scouts felt out the advance, followed by Company E under Winters, Company H, led by Parnell, and Company L in charge of Shelton and Brown. Bernard and Lieutenant John

Pitcher, to guard the right end of the line where the stock were corralled on a natural terrace, climbed a promontory offering distinct advantage.

When all troops had made the ascent they espied forty warriors lurking behind scattered rocks and mounds. The Indians opened fire when one of the scouts accidentally discharged his gun. Irrepressible cavalrymen charged in irregular line. Red men answered spiritedly with spurts of rifle fire, but failed to make more than a brief stand. They rapidly increased the distance between them and their pursuers, who had no immediate plan for further attack.

Casualties were light. Courier A. A. Froman was killed, another scout and a private of Troop E sustained wounds. Two Indian women fell captive, one a Paiute recognized by Sarah, the other a Bannock. They had retraced their steps to search for children the Paiute mother had lost in flight. She did not find her own offspring, but a leathery sergeant picked up a girl papoose whose tiny brown nose was poked into the dry dirt. Sarah permitted the Paiute searcher to care for the Bannock baby, clothed only in a soiled shirt covered with small beads. The infant was to spend three months with the troops before being restored to her prisoner-parents at Malheur Reservation.

According to plan, Forsyth effected a meeting with Sanford at Burnt River Meadows on the twenty-third. General Howard accompanied the latter, hoping to bring the Paiutes to quick surrender. He had advised Egbert to pick up any hostiles drifting across the Snake River to the Weiser and Payette country. The march was resumed to Malheur Agency over more rugged, desolate wasteland. On the trail, Brown counted a dozen carcasses of horses, lost by the Indians. The soldiers saw twenty-two of their own horses and eleven mules give out. For subsistence they killed four beeves.

They reached the Agency on the twenty-seventh and

the next day welcomed the arrival of Colonel Marcus P. Miller and Lieutenant William Crozier, Fourth Artillery, who brought rations from Baker City. Lieutenant Galbraith, of the Class of '77 and Troop F, First Cavalry, also appeared. Brown formed a friendship with Crozier which would endure throughout his lifetime. Malheur Agency was made a subdepot, temporarily garrisoned by Miller's force and Troop F.

Howard concluded, correctly, that the Indians had broken up into small groups. He ordered scouting from eastern Oregon into Idaho by veteran Major John Green with three troops, First Cavalry. Forsyth, with Bernard and Sanford, was to scour the adjacent region for fugitives before proceeding to the Boise district. Wheaton was to shift his field headquarters from Baker City to Boise City.

The General, wishing to go as far east as the Winnemucca stage road before returning to his headquarters on the Columbia River, was escorted beyond the Owyhee River by Troops D and L. Brown, while crossing the high desert country, learned more of its vastness from Captain E. V. Sumner of Troop D, who had been ordered into the field from Camp Halleck, Nevada. On August 3, the Lieutenant bade good-by to Shelton, who, commanding Howard's escort of ten men, was to return to Walla Walla.

A week later, Brown, commanding Company L, joined Major Green's forces and volunteers in protecting settlers near Dixie Stage Station, on the road from Boise to Kelton, Utah. For on the ninth, Captains Egbert and William Dove had, after a sharp skirmish, driven toward Big Camas Prairie a hundred hostiles found on an island in Bennett's Creek, a tributary of the Snake River east of Rattlesnake Creek.

Other parts of Idaho were scouted for Bannocks trying to reach the Fort Hall Reservation or their old haunts, while in Oregon the military gathered in prisoners. By mid-August some four hundred Indians, including sobered

Oits, had surrendered at various places within the department. Captain W. F. Drum and two companies of the
Second Infantry crossed the Snake at Brownlee's Ferry and,
while marching to Camp Howard, near Mount Idaho,
bolstered settlers alarmed by stray red men.

Cavalry horses now were in a jaded condition, some having to be abandoned. A dispatch from Boise informed
Brown "that at such times as you find it absolutely necessary to do so, you may mount the dismounted portion of
your company with horses from the country through
which you are marching." Little luck there was, however,
for, by the middle of August, Major Green ordered Troop
L to proceed to Fort Boise for refitting.

Brown and his tired troop entered the post on the
twenty-second. Five days later, Bernard and Winters also
came in. Then Forsyth, commanding the District of the
Boise, received a disturbing message from Captain Drum.
He had written on the twenty-fifth from his camp near the
Falls of the North Payette River stating he had found and
buried the bodies of three citizens slain by Indians on the
Gold Fork, and, near the Payette Falls, had also discovered
and interred the bodies of two slain prospectors. Some of
his soldiers and Idaho volunteers were scouting the trail
of the murderers. He asked that a company of cavalry,
with needed rations, be sent him.

Brown and his Troop L, supplied with transportation and
fifteen days' rations, left for the northern mining country
on the twenty-eighth. Though the going was rough after
leaving Garden Valley, the soldiers and packers joined
Drum on the Gold Fork the first day of September. They
could see snow on the mountains west of the valley, peaks
rising to a height of more than 7,000 feet.

Scouting of the wilderness, joined in by Lieutenant
Abner Haines, Jr., of Drum's command, availed little except first-hand glimpses of an area previously unexplored
by whites. The Indians had found refuge in the mountain

fastnesses or had followed trails to the east. Packers were discharged by the fifth. Several days more were spent in camp, until further orders came from district headquarters. When the courier arrived, Drum made ready to move on to Camp Howard. Brown, under the instructions, led his company back to Fort Boise, arriving on the seventeenth.

Field reconnaissance of the campaign within the Department of the Columbia now was virtually at an end. Meanwhile, the small bands of unappeasable Bannocks who had escaped the cordon in Idaho and Oregon wended their way to the region of Yellowstone National Park. On August 25 some of them attacked a party of government surveyors near Henrys Lake. The white men, led by A. D. Wilson, comprised a primary triangulation group co-operating with Geologist J. V. Hayden, then camped in Upper Geyser Basin. They left mules and horses behind them as they escaped on foot to tread sixty miles before reporting their plight to Hayden.

Troops of the Department of Dakota, aided by Indian scouts, rushed into action and captured the stray parties of Bannocks. A vacation trip in Yellowstone Park, planned by Colonel Nelson A. Miles commanding the Fifth Infantry at Fort Keogh, Montana Territory, was turned into tragedy by the surprising turn of events. Women, including the wife of Captain Frank D. Baldwin, an officer who had won sweeping acclaim for his fight against Chief Grey Beard's Cheyennes in Texas in 1874, were in the holiday group.

The quick-acting Miles, with Captain Andrew S. Bennett, twenty-seven soldiers of the Fifth Infantry, and thirty-five Crow warriors, moved up Clarks Fork of the Yellowstone River. They surprised and attacked a Bannock camp near Heart Mountain September 4. Captain Bennett and a Crow interpreter were killed in the charge that resulted in the capture of thirty-two red men with nearly two hundred horses and mules. Eleven Bannocks were reported slain. The vacationers stood in silent tribute as a stretcher bearing the body of the Captain rested at their feet, the first halt in the long journey to a family burial plot in Wisconsin.

On September 12, Lieutenant Hoel S. Bishop, Fifth Cavalry, accompanied by thirty soldiers and 150 Shoshone Indians under Chief Black Coal, Arapahoe warrior, struck the fleeing Bannocks at the head of Dry Fork, a tributary of the Snake River in Wyoming south and west of Yellowstone Lake. One Indian was killed and several others, with stolen horses and mules, were captured.

Only a few straggling red men were left to be picked up by troops who, in the shredded final stages of a futile widespread revolt, returned to their frontier posts. Until the captured malcontents were properly disseminated by the Department of the Interior some months later, they remained under military care.

At Fort Boise, Forsyth instructed Troops L and C to proceed to Camp McDermitt. The latter troop, under Captain Henry Wagner, after reporting for duty at the Nevada post, was to accompany Brown as far as Camp Bidwell, California. Troop L held orders to take station at Fort Klamath, near the northern edge of Klamath Lake, Oregon. All Indian prisoners in the district, nineteen squaws and papooses and three men, were to be delivered to the commanding officer at Camp McDermitt, then "to be sent by the first opportunity to Camp Harney, Oregon."

The wagon-and-horse train, Indians riding their own ponies, set out for the Nevada post on September 21. The journey consumed a week. On the thirtieth, Brown saw Sarah Winnemucca and her future husband, Corporal Hopkins of Troop A, First Cavalry, come from Camp Harney to aid in transporting Paiute prisoners back to Malheur Agency. From there, at the beginning of the new year, they would be conducted by two cavalry companies under Captain Winters to the Yakima Agency in Washington. And their Oregon reservation, in 1883, would again be part of the great public domain.

After arrival at Camp Bidwell on October 14, Troop L rested for two days before proceeding northward. Nine days later, Private Frederick Mayer of the command, spending his first night at Fort Klamath, wrote in the last line of his diary of the campaign of 1878, "Welcome home again." The German-born Mayer, who had also gone through the campaign of '77 with Troop L, and who was to serve in the Engineer Corps until his retirement as a sergeant, had not seen the Klamath post before. But it meant "home."

From August 3 until October 28, Lieutenant Brown had been troop commander because of the absence of his superiors on other duties. He had carried on exceedingly well. In his diary he jotted down the fact that in four months and twenty-five days he had marched more than twenty-seven hundred miles.

The Bannock-Paiute uprising had been quelled without great loss in battle. Of forty soldiers and citizens killed, only nine were army men, and fifteen soldiers survived serious wounds. About eighty Indians had been slain. Yet many troop mounts were half-broken broncos, frequently overloaded and underfed, not always having shoes replaced when needed. The Indians, with fresh unshod ponies, did not need or use heavy traveling equipment. Although the United States Army had been getting better equipment to facilitate transportation, the Department of the Columbia paid $960 for a dozen oxen in the year 1878.

In their last major uprising, the red warriors had seized or bartered for rifles, such as Winchesters, Sharps, and Centennials. Upon their surrender, they handed over mostly out-of-date models and little ammunition. Citizens' groups also had relied upon old-fashioned weapons, including needle gun and muzzle-loader.

William C. Brown as a second lieutenant, First Cavalry, taken about 1880. Frank G. Abell, photographer, Portland, Oregon.

Troopers prized their steel-barreled Springfield rifles, Model 1873, the rifle carbines and revolvers. Useless was the saber in the seventies and eighties against Modocs, Bannocks, Paiutes, Sheepeaters, and Apaches. In the Nez Perce and Bannock Wars, the Gatling gun, forerunner of the machine gun, and the howitzer, short and light cannon, had written awe on streaked faces of courageous warriors.

Lieutenant Brown and his comrades let down the curtain on a stage from which warring red men disappeared for all time. Indian campaigns of the Pacific Northwest, save for the Sheepeater struggle of 1879, were of the past. Fast fading into history were military figures who had procured invaluable experience in the region that once had been the old Oregon Country before they climbed the ladder to national fame. Among them were George Crook, U. S. Grant, Philip H. Sheridan, D. A. Russell, and John F. Reynolds.

Sheridan and Russell had cemented friendly ties at old Fort Yamhill, Oregon, tragically broken by the mortal wounding of Russell on a Virginia field in 1864.

In Oregon's sage land, Brown forged a friendship with Captain A. G. Forse, destined for severance on a sun-stippled hill in Cuba's perforated jungles.

CHAPTER VI

The Sheepeater Campaign—1879

BEFORE the final exodus of Indians from Camp Henry in 1879, some slipped stealthily past their guards. Lieutenant Brown, on March 21, proceeded with a small detachment to Yainax Subagency of the Klamath Indian Reservation to assist the agent in capturing a number of the "renegades" who fled confinement. A month later, he was ordered to visit Yainax again while on a dispatch-bearing mission to Camp Bidwell.

By the last of April, there were thirty-one Indian prisoners at Fort Klamath ready for transfer to a more distant location. At the head of a group of four noncommissioned officers and eleven privates, Brown broke garrison duty early in May to escort the Indians to Vancouver Barracks.

Upon returning to Department Headquarters, he received instructions to proceed to Umatilla Indian Agency for the purpose of joining and assisting in the organization of a company of Umatilla Indian scouts and guides. Violence on the part of red men again had burst forth.

The disturbed region which commanded the attention of the military in the Columbia Department lay between the Snake and Little Salmon rivers. In this wild and inaccessible country of Middle Idaho, half a hundred renegade Bannocks, Paiutes, and "Sheepeaters" had been dealing severely with Chinese and white miners, regarded by the Indians as trespassers. And they displayed a marked obstinancy in clinging to their wild retreats. Whether or not the disturbance was a repercussion of the Bannock War was open to argument. The bands were very much isolated, although the militant leader, Tamanmo, or War Jack, was of Bannock and Nez Perce blood. He had participated in the outbreak of the Bannock War and, finding refuge with the non-reservation group in Middle Idaho, claimed to be the successor of Chief Eagle Eye.

The chase of the Cavalry and Infantry, because of indirect rumors concerning the hostiles' whereabouts, and bewildering factors presented by rugged terrain, resulted in prolonged reconnoitering. Circuitous courses were followed from the Payette River and Lakes to and across the South and Middle Forks of the Salmon River. The several military units which entered the field were directed to come under the command of Captain Bernard, who had added to his laurels as troop and battalion commander in the Bannock War.

Bernard and sixty-odd soldiers, answering the trumpeting of "Boots and Saddles," left Boise Barracks on the last day of May. They were followed by a pack train which ten civilian packers had loaded with two months' rations. Scouts and guides included the persevering Rube Robbins, Johnny Vose, and John S. Ramey.

In the first week of June, Lieutenant Henry Catley with Lieutenants W. C. Muhlenberg and E. K. Webster had moved northward from Camp Howard, near Grangeville, Idaho, and from the Salmon River. They led a mounted force of forty-eight men of the Second United States Infantry, assisted by packers, scouts, and Medical Officer E. J. Pring.

On June 9, Lieutenant Edward S. Farrow of the Twenty-first Infantry and cavalryman Brown enlisted twenty-seven Indian scouts at Umatilla Agency. Equipment and clothing came from Fort Walla Walla. Although the scouts received pay for the use of only one horse and equipment each, they took forty ponies. Ya-tin-ow-itz, Cayuse war chief and son-in-law of Chief Howlish

Wampo, who possessed several thousand cayuse ponies, went into the campaign with five of his best horses.

The Umatilla Reservation was scouted between July 1 and 5. On July 8, the Indian scouts, seven enlisted men, and a pack train of twenty packs, with four packers headed by John Corliss, left the Agency to cross the Snake River into Idaho. They arrived at Upper Payette Lake eleven days later.

The entire group, commanded by Farrow, scouted the Seven Devils Mountains area before meeting up with Bernard in Long Valley and Catley on Elk Creek. In the meantime, after searching by all, Catley had been the only one to contact any hostiles. His small force had been obliged to retreat after a running fight in the Big Creek country. The denouement led to Bernard's shifting of the search to this particular region.

With the force of Farrow and Brown in advance, it attacked and captured a camp of the Indians on Big Creek, August 19. But the hostiles made a hasty flight, skins and cooking utensils being among articles left behind. Further pursuit by all the troops soon was out of the question, for a sorely needed supply train had failed to overtake the soldiers. Bernard, after giving the bulk of his rations to Farrow, was compelled to report his predicament.

In his march of 1,168 miles, the greater portion over baffling mountains, he had lost forty-five pack mules and eighteen horses. Men who had been worn down battling mushy or high-banked snow shot deer or grouse and, in one instance, raided a Chinaman's isolated patch of green onions. A meager supply of bacon and hardtack did not make for restraint.

Authorization came for Bernard to return to Fort Boise for refitting. After having overcome innumerable obstacles, he was back at his original post by September 8. Yet the relentless drive he had started was not doomed to failure.

The wind-up of the campaign—its success being made more dubious by fresh falls of snow—belonged alone to the small contingent under Farrow and Brown. With perseverance and fortitude that far outweighed means and supplies, about two dozen men, including the sturdy packers, repelled fretting. Only half the cayuse ponies were left, and these and pick-up stock displayed more skin-rippling ribs than signs of endurance.

The party started from Rains' Ranch on September 17 and, facing northeasterly, marched toward the region lying south of the Salmon and west of the Middle Fork. On the second day they picked up two squaws, a papoose, and a young boy. Another boy proved too fleet of foot to be trapped. Soon the fresh trail of a hunting party was easily detected, leading north to the high plateau above the main Salmon. Further search brought the pursuers to a hastily abandoned camp, where they seized four horses, and 600 pounds of meat not yet fully cured. Feasting on venison and elk alternated with relished naps.

On the twenty-third, after the following of a circuitous trail, a base camp was pitched eight miles west of the Middle Fork. Two men were sent to Warren for flour and fresh horses. Farrow and Brown, with sixteen of their command, accompanied by the papoose and its mother, left brightly burning campfires to press forward. They halted in a gulch the next day, sending the squaw ahead to intercept her people. The papoose, held as a hostage, wailed so loudly that the camping spot became Papoose Gulch on the official map. The squaw failed to bring in a report from her kin, but two camps revealed signs of four to six lodges quitted precipitately.

On the second day at the base camp, a sharp yell from the near-by timber rent the air. A hostile was ready to parley. Lieutenant Brown and his interpreter, Wa-tis-kow-kow, approached him in a spot hidden from view of the camp. The enemy, possessed of a Henry rifle, was advised to drop it. His interviewers pointed out the fact that they were unarmed. Answering a query as to the identity of the officer, the interpreter explained crisply, "Tenas Tyhee."

It meant "Little Chief." On that reply rested Brown's life. Had the words been "Hyas Tyhee" (Head Chief), so asserted the scout later, the questioner would have shot down the peacemakers.

The Henry rifle, however, was discarded, the captors grasped by the hand. When facing Farrow in the camp-fire parley, a bulge was detected in the back of the guest. The bulge proved to be a revolver. Its owner then bared his identity. He was Tamanmo. Of fighting he had had enough. Still he was deeply envious of the pursuers. The previous night, he revealed, he had crept cautiously to the edge of the camp, had noted the Indians therein were Cayuses, and had returned to his fellows with a plot to steal a few of the best horses.

Now he was ready to make peace. The beleaguered Indians, in destitute condition and altogether disheartened by the toe-to-heel chase, would hide out no more. Tamanmo, swearing that some of his people held forth at the mouth of Big Creek, gained permission to leave and round up his scattered followers. A white flag was hoisted in the camp. It fluttered there for the next few days. Rain, snow, and sleet added to the discomforts. Subsistence was reduced to half rations. A change in camping places was made September 30.

On the first day of October, in another shifting of camp, Tamanmo reappeared. With him came eight men and twenty-four squaws and papooses. Mostly Sheepeaters, they did justice to the occasion; they donned full dress of feathers and paint. The arms they boasted were one double-barreled shotgun, two muzzle-loading rifles, two Henry carbines, one Sharp's carbine, one Springfield carbine, and a Springfield breech-loading rifle. The final count of ragged and half-starved red persons who surrendered to the dogged pursuers was fifty-one. Fifteen rated as warriors.

The captors, in the position of sharing rations with their prisoners, found the demand imperative. Farrow sent Brown ahead to Warren, there to obtain food being brought from Camp Howard by Captain Forse and Lieutenant Muhlenberg. To procure the necessary supplies, the returning party followed the winding route through Camp Howard, Forts Lapwai, and Walla Walla.

Snow, dense in its fall and driven by biting winds, whirled down from the mountains to the troughs of the valleys and the level expanse of the plains as the Sheepeater Campaign ended. The prisoners, and the soldiers and scouts who had charge of them, faced a long and cold journey as they forsook the isolated fastness which, to them, had seemed impregnable. They marched and rode many lean miles before espying their temporary destination, Umatilla Agency, on October 22. Farrow then conducted the prisoners to Vancouver Barracks, where they would remain until transferred to Fort Hall Reservation the next year.

Duty done, Brown gave unhedged praise to the white and red men who aided Farrow and himself. Sergeant Charlie Shaplish (Whirlwind), Umatilla scout, "spoke a little English, was of the Fenimore Cooper type, and as handsome a warrior as ever wore moccasins. Whenever there was a difficult piece of scouting to be done, Shaplish was usually selected to do it." And "Corporal Wa-tis-kow-kow's knowledge of Shoshone enabled him to assist materially at the surrender of Tamanmo, or War Jack, in which he took risks which should have won him a decoration."

The cavalryman could not forget that the Indian "is more expert at hunting and fishing than the white man, an important consideration when the regular rations run short, which was frequently our misfortune."

Guides and couriers, carrying food and bedding on their saddles when separated from the command, often were in danger of sudden attacks on covered trails. Though they usually traveled by night on the plains, they were compelled to take unfamiliar mountain trails in the light of day. Packers always rose before sunrise, to pack the mules with ropes made rigid by frost. Those under Bernard, in thirty-seven days of marching in a so-called "midsummer campaign," encountered thick falls of fresh snow as well as solid drifts twenty to thirty feet in depth.

Among the guides, couriers, and packers who participated in the Indian campaigns of 1877, 1878, and 1879, and whom, Brown pointed out, "the State of Idaho should hold in grateful remembrance," were George Shearer, Josh Falkner, Calvin R. White, Levi A. White, David R. Monroe, Johnny Vose, J. W. Redington, Jake Barnes, Alexander Foster, Harry Serren (Lemhi), Uncle Dave ("Cougar") Lewis, the Parker brothers, Corliss, Ramey, Bright, and Robbins. None, however, approached as closely to Bernard in his effective style of fighting as did Robbins.

Of the stout-hearted men who brought an end to the Sheepeater Campaign, General Howard wrote in an official dispatch to Division Headquarters:

Lieutenants Farrow, Twenty-first Infantry, and W. C. Brown, First Cavalry, with the seven enlisted men, citizen employes, and Indian scouts, deserve special mention for gallantry, energy, and perseverance, resulting in success. There is not a rougher or more difficult country for campaigning in America.

Further, the Department Commander, in a communication to the Adjutant General of the Army, October 20, 1879, asserted, in part:

. . . . But for gallantry, skill and energy of Lieutenants Farrow and Brown I should have been obliged next summer to put another and larger force into the field. . . . .

By his action Lieutenant Farrow, then, has not only given security to the numerous scattered and weak settlements of Middle and Northern Idaho, but has also saved many thousand dollars of expense to the government.

Therefore I recommend that for this the brevets of 1st. Lieutenant and Captain be conferred upon Second Lieutenant Edward S. Farrow, 21st Infantry for distinguished ability, perseverance and gallantry in conducting operations, expedition of 1879, against hostile Indians in Middle Idaho, resulting in the capture of the entire band, and that the Brevet of First Lieutenant be conferred upon 2nd Lieut. W. C. Brown, 1st Cavalry, for distinguished perseverance, energy and gallantry in action against the hostile Indians of Middle Idaho, expedition of 1879, which operations resulted in the capture of the entire band. . . . .

Brown received an official copy "for his information." With no little pride, he filed it among his papers, to await the outcome. Generally, brevet title called for courteous social discernment, although the officer awarded it was listed on the official roster of his command according to actual rank. It had its advantages. Brown recalled the case of Captain Sylvanus Thayer being made a Brevet Major before his going abroad in 1815. James Monroe, Secretary of War *ad interim*, had foreseen that major's epaulettes would give Thayer increased prestige and make easier any opportunity to study the military establishments of Europe. Yes, a brevet could be useful.

The hopeful Lieutenant rejoined his company at Fort Klamath on November 14, after having spent six months and ten days in field service, and marching 2,365 miles in the year. The campaign had given him the chance to make the first map of Middle Idaho. From his notes he marked out trails blazed by the troops, submitting the sketch to the Office of the Chief Engineer, Department of the Columbia. Late in February, 1880, First Lieutenant Thomas W. Symons, Chief Engineer of the Department, replied:

I have the honor to acknowledge receipt of a map of the country which is the scene of the recent Indian hostilities.

I take pleasure in testifying to its excellence and in thanking you for it.

It is a valuable addition to our knowledge of an almost unknown section. . . . .

The brevet, however, Brown came to consider as a matter forgotten by superiors who thought of things more important. There was reason to change his mind. The author of *The Sheepeater Campaign* wrote in his laconism: "Lieuts. Farrow and Brown were each subsequently awarded (February 27, 1890) the brevet of First Lieutenants for their service."

There had been hitches. In the final recommendation resulting in the bestowal of the brevets, General Howard requested that the words "in the field" replace "in action" as set forth in the original citation.

The year 1918 lay far distant in the future. It would find Brown in France, one of six survivors on the active list of the United States Army breveted for courageous conduct in the field or in action.

Last Days in the Pacific Northwest

ALONG with regular garrison duty at the Klamath post, Brown shouldered quartermaster and commissary worries the first three months of 1880. More than a few times the delayed arrival of a freighter, struggling over Cascade Mountain passes with supplies, provoked moments of anxiety and strain. Though roads were fair, the snow, especially on the eastern slope, was flung again and again onto ever-mounting drifts. Four- and six-team wagons were required for transportation. The 200-mile haul from Roseburg to Klamath cost about nine cents a pound, the rate being halved in warmer seasons.

It was at Roseburg, humming stage-and-rail terminus, where General Howard had met President Rutherford B. Hayes, General Sherman, and their party on a visit to the "Web-foot," or "Beaver" State, in the fall of 1879.

Military mail between the post and Linkville (Klamath Falls) was dispatched three times a week. Weather permitting, Brown and his companions sought relief from dull routine in hunting and fishing trips, to bag a full share of deer and trout. Too, they benefited from the hospitality extended by civilians who lived at or near the post.

Out of everyday neighborly discussion came the ever recurrent "new tip" on the Blue Bucket Mine. It was a rich deposit of gold, supposed to have been discovered in eastern Oregon by early-day emigrants, yet never rediscovered. Officer Brown recorded information on the subject as passed on from Mrs. W. G. Parker. Her husband kept the stage station near the summit of the Cascade

Mountains, about midway between Linkville and Ashland. Hardly a traveler passed through but whose ears tingled to the various tales which "located" the "lost" bonanza.

Target practice, indulged in only slightly by the army when Brown gained his first commission, virtually became a craze in 1880. Troops in the Department of the Columbia, as well as those elsewhere, waited eagerly on the range for sunrise. And their firing did not cease until twilight. Department commanders published reports of competing units as they reveled in the marksmanship trials.

On June 5, Brown began a march to Vancouver Barracks with Company F, Twenty-first Infantry, commanded by First Lieutenant Joseph W. Duncan. All but a few men rode in creaking wagons, at four dollars a head. In a twenty-mile march on the sixth, Brown lost his saddlebags near Chiloquin bridge. At Modoc Point, sanguinary landmark near the shore of Klamath Lake, he counted more than a hundred snake trails in the road an hour after wagons had passed. Rattlesnakes abounded in the tall grass so tempting for the grazing of animals.

Four days later, the troops crossed Green Spring Mountain, and on the sixth day camped beside the Rogue River. Then, contrasting with the chilling winds and muddy roads of the mountains left behind was the hot and dusty journey northward. On the fifteenth, Brown sat in the saddle for eleven hours, riding thirty-eight lip-cracking miles before arriving at Roseburg. The infantrymen camped at Oak Grove. So wearisome had been the ride, that a measure of mutiny prevailed in the ranks until an hour after midnight.

After the train ride through Eugene, with its six-year-old State University, Salem with its gray-white Capitol, and rose-embowered Portland, the Lieutenant wrote in his diary for June 17: "Arrived at Vancouver Bks. Men noisy & disrespectful at Reveille. Gen. Morrow and Gen. Howard very indignant about the mutiny & talk of disbanding the Company."

He spent the next day listing the mutinous men and specifying the charges against them.

Soon he was informed that Captain Bendire was preparing his company for scouting between the Palouse Ferry on the Snake River and the Spokane River, also the adjacent region. The assignment, of benefit to the Smithsonian Institution, was for a topographical survey and the collection of specimens, chiefly mineral. Brown rejoiced in instructions permitting him to accompany the expedition.

For the next several days he worked on the mutiny cases, made trips to Portland, visited with officers in quarters and on the target range, and drew maps in Symons' office. On the thirtieth, an order was published directing Private C. C. Manning, topographical assistant, and Private Emerie Lane, Company A, Twenty-first Infantry, to aid the Lieutenant in the scouting and surveys. They started labor on an odometer cart harness.

Three days later, Brown left by boat for Walla Walla, where Bendire's company had preceded him. The Columbia was at flood stage when he arrived at The Dalles in the evening. He reached Celilo by rail July 5 and, the next day, took the steamer *John Gates* to Wallula, having to "camp out" on deck because all the staterooms were occupied by ladies. Having arrived at Wallula by midnight, he fretted two hours waiting for ferry service to the railroad track. Abreast of daylight, he sauntered into Walla Walla, reporting to Bendire and Major John Green. The older officer was looking forward to happy retirement in Boise City.

Further prepartions included more work on the odometer cart. Edmund Schriver, inspecting General, graduate of West Point in 1833, and now in his late sixties, arrived with General Howard and Aide-de-Camp Wood. Review and inspection were in order. Emphasized was the wearing of government boots but *not* white collars by soldiers. Bedding and mattresses were closely examined. Because they had been forewarned by letter from an officer of a previously inspected unit, the men at Walla Walla avoided cause for barks by a puzzled scrutinizer.

Brown left for the Snake River country July 17. Roads were rough, the weather hot, and the odometer cart demanded frequent repairing. Good camp sites, however, were found, water and grass obtained readily. By the twenty-sixth the party made camp on the Spokane River, near Spokane Falls, and two days later pulled up at Fort Coeur d'Alene.

New quarters for fifteen officers at the post neared completion. The buildings were spacious and their location was one of rare beauty. A steamboat had been launched on the lake, and a merry group busied itself for a trial run. Captain Charles A. Dempsey and Lieutenant Haines were out working on the Mullan Road, an important link of travel with posts east of the Bitterroot Mountains. On Sunday, August 1, Brown witnessed the first military funeral in the heart of the mountains.

On the morrow he left the post with Bendire's expedition. They wended their way to Pend d'Oreille Lake, Hayden Lake, and other scenic spots, gathering specimens of minerals, making surveys, and angling for trout. Supplies were replenished at Fort Coeur d'Alene before venturing into the more inaccessible regions.

Camp was pitched at Fort Lapwai on August 19, and Bendire visited Lewiston. Soon the party diligently resumed its task. At the end of the month they were on the shores of Wallowa Lake, in Chief Joseph's original haven where tall, luscious grasses grew. Fishing luck held good, for Bendire landed a seven-pound trout.

Reluctantly the men moved on, raking in material and drawing up reports. They avoided, as much as possible, the higher reaches of the Blue Mountains. Their trek back to Fort Walla Walla ended September 9. They had noted the upsurge in settlement on range lands where bunch or swamp grass grew plentifully. Too, whites were getting more timber out of the hills, and new roads demanded new toll fees.

Again at The Dalles on the thirteenth, Brown took a Columbia River steamer and arrived at Fort Vancouver the next day. His efforts resulted in furnishing a complete and accurate map of the region about which little had been properly registered. Ordered to return to Fort Klamath, he journeyed to Roseburg.

He left the railhead with instructions to follow a trail which might be made into a wagon road. It led through heavy timber, over rocky slopes, to depressing Mud Lake. Next, the struggler and a few companions camped on Indian Creek. In gaining the sandy and pumice country east of the Cascades, the group sagged with fullest fatigue.

By the time Fort Klamath was in view, September 26, one mule had been lost, and Brown had not tasted food nor water for more than twenty-four hours. He totted up his field service of two months and thirteen days, the marches totaling 1,052 miles.

The soldier-explorer soon applied for, and was granted, one month's leave of absence. But it was not to take effect until other duties had been performed. On November 1 he was given an escort of one noncommissioned officer and six enlisted men of Troop L to complete reconnaissance of the proposed road to Roseburg. Rationed for ten days, the detachment was furnished a pack train of four mules and a mounted Indian guide who drew compensation of a dollar a day.

To be guarded against were sudden and severe storms which swept the mountains. On the second day of the reconnaissance, the party attained the vicinity of peak-cupped Crater Lake, a mammoth bowl of icy depths that, when becoming more widely known, would draw tourists from afar. A blizzard drove the searchers to wooded shelter. In the emergency, Brown turned back to the post.

In the latter part of the month, he accompanied quartermaster wagons to Yreka, a trading center for miners of northern California, whence a start might be made on his delayed vacation. He bought, among other supplies, turkey and butter, to be sent to the post for the Thanksgiving table. A stage carried him on to Redding, to catch the train bound for Denver. He arrived at the Colorado metropolis, he admitted to himself, as a grown-up fighter at last.

Already the young soldier had campaigned much and explored more. Relatives and friends extracted details that had been sore roots too long. The homey aspects of fireside chats paled in comparison with the tales yanked out, and adolescent guests boosted the officer to higher rank. An explorer at heart, William made a serious study of metals and minerals. Between the ruled leaves of a well-preserved "Note Book on Assaying," dated at Denver, December 27, 1880, he left a small card which had been attached to a gift. It read:

> CAPT. BROWN
> Merry Xmas
> from
> Susie Frances
> and Julie Goode

The leave of absence granted as of November 1 was extended three months. Mineralogy received further attention.

The Lieutenant, out of Denver once more, returned to Oregon on March 15, 1881. On that day, Colonel Upton fatally shot himself at the presidio of San Francisco. He had sat down the day previously to resign as colonel of the Fourth Artillery and to write a note that "unbearable" illness was the cause of his final dual act. Upton's death, coming when he was only forty-two years of age, startled the nation. The officer had overtaxed himself with many studies. Left unfinished was his monumental work, *The Military Policy of the United States from 1775*, to be dusted off and published by order of Secretary of War Elihu Root in 1904.

Also on March 15, Robert Todd Lincoln became Secretary of War, to occupy the office until March 5, 1885.

By the first of April, Brown had taken over the duties of Post Engineer and Signal Officer at Fort Klamath, relieving Lieutenants G. B. Backus, First Cavalry, and E. H. Brooke, Twenty-first Infantry. Meanwhile, General Howard had become superintendent of the United States Military Academy. Headquarters of the Columbia Department, for the time being, were in charge of Brevet Brigadier General Frank Wheaton. Nelson A. Miles, given the star of a brigadier December 15, 1880, soon was to command the Department and fill the office until 1885.

Convened general courts-martial at the post, from time to time yielded Brown experience in acting as Judge Advocate of the Court. On days set aside for such sessions, the Court sat without regard to hours as the prisoners were brought before it. At midnight of June 22, Brown galloped out of the fort in search of a deserter. That night and the next day the pursuer rode fifty-six miles, returning without his man, but with an urge to spout a stream of expletives.

Then there was the buying of horses for the troops in June. As junior member of the Board of Officers who visited stock dealers in the vicinity of Klamath Lake, Brown recorded the transactions. As much as $125 was paid for a cavalry horse. Stablemen had to make frequent count of the mounts bearing the brand of U. S. Sometimes, when turned out in pasture, a few of their number fell into the hands of rustlers, men all too adept at altering scorched initials.

On July 20, the Lieutenant and a detachment of five

men from Troop L set out to continue observations on the trail to Roseburg. In rough country from the beginning, they encountered heaping trouble the second day. South of Crater Lake, a mule rolled down a gulch into a roaring stream. With its head held under water by a log, the animal was retrieved after strenuous pushing and pulling. One of the men who strayed from the group in dense undergrowth was picked up only after a four-hour search. Rank rhododendron was beautiful but also entangling.

The same man, on the march to Skookum Prairie next day, suffered a bashed leg when knocked down by his horse. And at the same moment another pack mule fell into another gulch, necessitating prolonged rescue. The trail, obliterated by fallen timber, was struck near Indian Creek. An abundance of game and grass greeted the men in the mountain camp. Next day they climbed a steep trail to obtain a commanding view from Black Rock. They spread blankets at Mud Lake, checking a march of fourteen miles.

On the twenty-fourth they pitched shelter at Snow Bird and met R. L. Cavitt, reliable guide. Brown arranged for the guide's going with him to Crater Lake, by way of Fish Lake Gap, to mark the trail or wagon road. Next morning the two men explored the area between the head of the East Fork of the North Umpqua River and Snow Bird. The officer was of the opinion that a zigzag trail could be made, but the steep grades would make a suitable wagon road too costly. They returned to Mud Lake for camping.

Cavitt and a sergeant left on the twenty-sixth to find a way to take the pack animals down to the forks of the South Umpqua River, then up Quartz Ridge, while blazing a trail into the old path. Brown pictured the difficulties:

It is a noticeable feature in the Cascade range that on the western side the air is more moist, trees much larger & thicker together, more undergrowth and hardwood trees than on the eastern side. The country seems also more impassable on the western than on the eastern side. The variation of the compass in these mountains owing to local attractions seems to be so great that it would be desirable to take angles with a sextant or transit rather than by the magnetic needle.

The diarist, however, found the Douglas fir belt of southern Oregon exceptionally alluring. A typical entry, for July 27, set forth:

Mched 17 m[iles]. Camped on Rogue River northwest of the Rogue River Pass. Found a tree about two miles from camp measuring 32.2 feet in circumference. We marched today to Black Rock about 4 miles. Just east of Black Rock [we] took an old Indian trail which was followed and lead[s] to high ridges overlooking the Rogue R. country & then across Fish Lake creek valley south of Fish Lake Gap. Reaching the summit overlooking Rogue R. we left the trail[,] it being difficult to follow & would probably have led too much to the left; found a fair grade to a large stream containing waters from Skookum Prairie & Indian Ck, then crossed a number of small gulches and came to Rogue River where camp was made.

After fording the whimsical Rogue on the twenty-eighth, the group hit the old John Day wagon road for a few miles. Serrated ridges and slashing canyons made the going tough. The day's march of eleven baffling miles ended when blankets were unrolled in a grassy plot encircled by toppled timber northwest of Crater Lake. A swing around a high ridge in a twenty-eight-mile ride the next day brought the men back to Fort Klamath.

Department Commander Miles now decided to locate the military telegraph line between Fort Klamath and Ashland. On August 9, he instructed Lieutenant J. F. Reynolds Landis, First Cavalry, the department's chief signal officer, to proceed to Ashland and the fort, and to make a report on the contemplated line. Accompanying him was Private W. L. Whiting, Company G, Twenty-first Infantry. Lieutenant Brown and two troopers were to meet the men with two saddle horses at Ashland. It was also made known that Brown later would be given a working organization to get out poles for building the line, although much of the wire was to be strung on standing trees.

The mounted trio left the post on the twelfth. They rode twenty-six miles, to Tom McKay's ranch where they put up for the night. An early start the next morning enabled them to cover the remaining forty-four miles to Ashland before nightfall. The seventy-mile journey, called the Dead Indian Canyon route, Brown reported as passable for uncovered wagons, provided a driver was willing to hack away prone logs and throw out countless rocks. Return to the post over the more traveled route was a march of ninety-nine miles. It led by way of Parker's Station, atop the Cascades, then down to Linkville, whence the distance to Fort Klamath pegged thirty-seven miles.

The cutting of poles started on the twenty-seventh. Brown's initial working party consisted of Private Whiting, three men from Troop L and three from Company C, Twenty-first Infantry. They had a four-mule team. Within a few days all men of Company C joined in the task. Captain George H. Burton and Lieutenant Brooke cooperated, but the greatest measure of credit for carrying the work to completion fell to Brown and Lieutenant Charles Hartwell Bonesteel, Twenty-first Infantry. The name Bonesteel, title of Major General as prefix, sixty-one years later would become synonymous with defense pioneering in Iceland.

Actual construction of the line began October 5. Snow and rain produced serious handicaps, but the job pushed forward at the rate of 4.31 miles a day. The last insulator went onto the last pole on the last day of the month. In twenty-three working days the wire was strung nearly one hundred miles. The feat drew high praise from General Miles. Except for a few days spent in a rifle contest at Vancouver Barracks, "tops" among the marksmen, Brown had labored unfalteringly on the telegraphic prolongation.

His record of accomplishments had not been overlooked by members of the General Staff. The Adjutant General of the Army had notified Miles that Lieutenants Brown, Muhlenberg, and Brooke were to be relieved from their duties within the Columbia Department in order that they might report for enrollment in the School of Instruction for Infantry and Cavalry at Fort Leavenworth, Kansas.

Informed on November 11, that he was to reach Fort Leavenworth by the twentieth of the next month, Brown started for Fort Vancouver nine days later. Astride his iron-gray mount, he bade farewell to comrades of Fort Klamath. In a few minutes, a curtain of fast-falling snow shut off his view of the post. Accompanying him were four prisoners and a quartet of guards and witnesses, huddled in a wagon pulled by a six-mule team.

Confirmation of the order for conduct of the prisoners, awaiting trial by general court-martial, to Vancouver Barracks bore the signature of Frederick Schwalka, aide-de-camp to Miles. Lieutenant Schwalka had, in 1879-80, penetrated deep into the wilderness of Alaska in search of Sir John Franklin's men. In 1883, he was to win further acclaim in leading another expedition from Portland to the Yukon's wildest tappings. The explorations by army men opened the way for further incisiveness and the establishment of meteorological stations around the Arctic Circle.

In leaving the Klamath country, Brown's baggage tipped the scales at 563 pounds. From Parker's Station to Ashland he rode in a buggy. Three prisoners and two guards took the stage at Rock Point, and the remaining prisoner and two guards boarded a stage with the Lieutenant at Ashland.

Brown reported at Vancouver on the twenty-eighth. Thee days previously, in Washington, D. C., Commissioner Spencer F. Baird of the United States Commission of Fish and Fisheries had sent him a letter addressed to his late station:

Captain Bendire has mentioned to me your interest in natural history, & your willingness to make collections for the National Museum. He informs me, however, that you will probably be transferred to Leavenworth for special duty.

Will it be agreeable to you if I ask the Secretary of War to keep you at Fort Klamath, if the interest of the service will not be thereby disturbed? I of course, very naturally wish to secure some help from you if I can. We are particularly desirous of obtaining a first-rate collection of the fishes of Klamath Lake, as also of any frogs, toads, lizards, salamanders & the smaller snakes.

Prof. Cope has published lately an account of the fauna of the lake, in which he says that it contains some species of fishes living, that have hitherto been only known as fossils, from the tertiary beds of the country.

In addition to the collection of fishes etc. we are extremely anxious to obtain all we can of the fossil remains of the vertebrate animals, of which so many have recently been collected.

Anything we can furnish, in the way of publications, material for collecting etc. will be cheerfully supplied.

To serve Baird, the great ornithologist and teacher of natural history, the young officer knew, would indeed be an honor. Selected by President Grant to head the Commission of Fish and Fisheries when formed in 1871, he had contributed unceasingly to the movement for the preservation of wild life.

The recipient of the tardy letter, however, realized that his sojourn on the frontier of the Pacific Northwest must become only a memorable picture, to be recalled often because of its fadeless colors. He sailed from Portland for San Francisco on December 4. His ship, next day, had to lay by at Astoria while waiting for the tide which would carry him away from Oregon's shore.

In San Francisco he mingled with men of the Far East, with men from all corners of his native land. He called upon officer friends at the presidio. General McDowell was there.

The man whose unfortunate lot it had been to take the blame for the ill-prepared Federal Forces at the First Battle of Bull Run had returned to San Francisco in 1876 as Commander of the Military Division of the Pacific. He would retire from the Army there in 1882, becoming Park Commissioner and serving in that position until the last year of his life, 1885. The Presidio Reservation, whose park improvements he fondly planned, would become his burial place. Testifying to his appreciative vision would be the enticing roads coiled high above the Golden Gate.

Lieutenant Brown, like other officers, knew that Mc-Dowell's efficiency as a staff officer outshone his record as a field general. He was admired as a champion of all-for-the-service discipline, a man who was temperate, loyal, and truthful, with no political aspirations.

On the train roaring toward Denver, and in the months and years to follow, the cavalryman was to balance delicately those requisites which were possessed by men of cool vision as well as of impregnable judgment.

At Fort Leavenworth

AFTER hail and farewell to Denver, Lieutenant Brown obtained his first glimpse of the School of Application at Fort Leavenworth on December 20. He gazed at new buildings being erected and old ones undergoing repairs to accommodate the influx of troops. Two days later, he reported for duty with Company H, First Infantry.

Need for the training offered was plainly evident. There were no schools for officers of the Army save that for engineers at Willet's Point on the Hudson River, and another for artillerymen at Fort Monroe. The capacity for each was about thirty officers. The United States Army between 1877 and 1897 did not attain impressive size. Its hinges swung on the shoulders of 25,000 men and 2,000 officers, eleven of the commissioned ranks being general officers.

Organization of the School for Infantry and Cavalry, patterned after the artillery establishment at Fort Monroe, was provided for in General Orders issued by the War Department, May 7, 1881. Actual inauguration by General Sherman came December 1. Lieutenant Colonel E. S. Otis, Twentieth Infantry, another hardy veteran of Indian campaigns in the Pacific Northwest, stepped in as the first commandant.

The minimum of the garrison was set at four companies each of cavalry and infantry, and a light battery. Three field officers were assigned. The student group, consisting of one lieutenant from each regiment of infantry and cavalry, went into two classes which in turn were split into sections. A qualifying examination determined the grouping of students. The War Department having detailed no special instructors, officers on duty at the post and students themselves served on the faculty.

By November 25 there had arrived units from the First, Fourth, Eleventh, and Twentieth Infantry Regiments; troops from the Third, Fourth, Seventh, and Eighth Cavalry Regiments and Light Battery F, Second Artillery. These, with the general staff, numbered thirty-nine officers and 403 enlisted men. Before the end of December accretion of recruits swelled the enlisted ranks to 550 men.

Here was a fresh experiment in army schooling beset by multitudinous problems. Both officers and men, coming from varied commands and widely separated regions, possessed highly divergent opinions as to what made a smooth-working armed force. Military policy at an isolated post called for a certain resiliency dictated by exigencies not encountered in the normal sway at a garrison far removed from the frontier. To instill a harmonious desire for a blending of discipline and study became an administrative task in dealing out the proper apportionment of duties and studied pursuit of cultural aims.

The burden of regulation and of outlining courses of study for the school fell chiefly upon its staff of five senior officers. The staff, aside from Commandant Otis, at first consisted of Majors John J. Upton, Fifth Cavalry, and John S. Poland, Eighteenth Infantry; Captains E. B. Williston, Second Artillery, S. B. M. Young, Eighth Cavalry, and J. S. McNaught, Twentieth Infantry. Subject to the approval of and amendments by the General of the Army, the course of instruction and system of training evolved into a procedure of orderliness.

The first term ran for four months, ending June 13, but plans were laid for the next term to cover the period between October 1 and the same date in June. Except on Saturdays and Sundays, each class and section met twice daily for recitation. Some forms of teaching went begging because of the lack of determinate facilities. Rooms for recitation and practice bulged with officers and enlisted men. In the beginning, the post library boasted only a few books, and appliances for instruction were restricted by meager appropriations.

Attention had to be paid to a wide range of subjects, from the elementary to the more advanced. Lessons varied in number, recitation standings of every scholar were kept and posted, and absence without good excuse evoked more than frowns. Difficult indeed was the classifying of officers for instruction. Some had come from West Point and some had attained a liberal education otherwise, a number of them still short of practical military seasoning. Others had seen a great deal of active field service after having procured an average amount of schooling, while there were those who had never looked far past the covers of common-school books. All had to be prepared for a measure of efficiency in tactical practices.

Lieutenant Brown's high qualifications placed him in the first section of the first class. He commenced work on the regular course March 13, and also taught "Harper's Geography." In April, the students and instructors began shooting on target ranges of varying distances, the practice holding through fair-weather months along with other field training and drill. At the end of May, Brown relieved Major Poland as preceptor in "Woolsey's International Law," a course demanding no small amount of application. At the close of the first year, he ranked number 5 in the first class.

He received a summer month's leave of absence, being privileged, also, to wear the freshly won marksman's button bestowed by the Office of the General Instructor of Musketry, Department of the Missouri. On October 4, after his return to duty, he was transferred from the roster of Troop L to Troop K, First Cavalry.

In his annual report of October 11, 1882, Colonel Otis quoted the "final deliberations" of his staff as of that year:

The progress of the first class has been entirely satisfactory, and the officers composing it have shown a degree of application and appreciation of the course that is alike honorable to them and deserving of commendation. The following named officers of the first class, having been instructors of either the first or second class in addition to their individual studies, and having acquitted themselves creditably, are especially recommended to superior authority:

1st Lieutenant *T. E. True*, 4th Infantry.
2d Lieutenant *Arthur Williams*, 3d Infantry.
2d Lieutenant *W. C. Brown*, 1st Cavalry.

Though the commandant felt encouraged by the headway made in many of the school's endeavors, he did not fail to mention its shortcomings. Especially worrisome was the conduct of some men who, coming to a long-established post, found in its vicinity more "demoralizing tendencies" than had been the customary lure. The result was a mounting list of trials of enlisted men. The courts-martial loaded officers and post headquarters with extra toil. In seeking a solution of the problem of the division of labor between post administration and education, Otis created the position of secretary of the school. Thereafter, the Post Adjutant had fewer papers and records to keep.

Years later, in 1930, Brown was to tell reserve officers in Denver how the technical training along with educational courses in grammar-school subjects did not readily appeal to some of the rowdies at Leavenworth.

"I have vivid recollections of having certain officers up at the blackboard struggling ineffectually at such problems as adding 2-11 to 3-13. The school was, of course, unpopular with many of the officers who needed it the most; a few were dissipated and treated the thing as a joke. General Sherman, hearing of this, visited the school personally and, calling the officers together, he in a memorable address 'laid down the law' in unmistakable terms."

Sherman reminded his listeners that they could not take their career and ranks for granted. Other men, desiring their pay and opportunities, could easily be gotten to displace them. Theirs was an honorable profession in which all should maintain ambition.

"That plain talk from a man of General Sherman's prestige had a salutary effect." The type of officers to whom the remarks were aimed became a rarity.

By command of Sherman, Adjutant General R. C. Drum, on January 3, 1883, issued General Order No. 2, stating that a manual prepared by Brown and recommended by a board of officers at Leavenworth's School "is approved, and will be used for all arms provided with the *stacking swivel. . . . .* " In the long-standing exercise, front and rear ranks and file-closers of the infantry were enabled to stack their barreled "pieces," bayonets unfixed, with ease and precision of movement.

When sunflower stalks again grew thick on the prairies of Kansas, Brown applied for a month's leave. Commandand Otis indorsed the application.

Post of Ft. Leavenworth, Kans., May 22, 1883. Respectfully forwarded to Headquarters Department of the Missouri. Lt. Brown has been a most useful officer during his tour of duty at the Post, both as an occasional instructor in the School and as a duty officer of the garrison. As a student he has taken the full course of instruction prescribed for the first class of the School and has therein shown marked ability. He deserves the indulgence requested. . . . .

The leave of absence not only was granted, but was extended by Lieutenant General Sheridan, Commander of the Division of the Missouri.

At the conclusion of the course of instruction, nearly two years in length, the school staff, in a circular of July 3, reported the ranking and proficiency of student officers. Brown stood number 2 in his class for the second year, with the rank of number 5 for the entire two-year course. The staff also reported those student officers showing aptitude for command, or placement in staff departments, and those fitted best for professional employment in the Adjutant General's Department, Quartermaster and Subsistence Department, Judge Advocate, Surveying, Topography and Field Fortification, Signaling and Telegraphy, Field Officers of Volunteers, and Battery Commanders.

Brown was one of two officers recommended for professional work under all the classifications. Furthermore, he became one of a pair named by the War Department as instructors immediately after graduation. His diploma from the school was transmitted July 23 by H. A. Greene, Second Lieutenant, Twentieth Infantry, Secretary pro tem.

On August 28, the graduate drifted away from temporary assignment with Troop B, Third Cavalry. In a few days he was attached to Light Battery F, Second Artillery, where, in addition to other duties, he would serve for the next two years.

By special orders of Major General Pope issued from Department Headquarters at Fort Leavenworth on September 12, the artillery fledgling received an assignment in which he gloried. For a brief period he competed in regimental rifle contests under Captain J. C. Gilmore, Twenty-fourth Infantry, commanding the Musketry Camp. Competitors for positions on the department's target team numbered seventy-two officers and enlisted men. The possible grand total score at all ranges was 315. Brown, who had placed sixth in preliminary practice, came out tenth with a grand total of 245. He won a place among the fourteen competitors for positions on the Department of Missouri rifle team for 1883, the aggregate scores being compiled from firing at distances of 200, 300, and 600 yards.

On November 1, Sherman's long tenure as General in Chief of the Army came to an end. The forces of which he had demanded much advanced still further under his successor, Sheridan, who held sway until August 5, 1888.

Brown salvaged enough time in the winter of 1884 to

compile a memorandum of "Decisions on Points of Tactics" for study at the school. It called for a clearer definition of prescribed movements of cavalrymen and infantrymen, along with suggested improvements for prevailing practices. The pamphlet, finding its way to the Adjutant General's Office in Washington, won ready approval. Later, it was reprinted for the National Guard of Wisconsin, New York, and Pennsylvania, then reprinted by the War Department.

Participation in the Department's rifle contests of 1883 had proved to the Lieutenant that allowances for the strong winds of Kansas were an important factor on the target ranges. Tables prepared by others enabled him to make diagrams presenting wind allowances. By the spring of 1884, his inventive mind conceived the automatic correction for the drift of the bullet in the Springfield rifle. The annual report of the Chief of Ordnance asserted:

> Lieutenant W. C. Brown, 1st Cavalry, proposed that drift lines or curves be marked on the leaf of the rear sight, Model 79, so that adjustment could be made for drift; on this basis for which credit is due him, the automatic arrangement was devised . . . . it follows that correction for drift is thus secured automatically, requiring no thought or adjustment of the marksman for any range.

No patent was obtained on the device, but after 1884, except for a few years in the nineties, the automatic correction remained on the Springfield rifle so long as it was fired. Its saving in ammunition and as an aid to the marksman's skill restored its usage after the temporary removal.

The inventor had well earned the month's leave of absence granted him in June by Brigadier General C. C. Augur, then head of the Missouri Department. No doubt the vacationer spent part of his holiday practicing with the service rifle, for upon his return to Fort Leavenworth his firing skill had improved smartly. On September 20, a sharpshooter's certificate, entitling him to wear the Sharpshooter's Cross until September 30, 1885, was issued by

Department Headquarters. He and six others comprised the School of Application's list of sharpshooters for that year.

On September 23, he was named with four officers on a board to consider and report on the handling of the blanket-bag, inspection to be of two infantrymen equipped for heavy marching. Captain Evan Miles, who had hurled back the Bannocks and Paiutes on Umatilla Reservation in Oregon, had prepared the new manual for blanket-bag inspection. The board, after accepting the amended manual, recommended its adoption in displacing certain portions of Upton's *Infantry Tactics.*

A measure of Brown's happiness because of his progress during the year was drained away by the death and burial of his father in Denver. A sturdy shelter against life's storms had been carried away. The sorrowing son, who ever felt deep responsibility to his parents, procured a twenty-day leave in mid-October.

Now, upon him and his mother fell the duty and privilege of providing gainful education for Helen and Grace. When he received promotion to a first lieutenancy on December 19, there was a renewed desire to study for further advancement.

Yet the winter of 1885 ushered in many drab days. Welcome changes were the drill and other outdoor movements which came with spring. At the end of May orders went out for the school staff's supervision of infantry drill examinations. Lieutenants, acting as company or battalion commanders, shouted in tension under watchful eyes. Brown assisted in special duties.

So efficient was his performance that on June 1 he became Post Adjutant, relieving Lieutenant George D. Wallace, Fourth Cavalry. Having been under orders to rejoin his regiment, however, Brown's tenure was short. On the fourteenth, the day before he turned over the files to Lieutenant R. F. Bates, Eighteenth Infantry, he signed orders of the Commandant for re-examining student-officers in subjects that had tripped them in their first trials.

Relief from duty at the school came on the first day of July. The polished cavalryman, ready to join his old field command, invaded the Colorado home once again. With undeniable pride, he recounted how the School of Application, despite its weaknesses, was creating a vastly improved personnel for an army no longer mired in stultifying complacency.

Umapine, hereditary chief of Cayuse Indians. Photo by Bradley &
Rulofson, San Francisco, Calif.; procured by Lieut. W. C. Brown about
1879, probably at Pendleton, Oregon.

CHAPTER IX

Adjutant at West Point

TO Number 32 South Thirteenth Street, Denver, came a Western Union telegram July 22, 1885. Signed by Adjutant General Drum, it read:

ORDER ISSUED TODAY DETAILING YOU AS ADJUTANT MILITARY ACADEMY   THE SUPERINTENDENT DESIRES YOU TO REPORT AT AN EARLY DAY

By command of General Sheridan, ruling at Headquarters of the Army, Washington, Cavalryman Brown was to replace First Lieutenant Eli D. Hoyle, Second Artillery, at West Point.

On the first day of August, the Westerner once again tread familiar ground, taking over the assignment in which his stature as a soldier would lengthen and his contact with notables widen. The "Supe," Colonel Wesley Merritt, who had succeeded General Howard in 1882, greeted him warmly. Merritt, of the Class of '60, had, after a promising record in the Civil War, performed with brilliancy on the Western frontier. A discerning judge of men, he employed quiet yet forceful means of obtaining laudable results.

Leaders of the Civil War period now were giving way to leaders of Indian campaigns. Each year an increasing number of former Union Army commanders reached the journey's end. Only a week before Brown reported to Merritt, the Cadet Corps had crossed the Hudson River to Garrison, there to pay respects as the funeral train of U. S. Grant rolled slowly past. In six more years, the Corps would be journeying to New York to render honor to Sherman, his sword sheathed for all time.

As always, younger men had emerged from the towers, while others still behind the gray walls prepared to take over when their elders dropped the load. George W. Goethals, graduating in 1880, two years later was refreshing himself at Willet's Point while keeping a news eye on the Panama Canal venture which the French had just initiated. From 1885 to 1889, with Brown as Adjutant, the Academy claimed Goethals as an outstanding teacher and professor of civil and military engineering. He would prove himself, in the next decade, master of the project taken over from the French by his government.

In 1881, Joseph T. Dickman received his diploma and handshake. Robert L. Bullard had gone out with the Class of 1885, to be followed the next year by John J. Pershing. Dickman and Bullard, along with Liggett, '79, were to be Pershing's trio of army commanders when the erroneously named World War would call them overseas. And forming deep friendship with Adjutant Brown were Charles P. Summerall, to bow out with the Class of '88, and Charles D. Rhodes, to graduate in '89.

The tempo of life at the Point in 1885, Brown learned, had quickened perceptibly. Talk was going round that even telephones would be installed—talk for two more years. There was still a preponderance of things wrapped in old traditions, but new and broadening light was scattering drabness. Modern languages had gained a firm foothold, and history, shunted aside in 1862, again was being taught. The learned Michie, producing his *Life of General Upton* in 1885, revealed the old army ways in contrast with the new, and pointed out basic elements not soon to be outmoded. Fresh textbooks induced livelier interest in studies. The library flourished in renewed attractiveness under Michie's supervision. Increasing in numbers were the men from West Point who gave impetus to their nation's higher educational institutions.

Athletics at the Academy, in conformity with the grow-

ing desire throughout the country for a wider variety of
sports, began to perk up a bit. The new Adjutant watched
with fascination as Herman J. Koehler, Master of the
Sword, inaugurated his calisthenic and gymnastic program.
From it would come the rush to virulent football and a
system of athletics in which every cadet could participate.

There was something more to this than swimming in
ponds and the river, or in boating, drill, and equitation. It
would finish off the ruder forms of hazing. The public
never failed to keep a vigilant eye on the Military Academy.
Its hazing "scandals," though some quite trivial, would be
aired and Congressional investigations made. The end to all
hazing was to follow—in January, 1901—its abolition
emanating from the action of the Cadet Corps itself.

Like the majority of officers at the Point, Brown knew
that reports of misbehavior on the part of a cadet, if set
adrift, often were enlarged upon. To stop rumors from
becoming elastic, the Academic Board took definite action.

On May 17, 1886, the Adjutant affixed his signature to
"Circular No. 13," published by order of Colonel Merritt.
The resolutions prohibited certain officers "from making
to others than members of the Board any statement, oral or
written, expressing an individual opinion as to the conclusion or probable action of the Academic Board in regard
to any cadet; or concerning matters relating to any cadet
which may, in their opinions, come before the Board; unless
called upon to do so by proper authority." Further, the
officers named were restricted to the Academy's authorized
published statements when certifying or writing an opinion
relative to any cadet's record.

Before the year was out, Adjutant Brown journeyed to
Baltimore on an official errand. Mayer, painter of early-day
scenes in Minnesota, having reached mellow age, dropped
in to see the son of his old friend who had kept store near
the banks of the Minnesota River. The artist, living in
Annapolis, invited the grown-up soldier to visit his home

on Chesapeake Bay where he might view the large painting of the Traverse des Sioux Treaty.

Brown jumped at the chance. And he saw many other historical sketches which brought boyhood days swimming into wistful eyes again. Familiar indeed were some of the Indian characters, like Red Iron and Sleepy Eye.

Not long after the meeting, Mayer died. Presumably, he did not reveal to Brown where the products of his keen observation and high talent would finally repose. Many years later the caller would find them safely preserved— half the width of the country from Baltimore.

Two years in the adjutancy slipped by for the Lieutenant, his meticulous work and co-operative assistance to staff and cadets alike making him a popular figure. If he reported the many trivial "slips" as well as the bulking breaches, it meant only that each link in the chain of discipline must be of equal strength. A corporal who stood on authority to order "fins around" some day might be a general directing an army corps to turn a flank.

Merritt, finishing his fifth year of superintendency, bade farewell to the school on the Hudson. Appointed to succeed him August 28, 1887, was Colonel John G. Parke, who had carved out a well-shaped reputation in the Corps of Engineers.

Parke had graduated from the Academy in 1849. A few years after his departure he, with Sheridan, McClellan, John B. Hood, and many other former cadets, served their government in steps toward the railway-spanning of the country. Their labors in topography made easier the future intensive construction of routes by rail beyond the Mississippi River.

The day after Parke's appointment, the Adjutant penned a letter to the new superintendent:

SIR:

In order that you may not be embarrassed in entering upon your duties as Superintendent by having as Adjutant an officer who is a total stranger to you, I have the honor, in case you may desire to have in my position an officer of your own selection, to tender my resignation as Adjutant of the Academy.

Should my resignation be accepted, I would request that I be relieved of my duties at as early a date as may be convenient.

I am Sir

> Very respectfully
> Your obedient servant
> W. C. BROWN
> 1st Lieut 1st Cavy.

The letter came back quickly to the sender. He appended to it a penciled note: "Gen. Parke refused either to accept this or to receive it to be placed on file."

Brown had been partly in error. His acquired chief was not a personally met friend, but he had become familiar with the writer's record.

Meantime, the Surgeon General of the Army, John Moore, was having prepared for the Medical Department its first *Drill Manual for the Hospital Corps and Company Bearers*. Changes in the Hospital Corps organization caused by the injection of new tactical formations necessitated collaboration by experienced officers of the line. Lieutenant Brown took time to lend able assistance. He received special thanks from the Surgeon General in a letter of February 1, 1888, stating that the manuscript of the manual had been approved and handed to the Public Printer. In due course the army received bound copies.

A pleasing communication from Fort Leavenworth also came to the Lieutenant in February. It carried his certificate of membership in the United States Cavalry Association (admittance being on the sixth of the previous December), signed by "W. Merritt, Brigadier-General, Brevet Maj.-Gen. U. S. A., President."

Then Brown became absorbed fully in a pressing matter. On April 19, Secretary of War William C. Endicott, in Special Orders, directed that a board convene at the earliest opportunity at West Point to consider the extension of the southern limits of that post's reservation. Named on the board were Parke, president, Professor James Mercur of the Academy, member, and Adjutant Brown, recorder.

The reservation, purchased originally in 1790, contained 1,793 acres when Thayer became superintendent. The Gridley property was added in 1824 and Round Pond two years after Brown's graduation from the Academy. In 1888 came the move to acquire 225 acres of an estate left to heirs by Edward V. Kinsley, deceased.

Edward had inherited the property from his father, Zebina J. D. Kinsley, known as "Old Zeb," and who had been an instructor in artillery at the Academy. The history of the Kinsley family was intertwined with the story of West Point. "Old Zeb," who died in 1849, had two sisters numbered among the belles without whom early dances at the post would not have been such a magnet.

More than one good reason was given for acquiring the Kinsley estate. Until the day of his death, Edward had held it intact, and by so doing had prevented the growth of the village of Highland Falls toward the reservation. The board, in its investigations, emphasized the fact that, "A piece of land not far below his property was in recent years thrown into the market, and was bought in small lots, upon each of which was erected a saloon or barroom." The same procedure in regard to the Kinsley land, with the resultant demoralizing influences, it was argued, would indeed be a catastrophe.

As a result of recommendations made by the board, title was obtained to the Kinsley estate in 1889. Successive acquisitions would give West Point Reservation the several thousand acres needed for field training and other activities.

From reservation enlargement Brown turned his attention to graduation exercises for the Class of '88. He took special interest in handing a diploma to young Charles Summerall. Four years previously the recipient had come from Florida to the Point as a green civilian. The Adjutant, among others, had taught and advised him well, lending sincere encouragement that was to bear rich reward. Brown, presenting the graduate his first commission, would see the happy day when he, as a colonel, would be serving under Brigadier General Summerall.

At a time when he could indulge his liking in research of old files, the ever-curious Adjutant dug up the original name of General "U. S." Grant—from an enrollment register of 1839, the year Grant had entered the United States Military Academy. A clerk had written in the name "Ulysses S. Grant" on the school's books.

The initial "S." was for Simpson, the name possessed by the mother of the entrant. Young Grant objected, unhesitatingly. He had, however, to learn that some officials did not seem to worry about such trifling mistakes. The name, as listed, remained. Ready use was made of the initials "U. S.," classmates dubbing their fellow as "Sam."

Brown, with a piece of blueprint paper, transferred the true signature of "Hiram Ulysses Grant" from the register. He gave it to the public. The public, like the classmates, persisted in using the more popular initials to which it had long been accustomed. For his own satisfaction, however, the debunker produced a film negative of the original signature from the blueprint and retained it among his rare papers.

The army's new General in Chief, John McAllister Schofield, who assumed on August 14, 1888, the position to which Sheridan had brought high color, was a man who could chuckle heartily over one soldier's debunking of another. At any rate, during the next seven years Brown was to find that he had a kind and helpful friend in the man who headed a fast improving military body.

Soon Superintendent Parke packed his personal belongings, and Colonel John M. Wilson, also of the Engineers, came to take his place. Brown remained. His persistent application to duties and alacrity in making shortcuts

through ever-mounting paper work drew satisfactory nods
from superiors. The Lieutenant labored mightily as a new
academic year spun around. Then he left for a much-
needed vacation. And Colonel Wilson, with yuletide
generosity, consented to extension of the leave to four
days past Christmas.

Icy winds and a new year brought the usual serious
season of study by the cadets. Brown, finding it easier to
keep up with routine, thumbed his mail leisurely in a comfortably warm office. He opened a letter from the Assistant Adjutant General in Washington, dated February 5,
1890, two paragraphs reading:

For the purpose of aiding General George W. Cullum in the completion of his "Biographical Register of Officers and Graduates of the
United States Military Academy," I have the honor to request your
verification or correction of the inclosed statement of your military
record since 1878, and that you will also add thereto the names and
dates of any actions with Indians in which you may have participated
since the end of the Rebellion.

After examination and completion of the inclosed paper, please return
it to this office.

The Adjutant, making certain corrections for the en-
closure, reflected on the monumental work for which it was
intended. Cullum had started on his biography of graduates in 1855 and, thirty-five years later, had brought it up
to date. Having been in Thayer's last class of 1833, and
superintendent of the Academy from 1864 to 1866, the
soldier-scholar was especially fitted for his great task.

Brown, wondering how much longer his own stay on the
Hudson might be, received word March 10 that he would
be relieved from duty at the Academy July 1. He and four
fellow officers were to join their respective regiments.

His departure, nevertheless, was postponed as he strove
for the privilege, once relieved, of spending a five-month
leave outside the United States. A letter of April 28 from
the General of the Army, concurred in by the Secretary of

War, dashed cold water on his hopes for a trip abroad. The applicant was advised tersely that, when replaced at West Point, he should join his troop "without delay."

Yet the Adjutant was entitled, according to academic regulations, to an immediate twelve-day leave. It was granted in May by direction of Colonel Wilson. Within a few weeks, the order of March 10 was amended, General Schofield requesting that Brown be relieved at the Academy September 1. A longer leave was in order.

Except for the disappointment in not being permitted to travel and broaden his military knowledge beyond the boundaries of his country, the Lieutenant had reason to feel elated because of the hurdles he had taken without tripping. Upon the relief of his adjutant, Colonel Wilson published an order revealing appreciation of no little depth. It stated in part:

> In severing the close official relations that have existed between the Superintendent and the Adjutant during the past year, the former desires to express his sincere thanks for the energy, skill and ability displayed by Lieutenant *Brown* in the discharge of every duty devolving upon him.
>
> Faithful, energetic and untiring, his earnest efforts have been to uphold the dignity and maintain the high reputation of the Military Academy.
>
> He carries with him to his new sphere of duty the respect and regard of his brother officers and the sincere wish of the Superintendent that his future may be one of happiness and success.

The years spent with his Alma Mater became a rich memory to the soldier when a down-river boat carried him beyond sight of flinty towers and barracks. Perhaps it was at that moment he decided he would like, when his course should be run, to be brought back to rest in the cemetery of the Point.

Meantime there was work ahead. Again the Lieutenant of Cavalry faced westward.

Fort Assiniboine and War Rumors

A TRAIN roared out of Cheyenne. The clean-shaven army officer, heading northwesterly to take station at Fort Assiniboine, Montana, set his thoughts adrift. There was a plaintive "Theme Song" of soldiers not so close to Cheyenne as he.

> Boys, stay at home,
> Stay at home if you can.
> Stay away from that city
> That's known as Cheyenne.
> For Sitting Bull's there,
> Also Wild Comanche Bill,
> And he'll sure lift your scalp.
> In the dreary Black Hills,
> And still we kept marching
> To the dreary Black Hills.

But Sitting Bull, in 1890, was nearer the Black Hills of Dakota than to the cowman's metropolis of Wyoming. He was a peaceful man at last. The West had grown up. Washington, North and South Dakota, and Montana had added stars to the Union flag in 1889, followed in a year by Idaho and Wyoming. In six more years Utah would no longer be a territory.

Yet pacification of the red men in the region through which the train rumbled still remained a story fresh in Lieutenant Brown's mind.

Only two dozen years had passed since soldiers had come into Fort Laramie to build and maintain a wagon road through the Powder River country. White men had urged

guarantee of security over the Bozeman Trail to newly dis-
covered gold fields in Montana. North of the Platte, mili-
tary posts were built for protection: Fort Reno, on the
Middle Fork of Powder River; Fort Phil Kearney, on the
Powder's Clear Fork, and Fort C. F. Smith, on the Big Horn
River.

Still Sioux and Cheyenne, warring until 1868, caused
inevitable delay. Red Cloud of the Oglala band of Sioux
led his red-blanketed horde of horsemen against blue-coated cavalry. Eighty-two men, including Brevet Lieutenant
Colonel William J. Fetterman and Captain F. H. Brown,
of General Henry B. Carrington's command, failed to return from a fight near Fort Kearney.

Later, there were attacks upon Forts Buford and C. F.
Smith, and Red Cloud and Crazy Horse inflicted severe
punishment with mordant forces upon a small detachment
under Captain James Powell. The primed Captain had
not tasted defeat in the Wagon Box Fight of August 2,
1867, but wagon trains failed to get through from the
summer of 1866 to the fall of 1867. A peace treaty signed
in the spring of 1868 acknowledged Red Cloud as victor,
for whites were to withdraw from the Sioux country. The
Montana road and its forts were to be abandoned.

Red Cloud was content to be peaceable thereafter, argu-
ing against strife, which came eight years later. He and
Spotted Tail basked in the glory becoming to leaders of
agency Indians. Not so with others. Many warriors of the
Brulé, Oglala, Sans Arc, and Miniconjou preferred hostility.

The railroads pushed on westward, while their builders
sounded a challenge with both guns and tools. As the
Kansas Pacific lines snaked forward, as white hunters and
settlers shot down the buffalo and antelope, the Indians became aggrieved over depletion of their game preserve. By
1870, in spite of regrouping and pacifying of Indians in a
fashion, disturbances cropped up here and there. Cavalry-

men disarmed a number of Piegans of the Blackfoot tribe who had murdered Montana settlers. Utes showed discontent. Cheyenne and Arapaho sent word to Kiowa and Comanche to meet with them and obtain in war what they could not get in parley. Peace on the plains had not yet been secured.

After General Custer and his expedition had explored the Black Hills in 1874, and the wind had carried fast the news that the hills would yield gold to the white man, it was certain that the Sioux country was to see more trouble. The Pawnee veered, seeking safety on a reserve. Thousands of Sioux were enrolled and given supplies by Indian agents, but the Government could not be certain how many held back. Reluctant to forsake the idea of resistance were leaders like Crazy Horse of the Oglala, Two Moons of the Northern Cheyenne, and Sitting Bull and Gall of the Sioux, Hunkpapa band.

After the group under Sitting Bull, on the Yellowstone, refused to come to the agency and enroll with placated Indians by the beginning of 1876, the Army prepared to round up all hostiles. Sitting Bull's emissaries, however, had already been busy. They carried his message of revolt to various tribes far and near, to the Chippewa on the east and to others far west of the Rockies. From these and from a dozen Sioux agencies Sitting bull drew to his camp the malcontents and war-seeking youths.

Three blue columns of soldiers had set out to gather in the enemy. From Fort Abraham Lincoln, on the Missouri River, Custer and his Seventh Cavalry galloped westward in movement with General Alfred Terry. From western Montana came General Gibbon, and from the south General Crook set forth. Newspapermen with Crook's command forsook the railroad cars at Cheyenne City to proceed northward by way of Fort Laramie, over much of the road Red Cloud had closed eight years earlier.

The story of the campaign of 1876 became a story told

and retold around the world, the Last Stand of Custer thrusting other critical phases into deep shadows. Against Crazy Horse on the Rosebud River, June 17, the ever-dogged Crook saved his men from a perilous trap, though his victory was not complete. Sioux and Cheyenne revealed the Indians' hesitancy for pitched battle. Yet they suffered sorely at the hands of Crook's allies, Crow and Shoshoni led by Chief Washakie.

Custer had not learned of Crook's engagement when, within a few days, he left camp on Powder River. Under orders to meet Gibbon near the Little Big Horn on June 26, Custer arrived a day early, to face a mighty assembly of war-ready Indians. Against an estimated three thousand warriors, Custer divided his force of 600 into three detachments. Then he of the yellow hair, with 264 officers and men, rode to quick death. Major Reno was driven back. Soldiers under Gibbon and Terry found the scene of massacre one of indelible memory. Victorious red men had separated, like wind-blown chaff.

On July 17, Colonel Wesley Merritt, hard-hitting campaigner, had met delay in leading his Fifth Cavalry Regiment northward to join Crook when, with seven troops, he trounced a band of Cheyennes bent on quitting the Red Cloud Agency. The fight had been at War Bonnet Creek—now Hat Creek, Montrose, Nebraska. From the first onslaught, when Buffalo Bill, chief of scouts, did away with scrappy Yellow Hair, until the troopers drove the red people back to the agency, Merritt had been the master strategist. It was for Captain Charles King, Fifth Cavalry, to write radiantly of this and the paths he followed with Crook.

Other scattered fights were staged and, before the year's end, the main resistance had crumbled. Sitting Bull and Gall, fleeing from General Miles, found refuge in Canada. On January 7, 1877, Miles dealt Crazy Horse a blow hard enough to bring, in the spring, the surrender of that chief and most of the unappeased.

Followers of Sitting Bull and Gall, facing season after season of scanty living, returned to the Dakota lands. But five years passed before Sitting Bull came back to say he wished to round out his years in peace.

Peace there was for several years thereafter. Many who had fought the Sioux tried to aid them. Among the most helpful was General Crook. The red men had known him as a warrior to fear, then found him a friend on whom they could rely for justice. Thus it was essential that Crook be one of the commissioners to go to Standing Rock with a view to opening the Sioux Reservation, lapping in both South and North Dakota—adjustments were made.

Now Crook was dead—since March 21—his body interred at Oakland, Maryland. This as well as other events had brought sorrow to both reds and whites. From a brew of economic troubles and hopes of cure in revived religious fervency, the Sioux again were seeking relief in their own manner. And new posts as well as Indian reservations had sprung up since the outbreaks of years gone by.

The mining Titan, cattle baron, and railroad builder had brought sweeping changes to Montana, although certain rugged sections of the Treasure State still invited exploration by white men. Completion of the Northern Pacific Railroad in 1883 quickened service out of Helena and other stations by stage coaches and freighters. In 1887, the Blackfeet permitted whittling down of their reserve, followed by the granting of a right of way for the extension westward of James J. Hill's railroad.

The problem of crossing the Rocky Mountains proved more formidable than the placating of red men. Yet a way was found. Hill's engineer, John Frank Stevens, defied winter's blasts in December, 1889, and in his reconnaissance snowshoed his way through the famed Marias Pass. He was the first white man to set forth its existence in a permanent utilitarian manner, although the location of the pass had been known in the first years of the century. The name stemmed from Marias River, found by Captain Meriwether Lewis and honoring his cousin, Maria Wood. It had remained actually "undiscovered" after its early use by red men and, doubtless, trappers.

On January 31, 1890, the Great Northern Railroad was born. It would thread its way through Marias Pass the next year and, in 1893, the line of steel would connect northern Montana with the Pacific coast. Engineer Stevens, going on to initiate work of the Panama Canal for the United States, would time and again, in more mellow days, clasp hands with the army officer, late of northern Montana's garrison.

Brown, brushing aside the web of history, reported at Fort Assiniboine on September 8. With zest he took command of Troop C, First Cavalry. The post, one of the largest and best of its type in the West, had been built in 1879 as a bulwark against Indians who roved along the Canadian border. An earlier Fort Assiniboine had stood west of Fort Union and at the head of steamboat navigation on the Missouri River. It had served as a depot for the American Fur Company's bartering with Assiniboin, Blackfeet, and Piegan. But that post's life—1834-35—was long past.

About forty miles south of the international boundary and southwest of Havre, the new post's location near the Milk River lent fascination. No matter if the next settlement might be a hundred miles distant. Sprawled across the military reservation were the Bear Paw Mountains where Chief Joseph had met his Waterloo in 1877.

Living quarters at Fort Assiniboine were fairly comfortable. Frame and log buildings prevailed. The mess on the frontier did not offer the side dishes sometimes served at West Point, but it was substantial. Fresh fruits and vegetables came at a premium. Of "Articles Composing the Ration" shortly after his arrival, the Lieutenant listed:

Meat (1 pound)—3/20 pork; 3/20 bacon; 14/20 fresh beef.
Bread—18 ounces soft, or 16 ounces hard bread.
Articles (per 100 rations)—beans, 15 pounds; sugar, 15 pounds; coffee, 10 pounds; soap, 4 pounds; salt, 4 pounds; yeast (powder when in the field), 4 pounds; pepper, 4 ounces; vinegar, 4 quarts.
Vegetables (1 pound)—4/5 potatoes; 1/5 onions.
Rice or hominy, in lieu of beans—10 pounds per 100 rations.

A two-weeks practice march for all troops except the sick, general prisoners, and skeleton details in charge of barracks commenced September 22. The command, under Major Van Valzah, Twentieth Infantry, consisted of five companies, the band of that regiment, and Troops C, F, and H, First Cavalry. A number of four- and six-mule wagons and an ambulance rocked along under the control of lashing drivers or "mule skinners." Full field equipment and tentage was carried.

Fair grazing was found on hillside and plateau. Small running streams furnished drinking water, and the banks of creeks or scattered clumps of pines yielded the necessary firewood. Relaxation could be had only on Sunday, when ladies were allowed to visit camp. The day before return to the fort, there came wind-driven rain and near-freezing temperature. Brown left camp on Beaver Creek to hunt prairie chickens.

On the threshold of winter—when forty degrees below zero might be the average reading at times—the garrison had little to look forward to other than usual routine. In October and November, by order of Brigadier General Ruger, from the Dakota Department headquarters, St. Paul, Minnesota, Lieutenant Brown aided fellow officers in the conduct of general courts-martial at the post. Among members of the court sat Major John M. Hamilton, First Cavalry, and Captain Frederick K. Ward, old friend of Bannock War days.

Courtesy of Mrs. M. B. Nash, Coeur d'Alene, Idaho.

Grave of Lieutenant S. M. Rains, First Cavalry, Fort Walla Walla, Washington, Cemetery. Killed by Indians July 3, 1877, at Cottonwood, Idaho, in the Nez Perce War. Photo by John R. White.

Soon Nelson A. Miles came to the Dakota Department. With him was Charles Baehr Gatewood, Brown's classmate, whose deep knowledge of the Apache character had been highly instrumental in bringing about the final surrender of the wily and obdurate Geronimo in 1886, after Miles had replaced Crook in Arizona.

Miles, lifted to the rank of Major General in April, 1890, while commanding the Division of the Pacific, had never attended the United States Military Academy, but his gallantry and efficiency in the Civil War and on the Western stage marked him for rapid rise. Vigilantly, he demanded quick and effective action, but handed out proper reward for hard-fisted discipline and fighting. His own body bore scars of four serious bullet wounds.

News received at Fort Assiniboine, though more or less delayed, conveyed word of unrest among the Sioux on their seven large Dakota reserves. Grasshoppers and drought had destroyed crops, rations had been pared in comparison with earlier issues, and recurrent attacks of what white doctors called "la grippe" caused increasing fatalities among the Indians.

Similar conditions and other woes had previously produced great Indian preachers with remedial teachings. James Mooney, doubtless best known for his ethnological papers concerning the Cherokee, produced a thorough study of the Sioux troubles of 1890. His findings, with others, revealed that Christianity had little influence upon the religious prophecies of the American Indian, despite seeming similarities.

Various crises among the red men brought "messiahs" to an elevated position, urging reform and harking back to the beliefs and customs of ancestors to instill virility and a conquering spirit. Prophets, after long meditation, pictured restoration by the supernatural power, of all that originally had been meant for red men alone. Land and game in abundance would again be claimed, free of intrusion by any alien. The Great Spirit was to bring the millennium to the Indians as the Chosen People, the souls of departed ancestors joining them. To achieve this state, new things had to be exchanged for the old, and prayer and watchfulness should displace warfare.

Thus, in their times, rose men like Smohalla, known among Nez Perce followers of Chief Joseph as the "Enemy of Agriculture." The influence of Smohalla the Dreamer ran narrowly, but it found fertile reception in the valleys of Nevada's mountains. From there came Tavibo the Ute, last and ablest messiah of North American red men. His evangelism centered around the dance, and from the core of the ritual sprouted the name Ghost Dance religion. Tavibo's ministry bore much fruit by 1870.

Another Paiute, Wovoka, or Jack Wilson, appeared as a new messiah about 1886. Born of the same family and tribe from which sprang Tavibo, he never forsook the place of his nativity, but Indian leaders and medicine men traveled westward from the plains to obtain instructions from him. Then they carried the instructions back to their peoples. Of all this, in grapevine fashion, Brown and his comrades had heard.

The Ghost Dance religion spread rapidly from the Arapaho and Cheyenne of Oklahoma to the Sioux at Standing Rock Agency and Sitting Bull's camp on Grand River. The majority of the Sioux remained unimpressed, but Sitting Bull and his band, sourly aggrieved, took to dancing with zeal. At Pine Ridge, where Indians of the several reservations assembled, their frenzy caused Agent R. F. Royer to wire for military intervention. Troops arrived October 19, and thousands of red persons scurried pell-mell for the Badlands.

Newspapers, with graphic picturization of wildly dancing hordes, added fuel to the racing fire of rumors among the white men. In truth, the flame of danger was localized, but white people began to think of a sudden uprising in many quarters. Settlers fled their homes.

Sitting Bull had toured America and Europe with Colonel William Cody's Wild West Show. The Army thought it best to send Buffalo Bill to arrest his friend. But Major McLaughlin, the agent at Standing Rock, hoped that the rigors of winter would cool the ardor for dancing and, to avoid any flare-up, asked for postponement of the arrest.

As long as the Indians danced, however, the whites had no feeling of security in villages or on ranches. Flight of the Indians to to the Badlands stirred the military in Montana. A message was received at Fort Assiniboine ordering its three cavalry troops and two companies of the Twentieth Infantry to entrain for Fort Keogh, at the confluence of the Tongue and Yellowstone rivers, near Miles City. Units of Infantry under senior officers were chosen; Company G, Captain Abram A. Harbach, and Company H, Captain John N. Coe.

The post shook off its lethargy. From barrack to stable to cars on near-by tracks, the men skidded on glazed paths, in their haste to be off.

Brown, too, was in a hurry; he did not pause to wonder if it was safe to assume his days of Indian fighting were all in the past.

CHAPTER XI

Last Campaign Against the Sioux

IT WAS midnight of November 29. The steam-veiled troop train on the frost-crusted rail bed a mile from the fort inched its way along the loading platform. Then sparks flew from spinning wheels, and men from lighted windows waved to other men engulfed by darkness.

Lieutenant Brown exchanged banter with sleepless soldiers. Nothing, it seemed, had been overlooked. They were fully armed and equipped for the kind of field service ahead of them—each man carrying 200 rounds of ammunition. Piled into corners, were rations sufficient for thirty days and forage enough for twenty days. As usual, it was to be expected that hay and grain could be obtained from friendly ranchers.

On the evening of the next day, the soldiers arrived at Helena, the State's Capital, of gold gulch lineage. The train, transferred to tracks of the Northern Pacific Railroad, dallied briefly before resuming its journey. That night and all the next day it puffed through snow-roofed watersheds of the Rockies, curved with river valleys, and swept across flat sagebrush land as it neared its destination.

At Fort Keogh, headquarters of the Twenty-second Infantry, the men from Fort Assiniboine went into camp in a forested area on the cobbled banks of the Yellowstone. Other regular troops also were on the ground, along with a company of Crow Indian scouts under command of Lieutenant Edward Wanton Casey. Here the men were to remain a month while troops were filled out with recruits and remounts.

Deep snow was pitched aside to make room for the community of canvas. Wall tents having been found unsatisfactory for cold regions, the conical tent, called the Sibley, was preferred. The Sibley's full-sloping sides, like the Indian tepee, could be drawn snugly to the ground to afford greater warmth. The cotton duck was of strong texture, heavy enough to be durable, not tearing easily. The irritable factor was the fire hazard caused by overheated stovepipes, and the tin shield protecting the canvas from the pipe served none too successfully. In thirty-below-zero weather, Brown began to think of a remedy.

Fuel was plentiful for the many and constant fires. Hauled by six-mule teams, wagons were heaped high with firewood. Lack of water, however, hampered company kitchens. The river was a ribbon of ice. Teeth-chattering men melted snow in their quart cups to deliver water to the cooks. Any man shunning this duty was deprived of his supper—few went hungry.

The weeks passed and the camp grew restless in the forest. Then Brown and his fellow officers at Fort Keogh received enough information for them to believe that Sitting Bull had been slain, and fighting was imminent in the Badlands.

Indeed, the Messiah War, of Ghost Dance propulsion, was whirling with the blizzards. Dancing and dreaming had continued on Grand River in December's icy blasts. Indian police, loyal to their agent, revealed that Sitting Bull and his band were about to leave for the Badlands. General Miles ordered apprehension of the chief, who had set up camp thirty-eight miles from Fort Yates. Soldiers of the Eighth Cavalry, stationed at that post, were anxious to do the job, and there were willing troops at Mandan, sixty miles north. But a more tactful arrest was decided upon by the agent and Miles.

Forty of the Indian police, many of them former members of the Wild West Show, faced the task of going to

Grand River. They were to arrest the aged chief and medicine man and take him to the agency. Two troops of the Eighth Cavalry were to follow and halt at some distance from the camp, a shielding force in case of hostility.

The police reached the shelter of Sitting Bull the morning of December 15. In the piercing cold, accentuated by a gloomy haze, they waited impatiently while the unprotesting chief had his two wives get his best wearing apparel together. By the time Sitting Bull stepped over his threshold, 150 of his strongly armed men pressed around him.

The old warrior displayed no sign of resistance. His youthful and impetuous son, Crow Foot, rebuked him. Words and guns spat in the same second. Sitting Bull crumpled to the ground, along with Lieutenant Bull Head and Sergeant Shave Head, Indian officers. The wounded Bull Head, it was later told by cavalrymen, shot the Sioux leader once, and Red Tomahawk, pulling his gun's trigger twice, ended Sitting Bull's days.

Out of the resultant exchange of deadly cross fire a red man dashed off on a pony to obtain aid from the soldiers. From a ravine two miles away, the troops spurred their horses into a gallop, with a line of skirmishers thrown ahead. When they opened up in firing order, hostiles fled and the police signaled with a white flag.

The troopers made temporary camp at the scene of sharp and bitter fighting. It had cost the lives of six Indian officers and eight of Sitting Bull's people. Shivering cavalrymen devoured a hastily cooked meal, fed their horses, and collected souvenirs. Sergeant George B. DuBois of Troop F watched with pinched face as Indian knives and medicine bags disappeared into saddlebags. Without wagons or bedding, a start had to be made toward Fort Yates. At midnight, in bivouac at Oak Creek, they rushed out to grab buffalo coats and supplies brought by two companies of infantry.

Drooping from lack of sleep, the men arrived at the

fort the next morning with increased liking for spring bunks. The slain Indian police received burial with military honors and the entire garrison participated. Yet thoughts turned to the probability of a call to saddles again.

Flight of the Indians to the Badlands drew skirmishes and pursuit from units of the Seventh Cavalry in that area. To the regiment which Custer once had led against the Sioux, fell the task of writing the last chapter in the warfare of the tribe. Major S. M. Whiteside, at Wounded Knee Creek on December 28, came upon the major portion of hostiles. Led by Big Foot, the warriors of the camp agreed to surrender to Whiteside's force.

At eight-thirty that evening, Colonel Forsyth, Brown's commander of Bannock War days, arrived to take charge. With him were four troops of Seventh Cavalrymen carrying two Hotchkiss guns to implement their effectiveness. Three nights after Christmas, just a decade short of the twentieth century, no soldier could have wished to entertain any suspicion of the tragedy the morrow would bring.

Troops and Indians stirred at dawn. Not later than seven-thirty, Big Foot and 106 of his blanket-wrapped warriors were assembled a hundred yards from the main camp. Midway between the two groups stood Troops K and B. Informed that after their formal surrender they would be considered prisoners of war, the warriors were divided into groups of twenty and advised to lay down their weapons in a selected spot. Only two useless carbines were offered.

The military, not found wanting in alertness, kept the warriors to themselves while an inspection was made of the camp. The search yielded four dozen guns, pulled from under sitting squaws and places of concealment in and among the tepees.

Meanwhile, an Indian in the garb of a Ghost Dancer railed at his fellows. An interpreter informed the inquiring

Forsyth that the haranguer was merely advising submission. Yet in a few moments, the dancer had changed his plea to one for revenge. Officers and men jerked out guns hidden by the blankets allowed the warriors as a shield from the penetrating cold.

Another dancer flung upward a handful of dust. At the signal, warriors fired upon Troops K and B, streams of their bullets splattering the camp of Indian women and children. The warriors then raced for the tepees. So quickly had they accomplished their maneuver and so constant was their fire upon the soldiers, the men in uniform had no choice but to encircle the camp. As the ring squeezed inward, the return fire grew in intensity. All too suddenly mounted the toll of the dead.

For twenty minutes the cross fire blazed while Indian families of young and old rushed afoot or on horseback for the hills. Although a dry ravine afforded a degree of protection, three troops charged up the gully, killing half a dozen warriors and capturing about twenty men, women, and children. Skirmishing continued.

Brulés, at the near-by Pine Ridge Agency, had heard of the struggle, and 125 of them leaped out to engage the cavalrymen. The troopers, paying no heed to captives, drove the challenging Brulés toward the agency.

Frustrated red men attacked the agency and scouts and police opened with a protective fire. Word that Big Foot had been killed jumped like a prairie blaze from one group of Indians to another. The day wore on, and three thousand of them became hostile in thought or act. By nightfall, Kicking Bear and Short Bull had led their people from the Badlands to No Waters, seventeen miles from the agency and half that distance from the mouth of White Clay Creek. A thousand warriors in a camp of four thousand irate Indians had to be persuaded that resistance was folly.

Out on the frozen ground were too many casualties. Scattered among the carcasses of horses and mules lay more than two hundred Indians. They would never stir again. Many who were wounded died that night because of a blinding blizzard that forbade their rescue. Twenty-three white men met death, Captain George Daniel Wallace among them. Thirty-three had sustained wounds.

The last stand of the Sioux has been labeled a massacre, but it could not have been intentional. General Schofield, in his report to the Secretary of War, was hesitant in blaming the troops. Colonel Peter E. Traub, long a friend of Brown's, in recent years set forth the results of careful research. A portion of a paper he read to a meeting of the Order of Indian Wars in 1926 asserted:

The Secretary of War, Mr. Redfield Proctor, completely exonerated Colonel Forsyth and the Seventh Cavalry. After carefully reviewing the circumstances, he said:

The women and children were never away from the immediate company of the men after the men broke from the circle. Many of them, men and women, got on their ponies, and it was impossible to distinguish buck from squaw at a little distance when mounted. The bucks fired from among the squaws and children in their retreat. Cautions were repeatedly given by both officers and non-commissioned officers not to shoot squaws or children and the soldiers were cautioned individually that such and such Indians were squaws. Some were unavoidably killed and wounded—a fact which was universally regretted by the officers and men of the Seventh U. S. Cavalry. The Indians themselves were entirely responsible for this unfortunate phase of the affair.

Though there were no more battles, troops of the Dakota Department faced winter's defiance in cleaning up the battle ground and in restoring order. Not until the first few days of a new year had passed would Miles effect full surrender of the Sioux at Pine Ridge Agency. Murder of Lieutenant Casey by Brulé ruffians on January 9 was to be a costly sacrifice.

Word for which the men had been waiting at Fort Keogh came tardily. On the last day of the year 1890,

Lieutenant Brown and his officer companions ordered their units into march formation. The three troops of First Cavalry and Indian scouts led the way, followed by the two companies of Twentieth Infantry.

Woolly snow spun about them as they passed in a lane formed by arm-swinging well-wishers. Purple-lipped newspaper reporters and photographers turned backs to the frigid wind. On both flanks rose full-throated war songs of Indian women with papooses strapped to their backs. The singing changed to a shriek as a remount slipped on the ice-crusted earth. The animal, with a broken leg, turned glassy eyes toward a man who whipped out a pistol.

The going was no better once the post was left behind. Stern-faced men, enveloped by long and heavy buffalo coats and muskrat caps, rode awkwardly. When time came for halts and the chance to warm stiff legs and feet, men on new horses could not dismount for fear of being unable to get back in the saddle. The foot soldiers, trudging in the trail blazed by the horses, carried haversack, knapsack, canteens, guns, and web belts weighted with 100 rounds of ammunition.

After a flailing march of only thirteen miles southeasterly, camp was made on Tongue River. Sibley tents sprang up in a saucerlike valley. Cooks pounded on pans, and the men came running with armfuls of wood hauled along in the wagons. Frugally, fires were fed during the night.

In the clear, crisp cold of New Year's Day, breakfast was gulped down, wagons again were loaded and the march resumed. The cavalrymen and scouts gained a long lead on the infantrymen, a lead that lasted for several days. Averaging eighteen to twenty-three miles a day, the mounted men pitched successive night camps at Pumpkin Creek, Mizpah Creek, Powder River, Timber Creek, and Box Elder Creek. A ride of twenty-five miles on January 7 brought them to the Little Missouri River. There, on

the South Dakota-Montana line, they awaited further
orders.

Brown scribbled only laconic entries in his diary, noting
mileage and locations. The monotony of the winterbound
landscape froze his well of inspiration. Yet there were to
survive fairly accurate records of this drab reconnaissance,
unsparked by any clash with Indians. One of the most
illuminating would come from Sergeant James E. Wilson
of Company H, Twentieth Infantry. At the end of the
day on which the mounted force disappeared, the infantrymen camped in the only available shelter among wind-torn
pine trees atop a ridge. Of trouble encountered, Wilson
wrote:

> After setting up our tents and banking up the snow to keep the wind
> out and from flapping the tents as it was blowing a gale through the
> pine trees, we were told to melt snow in our tin cups for water for our
> coffee.
> Our squad had built a fire beside a fallen pine tree, and it being very
> cold we had taken off our overshoes and sat around the fire with our
> feet probably too close to the coals, and before we knew it the intense
> heat was cupping the soles of our shoes.
> The next morning many of the boys could not get their shoes on and
> were obliged to march in their overshoes.
> That was a weird night on "Tin Cup Ridge."
> The wind howled, and the timber wolves also. There seemed to us to
> be thousands of them and they would come very close to our camp as
> if to attack us.
> They howled the whole night through and then slunk away at the
> break of day, and the wind died down as we broke camp at
> sunrise. . . . .

Two days later, the plodders reached the west bank of
Powder River. An easy crossing was possible on the wind-
swept ice. To gain the top of bluffs on the other shore, men
put shoulders to wheels of wagons while others tugged at
ropes. The snow got deeper, clinging to and oozing into
loose overshoes. The temperature dropped lower and
floundering humans cursed heatedly. They had marched

fourteen miles when they set up camp on timberless Timber Creek. Sagebrush was the only fuel for weary builders of fires.

Many feet showed raw the next day, yet the march went on. Atop a high and broad plain, the men at first saw nothing but snow stretching out to meet a steely sky. Then a ridge rose on their flank. In a twinkling, a thousand antelope turned tail and vanished over the crest. Sergeant Wilson thought it "one of the most beautiful sights we had ever witnessed." Hundreds of rabbits, their color of the snow, and sage hens in the camouflage dress of their habitat bounced and fluttered across the terrain. They were searching for food.

Against the ripping wind and stinging icy arrows the men pushed for twenty miles. By four o'clock the sun no longer glared at them, and in early twilight they unrolled crinkling canvas. Dreariness reigned in the "Blue Mud Hills" of Montana's Badlands. Tattered figures asked how close they were to hostile Indians, but officers professed not to know. Wilson could not forget the disconsolate mood.

As we sat in our tents that bitter cold night with out furs to keep from freezing, one soldier spoke up in a very weak voice and said, "I wonder when we will find them Indians." Another replied, "I hope we find them soon and don't care if they kill us all and put us out of pain."

We had experienced much difficulty during the day in keeping some of the men on their feet.

We had no ambulance and only one six mule team to each company. . . . .

Seasoned officers, however, knew full well that inaction dulled the zeal of men who proved valorous in a crucial moment.

Two more days of sloshing and the foot soldiers reached the camp of the cavalrymen and scouts on the Little Missouri. While they thawed out around full-blazing campfires, the bluecoats forgot the aching trek of 140 miles.

Settled in camp for two weeks, the hungry filled up on warm food. Water was fetched from holes cut in the ice-locked river. Clothes were laundered, though soap brought a skimming of alkali in the process. Faces were left un-shaven. The Indian scouts, except for occasional recon-noitering with troopers, made little disturbance in the short days. When darkness fell they sang their songs of the hunt and the battle to the throbbing of barrel-like tom-toms.

At noon of a clear day, Brown and a group of officers, squinting through field glasses, discovered a shifting object on the horizon. It moved closer—a man astride a mule. He asked for the commanding officer and was directed to the tent of Captain Harbach. Chafed fingers extracted a large envelope from an inside pocket. The man explained that he came as an orderly from field headquarters, sixty miles away.

Irritable humans swarmed around the messenger. Ques-tions and answers multiplied as the piecemeal story of the tragedy at Wounded Knee was unfolded. The soldiers learned, for the first time, that they had made their march to round up any red men who might have wished to hide in the Badlands. Now their help was not needed.

On January 24, the march back on the same trail to Fort Keogh commenced. Cavalry and scouts again set the pace, quickly outdistancing the infantrymen. Rations had run low, but there was no suffering from lack of fresh meat. Scouts killed fifteen antelope the first day, twenty-five the next day, and thirty on the third.

The hikers started to discard worn-out overshoes a hun-dred miles from their destination. But on the fourth day frigidity lost its grip—a chinook wind blew in from Da-kota. Buoyant cheerfulness replaced dejectedness; carefree soldiers tilted ear flaps on their caps and, now and then, a man bounded out of ranks. A rifle cracked, and another sage hen or rabbit was added to the supply that would be devoured in camp.

The cavalrymen and their scouts re-entered the post of the Yellowstone on the twenty-ninth. They gloried in the boisterous welcome of the garrison and gleeful Indian women. Lieutenant Brown, adding up the distance marched to and fro, found it to be 264 miles. Then whiskers came off, and water was heated for baths.

Dressed out in a change of clothing, the men from Fort Assiniboine boarded a train February 4. Two days later they told their story to eager listeners on Milk River, a story never fully repeated.

Action-loving Brown had not had the luck to add another fight to his record, but the troubles encountered with tents burning from glowing tin pipes gave him an idea for which the Army would forever be thankful. In garrison routine, he turned to the development of a protective shield of asbestos.

Too, the discoveries made four years previously by Charles M. Hall and Paul Heroult, defining the commercial possibilities of aluminum, could be a blessing to the soldier of the American Army. At least Lieutenant Brown considered it worthy of serious thought.

CHAPTER XII

Exploration of Basin of St. Mary North Fork

FOR nearly one thousand miles, almost unbroken by hills and tragi-cally scarred by ravines, the vast sod plains of the west sweep upward to end abruptly against the stark, gaunt Rocky mountains that stretch out, windblown, snow-crested and ice carved across all trails to the western sea. From these mountains flow the rivers that served as the earliest highways, and from one distinctive peak—in that pre-eminent position of the range marked by Glacier park—the water flows into three oceans: Through Norris creek and St. Mary's lake to Hudson bay and the Arctic; through Cut Bank creek into the Missouri and the Gulf of Mexico, and through Nyack creek into Flathead river, thence to Clark's fork of the Columbia and the Pacific. Sheltered here in the maze of mountains that surrounds this triple divide peak is Marias pass, long named, long known, long sought for, yet unfound—the elusive will-o'-the-wisp of the Rockies.—GENEVIEVE MURRAY in *Marias Pass.*

Prior to the pushing of the Indian westward from the Atlantic by America's first colonists, the world of grass, running up to the Rockies, gave good hunting to many red men—Selish, or Flathead, Kootenai, the Shoshone, or Snake. Later, these were driven westward and scattered by tribes of the strong Algonquin nation. Principally they were the Blackfeet, the Bloods, and the Piegans, or Pikani. The red men found use for what came to be known as Marias Pass.

There came men of the Hudson's Bay Company to hunt, trap, and trade with the Indians. David Thompson appeared in 1786, to learn much of the northern Rockies. He returned to Piegan country again in 1800, but passed a great distance north of Marias Pass. Men representing the Northwest Fur Company examined the new country but not Marias Pass. Lewis and Clark reached the mouth of the

Yellowstone River May 6, 1805. When they ventured northward and westward they discovered new things. Captain Clark plotted rivers. Captain Lewis, however, was credited with surveying the Marias River. The thick and colorful series of rocks which, in millions of years, had been formed in a sea created by waters from the Arctic Ocean, he called "shining mountains."

Because of Thompson's persistent exploring, three men of the white race went through Marias Pass, east of Flathead Lake, in 1810. Red men continued to use it, but from that date until about eighty years later no white man seemed to be able to guide travelers to its location. When John F. Stevens and a renegade Flathead named Coonsah struck out from the Blackfeet Indian Agency to find the pass, they comprised a ludicrous "expedition." Fitted with improvised snowshoes, each carried a pair of blankets and a small supply of food. The Indian gave out before gaining the summit. Of their venture in 1889, Brown was to write:

It was a situation which had in it an element of humor worthy of the pen of Mark Twain or Will Rogers, for they were attempting in mid December to find the low pass over the Continental Divide which had been talked of for eighty years, which Lewis and Clark failed to note; which Greenhow, making a shrewd guess had put on his 1840 map, only to omit it four years later, and finally which had been missed by Gov. I. I. Stevens' large and well-equipped expedition of 1853-4 which included scientists, guides, voyageurs, explorers, Army officers and soldiers and was supplied with abundant transportation. The bare publication later of I. I. Stevens' voluminous reports and maps must have cost a good round sum.

Other parties crossed the Divide at points higher than the 5,216 feet of the elusive pass. The rough-hewn region that was to become Glacier National Park obtained wider recognition in the eighties when George Bird Grinnell, editor of *Forest and Stream,* broke trails through patches of its wilderness. The fitting names he gave to numerous natural wonders still hold out.

Courtesy of Mrs. M. B. Nash, Coeur d'Alene, Idaho.

Grave of Charles C. Blewett, 19-year-old scout, in the City Cemetery at Walla Walla, Washington. He was killed along with William Foster and Lieutenant S. M. Rains at Cottonwood, Idaho, in Nez Perce War of 1877. Photo by John R. White.

The interest of the public increased in the area chiseled from mountains by great Alpine glaciers, in sheer cliffs rising as high as 5,000 feet, in U-shaped valleys, sky-reaching divides and peaks, cirques and ice-cold lakes numbered in hundreds, and sixty glaciers giving birth to thousands of streams.

The army, therefore, felt impelled to gain greater knowledge of the St. Mary Basin, in the central eastern portion of today's Glacier Park. Here indeed was a great natural reservoir of water. Upper and lower St. Mary Lakes, extending along the western bulwark made by the Hudson Bay Divide, had been christened in 1840 by Father Peter John De Smet, missionary to the Indians. St. Mary River flowed from the lower lake to and across the Canadian border. Orders for further exploration came to Fort Assiniboine in mid-September, 1891.

Colonel J. C. Bates, commanding, requested Lieutenant Brown to prepare a party for mapping and surveying the region northwest of St. Mary Lakes. On September 18, Secretary of War Proctor and his official party visited the post. Courteous was the reception and intense was the interest of the guests in plans for the enticing quest.

The "instruments" Brown jotted down in his notebook as needing prompt attention were pocket sextant, aneroid barometer, two prismatic compasses, hand level, thermometer, odometers, and two notebooks. His troop busied itself assembling equipment, rations and forage, to be hauled in wagons and on mules. Lieutenants Frederick S. Foltz, First Cavalry, and J. F. Morrison, Twentieth Infantry, were to assist in the triangular surveys. Assistant Surgeon A. M. Smith was to provide medical aid. Others filling out the party would be C. S. Foltz, photographer Hunter, and guides and packers, all familiar with the region or requirements of exploration. They hoped to cross trails with Grinnell, then somewhere in the fastnesses.

Brown led his party forth on the morning of the twenty-first. Members of the troop rode unchecked and in high spirit. The two wagons with grease oozing from their axles, drawn by six-mule teams, and the four mules sagging under heavy packs, moved more slowly. For ten miles across the flat prairie the post remained visible. The men continued ten miles more to the left of Sweetgrass Hills, finding little water in the shallow coulees. Sage Creek provided a good camp site. The grass was plentiful, and the summer camp of a sheepherder was spotted near by. Twenty ducks the command had shot added to the appeal of the evening meal.

In the dewy morning, the bugle sounded reveille and two hours later the group affirmed its readiness to wheel and ride. The tracks of the Northern Pacific were crossed. The wagon road veered toward Middle Butte, then lost itself in high grass. Some good water lay in a coulee on the way, but cattle had riled up Buffalo Coulee where the night's rest fell due. After the men had pitched their Sibley tents, a violent wind swept across the spaces. Short poles had to be reinforced to avert the shaking down of shelters.

The wind, smiting furiously, plagued the men all the next day. As they approached Sweetgrass Hills there was rain; then a spitting of snow, and the grazing disappeared. Two miles above G. G. Wood's ranch, shelter was available at a stockade. Wood, hay and bedding for the animals were bought from rancher Wood. Buckets dipped into Cottonwood Creek for water.

Travel on the fourth day revealed large herds of cattle in the valley northwest of Shark's Tooth. From a high plateau farther on, the group drank in the beauty of the Highwoods, the Bear Paws, and Mount Licatur of the Rockies. Brown took sextant bearings for camping at Symonds Creek. The stream abounded with small fish and luscious grass grew in spongy soil. A pile of poles provided firewood for cooking.

The next afternoon the adventurers reached a point slightly above Rocky Springs station on the Great Falls and Canada rails. Morrison, who had been detained, jumped off a northbound train and joined the westward march. No wood nor brush could be obtained that day or the next in two twenty-mile jaunts. When bearings were taken at camp on Flag Creek, a small alkaline stream walled in by a canyon, what proved to be Chief Mountain at the Canadian line reared up thirty-one degrees north of west. Brown, uncertain as to the name of the creek, called the place "Where Are We?"

There had been no trail to follow all day and the only targets were a porcupine and a swift. In the position south of Flag Creek's confluence with the Cutbank, however, it was noted there were three places where teams might cross Rocky Ridge south of Snake's Head, and the spot on which would rise the town of Shelby.

Thirty-two miles were chalked off on the twenty-seventh in the northwesterly trek to the South Fork of Milk River where the MacLeod road crossed. There was brushwood aplenty, sparkling water, and grass tall enough for mowing.

The next evening, the group had better protection against a bothersome wind in dense undergrowth and small timber at the outlet to Lower St. Mary Lake. But the rank grass and wet earth did not provide perfect rest for weary teamsters who arrived four hours behind the troop. It had been mostly an uphill pull. Not far from Henkel's ranch on Swiftcurrent Creek, Brown learned that Grinnell had passed on his way up Swiftcurrent.

The weather turned wintry and camp remained unbroken for several days. Brown, accompanied by Lieutenant Foltz, rode to the Norris ranch and engaged the owner as a guide for the mountain trip. Wagons were sent to Blackfoot station for more supplies.

September blew out on an icy wind from the north

which hurled a foot of snow on the ground. Mrs. Henkel parted with half a ton of hay and received five dollars. Food became scarcer. Two sergeants and two packers went with a mule to Norris for fish, and the soldiers returned to report no luck. Brown then sent Lieutenants Foltz and Morrison, civilian Foltz, surgeon Smith, two sergeants, a corporal, and a private to engage a Mr. Carter at the Norris ranch to guide them to Eagle Lake in a hunt for large game. They departed in the teeth of a raging blizzard.

Brown rose on the first morning of October to find eighteen inches of snow weighting down the wiry grass. Sodden flakes had to be wiped off the matted backs of horses which had spent the night munching hay in the brush. As they were led out to herd, Hunter focused his camera on them. Brown brought his journal up to date in spare hours. In the evening, he welcomed the return of the two packers with fish and, as his share, carried to the cook a seven-pound trout.

He and Hunter hiked through drifted snow to the Norris cabin the next morning. The two other lieutenants went back to the lower camp and welcomed the wagons which had returned from Blackfoot station after a sluggish journey. Brown, surgeon Smith and half a dozen fellows kept warm around a small sheet-iron stove set up on the earthen floor of the cabin. The leader shot a teal for his breakfast, and 100 pounds of fine trout went into the larder.

On the fourth, Brown, Hunter, and Norris climbed laboriously up Flattop Mountain. Once on the frigid tableland, the officer went to work with his sextant, and Hunter with his camera. Brown found Flattop to be 8,700 feet high, yet "simply a plateau compared to many others" in the vicinity. Upon sighting a trio of mountain sheep in the distance, he fired his rifle. But the cagey animals, bounding swiftly over the rocks, escaped singing bullets. On the same day, the main command, leaving two men with a few supplies at the lake, moved closer to the interior.

Anxious to contact Grinnell, Brown sent Norris and Sergeant Rogers with a note to the trail breaker. While triangulation was undertaken to determine the exact location of the camp, party members shot nineteen prairie chickens and twenty-six ruffed grouse. Brown, Officer Foltz, Morrison, and Hunter, with two packers and packs, spent two days atop Flattop making further triangulations and observations. They camped at the timber line, 7000 feet above sea level. On the summit, above stunted pines, waves of snow glistened under a strong sun.

The chapped group returned to camp at Norris in the afternoon of the seventh. Norris, after a hard ride, reported his failure to find Grinnell. The weather cleared and preparations for the mountain trip began immediately.

A start was made late the next morning. Brown's party, with fourteen days' rations, consisted of Lieutenants Foltz and Morrison, Mr. Foltz, Norris, Sergeants Murray and Shaffer, Hunter, and a trio of packers, Brims, Brackenridge, and Brigham. They found the trail stubbornly risky at The Narrows halfway along the upper St. Mary Lake. Upturned layers of age-worn limestone projected at a 45-degree angle. A mule fell over a rocky spur and had to be retrieved, another toppled on Murray. The sergeant was bruised severely and Brims took his place. Steepness forbade safe riding, for soon two more mules went rolling downhill. After a march of nine miles, the men pitched tents three miles below the upper end of the elongated lake. Grazing was scant, but the water was good.

On the ninth, Brown left camp with Norris and reconnoitered a portion of the North Fork of St. Mary River from the side of burnished Going-to-the-Sun Mountain. In halts between hard climbs, the men watched the antics of wild goats on the slopes of Goat Mountain, and their own fortress of rich Indian legend. Here it was that Napi, or "Old Man," supreme creator of earthly things, was supposed to have returned to the sun, from which emanated life and light. Back in shelter after a weary day, Brown, to lighten the packs, gave a tent to two men who had arrived in a boat. Mr. Foltz went downstream to procure horse and mule shoes and, on the trip, talked with Grinnell.

Early the next day, Brown drifted back to Norris by boat, hoping to meet Grinnell. The editor had left the previous evening, and the officer interviewed, instead, the explorer's guide. A horse was ridden back to camp in the afternoon, for the wind had suddenly whipped up huge waves on the lake.

A storm brought rain during the night and morning. Brown ordered camp moved four miles to the west to gain shelter in the timber and better grazing around sparkling springs. The conical tents were pitched half a mile west of Baring Creek and wood fires crackled. Four of the pack animals being team mules, Brown decided their loads were too heavy for the rugged country. A pine-bough shack, that had been constructed by Grinnell under a rocky ledge of the lake shore, came in handy as a cache for provisions.

Snow halted the party on the twelfth. A foot of it compelled the stock to rustle for feed. Stalking hunters blazed away at mountain sheep without success.

Weather that melted the snow stirred the men into further progress the next day. Brown led them on the Grinnell trail along the St. Mary Fork roaring with milky water debouched by the glacier. Under snow-daubed firs and cedars they marched, soaked by dripping branches. They made evening camp on the stream and faced Almost-a-Dog, perching twin of Going-to-the-Sun, in adoration. The density of the timber foiled erection of a tent. Morrison's tent fly was used with a lean-to, and in this shelter wet clothes dangled limply.

Brown took note of the fact that Grinnell had reported no signs of others than himself penetrating above the camp site. Norris found it necessary to return afoot to more urgent pursuits, but the Lieutenant felt confident he could carve out his own trail.

He and his followers started toward the southern slope of Going-to-the-Sun in the morning of the fourteenth, but Norris overtook them. Winded from haste, he handed over a letter from Grinnell and one from Sergeant Rogers. The sergeant reported that the men in the provisional retreat had procured whisky from a rash trader and were bent on mischief. Brown at once sent Morrison back with Norris to halt the quarrying of trouble. The explorers pressed on, slashing through thick timber and tangled undergrowth of black willow.

Two hours after noon, they struck a small stream gurgling its way from Going-to-the-Sun to the North Fork on their left. Brown noted the position carefully: "We are now in country never before visited by white men, I think rarely if ever by Indians." He and Foltz, climbing a promontory, saw that travel northward would meet with sundry obstacles. Three miles to the southwest Brown, through his glasses, located an area of swamp grass at the foot of Reynolds Mountain. There he decided to camp.

The greenish North Fork had to be recrossed. And the second fording proved defiant, with jutting slippery rocks and a series of cascades and waterfalls. The snow had melted from the trees, but it was soggy underfoot. One of the mules fell exhausted. Its bundles were transferred to the backs of the horses. The shuffling group reached the opening at five o'clock. Mountains, draped with clouds, no longer beckoned. Rations had diminished alarmingly, and soup tablets proved a salvation. Brown and Foltz then agreed with Mr. Foltz that it was too late to erect a tent. They eased into sleeping bags beneath the emerald canopy of a large pine.

As the frayed marchers fell asleep, a light rain began sifting through needled boughs. Intermittently, for the next forty-eight hours, the rain gave way to sleet and snow. Tents were staked out on the stream's graveled banks. Burning wood sizzled from dampness and flared up only when needles caught flame. Hunting yielded nothing. The animals, feeding on coarse grass, fared better than did their masters.

On the sixteenth, as the storm increased, Brown reluctantly exhaled hope of further penetration of the wilderness. He advised withdrawal, and the group struck out an hour before noon. The back-trailing throughout the day, southeast and east, depended upon the compass. An occasional glimpse of neighborly mountains aided in the mapping. Willow entanglements were avoided, and although little prostrate timber had to be cut through, snow on the trees and the ground made for a wet, annoying march. When the Grinnell trail was picked up a mile from the camp site of the eleventh and twelfth, the pace of the animals quickened.

By four o'clock the men reached their cache, and hastily they attacked the hard bread and cheese. There camp was made for the night, a blustering gale coming down the lake to fan the fires. Brown forewent the privilege of setting up Morrison's tent, and the fly was stretched over the chilled horses and mules.

Hunter procured an excellent view of the mountain to the west before the breaking of camp in the morning. On the back trail of twelve miles, to the troop at Norris cabin, he photographed the straggling explorers. The pictures were to become historical. But of more immediate urgency was Brown's investigation of carousing by the troopers. The commander dealt out ear-tingling "plain talk" at retreat while shamefaced men shivered in a howling wind.

Major Steele, Indian agent, appeared on the scene the next day, a balmy Sabbath. The soldiers pondered their errors while preparing to march back to their post or to near-by points of scenic interest. The agent, gravity stamped on his face, disclosed his earnest aim either to drive the whisky peddlers out of the region or conduct them to the agency's jail.

On Monday, Brown ordered inspection and verification of property before permitting the reloading of wagons and division of supplies for side trips to be made by detachments under Lieutenants Foltz and Morrison. On this last day of dispersal, with a surplus of rations to be loaded, the first large specimen of game was bagged. Norris and Surgeon Smith strode proudly in from a hunt with the hide, head, and meat of a splendid mountain ewe, which the medical officer had brought down with deadly aim. And, more ironically still, now that trail breaking was off the schedule, the wind blew so warm a fire was unnecessary.

Subsequently, however, in the Engineer's Office, Department of Dakota Headquarters, there was to be prepared an invaluable map of the St. Mary Lake region as compiled from the triangular surveys made by Brown and his assisting officers, and from a "Sketch Map by Geo. Bird Grinnell 1885-91." On May 11, 1910, the area which had been nature's tight secret so long, and which now invites tourists by highways and trails, would become Glacier National Park. In 1932, Brown was to see, happily, the joint establishment of Waterton-Glacier International Peace Park. The American section, embracing 1,538 square miles of the Rockies, would rank third in size among the national parks of the United States.

During the remaining months spent at Fort Assiniboine, Brown did not allow his inventive ideas to grow cold. His suggested improvement for the stovepipes of tents, after hearty indorsement by Colonel Bates, was communicated to St. Paul. On December 31, 1891, Department Commander Merritt forwarded the Lieutenant's communication to the army's adjutant general, while suggesting that the device was "worthy of adoption" and that Brown "should have a patent for it."

The researcher, citing advantages that should accrue in substituting aluminum and its alloys for other metals used in equipment of cavalry and infantry, received further encouragement. On February 1, 1892, General Merritt wrote quite informally:

DEAR BROWN: Your note with enclosures received today. Certainly your effort in favor of aluminum can do no harm and ought to result in much good to the army. A pound saved in the weight carried by each soldier is a great gain. Your device for stovepipe hole in tent must commend itself to all who have had experience in matters of the kind. . . . .

In April, the cavalrymen at Fort Assiniboine prepared to quit Montana's prairies for the more arid expanse of Arizona. Merritt, as persistent as Brown, recommended strongly that fitting tests be made of aluminum equipment.

Lessons learned in many arduous campaigns by the venerable commander at St. Paul and in the fewer years of service by the young cavalry officer, proved much. But, seemingly, the knife for cutting the tape of time would have to be held firmly to the whetstone for countless days.

CHAPTER XIII

New Steps in the Department of Arizona

AMID bustling, in the loading of horses, baggage, equipment, and supplies, Lieutenant Brown stole time to attend the farewell dance at Fort Assiniboine the night of April 20, 1892. Immediately after, the troops marched out of the lighted garrison in step with buoyant music played by the Twentieth Infantry Band. Two hours past midnight, the cars rolled out of the station. And twenty-four hours later, the cavalrymen left the metropolis of Butte where King Copper ruled with a polished scepter.

Travel southward lay through Denver and La Junta. Brown's family table beckoned irresistibly. There was a visit, but all too brief.

In the still of night on May 6, the sleepy officer sauntered into the Southern Pacific depot at Willcox, Arizona. Not far away loomed the Chiricahua Mountains, running into the southwest corner of New Mexico. The railroad, after leaving the town, curved southwesterly to breast the Dragoon Mountains and cross the San Pedro River.

Brown, bent on reaching Fort Grant, dozed behind a team for four more hours. The post, almost straight north of Willcox, rested in a foothill arc a short distance southwest of lofty Mount Graham.

As spring met early summer, the cactus-spangled desert offered a stimulating tonic in wide-sweeping, scented breezes. The time was ideal for following cattle trails and interlacing footpaths. Remoteness sharpened initiative. Brigadier General McCook commanded the Department from headquarters in Los Angeles, California.

In June, Brown served in general courts-martial at San Diego Barracks as well as at Fort Grant. Detailed with him at his regular station were several officers who had fought in the closing Indian campaigns of the Pacific Northwest. Thomas McGregor was there as a Major, Second Cavalry, also Captains F. A. Boutelle, Ward, and F. A. Edwards, and First Lieutenant John Pitcher, all of the First Cavalry. Present, too, was Second Lieutenant Edward Anderson, who had joined Brown's Troop C at Assiniboine.

"Bad men" still remained at large in the Southwest, but no longer was there warfare with red men along the history-cloaked Santa Fe Trail. Deeds of famous Apache Chiefs Cochise, Victorio, and Geronimo belonged to a day never to return.

Brown recalled the experiences of his leaders who had come and gone.

Arizona's lawmakers had handed Crook tokens of deep gratitude for his controlling of the Apaches in 1871. Howard, prior to his term as commander of the Columbia Department, had been peacemaker with the Apaches. But the red men had not been tamed.

Again in 1882, Crook was called back to Arizona, and he finally encircled Geronimo and his band in the Sierra Madre Mountains. In July of that year, Lieutenant Thomas Cruse, Sixth Cavalry, gallantly charged hostile Apaches, rescued a wounded soldier, and in 1892 would receive a Medal of Honor for the act. Captain Adna R. Chaffee had been cited for gallantry in the same fight, at Big Dry Wash, Arizona. For a third time Geronimo went to San Carlos Reservation. In 1884 he started his last revolt, a lengthy, strategical hit-and-run race. Miles came to relieve Crook, the older man taking command of the Department of the Platte. In abbreviated time, Miles, with the aid of Mexican troops, had forced the surrender of the wily and obdurate Geronimo. Columns of sweating, fighting cavalrymen had had their day.

But it was in the story of rough-and-ready Bernard that one who knew him as battalion leader could picture best the early days of the Southwest. Here it was that Bernard first met General (then Colonel) Edward R. S. Canby, destined to die at the hands of the Modocs when both men were to see fateful fighting in Oregon against Captain Jack. Colonel Canby, recognizing the merits of the Tennessean who had become an acting lieutenant, appointed him second lieutenant, regular.

The New Mexican campaign of 1862, in which Kit Carson and Major John M. Chivington, among others, had played outstanding roles, resulted in the forced withdrawal of General Henry H. Sibley's Confederates to El Paso, Texas.

Bernard, as a major, had been in command at Fort McIntosh in 1886, when election day at the town of Laredo, Texas, saw arguments turned into fighting. When he heard that groups were crossing the Rio Grande River from Mexico to enliven the melee, he marched into the town with his troops. His restoration of order was prompt and effective.

Peace and all its benefits were finally enjoyed by Mrs. Bernard, mother of seven children. In 1891 she had died, only a year after her husband had been breveted a brigadier general and five years before he would retire.

In 1892, Brown realized that even political feuds were getting less violent in New Mexico and Arizona. Yet the military and responsible citizens saw there was much work to be done before the territories might provide the last two stars in the Union's field of blue. An abundance of minerals proved a boon, as did the rich ranges for thousands upon thousands of sheep and cattle, but the irrigation of the vast reaches of arid and semi-arid lands loomed as the vital problem. Meanwhile, cattle-thieving remained a thorn in the side of settlers.

The renegade Apache Indian, "Kid," had driven off cattle at his will. Pursued, he stole fresh horses to ride. When mounts gave out, he killed them. Once, a squaw of his showed up in Mammoth to buy some things with a twenty-dollar gold piece. The sheriff followed her into the hills, but she also escaped rather easily, leaving her horse dead on the trail.

Brown got the chance to lead a mounted scouting party of ten privates in chase of the "Kid" in the Galiuro Mountains. The search, between July 19 and 28, led up from the Aravaipa Valley to the vicinity of Stanley and Sombrero Buttes and beyond.

In and out of rocky canyons, the Lieutenant and his men lashed their horses. They camped at widely spaced water holes or visited isolated ranchers for information or the purchase of forage. Rumors concerning the whereabouts of the desperado were never lacking, but he kept on going. On the twenty-third, the scouts and packers suffered a thorough drenching while trying to outrun a cloudburst. Brown ordered a return to the post.

Something more important was on his mind. It was experimentation with lighter and more durable articles for the Army. A board, Captains Boutelle, Ward, and G. S. Hoyle, met at regimental headquarters "to examine and report upon the merits of a picket pin, of an alloy of aluminum and titanium, with iron head and swivel; and an aluminum cup." These Brown presented, and the board reported favorably. Before long, higher authorities would do more than raise eyebrows. For the time being, August days flared intensely hot and the inventor battled forest fires on Mount Graham.

Then attention turned to the Navajos. In the long period since their release from Fort Sumner at the Bosque Redondo in 1867, they had occupied a vast area while tending their sheep and cattle. Yet not all were happy. Of the situation, T. J. Morgan, Commissioner of Indian Affairs, reported in part to Secretary of the Interior John W. Noble:

SIR: The relations between the Navajo Indians of New Mexico, Arizona, and Utah and their white neighbors have been much strained for some time. The Navajos, on account of a lack of water and grass upon their reservation, located in the Territories named, have been forced to go beyond its boundaries to sustain their flocks and herds.

A few have settled upon the public domain with a view of securing title to their homes under existing public land laws. The whites have sought the use of the public lands in the vicinity of the reservation mainly for grazing purposes and the interests of the two races have thus conflicted. Difficulties have occurred between them, resulting now and then in the loss of life both to Indians and whites.

This office has endeavored to maintain peace and harmony among the Indians and whites and to return the nonreservation Navajos to their reservation; but the want of a water supply and grazing facilities thereon have hindered their return thither; notwithstanding these needs the Navajo Indians are self-supporting.

The Navajo agent stated that nine thousand, or half of the eighteen thousand Indians of the Navajo nation, were forced to seek water and grass off the reservation. General McCook, recognizing the problems, submitted recommendations for a survey of the reservation to locate artesian wells, to bore wells and place windmills at them, and to select sites for water storage and ditches for irrigation. McCook believed that it would "be inhuman to drive the Navajo Indians, with their large flocks and herds, back to the reservation as it now is....."

Lieutenant Chauncey B. Baker, Seventh Infantry, in the Engineer Office, Headquarters of the Department of Arizona, on August 22, apprised the department's Assistant Adjutant General that, "It would require at least two years for the completion of a topographical survey" for mapping correctly the Navajo reserve, containing 12,821 square miles, "a territory larger than the combined areas of Connecticut and Massachusetts." He advised that maps be drawn of localities and accurate markings made on Powell's existing Geological Survey Map. For surveying the water resource areas, the acting engineer officer divided the work into three parts.

On September 2, President Benjamin Harrison ordered the survey, and eleven days later Lieutenant Brown received instructions to take charge of it. Second Lieutenants Odon Gurovits, Eleventh Infantry, and Edwin M. Suplee, Second Cavalry, were named to accompany him to Fort Wingate, New Mexico. There, while preparing to go afield, they were to await further orders and the arrival of three noncommissioned officers and sixteen privates of the Second Cavalry from Camp Doane.

Meanwhile, back East, old friends were recommending Brown for detail in the Bureau of Military Intelligence. Superintendent Wilson, writing from West Point, pronounced him "peculiarly well fitted" for duty in the bureau.

On the twenty-second, Brown and Gurovits arrived at Fort Wingate, followed the next day by Suplee. Gurovits was assigned the northwestern part of the reservation and Suplee the southwestern area. For his portion, Brown took the territory east of the Lukachukia and Tunitcha Mountains, north and east of Cañons del Muerto and De Chelly on the south. In his party were Acting Hospital Steward G. G. Roberts, a lance corporal, three privates of Troop D, Second Cavalry, and, so reported the leader, "four privates (Navajos) Troop L, Second Cavalry; one civilian packer, and one teamster driving the buckboard, which was returned to the post on October 14; my transportation consisted of 11 pack mules."

There was a scarcity of surveying instruments in the Department of Arizona, and Brown obtained on the twenty-fourth, except stadia rods, chains and pins, certain

Courtesy of Dr. G. H. Gilmore, Murray, Nebraska.

Grave of John B. A. Rhoden, aged 24 years, near Murray, Nebraska. He was killed by an Indian at Ross Fork, Idaho, November 23, 1877, in a prelude to Bannock War of 1878.

instruments sent from the engineer depot at Willets Point, New York. On the twenty-fifth, the three groups left Fort Wingate, arriving at the Navajo Indian Agency at Fort Defiance, Arizona, the next day.

Transits and levels being too heavy for the pack mules, Brown had telegraphed to Willets Point "for three hand levels, three clinometers, three pedometers, and one aneroid barometer, leaving instructions at Fort Wingate to have these instruments forwarded to us upon receipt." The postmaster who received them forgot about them for a week. Brown and Suplee would get theirs a month later, but Gurovits would have his work finished by the time his came to hand. The stadia rods, Brown explained, were "strips of lumber 15 feet long and could not have been carried on pack mules even had I known of their being at Fort Wingate when we left."

Though handicapped, the surveying parties produced a valuable quantity of maps and reports for future projects. In his officially printed report, Brown spiced staid impressions with sharpened wit:

Learning that the agent contemplated a visit to the camp of Manuelito, chief of the Navajoes, on September 28, I accompanied him. Here I found the largest collection of Indian farms seen on the trip, the camp and farms extending over an area about a mile long by about one-fourth of a mile wide, with about ten to forty families, according to season. The water for domestic purposes was obtained from holes 3 to 4 feet deep in the sandy bed of a "wash." At this depth there is a stiff clay subsoil perfectly impervious to water, the method of irrigation here as in many other parts of the reservation, I found to be to flood the surface during the season when the snows are melting on the mountains, and water in streams and "washes" is plenty, holding it on the surface by means of small dams about 12 inches high, at a distance apart from 15 to 50 yards, depending on the natural slope of the ground. The water soaks through only as far as the clay subsoil, and one irrigation is found sufficient to raise a crop of corn. This is a place of importance and an artesian or bore well should be located here.

Manuelito was informed of the object of our visit, and with him I visited Heavymans Springs, where the herds were watered, some 5 miles to the west. Here was found an excellent opportunity of instructing the chief, and through him the Indians of his camp, in the proper method of developing these springs and storing the water from them. By a few minutes' work with the shovel the flow of two of the springs was materially increased under his own eyes, and he was shown how, by the labor of ten men for a day, a dam could be constructed holding a considerable volume of water and which would give the herds watering there relatively pure water instead of the muddy, polluted stuff which the large number of sheep, goats, and ponies watering here were drinking. The desirability of this he frankly admitted, saying that "goats would drink only pure water," but on the principle that "everybody's business is nobody's business," doubted whether his young men would do the work, but promised to talk to them about it. Seeing him some six weeks later, I questioned him in regard to the matter, but found, as I had suspected, that nothing had been done.

The condition of these springs is about the same as many others. Neglected partly because the Indians do not know how, but chiefly because they are too lazy and shiftless to care for them. While thus neglecting to care for what he has, Manuelito asks that the reservation be enlarged, which I do not think at all necessary.....

In continuation of his survey, however, Brown saw more progressive steps already taken. Tom Terlino, a Carlisle graduate, welcomed the officer to a stone house instead of a makeshift abode, also to fresh-water springs. At other points, he found good adobe houses along with some of stone, especially at the favorite Sheep Spring.

On the San Juan River, where the whites had orchards on their side, the Indians recognized good neighbors, and were on friendly terms. Citizens had constructed an irrigation ditch at a cost of $75,000, to make a fruitful Eden.

At Sandival's farm on the San Juan, ditches were being dug and fences built by ambitious Indian farmers. Yet here, as elsewhere, Brown lamented the fact that the Indian "almost invariably makes a poor ditch heading, on which the efficiency and permanency of a ditch largely depends." Moreover, the red man in wishing "to handle only a minimum of earth," shaped the cross section of his ditch with perpendicular sides. This faulty practice, instead of approved sloping banks, or trough form, led to frequent cave-ins and excessive repairing.

North of the Lukachukia Mountains, the Lieutenant visited an area which could be irrigated by running flumes across numerous arroyos. Standing Red Rock Valley, controlled by Black Horse, offered great fertility but the officer saw neither a plow nor a wagon. He received a message asking him to hasten from Tsa-a-no'-sti across the Tunitcha Mountains to investigate trouble at an Indian store at Tse-a-lee. Brown went, viewing an open timber country where plenty of water could be had for developing rich tracts of from five to twenty acres.

There was a rumpus at the store. The Indian agent and a few of his assistants were barricaded within. Black Horse and his people, in a near-by camp, threatened reprisals for the taking of Indian children "too far away in cold, bad cold, bad wind and snow."

Brown sized up the situation calmly. He talked with the agent and with the chief. The children must go to school, but then, too, the agent must provide better facilities.

"Black Horse," he said, "it is good to love your children. Keep them warm until better things come. Do not harm the agent or his police. That would bring many soldiers and guns."

The issue was settled on the spot. The chief and the agent made their promises to each other.

The army man turned to the inviting Wheatfields area north of Whisky Creek. There a number of Indians tilled the soil. In Bonita Creek at the Agency, the water volume was six and a half gallons a second, being doubled in irrigating season. It was November and the survey drew to a close.

Of the reservation as a whole, Brown reported:

In general terms it may be said that the mountain range, extending for 70 miles north and south through the reservation, constitutes in itself a vast reservoir, as the winter's snows melt and run down the numerous cañons and washes, at almost the very time when water is most needed for purposes of irrigation.

If whites were in possession of this country the greater portion of this water would be utilized. . . . . The soil is generally sandy, but, so far as could be ascertained, quite fertile, and along the San Juan well adapted to fruit-raising.

The officer warned that money spent on sorely needed irrigation projects for the Navajos would be wasted unless proper farm implements were furnished the red men, along with practical farmers who could provide proper instruction.

That his observations, as well as those of his fellow officers, carried weight was borne out in recommendations made by Commissioner Morgan. Early the next year, he drafted an appropriation item for $64,000 to aid the Navajos in accordance with the general plan submitted by the army men. Congress, ever watchful of disbursements, in June, 1893, was to allow $40,000, presumably in pursuance of the report made on behalf of the Navajos. From funds it had previously appropriated, the Commissioner could add the available tidy sum of $20,000 for the Navajo Reservation's irrigation and water supply.

In a special order, November 14, Brown was requested to appear in person before an examining board at Fort Grant. The board, with Colonel Abraham K. Arnold, First Cavalry, as president, was to look into the Lieutenant's fitness for promotion. A practical examination in drill regulations was held two days before Christmas.

The troop, in undress uniforms and forage caps, carried all arms. The saber was attached to the saddle. Adroitly, Brown thwarted "staged" confusion. And the troopers learned several new lessons. On January 17, 1893, the Adjutant General's Office at Washington informed the tested officer that he had qualified satisfactorily. The Secretary of War approved, therefore he would receive promotion when a vacancy occurred in the next grade for which he was eligible. The wait was to drag out for three years.

Near the end of January, General McCook, by authority of the President, tendered Brown the office of acting agent for the Navajos. Their agent had just left. The Lieutenant wired kind thanks, but added, "I do not wish it and earnestly hope that I may not be detailed."

An all-prevailing desire to push ahead with experiments in aluminum won out. Yet special duty in surveying and superintending the extension of Fort Grant's water system took up most of Brown's time for a while. Early in April, the experimenter received an official copy of a letter addressed to the Department of Arizona's head by Adjutant General R. Williams, Hadquarters of the Army. Here was encouragement:

Referring to your endorsement of February 11th, 1893, forwarding approved, letter of First Lieutenant W. C. Brown, 1st Cavalry, dated Fort Grant, Arizona, February 7th, 1893, in which he requests authority to test at that post the serviceability of saber belt plates made of aluminum by distributing about thirty plates among the various troops stationed there for trial and report, troop commanders having expressed their willingness for the trial to be made in their troops, and also asks, that, if possible, a practical test of the serviceabiliy of aluminum cartridge plates for infantry be made by sending a few for trial to some of the infantry regiments, as to the 2nd and 7th Infantry, and the Infantry and Cavalry School, and further states that he expects to have a number of cast aluminum horse shoes sent him for trial by officers stationed at the post and if the test is favorable he expects to submit a report on their merits particularly as to their use in the field. I have the honor to inform you that the Major General Commanding the Army authorizes Lieutenant Brown to test the saber belt plates and horse shoes in question at Fort Grant under the direction of the post commander, and also authorizes Lieutenant Brown to send at his own expense a few cartridge belt plates for the infantry at Forts Omaha, Logan, and Leavenworth for trial. Full reports of these tests to be forwarded to this office for the information of the Department.

Highly elated, the Lieutenant offered his wares for thorough testing. At the end of May, he sought and procured a two-months' leave in order to continue his studies. However, a pleasurable assignment altered well-laid plans. On June 9, the Secretary of War directed him to report to the then Major General Miles, commander of the Department of the Missouri, for duty at the World's Columbian Exposition.

A week later, the bronzed officer from the desert took command of a group of companies detailed as guards at Jackson Park, Chicago. The roster of the Columbian Guard, headed by Colonel Edmund Rice, carried the names of well-known officers representative of regular regiments of the army.

The Lieutenant seized opportunities to investigate, directly or indirectly, the progress of aluminum manufacture. On a holiday at Denver, he informed the Brown family that he hoped soon to begin a tour of Europe for further research.

Before the end of the month, the traveler was back at Fort Grant. Weeks of routine passed slowly. On November 20, he and his Troop C changed station to San Carlos, in the Department of the Colorado. Tasks were placid enough.

Yuletide came to Arizona's hills and valleys. And to Brown, the Commissioner of Patents in Washington granted letters of patent on the asbestos stovepipe shield for tents, the device which had received its stimulus on the banks of the ice-locked Yellowstone.

On the brink of 1894, the troop leader opened a letter from I. H. MacDonald, friend and patent authority of New York. One sentence called for rereading: "I suppose you will soon be deluged by circulars from claim agents & so called Patent Attys of every degree & kind."

The winter, with time for acquiring a sharpshooter's

certificate, and a lengthy study of the uses of aluminum, slipped by. The Lieutenant kept hoping for a move that would place him in closer contact with Washington.

Hope flared into reality on April 28. Orders directed that he report May 10 for special service under Adjutant General George D. Ruggles.

CHAPTER XIV

To Europe—Investigation of Aluminum

THE summer of 1894 in Washington was not one of quiescence. President Grover Cleveland had his economic problems to fathom. The Secretary of War, Daniel Scott Lamont, provided Federal troops to prevent recurring violence or keep it under control. Hordes of skilled and unskilled men, thrown out of regular employment, knew not where to seek a livelihood.

Thousands of disappointed jobseekers endeavored to find refuge in the armed forces. The army took its pick, gained full strength with unprecedented quality that would prove needful in a war that drew ever closer. Organization and equipment demanded intensive study and all-round improvement. Each branch of the service made its surveys, confined not alone to the Western Hemisphere.

Under Adjutant General Ruggles and Assistant Adjutant General John B. Babcock, Lieutenant Brown breathed the invigorating air of painstaking research, wide observation, and careful direction. His aptitude met its reward. At the end of September, he was granted leave for four months to investigate the use of aluminum in the manufacture of military equipment in England, France, Germany, Austria, Belgium, and Italy. Aluminum—"aluminium" to researchers—had recruited few converts in the United States compared with those in Europe. Gainful observation also was to be made of habiliments, housing, arms, or any essential development.

Brown set foot in Southampton October 10. Proper credentials paved the way to military and naval establishments.

He was elected an honorary visitor of the Army & Navy Club at Pall Mall for the period of his official stay in England.

The visitor first went through the troopship *Britannia*, emerging as spotless as the vessel itself. Then he made his debut at humming Aldershot. Men in troops and batteries lived over the stables, and mess was in their sleeping rooms. Officers fared better in one room and kitchen, possessing two horses which cost $400 each. Most of the garrison, including the Highland Light Infantry, Hussars, Scots, Greys, and three batteries, bespoke cleanliness. The washroom of the Hussars, however, was "filthy & wet" and had "but one dirty bath tub for the troop."

The canteen of the English cavalryman, like that of the American, was of tin and small in circumference. All leather work on battery harness and cavalry equipment gleamed in natural yellow. Traces were of rope covered with leather. Unlike the Americans, the English and Belgians did not discard half-worn horseshoes, for when made over they were supposed to be more durable. Some of the shoeing was done "without heating the shoes—this to accustom farriers to properly prepare the horse's feet to receive shoes previously fitted to the horse, as would be required in the field." The pistol was little used, it being regarded as dangerous to friend as to foe.

Upon inspecting informally the First Life Guards, Brown saw horses which had been shipped from America. Troop designation had been dropped for squadron. Remount horses went through six months of preliminary drills before being put into the squadron. The noncoms' mess stood forth "very handsome with table linen &c." Uncomfortable, however, were the heavy iron beds which supported mattresses, stuffed with straw. The riding hall was somewhat smaller than that of which West Point boasted. At the riding school, the men, wearing white buff-leather breeches, boots, and short red jackets, cut and thrust poorly. Brown wondered why they did not lean over in taking rings and bends. The fleshy and well-trained horses, nevertheless, jumped in fine manner.

There were two riding halls for six companies of cadets at Sandhurst. Riding, grooming, and athletics created keen rivalry between companies. Yet, Brown lamented, "Sandhurst cadets only clean their own guns & equipment once or twice a year, so as to learn how to do it."

In the Royal Military Academy at Woolwich, as at Sandhurst, Swedish exercises were given in the gymnasium. Mechanical maneuvers in inclement weather could be carried on in a large drill shed. The cadets wore white clothing, similar to stable apparel, at standing gun drill. They lived one in a room, a servant on call for every three or four boys. A cadet unlucky enough to be expelled could never hold any position whatever under Queen Victoria.

On November 10, the observer left for Brussels. Through the land of huge windmills and thick chimney pots he rode into the Belgian city, curious about a river under one of the principal business streets. He enjoyed the courtesies extended by the Second Belgian Guides and their fellow infantrymen. Large barracks with high ceilings contained numerous improvements, for there officers had their mess and offices. Noncoms, required to take fencing lessons, kept their tables covered with clean linen. The men's mattresses bulged with hay. Coarse blankets, neatly marked and piled, contrasted sharply with scaly iron bedsteads. In the absence of tubs, douche baths sufficed. Boxes and hooks back of bunks held clothing and sundry articles. Cooking, done by steam, was on the consolidated plan. Metal plates lined with white porcelain lay evenly spaced on long tables.

The cavalry horses, of average Irish stock, were well bedded in paved stables. Manure was carried out in hand barrows; to the American officer, "a very poor way." Each *escadron* afield bore a couple of spades, picks, hatchets, and a pouch of explosive for blowing up bridges or barricades. Brown liked the Belgian method of carrying the saber by strap and frog on the rear side of the saddle near the cantle.

In place of picket pin or rope, each platoon possessed a large ring. When the troop dismounted, twelve to sixteen horses were secured to the ring. Canvas bags hung at the rear of saddles which had open stirrups of metal. Only noncoms carried revolvers.

The Belgian Military Academy, where youths between seventeen and twenty-four years of age were admitted, carried on in old convent buildings of twelfth century design. The privilege of being a cadet cost two francs a day. For cavalry and infantry, the course ran two years; for artillery and engineers, twice that time. The buildings also contained the War College and Post Graduate School for officers of all arms. A chemical laboratory held equipment that denoted wide knowledge of powders and explosives. The visitor was shown the "light prison" in which prisoners obtained light, heat, and air but could not see out.

Anxious to see one Herr Doew's bulletproof cuirass, Brown attended an exhibition at the Cirque Royale. Description went into his diary: "Present cuirass covers front of body & is about $3\frac{1}{2}$ inches thick due to being covered entirely with leather cloth &c to prevent an examination of material of which it is composed. The shield itself is a little less than 1 inch thick & weighs 8 8/10 lbs. The one now used is quite heavy due to being filled with bullets."

An expert marksman fired shots into the shield as it was placed against a horse and then against Doew. Brown saw no splash or ricochet of bullets. Foreign officers told him infantry could use it best, during rushes in attack, giving them something to lie down behind. Further inquiry revealed that the owner of the shield wanted 50,000 marks for his invention. But the American was not in a bartering mood.

He decided to spend a day on the battlefield of Waterloo.

The wind of mid-November blew much colder than that which bore the fragrant odor of bending flowers on the fateful June 18, 1815. Strides over the frosted terrain brought vividly to mind the carnage which engraved the last battle Napoleon had fought. Strategy, studied over and over, could be visualized without the printed page.

Here had come Napoleon with 200,000 men, from Paris, across the Belgian frontier. This far had he come after crunching tarrying outposts. Then the wall. To stop again the man who had conquered and reconquered, Wellington's 100,000 British, German, and Dutch soldiers marched towards Brussels to move with Blücher's 120,000 Prussians. To the Rhine swept Schwarzenberg with his force of Austrians.

Wellington, arriving first, had made an impenetrable curtain of fire. Even the Old Guard of the Corsican-Frenchman could not pierce it. The cutting, the slashing, the shredding brought a mighty armed host to its knees. Then, as nightfall and respite drew near, came the storm that was Blücher and his Prussians. Consternation, flight, despair ensued. Exhausted soldiers and a humbled and beaten Napoleon were back in Paris three days after—a Napoleon overthrown forever, with the Bourbons again ready to take over for a decade and a half.

Waterloo! If Wellington had not defeated Bonaparte at exalted Waterloo, another gory battle would have been decisive. To have plunged against Blücher, then against Schwarzenberg, would only have postponed the hour of Napoleon's crumpling before a foe given time to grow in sinew. Waterloo had spared the lives of many brave men.

Waterloo was an oft-recalled lesson, soldier Brown knew. He went on to Paris, to see its many sides, to watch it from a boat on the Seine. Familiar with the military establishments, he gave them scant attention while taking notes on the latest equipment. Thousands of pieces of aluminum were being ordered by the French Government, and the guest procured samples of aluminum horseshoes.

The French service, unlike others, had a two-neck canteen for double compartments, holding wine and water. Each fourth soldier carried a large pan to serve as a cooking utensil. The cavalry saddle was similar to that of the English and the Belgians, having metal stirrups without hood. Instead of a heavy and sometimes stiff nosebag as used by the Americans, the French, English, and Belgians fared as well, if not better, with a lighter one made of durable linen. Its cost was small.

In the first week of December, the Lieutenant entrained for Berlin. A stop at Cologne permitted an initial inquiry concerning the German army. Every fourth man was chosen to serve in the military for two years. Privates drew eight cents a day, and second lieutenants were paid twenty-five dollars a month.

Several days spent in Berlin disclosed how intensively the Germans labored for scientific efficiency. Brown, seeing the Geneva cross used as a sign for drug stores, opined: "Good thing to adopt." The Second Uhlan Garde regiment (cavalry) was well armed, with saber, lance, carbine, and revolver. Recruits drilled five hours daily with horses that were "excellent & well gaited." They groomed three times a day. Saddles had a padded guard in front of the knee. Screws held spurs to the boot of the rider.

Of the Germans, who carried the saber on a single strap and band hung from the saddle, back of the left thigh, Brown noted: "Several squadrons of the regiment of hussars of the guard in Germany have received wooden saber scabbards covered with black rubber to replace the steel scabbard. These experimental scabbards are said to have the advantage of being noiseless and less conspicuous at a distance."

The diary had something to say about the squad rooms,

each of which was occupied by a noncom and eleven privates.

.... Room visited was very dirty & with no ventilation & odor from dirty bed clothing was simply disgusting. Bunks are with two stories. No springs whatever. Thick straw mattress (straw rarely changed). Covering consists in a coarse horse blanket sewed or buttoned up in a calico cover or sack.

Rooms inspected by an officer once per week only.

Soldier has one pair of leather reinforced trousers issued each year & a coat for each two years.

Pay for private 27 pfennigs a day in clear money.

Ration. Bread & coffee for breakfast. Meat & peas for dinner.

Bread & coffee (with the addition of meat on Tuesdays & Thursdays) for supper.

Dining room in basement, gloomy, unattractive & not clean. Rough tables & benches. Canteen rather better than dining room but not clean. Kitchen large, good tiled floor, cooking done by steam.

It was in field equipment that the German Army excelled. Adopted or under trial by the Germans were many pieces in which aluminum was employed: cooking vessels, canteens, tent parts, ration boxes, haversack rings, drinking cups, carbine hooks, buttons, horseshoes, stirrups, curb bits and chains, snaffle bits, spoons, and forks.

For individual water carriers the Austrians used flasks, and Italians small wooden kegs. The Germans, Brown emphasized, "are ahead of all of us" with a light aluminum canteen. "Its shape—like a flask—recommends itself quite as much as the material from which it is made. The concave side being next to the body, the canteen oscillates less from side to side than does our own." In due course, the American officer would see aluminum canteens with concave sides suspended from the belts of his country's soldiers.

Two days in Dresden permitted visits to the Royal and Porcelain Galleries, the Historical Museum, and the Thiergarten. Next stop was Vienna. After quaffing the beauty of Austria's arts, Brown turned to the Emperor's stables which sheltered more than a thousand horses. An eye-opener was the fact that the Emperor retained "1100 servants &c and has an annual income of $7,000,000."

The Lieutenant also found blooded and well-kept horses at the remount school where officers pursued a two-year course in horsemanship. They rode five or six hours daily. Noticeable features were that riders used both hands, always keeping them low, and toes were turned outward. But spurs did not touch hide except where intention compelled. The men lived in barracks over the stable. Their riding hall outspanned the one on the Hudson, and they provided a place for horses to stand in water eighteen inches deep.

A more thorough study of Austrian field equipment was gained at the barracks of the Thirteenth Dragoon regiment. Brown, shown infantrymen equipped for summer and winter field service and a trooper fully armed and equipped with saddle packed, observed:

The cowhide knapsack, with hair on the outside, seems to be used universally in Europe. To accustom men to its weight, they drill constantly with the full pack, which in some services is carried even on guard.

A roll of cloth on the right shoulder of the coat kept the gun sling from sliding off. Shoes had hobnails and the usual U-shaped protection for the heel. This was something with which the American doughboy of 1917-18 would become painfully familiar.

In all countries visited, Brown saw the cartridges carried in boxes, commonly two in front of the body and one or two in the rear. The American soldier did better with the Mills belt, easily accessible and unobstructive. His meat can was not as large as the cooking utensils carried by the Europeans on the outside of their packs. All had handles on the cover to be used as a frying pan.

Tents, of course, were used less in Europe. Closely spaced

settlements permitted billeting in houses. The Austrians used waterproof linen pieces for a tent, which could also be converted into a light storm coat. In Russian Poland had been developed a "Kamtschatka tent," to offer secure shelter in angry weather of many degrees below zero. Made of various sizes, for groups of from eight to forty men, they retained the heat of a sizable fire.

Brown pronounced the Austrians the best mounted troops in Europe. They, with other foreign cavalry, used both the curb bit and bridoon. Because of this, and six more months of training for remount horses, the animals gave better performance and appeared to better advantage than those in the United States. Although the McClellan saddle had many champions, it did not always fit well. The Lieutenant praised the Austrian practice of having saddles made in four or five sizes so that a fitting of the horse as well as the rider would become possible. The Austrian, however, carried too many things on his horse, things he could easily discard. In winter, stirrups were wrapped with straw to protect cold feet.

As with the Belgians, the carbine was slung over the back of Austrian troopers, it being drawn tight to prevent slapping the body when fast riding was required. The English and French carried the carbine in a boot on the off side, near the cantle, but for the former, a sling had been devised for attaching the gun to the trooper.

Stables in Austria, as in England and Germany, generally were paved and tidy. Horses received more bedding than that provided in America. Plaited straw braid on heelposts and poles dividing stalls kept horses protected from injury. A woven border of straw along all heelposts was used at inspection. "Certainly," the visitor declared, "in the matter of neat, attractive-looking stables, the English, Germans, and Austrians can teach our stable sergeants valuable lessons."

Before quitting Vienna, he made inquiry concerning the

invention of one Captain Klima of the military swimming school—inflated swimming sacks or balloons. Experiments with them had been made in Hungary. A pair of the balloons, attached to a breast belt, floated men and horses across deep streams. Here was "hydro-balloon" transportation!

In the last week of the year, Brown journeyed through Italy. Christmas Day in Venice denied him a roaring fire, a tree in the corner, unwrapping of gifts, and heaped-up servings by two sisters in the home of far-away Denver. The Lieutenant walked out of the Grand Hotel, took a gondola and rode the length of the Grand Canal. He sharpened his pencil afresh for his diary:

Robt Browning died in a house on Gd Canal. Byron wrote Childe Harold in one of these houses. Lucretia Borgia also lived in a handsome house on the canal.

Next day, he went to Florence, then to Rome. From all angles he viewed the city that men had made and unmade, rode out on the Appian Way, got marble from Seneca's tomb. Military establishments virtually were forgotten. On the first day of 1895, he went to Genoa and on the third sailed for the United States.

Three weeks later, he reported to Colonel Babcock in Washington. Subsequently he prepared a paper for inclusion in *Notes on Organization, Armament, and Military Progress in American and European Armies,* published in 1896 by the Military Information Division, Office of the Adjutant General. His article, "Notes on Equipment and the Use of Aluminum," proved to be of especial interest to those watching the progress of aluminum in its application to military purposes.

In the German and French armies its value in the manufacture of certain articles of military equipment seems to be thoroughly appreciated. It is reported that in the German army two corps are provided to a greater or less extent with aluminium equipments, and there are no less than 125,000 aluminium canteens or water bottles, 50,000 cooking utensils for the individual soldier, and 90,000 sets of mountings for shelter-tent poles in use.

In France it is stated that about 40,000 gamelles, or cooking utensils for the individual soldier, and 20,000 each of canteens and cups are either ordered or in use.

These numbers are approximate only, but indicate that in these countries the use of aluminium and its alloys has passed the experimental stage in several important articles of equipment.

In Belgium, aluminium canteens and cooking utensils for the individual soldier are being experimented with, but the results have not yet been made public.

In England, 1,000 aluminium cooking utensils for the individual soldier have been ordered for trial.

Alloys of aluminium, from their hardness and rigidity, are better adapted for most articles of equipment than the pure metal; it seems also to have been pretty thoroughly demonstrated that an alloy which is well adapted for one article of equipment may be entirely unsuitable for another, and the particular alloy adapted in each instance can only be determined by careful experiment. Fortunately the alloys are but little more expensive than the pure metal, and but little heavier.

An important feature of such articles as canteens, cups, cooking utensils, etc., made of aluminium alloys, is that they can, by means of stamping and spinning, be made entirely without soldered joints, and however badly crushed and dented in service, can readily be hammered back into shape—an important consideration in the field.

The production of metal has increased so enormously in the past decade that the development in working it has also been great, and we find results to-day which three years ago were hardly believed to be possible.

A recent invention in aluminum alloy is Wolframinium, discovered by William Berg, a German contractor of aluminium military equipments, who also invented the victoria alloy.

The composition of Wolframinium is a trade secret, and it is said to be stronger than the victoria alloy, and double the strength of pure aluminium.

In this country the most promising alloy is nickel aluminium which, like the victoria alloy, seems to be remarkably well adapted for castings. .... In the 7th Infantry it has been used, quite satisfactorily, for over a year in shelter-tent pins.

A few meat cans have been made at Rock Island Arsenal of stiffened aluminium sheets. These weigh but 6 ounces while the regulation meat can of tinned iron weighs 16 ounces. The only fault found with the aluminium meat can is that if placed in a fire without food, or some such material in it to conduct off the heat, it will melt. . . . . The suggestion that the outside of aluminium meat cans be artificially blackened as is done with the cooking utensils carried in Germany by the individual soldier is deserving of experiment.

. . . . The German canteen of aluminium alloy is spun without joint or seam. It should therefore last indefinitely, as it can not rust as is the case with the regulation canteen, which is heavier by several ounces than the aluminium article. . . . .

Of the three articles—meat can, canteen, and cup—it is believed that a pound in the weight carried by the soldier can be saved by making them of aluminium.

The reports on the durability of steel-faced aluminium horseshoes are sufficiently favorable to justify more extended trials with a view to their adoption for field use, especially to take the place of shoes (one fore and one hind) carried in the saddlebags of each trooper. An advantage possessed by these shoes is that they can be fitted cold. Aluminum gun-sling hooks have been reported upon favorably, and aluminium belt plates having been given thorough tests in a number of companies are regarded as entirely satisfactory. . . . .

Other articles which seemed to be viewed with favor in foreign services are aluminium hobnails and heel plates for shoes, aluminium drum shells, castings for range finders, spurs, stirrups, and parts of limbers.

Among the novelties are camp cooking outfits suitable for small detachments or for officers' messes, each piece being spun from a single piece of metal without seams.

So wrote the cavalryman as the nineteenth century drew its last breath.

Shortly, the United States, with other nations, would be seeking feverishly deposits of bauxite, the only practical source from which to extract aluminum.

Airplanes, warplanes, darkening the skies—aluminum is essential for one and all.

In less than half a century, the war of the world would begin. And by his conquests Adolf Hitler was to hold in his reeky hands most of the coveted practical aluminum reserves of the earth.

CHAPTER XV

An Earned Captaincy

RELIEVED by the Adjutant General's Office at the end of January, 1895, Brown was to rejoin his troop at Fort Grant by February 18. Interested in Jerome's patent-seeking on steel and aluminum articles, he stopped in Pittsburgh to inspect manufacturing before proceeding to Denver for a brief greeting.

Horseshoes of aluminum from Jerome were given a stout test on the trails of Arizona. Brown, shoeing anew his horse, Dick, recorded the experiment:

```
Al. shoes from Jerome
Feb. 1st, 95                            lb   oz
    Hind shoes weigh                    1  -  6
    Fore    ”      ”                    1  -  6
                                       ──────────
                                   4)2    12       11 oz each
Put on Dick Mch 26)
Taken off ” May 10) 45 days
Weight of worn shoes when taken off:
                                        lb   oz
    Hind shoes weigh                    1  -  0
    Front    ”      ”                   1  -  2oz   (sent in
                                       ──────────   (official report
                         Total     2    2oz        (on same May 20
```

Results provoked dissatisfaction. The army animals continued hoofing it on heavier, more durable shoes.

While Dick was trying out his new footwear at Fort Grant, Brown spent happy hours entertaining his old classmate, Lieutenant Gatewood. The officer so well respected by the Apache "from the Mescaleros of New Mexico to the Yumas of the Colorado River" was no longer a robust man. He had been in poor health when participating in the Sioux War of 1890-91. The next year he had seen duty at Fort McKinney, Wyoming, and field service in the Cattle War of the Big Horn and Jackson's Hole country. Then, injured grievously in fighting a fire which left half the post in charred ruins, he had received orders to return home.

Arizona's desert lay hushed under starlit skies as the pallid Gatewood related hesitantly to Brown his most dangerous and historical mission. General Miles, failing to round up the band of twenty-two warriors under Geronimo and Natchez, had sent him with two Chiricahua scouts to Geronimo's camp to ask for surrender. He left Fort Stanton, New Mexico, and with his scouts went deep into Mexico. They entered the Indians' camp, received promises of surrender from Geronimo and Natchez. The Apache chiefs, demanding protection, were guarded by the command of Captain H. W. Lawton, who also was scouting in the vicinity, when they rode back to a meeting with Miles.

Brown urged Gatewood to write his account for publication, and corresponded with the owner of *The Cosmopolitan*, John Brisben Walker. Walker expressed a desire to print the article, in restricted length. But Geronimo's interviewer was to go to his grave in Arlington Cemetery in the spring of 1896.

The story would not appear in print until 1929, a compilation by Major Charles B. Gatewood, U. S. A., Retired, son of the ingenious Lieutenant. Of the pamphlet, which finally appeared under the editorship of General Edward S. Godfrey, Brown was to assert:

Gatewood wrote it in pencil, essentially as it appears here. This was found by his son 10 years after his father's death, when the matter of publication was taken up with the Order of Indian Wars of the United States resulting in this publication.

It is important historically as it gives at first hand the account by the officer who was most instrumental in the surrender of this hostile band which I came to know later when at Ft. Sill, Okla., under charge of Capt. (later Maj. Gen.) H. L. Scott.

On April 2, 1895, while the former classmates chatted together for the last time, Brown received letters patent for his improvement in cartridge belts. The belt, with loops and body woven in one piece, was intended particularly for cavalrymen. It carried cartridges for both carbine and pistol.

The G. I. (Government Issue) belt had loops only for carbine cartridges. Revolver cartridges reposed in a bag or pouch usually fastened on the right side near the buckle. Brown listed objections to the prevailing method:

First, the pouch if placed at the right side, is in the way when handling the carbine. If on the left side it interferes with the saber, and in either case is likely to interfere with the trooper when mounting and dismounting. At the trot or gallop the pouch is apt to and often does become opened and the cartridges thrown out. Again, it is inconvenient to open the pouch to obtain the cartridges, more especially if at a trot or gallop, as the trooper must use the bridle hand to hold back the cover of the pouch. Finally the weight of the ammunition is not properly placed either for the trooper or the horse.

The objector devised intermediate shell loops between the main loops in order to place pistol cartridges close to the belt proper while not interfering with carbine cartridges. Too, the pistol cartridge loops, aligned in a plane below the plane of the carbine shells, lessened the chance of error in handling. The pistol ammunition being secondary, usually twenty cartridges, he placed it at the middle of the belt, where weight was better supported and freedom of contact from the carbine or saber obtained. The trooper, even when his horse was galloping, could easily reach the pistol cartridges with one hand.

The troop leader's invention had distinct advantages. Yet its adoption was shied at, doubtless because of the danger of confusion in handling two kinds of ammunition in the same belt.

Brown changed station to San Carlos, Arizona Territory, on April 3. En route, he mapped the country. At the month's end, orders were out for the transfer of Troops C, F, G, and K, First Cavalry, to Fort Riley. But he was to report to Adjutant General Ruggles in Washington for special service.

The Lieutenant halted for a few precious hours in Denver. Ominous signs of the mother's failing health were distressing. With heavy heart, he arrived in the capital city in mid-May.

In the summer months, there was much of travel, visiting eastern military establishments and manufacturers of ordnance. Tedious hours were devoted to map work.

Schofield, General in Chief of the Army, left office October 5. Miles, whose term was not to expire until August 8, 1903, became the last General in Chief, his successors being designated Chiefs of Staff. Miles, hardly less hesitant than Schofield in recognizing the ability and initiative of younger officers, encouraged the alert. Brown's accomplishments led to his being placed in charge of the Militia Section, A. G. O., on November 2.

For the greater part of the next year, the hard-toiling, unruffled cavalryman served as chief. Glowing energy went into his compilation of *The Organized Militia in the United States in 1896*. Published as a document of the Military Information Division, it showed the ever increasing interest of the War Department in the potential usefulness of organized militia. Publication of such reports by the "M. I. D." dated back to about 1893, to carry on until formation of the Militia Bureau.

Inspection of State summer encampments by officers of the Regular Army and issuance of their reports had commenced in 1880. Drill competitions, as well as the encampments, aroused no little public interest in the National

Guard, but inspectors had all too rigidly adhered to Sherman's advice to avoid things political. Yet the violent labor strifes between 1886 and 1895, when Federal troops were compelled to restore order, revealed weaknesses in the militia.

How to share a closer unity of purpose by state and federal soldiers became a problem not to be forever postponed. Shadowy definitions partly were to blame. Brown would not have disagreed with Frederick P. Todd's explanations in *Military Affairs* in 1941.

The National Guard, popular belief and legislation to the contrary, is not descended from the common militia. In fact, its development has been in opposition to, and frequently in spite of, this body. It is a lineal descendant of the Volunteer corps, for the Guardsman is essentially an amateur soldier; the militiaman was ever a civilian.

Put briefly, the common militia was an impractical political concept, the Volunteer an inescapable military reality. Failure to understand this has meant failure to harness fully this great amateur force .... that nation which has directed its volunteer soldiery along useful channels has gone a long way in solving its problems of national defense.....

The basic militia law of the United States until 1903 was the Act of 1792 which, despite certain faults, did aid in bringing standardization of discipline and training to, and annual reports from, the States. Brown happily was to see Secretary of War Elihu Root and President Theodore Roosevelt, in 1903, win approval of the Dick Bill, placing a firm foundation under the National Guard. Although the bill would later need reinforcing, the National Guard could advance, divorced from the militia concepts, finding close kinship with the Regular Army in its several requisites of training, organization, discipline, equipment, and arms. The Guard, in due course, would become an integral, workable national defense body.

Brown, in 1896, realized there was much spade work to be done. And he kept on spading.

On March 28, the A .G. O. issued an extract of Special

Orders No. 74. It named a board of officers to meet in Washington three days hence, "or as soon thereafter as practicable, to examine the reports of the boards which were convened in the several military departments, 'to consider and recommend a proper ration for troops operating in emergencies,' and such views and suggestions as the Major General Commanding the Army and the Commissary General of Subsistence may lay before it. . . . . "

Lieutenant Brown received appointment to the board, along with Major Charles Smart, surgeon; Major Charles A. Woodruff, commissary of subsistence; Major Ernest A. Garlington, inspector general, and Captain Louis A. Craig, Sixth Cavalry. Their recommendations, when acted upon, provided the first emergency ration adopted by the United States Army. It was not tinned.

While following routine, Brown, at the direction of Secretary of War Lamont, participated in the unveiling of a statue to the late Major General Winfield S. Hancock. Ceremonial honors to the veteran of the Civil War, who, in the troublous times of 1867, had lent ear to the memorable defense of the Kiowas by Chief Satanta at Fort Larned, Kansas, were staged May 12.

Shortly after, the Lieutenant again saw the folks in Denver. Returning to Washington as June hastily fled, he attended Pennsylvania and Maryland Militia camps. From July 31, when an order transferred him from Troop F to Troop C, First Cavalry, until mid-August, he found himself heading the Military Information Division. For another two weeks he served as chief of the division's Map Section. At the close of August, he began reading proofs of the *Cavalry Drill Regulations*. The War Department had in 1891, for the first time, issued three sets of drill regulations for cavalry, infantry, and artillery. Brown finished his task October 24, and he relinquished headship of the Militia Section.

His desire for celebration increased. November 7 there

came, signed by the Secretary of War, his long-awaited promotion to captain in the First Cavalry, effective the previous day. The Senate, as a matter of form, had first to give its consent. The commission did not catch up with him until January 2. But folks in Denver were more readily informed. They lost no time in saluting the absent soldier as "Captain Will."

Meanwhile, high-ranking officers were commending him to the head of the War Department for promotion to the rank of major and assistant adjutant general of the Army. Of more immediate necessity, however, was further work in the field. On December 2, he reported to Lieutenant Colonel Kellogg at Fort Sill, Oklahoma Territory. Soon he joined Troop E, First Cavalry, at Anadarko. Sharing the post's command with the cavalrymen were units of the Tenth Infantry.

At his new station, Brown found reason to admire the unexcelled tact of Captain Hugh L. Scott in his treatment of the former war party of Apaches. Geronimo and those who had followed him into captivity in 1886 to Florida, to Alabama, and at last to Fort Sill, were far from contented, in spite of good treatment. The aged chief insisted, against argument to the contrary, that Miles had promised permission for his people's eventual return to the land of their fathers in New Mexico. He would keep on insisting until his death in 1909, four years ahead of the release of his band by the Government.

Violent dust storms frequently swept the Oklahoma post, resting on the short-grass prairie near growing Lawton and the Texas line. The onslaughts of wind-blown sand, sagittal and stinging, were all too lengthy in dry seasons. In the winter months a blizzard sometimes would unwind itself from out the Panhandle to swirl against near-by ridges of the Wichita Mountains, flecked with stunted and gnarled timber.

The newly made captain welcomed fervently the appearance of spring in 1897. He was aware that friends had not ceased to urge his further advancement. In his mail came a copy of a letter written at Milwaukee on May 11 by Author-Captain Charles King, still prolific in tales of days gone by, and addressed to Major W. W. Armstrong:

I learn that you are moving in behalf of the appointment of Capt. W. C. Brown, 1st Cavalry as Major in the Adj't Gen'l Dept., and if I may speak from the point of view of an older soldier who has had much occasion to study his work and character I beg leave to say that I know no man in the Army more deserving such appointment.

If high character, absolute fidelity, and most conscientious discharge of every duty are recommendations, Capt., Brown has no superior. He has had long and large experience in staff duty, notably as the Adjutant of the Military Academy under such admirable soldiers as Generals Merritt and Parke. He has served all over the wide West with his troop, the sternest work that falls to the lot of our officers nowadays. He is a model of discretion in the office and of diligence and efficiency in any capacity. I hope you may be successful.

A request that Brown had previously made of the War Department, to make a field test of the emergency rations, now was approved. The Captain led out his own troop onto the Kiowa and Comanche Reservation for the rigid trials. Reporting to him also were Privates Gustavus Johnson and Fred Wolf of the Hospital Corps, and Sergeant William M. Summers, Company E, Tenth Infantry. Major Charles Smart of the Medical Department, under orders of the Secretary of War, was on hand to make careful observations.

Between May 17 and 19, without other transportation than the saddle, the troopers marched an average of more than twenty-one miles a day. They subsisted on one-half the emergency ration, or a pound of food each day. The horses ate grass. In a controlled experiment, Lieutenant W. H. Osborne, First Cavalry, and ten men left the troop for ten days to take marches of the same mileage while subsisting on full field ration carried on two packs as well as on their horses. In Brown's command, the loss of weight for each man averaged three pounds, but physical strength showed improvement.

Cooking utensils and shelter tents of alien manufacture also got tryouts. Material similar to that used in the Austrian coat shelter tents proved unsatisfactory. It was not waterproof. Rain-repelling tents could be made of heavier cotton duck, but this, said the Quartermaster General's Office, was "very objectionable as the tendency of the time is to lighten, not to increase the soldier's impedimenta."

So the soldier, for many, many years, never quite kept dry in his pup tent when it rained.

Betwixt experimentation and adoption, as was too often the case, lay years of trial and error. Brown, temporarily, had to be content with mere commendation, and that somewhat belated. On November 2, 1897, Michael R. Morgan, Commissary General of Subsistence, was to write Secretary of War Russell Alexander Alger:

> I have the honor to recommend Captain W. C. Brown, 1st Cavalry, as a careful and industrious officer who would fill acceptably such position as he may seek. Captain Brown has been of service to the Subsistence Department as Recorder of the Supervisory Board upon the emergency ration, and in conducting a practice march where it was used. He was also of assistance in preparing the latest edition of "The Manual for Army Cooks."

Unforeseen were still later events. The emergency ration was not to "take" with the army command in the Spanish-American War, though there would be a distressing need for it.

CHAPTER XVI

A Bereaved Soldier Carries On

WEST POINTERS and Regular Army men, upon hearing of the Cuban Revolution in 1895, had sensed a call to action again. The democratic Western Hemisphere looked askance upon policies of monarchical Spain in the Caribbean. Economic and political interests conflicted. American national security faced danger if Spain should lose strategic islands to a stronger power in Europe. The Cuban Junta, with headquarters in New York City, and its American counterpart, the Cuban League, steadily gained sympathy for the insurrectionists through extensive operations and the helpful voice of the American Press.

Between 1895 and the early months of 1898, the army remained on the alert, although an apathetic Congress made no effort to add to its land forces. The country had expanded and the population had grown to about 73,000,000 persons, but the 25,000 regulars were, in proportion, the smallest effective force since the Revolution.

Perilously pruned, provincial, consequently defective, was the War Department's office group in Washington. Yet, as Colonel W. A. Ganoe, army historian, was to assert, in spite of its "newsstand size . . . . it was not inert."*

The West, finally won and beribboned with steel rails, permitted regimental units to assemble cohesively for war training. Still scattered to a great extent, the regulars achieved a degree of efficiency not hitherto possible. Those

---

* W. A. Ganoe, *The History of the United States Army*, D. Appleton & Co., New York, 1924 (revised 1942), pp. 371-72.

in Alaska patrolled and explored. Graduates of the various army schools energized troops on practice fields with tests ranging from strategy to new types of equipment. Notwithstanding, there remained a few tasks which engendered a bit of old-time excitement.

At intervals in 1897, Brown escorted funds for the Indian agent on the Kiowa-Comanche Reserve. He took the duty in stride as did others under Major General J. R. Brooke, Department of the Missouri. Protection of the Department of the Interior's money, however, was an assignment which, with some red and white bushrangers infesting Indian Territory, demanded a measure of vigilance.

The bags and packages of gold, silver, and currency were usually delivered intact by the men in blue. Their uniform had been altered but slightly after the Civil War. The crown of the fatigue cap was not as high, and the collar of the fatigue coat fell lower. Above the elbow of the noncom's fatigue blouse blazed large cloth chevrons. He wore them below the elbow on overcoats. His dress coat boasted gold chevrons. The cavalrymen, in dress uniforms adorned with shiny brass buttons, wide yellow stripes running up the sides of the trousers' legs, or yellow pompons dangling at the front of the flexible campaign hat, had a way of obtaining deep respect as well as lasting admiration.

Yet facing year-end weather on the open, crisp prairie offered little pleasure. In a mid-December "norther," Brown led his Troop E out of Fort Sill to proceed to the railroad at Rush Springs, twenty-eight miles away. Armed with carbine and revolver, each man carried forty rounds of ammunition for the carbine and twenty for the revolver. Responsible for the $40,000 "grass money" and annuity goods for the Indians was Captain Baldwin, acting Indian agent, and friend in whom Brown found rare qualities.

Baldwin, who as a lieutenant colonel had been mustered

out of the Union Army in 1865 at the age of twenty-two, had attained his captaincy in the Fifth Infantry in 1879. Twice he had won the Congressional Medal of Honor, at the Battle of Peachtree Creek near Atlanta, Georgia, and against Grey Beard's Indians of the Washita River in Texas. Victory at Byian, Mindanao, and the crushing of the Moros was to bring the veteran fighter the star of a brigadier, June 9, 1902.

From Rush Springs, Brown and his troops guarded the funds to such points as Baldwin selected. Sleet and rain, forming an icy crust, made the going slippery before the cavalrymen reached the issue station on Little Washita. There, as payment commenced in hurriedly sought shelter, Brown lost his "A" tent by fire. In a few days, a southerly wind melted ice and snow, and he detailed Lieutenant Osborne to witness issue of beef to the red men. The troop leader, marching on to camps in the Rainy and Wichita Mountains, did not return to Fort Sill until January 4, 1898.

Wintry February came and with it disconsolate news. The health of Captain Will's mother showed alarming decline. On the fourteenth, sister Helen sent a telegram: "Better come home." Colonel Kellogg granted, at once, a seven-days' leave and permission to apply for an extension of twenty-three days.

Next day, homeward-bound, the officer, more quickly than his fellow passengers, read a startling dispatch. It aroused the nation as had no other news since that of the last stand of Custer carried from the Little Big Horn. The U. S. S. *Maine* had blown up in Havana harbor!

At every station, bellowing newsboys sold out their papers. Editors of the Middle West, who had pleaded repeatedly for steps to guarantee the fulfillment of America's "manifest destiny" in the Caribbean, now urged vehemently the inevitable—aggressive action. This, Brown knew all too well, spelled hasty preparation by the undersized army to which he owed full allegiance.

The wistful son walked into the family home in the early hours of the sixteenth. In spite of death's lurking in the familiar rooms, he became the essence of encouragement. His very presence buoyed up the one woman whom, in her sixty-sixth year, he loved above all others. Her manner brightened and her willingness to talk exceeded the strength of her shaken body. Fondly, with misty eyes, she admired the military carriage of her "boy."

Feebly, she held between the thin fingers, which had performed so many parental tasks, a document she had longed to see. It was the District of Columbia Society's recent approval of Captain William Carey Brown's application for membership in the National Society of the Sons of the American Revolution.

Up to the noon hour, the cheered woman talked with Will, and listened to his reading of letters from close friends, some from the Minnesota neighbors of years gone by. How far and yet how close the rumble of wagon wheels at Traverse des Sioux!

The woman who had once been a plucky bride on the frontier slept soundly through the later hours of the day. She had had her last chat. And she had overtaxed her waning reservoir of fortitude.

A few hours before sunlight erased shadows from Denver's snow-swathed streets, she was seized by severe pains. Will sent for the family physician, Dr. Stedman. The doctor, on another urgent duty, sent up morphine for hypodermic injection. After its effect wore off, the son was compelled at daylight to go for the doctor. He gladly came. He bowed his head resignedly when he left. Yet, like all wise physicians, seeking assistance, he returned later with Dr. O'Connor. The two of them advised the sleepless family to prepare for the inevitable.

There was little left to do, except to make as comfortable

as possible the last hours of a patient fighting valiantly
against stabbing pain. Moments of consciousness and recognition of loved ones became fewer and briefer. The taking of teaspoonfuls of nourishment lessened. The kindly
doctor called more often, but his task was done. Sisters
Helen and Grace, ministering tirelessly, answered softly
as inquiring neighbors came and went.

Will, on each hour and its fractions, kept accurate
memoranda of pulse, respiration, temperature, the partak-
ing of medicine and nourishment, and reactions. In the
afternoon of February 20, he noted: "Commencement of
last sinking spell."

At 11:30 o'clock that night, his poignant grief expressed
itself in two words: "The End."

But vigilance had not ended. Hours later, the weary
soldier wrote: "Sat up till 7 A. M. Monday."

In the soft light of the next day, all that was mortal of
Sue Carey Brown was laid to rest in the family plot of
Riverside Cemetery. And in the evening of March 1, after
the will was probated, Captain Will kissed Helen and Grace
good-by. They thought of battle beyond his country's
shores.

When the cavalry officer stepped off the stage at Fort
Sill, he became, hastily, the full-fledged soldier again, for
the public and the press painted war clouds aplenty. The
taut Regular Army sniffed smoke. It prepared itself intensively to fight the blaze. Still Congress saw no immediate need for providing more firemen.

Earlier, men like Frederick Funston had listened to elo-
quent pleas for support of the cause of Cuban independence
made by men like General Daniel E. Sickles, and had forsaken their civilian ways. As a filibuster, and with the help
of the New York Junta, Funston had made a secret landing
in Cuba. With companions, he had joined the bush forces
under Chieftain Maximo Gomez, to taste failure in the
siege of Cascorra.

Then, marching eastward, the Americans had been received by the tall, white-haired and battle-scarred veteran of the war of the seventies, General Calixto Garcia. The awesome, deeply considerate leader had a staff of a dozen men from Cuba's best families, and an insurrectionist force sprinkled liberally with Cuban Negroes. Short, stocky Funston, one-time botanist, fought in guerrilla warfare against the Spaniards. He attained the rank of lieutenant colonel but, his health broken for a time, had returned to the United States early in 1898. At that time Brown could not envision the day when Funston's experiences in the hinterland of Cuba would be repeated with him in the Philippines.

In the second week of April, declaration of war ever coming closer, another of Brown's friends, Lieutenant Andrew Summers Rowan, Nineteenth Infantry, was embarking for Jamaica on a secret, but "regular," mission. President McKinley had inquired of Colonel Arthur Wagner, head of the Bureau of Military Intelligence, where he could find a man to carry a message to General Garcia, in command of Cuban troops "somewhere in the eastern part of Cuba." Colonel Wagner suggested the youthful Rowan for the onerous task of getting through hostile Spanish lines. McKinley gave the order to send him, promptly.

The President wanted vital information on both Spanish and insurgent forces, including numbers, condition, equipment, morale, efficiency of commands; transportation and sanitary aspects; what the insurgents might need until mobilization of American troops.

At noon of April 8, Wagner and Rowan lunched together at the Army and Navy Club. There they decided immediately on plans for the lieutenant's journey. There was to be no repetition of a Nathan Hale being caught with a dispatch. Wagner spoke coolly.

"Your problem will be to secure from Garcia information of a military character, bring it down to date and arrange it on a working basis. Your message to him will be in the nature of a series of inquiries from the President. Written communication, further than is necessary to identify you, will be avoided. . . . . "

No wonder that, later, Rowan would be quite surprised in reading Elbert Hubbard's *A Message to Garcia*, written in an hour after supper on the evening of February 22, 1899, many millions of copies of which came off the press. More than slightly askew was Hubbard's statement that Rowan "was sent for and given a letter to be delivered to Garcia." Doubtless, the supper induced further admixture of fact and fiction.

Interesting was this from the inspired writer: How Rowan "took the letter, sealed it up in an oilskin pouch, strapped it over his heart, in four days landed by night off the coast of Cuba from an open boat, disappeared into the the jungle, and in three weeks came out on the other side of the Island, having traversed a hostile country on foot, and delivered his letter to Garcia—are things I have no special desire now to tell in detail. The point that I wish to make is this: McKinley gave Rowan a letter to be delivered to Garcia; Rowan took the letter and did not ask, 'Where is he at?' "

The preachment was to keep rolling off the press in spite of Rowan's account in *McClure's Magazine* for August, 1898. Finally, after attaining the rank of Colonel, Rowan was to publish, with indifferent results, his paper-bound booklet, *How I Carried the Message to Garcia*. Too few have read Rowan's explanation of his going without a letter:

In instances of this kind, where one's reputation, as well as his life, is at stake, it is usual to ask for written instructions. In military service the life of the man is at the disposal of his country, but his reputation is his own and it ought not be placed in the hands of anyone with power to destroy it, either by neglect or otherwise. But in this case it never occurred to me to ask for written instructions; my sole thought was that

I was charged with a message to Garcia and to get from him certain information and that I was going to get it.

After leaving New York on the British boat, *Adirondack,* Rowan had only a fair start on his memorable errand when, on April 16, Fort Sill became electrified. At 2:30 in the morning, company commanders jumped from their beds to assemble in the adjutant's office. The War Department had ordered the cavalry to Chickamauga Park, Georgia, and the infantry to Mobile (although the latter place later was found unsuitable for the concentration of troops). They would leave as soon as transportation became available at Rush Springs. The men buzzed like busy bees in their packing.

Early in the afternoon of the eighteenth, the command left the post. The next day, alarming rumors of a threatened outbreak by Chief Geronimo's band dampened their ardor. Brown, obliged to return with Troop E to assume command of the post, called in Geronimo and Natchez for questioning. They explained that the rumors came from loose-talking younger warriors. Geronimo reminded the Captain petulantly:

"I am a soldier of the United States and wear a blue uniform, and it makes my heart sore to be thus suspected."

Brown sent off his report of the situation to department headquarters at Denver. Promptly came the reply that "Tommy" Tompkins' Troop B, Seventh Cavalry, would come from Fort Grant, and Captain Joseph A. Gaston's troop of the Eighth Cavalry from Fort Meade. Brown, anxious to get away, protested one troop was sufficient. But both were sent.

Tompkins arrived first, on the twenty-fourth, and fifteen minutes later Captain Brown "left for the R. R., this time at the trot!" Unlike Moses, never could he be resigned to being left behind.

Next day, the United States declared war. Five days previously, in Jamaica, Rowan had received a message in code from his government:

"Join Garcia as soon as possible!"

He had begun his journey at once. Always the Junta was ready to whisk the American on his way—by cab through Kingston's streets, by carriages beyond, by sailboat to Cuban shores, by an escort of bearers through the density of undergrowth and over steep slopes of mountains and through tropical forest by trail, then by saddle horses across less troublesome terrain.

On the day before Brown trotted out of Fort Sill, President McKinley had called for 125,000 volunteers. The Regular Army, after having been strengthened on March 8 by only two regiments of artillery, on April 24 was doubled in size. West Point's Class of '98 graduated the next day. On a peace-time footing, the Spanish forces boasted 128,-183 men. The hurried completion of coastal defense projects, for which Michie had pleaded and the Engineer Corps planned, was ordered.

Chafing at delay, the regulars moved toward cancentration points. The special train which bore Brown away from Rush Springs was indeed "special." It had two flat cars for one army and six escort wagons, three "streets W. S." cars for horses and one for mules, and a box car bulging with 13,000 pounds of baggage. Fifty-four enlisted men and two civilian teamsters rode in a tourist car and an antiquated Pullman.

Enthusiasm bubbled over the length of the route. Notwithstanding, the train sped along and pulled into Kansas City early the next morning. Somehow the men procured liquor. A corporal and a teamster got drunk. After that, Brown permitted no one to leave the cars except when the stock were taken off for watering in St. Louis and in Nashville.

When the train steamed out of Nashville for the last lap on the twenty-seventh, Brown forsook the stuffy cars. He

rode on the engine, and jotted down memoranda orders
concerning clothing:

Each trooper will wear a strong serviceable suit consisting of campaign hat, blouse, trowsers, leggings, shoes, blue flannel shirt, underclothing & gauntlets. Saddles will be packed and the extra suit of
underclothing carried will be strong & serviceable.

With the troop baggage each man will carry his second blanket, an
extra pair of shoes, an extra pair of trowsers, an extra pair of gauntlets
(if the man has an extra pair) & 1 pr of white gloves.

. . .   .

To be packed at post for future shipment: 1 Forage cap, 1 blouse, 1
trowsers, 1 suit underclothing & 2 Prs white gloves.

The full dress uniform will be boxed at post separate from the other
articles & each article stamped with name.

So it was decreed. Extra underwear and flannel shirts for
Caribbean weather! In truth, the weather was already
quite warm when the cavalrymen entered huge, bustling
Camp Thomas on the soil where had been fought the most
sanguinary battle of the Civil War. Scores of citizen
hawkers substituted for a post exchange.

Two days later, cavalrymen and infantrymen watched,
enviously, all batteries leave for Tampa. Shortly, however,
orders were received to make requisition for ordnance and
equipage for troops of one hundred men.

Brown and his men participated spiritedly in squadron
drills commencing May 2. After the drill, the officers submitted a proposition for a post exchange. Then came news
that was news, of Dewey's victory at Manila Bay. But it
would be some time before Brown—and the world—would
learn that on the first day of May, also, Rowan had made
his entry into Bayamo in central Cuba. There, while
Dewey's fleet was smashing Spanish ships, McKinley's messenger stood before Garcia for the first time.

Next day, "the hottest yet," the First Cavalry went to
the neighboring city of Chattanooga, to march in the
Spring Flower Parade. Brown, with a cold and a high fever,

went on sick report and added to his diary: "News received of promotion of Colonels Arnold, Young, Chaffee and Sumner, Samuel S., to be Brigadier Generals of Volunteers, and all the regular Brigadier Generals, except Coppinger, to be made Major Generals."

Immediately preceding the war, besides Miles, commanding the army, major generals were Merritt and Brooke. Seven corps were to be organized during the war, each commanded by two-star men. John J. Coppinger did become a major general, heading the Fourth Corps. The other corps commanders included James F. Wade, William M. Graham, Shafter, Fitzhugh Lee, Merritt, and Brooke, the last named of the First, at Camp Thomas, and having Major General James H. Wilson as a divisional leader. More than three times this number however, would attain the high rank as the army expanded to 278,000 in two months.

Captain Brown, yearning more for action than for promotion, awaited moving orders. Yet time was not heavy. The First Cavalry passed in regimental review. And General Bernard, now Deputy Governor of the Soldiers' Home at Washington, saw it and recalled some of its history.

The Twenty-fifth Infantry started for Tampa. Troops left behind gave attention to travel rations. News came that the First Cavalry was to go to New Orleans. Brown called on General Brooke, submitted names of corporals for promotion to sergeants, and issued clothing for recruits.

The Second and Sixth Cavalry departed. Orders came for all to go to Tampa.

The papers stated that the navy could not convoy from too many Southern ports. The papers also published lists of staff appointments, promotions in volunteer forces, and predicted Merritt's going to the Philippines.

Inebriated regulars initiated the sober recruits.

Rains came upon the red clay of Georgia, upon the soldiers. There came, also, a Chattanoogan who sold slickers.

Fever raged. Ominously, surgeons scanned the growing lists of the sick.

Captain Will sat down and wrote Sister Helen a long letter. There were so many things on his mind now, but not so many as to erase the picture of a flower-banked mound in a cemetery in Colorado.

CHAPTER XVII

Off to War in Cuba

WHEN on May 14 Troop E struck out for Ringgold, Georgia, half of the men lacked horses. They arrived at the rail yard perched atop wagons drawn by two six-mule teams and one four-line team. The ignominy stung, it snapped tempers. In the hurried loading of cars, a tipsy veteran scarified the scalp of a sullen recruit with his revolver. In addition to other worries, Brown had a patient and a man to be held for trial.

An impatient troop ate its next breakfast in Macon and overtook all previous sections. The train moved slowly through warm, dusty pine barrens. Tampa, with its single-track railroad, already was congested, so the cavalrymen unloaded the cars at Lakeland in the afternoon and evening of the sixteenth. The Tenth Cavalry arrived late that night. In the confusion, a private shot a civilian. The victim died.

For the next three weeks Brown, like other officers, struggled for supplies and against delay. He moved his camp into the timber, instructed the men to scoop up pine needles for bedding, and he sent in ration returns for the remainder of the month. He called on Colonel F. V. Greene, newly arrived with his regiment, and, between drills and dress parades, chatted with officers of the Seventy-first New York and Second Massachusetts Regiments. Some of the New Yorkers, meanwhile, looted the fairground buildings.

Then the camp heard that the Spanish fleet was at Santiago de Cuba. The regulars seemed to be getting nowhere.

Captain Brown thought he might as well try to become Colonel Brown of the volunteers. He wrote to General Merritt, and wrote and wired to Major Armstrong. They gave help, but orders kept him with his troop.

Ready to hurl himself against a new enemy, General Joe Wheeler, energizing ex-Confederate cavalry leader, visited camp. Sons of Yanks and Rebs cheered lustily the white-bearded soldier, now past sixty. In the veteran of small stature, Brown saw an entertaining person of grave dignity and pomposity, the qualities of a soldier, businessman, law-yer-planter, all seeking identification.

Joe Wheeler, Jr., aide to his father and only three years out of West Point, cultivated friends in his quiet way. Brilliant, self-composed, "always a first section man in mathematics," he looked forward to an unobtrusive career as an artilleryman. And in years ahead, despite his frail body, his high courage would not permit him to falter.

Greene, promoted, left for the Philippines. Scores of recruits, but only a few horses, arrived. Hay allowance fell off by half, and squadrons went out grazing instead of to drill. After sweating to complete a target range, Brown saw to it that recruits practiced on it.

Excitement swept camp on June 1. The First Cavalry's First Squadron received word from Lieutenant Colonel C. D. Viele, regimental commander, to hold itself ready for dismounting. Reports disclosed the futility of planning for the employment of large numbers of mounted troops on the ruffled terrain around Santiago. Moreover, the Cuban Expedition's Cavalry Division of three thousand men, under Wheeler, could not find space for horses on the transports. Each regiment was to send only two squadrons, or about five hundred men, to fight with their carbines as infantrymen.

Brown kept on making notes, the notes which, because of their value in clearing up some disputed points, were to be printed as *The Diary of a Captain* by the army's Publication Committee. The committee was to print virtually the entire diary, started at Fort Sill and continued until postwar return:

.... on the theory that the land operations were largely what President Roosevelt subsequently characterized the Naval engagement off Santiago —a Captain's Fight—and the experiences of the various captains were quite similar. . . . .

Practically none of the subordinate officers had ever participated in a real battle. A very considerable number of us had, it is true, participated in arduous Indian campaigns and engagements, but Santiago presented quite a different problem.

Many of the general officers and colonels were veterans of the Civil War, though, with but few exceptions, they had participated there in a subordinate role, and after a lapse of thirty-three years, with the Art of War gradually developing in the meantime, the value of their former experience was of limited value.

Santiago therefore led to many surprises, not the least of which were the merits of a uniform of neutral color and the advantages of smokeless powder.

Volunteers still carried the Springfield rifle, made in the United States Armory at Springfield, Massachusetts. The adopted model in service from 1868 to 1893, it first was a single-loading breech type with a triangular bayonet. Regulars could rely on a weapon which had been standard since 1892, the Krag-Jorgensen rifle. As a breech-loader used by Denmark and Norway, it had been named for Norwegian inventors. In 1892 had come its magazine, holding five cartridges, followed by the reduction in caliber. Steel barrel and smokeless powder meant much. With a muzzle velocity of about two thousand feet per second, no other step in small arms since the introduction of the percussion cap had been so important. Yet it would soon, in 1903, bow to the improved Springfield rifle.

As to clothing, the men would sweat and itch throughout the Cuban campaign in traditional blue woolen shirts and trousers. Even few of those going to the Philippines would get khaki before embarking.

Illustrative of what he later termed the small Regular Army's "*habitual* lack of any reasonable military preparedness," Captain Brown wrote in his diary for June 1:

.... A lot of Ordnance came today and I got nine nosebags, six surcingles, six lariats, eleven halters, eight picket pins, six saddle bags, five saddles, twelve links, ten watering bridles, twelve lariat straps, twenty-eight saber straps, four horse brushes, six curry combs, eight curb bridles complete with Shoemaker bit, eight carbines, twelve revolvers, fifteen sabers, seven saddle blankets and twelve revolver screwdrivers. ....

The next day, he learned from Major Forse, his immediate superior and constant friend, that their Second Squadron also was to be dismounted. While they prepared to turn over saddles and other property to the ordnance officer, Troops L and M received 124 horses from Tampa. But cavalrymen with new mounts had little cause to gloat over cavalrymen who packed with glee and drew ponchos if they didn't have any.

On Sunday, June 5, the troopers drew a month's pay and sharpened their sabers. They finished packing by retreat the next evening and went into bivouac alongside the railroad.

The bugler sounded reveille at three o'clock the next morning, but the soldiers' train did not start for Port Tampa until noon. Brown counted sixty-one men in his troop, including one not quite sober. They marched aboard the transport *Leona* early in the evening, hungry, and with only a small portion of hard bread. Four hours later, their Captain bought coffee and meat to go with it.

Up for breakfast at daybreak, the troop hastened to unload the cars. Lieutenants W. C. Rivers and A. L. Mills insisted that the baggage be placed aboard the ship systematically. But this day General Miles, down from Washington, was ranting at the general mixup of regulars and volunteers. Scattered facilities made for scattered units and scattered property. No matter, Miles wanted the

Leona and other ships to pack up and be off. "Orders then given by General Young, our Brigade Commander, to rush things," Brown argued, were obeyed "without regard to order or system and much confusion resulted."

Pantingly, the First and Tenth Cavalry, except for two troops, watched the *Leona's* crew pull in the gangplank at 9:30 A. M., only to drop anchor in deeper water. On jammed decks of Shafter's Fifth Corps transports, men with overcoats and blankets jested with men wearing khaki or white trousers, sombrero or felt or straw hats. Sixteen thousand men wanted to shove off. Some of the ships were under way, the *Leona* in midafternoon prepared to follow. But the naval convoy, thinking it had spotted too many Spanish cruisers, turned back its charges.

Next day, the First Cavalry again greeted Colonel O. J. Brown of the Second Georgia Volunteers. To friends of his old command, the former lieutenant of Bannock War days confided facetiously: "My regiment is all ready for the war, except we have no uniforms or guns."

Other visitors dropped over: the fuming Wheeler and his imperturbable adjutant general, J. H. Dorst; and Colonels Garlington and Leonard Wood, the latter far removed from a young surgeon's adventures in Apache country and, with Lieutenant Colonel Theodore Roosevelt, ready to lead the Rough Riders into a rough-scrubbing fight. Dorst, asserting there were forty thousand of the enemy "at or near Santiago," promised "fighting enough to go around."

Four more days the ships either lay out a little way for fresh air or eased up to the dock to let the men exercise. Poor food, pine-board cots, small dips of water, and foul odors did not produce a happy situation. Faces lengthened when the brigade commander ordered officers and men to cease all gambling. But a bit of compensation came to the *Leona* when two troops of the Tenth Cavalry shifted to the *Alamo*.

With some horses and mules reloaded, the transports sailed to the lower bay on the thirteenth. Cervera's Spanish fleet, they had been assured, was nowhere else but in Santiago harbor. The Americans furrowed through to open sea the next day, the *Leona* at the rear of the column. Brown, as officer of the day, had little chance to comment on the exceedingly fine weather. He had his hands full apportioning water and placing guards over the precious barrels.

The ships moved slowly, four to seven miles an hour. Fifteen miles south of Key West's string of palms, the *Indiana* and kindred warships lunged out of night to join the convoy. Torpedo boats skimmed outward from the flanks. Men who wished to get their feet on land stirred excitedly on the sixteenth when the *Indiana* fired a signal and compelled a Norwegian vessel to heave to for questioning.

Brown found more to write about the next two days.

June 17. About midnight vessel stopped by signal from Naval vessel to "Hold up," and about thirty minutes afterwards we were examined by a searchlight. Our Captain stopped for an hour and then ran ahead slowly. In meantime, the other vessels all got ahead of us, disappearing to the southeast. Then we went ahead again at speed and then stopped. Our Captain, it seems, did not know just where we were, and it is dangerous navigating through the Bahama Channel. Four (4) troops turned out under arms at 4:00 A. M. and E Troop went on [guard] with three others from 7:00 to 8:00 A .M. Torpedo boat and gun boat sighted about fifteen miles to the south at 10:00 A. M. No officers now allowed on the bridge except Regimental and Squadron Commanders and their Staffs. At 3:00 P. M. we sighted the *"City of Washington"* and her tow off our starboard bow slowly overtaking her during the afternoon. Target practice today with Hotchkiss guns. The *"Bancroft"* came down at Retreat to see what had become of us and was greeted with enthusiastic cheering. . . . . Making good time today and hope to overtake the fleet tonight, which the *"Bancroft"* says is fifteen miles ahead. Saw many flying fish this morning.

June 18. At 7:00 A. M., the fleet was finally visible about five miles ahead. An hour or two later a halt was called to let everyone catch up, to transfer the sick to the hospital ship, and allow proper formation to be again taken. This consumed about three hours and fleet started again at 11:00 A. M. . . . . Men are getting tired of the travel ration. Beans used up today, but the men don't like the meat, and permission was secured to cook bacon on the galley. North coast of Cuba visible at 2:00 P. M. Southern Cross visible tonight for the first time.

The next day, a Sunday, an east wind tossed the ships about in the Windward Passage. Seasickness swept soldiers off their food and feet. The *City of Washington* lagged provokingly, and the column had to halt and untangle itself. At night came orders that troops, upon disembarking, should have a day's rations in their haversacks.

An hour before noon on the twentieth, the Americans hovered off Santiago, then drifted to within six miles of grim-visaged Morro Castle at the harbor's entrance. Brown counted thirteen vessels with the blockading squadron. At suppertime a naval tug sped out. From it a man shouted through a megaphone:

"Take order of cruising—Course Southwest."

The fleet obeyed the instruction, but not for long. Civilian captains, neither then nor later, cared to expose their ships to any danger. Brown was noting by eight o'clock that "we were going due south or a little east of south. General impression now is that we are to describe a big circle to the left during the night so as to keep out of the range of Spanish torpedo boats, and that we will be before Santiago again in the morning."

They did set out in a beeline for Santiago before noon, but soon altered the course. The *Leona,* whipping toward Wheeler's boat, met it abreast a minute after the General had departed for Shafter's craft. While the First Cavalrymen turned over a scow to the *Alamo,* Brown hailed Tenth Infantrymen from Fort Sill.

As the setting sun attempted to paint the sea in scarlet, and soldiers wondered what the night might bring, a message-bearing craft glided in and out. It gave orders to land on Cuba's sands at the next break of day and to carry two days' rations. Immediate objectives were Daiquiri and Siboney. Thanks to Miles, there was to be no headlong attack upon Havana with the threat of excessive slaughter.

Naval guns began to clear the coast. They belched and roared in wreaths of smoke, driving the Spaniards inland. Still the uneasy captains preferred to keep their vessels far offshore.

Transfer of men in choppy waters had to be accomplished by the few boats and launches the navy had available. Animals, lowered into the water, had to swim. Two weeks would pass before the depositing of food supplies.

Of his landing at Daiquiri, eight miles below Siboney, Brown was not merely laconic:

June 22. Expected to disembark at daylight today as per orders, but waited till about 4:00 P. M., when General Young got permission to debark if he could do so with his own boats. Orders received from Corps Headquarters to take three days' rations in haversacks; also a blanket roll consisting of shelter half, change of underclothing, blanket, slicker or poncho. Each troop to carry three axes, three spades and three picks. Several boat loads of 10th Cavalry debarked in small boats and two of their men were drowned. We also heard that two men of the 17th Infantry were drowned in debarking. Finally, Major Webb C. Hayes went ashore and got the lighter "*Laura*," which took the remainder of the 10th Cavalry ashore. At about 10:00 to 11:00 A. M. the heights above Daiquiri were bombarded by the Navy and vessels up at Siboney were firing on Spaniards supposed to be collected there. It subsequently turned out that the Spaniards had burned as many as they could of the buildings of Iron Works, at Daiquiri, and that when the place was bombarded only insurgents were present, one of whom had his arm broken by a shell. The "*Laura*" returned and was on hand early next morning, leaving three men to each troop on board in charge of property.

June 23. Debarked about 5:00 A. M. from "*Leona*" to "*Laura*" and then went to the "*Alamo*" and took on Jones' and Grierson's troops and finally landed at wharf where men were obliged to jump from a moving boat to a wharf at considerable risk. Things in much confusion. Went into camp 400 yards from wharf. Went over and saw Captain Allyn K. Capron, Second Lieutenant, 7th U. S. Cavalry, in the Rough Riders' Camp and while there they got orders to move. About 4:00 P. M. a column moved out consisting of the Rough Riders and 1st Squadron

of the 1st [Cavalry] and 1st Squadron, 10th Cavalry. Went out in the
little town and found three carts with which to carry troop rations and
tools. One day's extra ration issued. Late tonight it rained and everyone
got a wetting. False alarm at night due to sentinel firing on some one
who failed to answer challenge.

Lawton and 6,000 men had landed at Daiquiri. Wheeler
had the remainder at Siboney. Shafter, tied to his ship with
gout, had planned that Lawton should stand in stout defense between Santiago and Siboney, with Bates holding
forth between Siboney and Daiquiri. Wheeler, however,
as senior officer ashore, just didn't like immobility.

He fretted at delay.

Shafter fretted at Wheeler and the gout.

Fighting Around Santiago

WHEELER learned that the enemy was lurking around Las Guasimas, in the direction of San Juan. He ordered Young to attack on the twenty-fourth. In his two advancing columns, the brigade commander placed First and Tenth Cavalrymen on the left, and the Rough Riders, now directly under Roosevelt, on the right.

All went afoot, and the Rough Riders gripped the Krags issued to them only the day before. They deployed at the embroidered edge of the enmeshing jungle. Roosevelt's column, tardy in scattering, suffered quickly from spitting Mauser rifles aimed by unseen Spaniards.

Camp at Daiquiri broke up early that morning. Preceded by numbers of the Tenth Infantry and Tenth Cavalry, Brown and his fellow optimists started for Siboney. They marched two abreast, sometimes in single file, on the narrow trail. Sultriness and stickiness added to the discomfiture of being overburdened with equipment. Overcoats, blankets, blouses, and other apparel were flung aside. A cart broke down. Others lagged far behind.

An hour before noon, the plodders reached Siboney. There, while resting for two hours, news of the fight ahead rekindled their belligerent zeal. After four more miles of trailing, they camped on the scene of the baleful engagement which had lasted an hour and a half.

Brown noted cryptically: "that Spaniards had shown themselves plainly on fortifications on a high ridge, but had concealed troops in the undergrowth close to the trail. The only advance guard was Lieutenant Charles M. Saltz-

man with ten men a short distance ahead of the column.
Spanish opened with volleys well fired but too high. . . . .
G Troop, 1st Cavalry, charged the fortifications on ridge
under heavy fire, which position was also exposed to a
raking fire from Rough Riders. Spanish retreated when
our troops were within 200 yards. Hotchkiss gun did good
work here. . . . . "

He listed nineteen Americans killed, among them Captain Capron, so recently conversant and fervent. Forty-five
wounded, including Lieutenant Colonel George Bell, Jr.,
needed urgent attention. That evening, on ground dedi-
cated with blood, and across which a tropical forest cast
softening shadows, Brown, tight-lipped, helped to bury
the dead.

When sunlight again flooded the resting camp, he explored the abandoned fortifications. All day troops
streamed forward. All day men toiled with picks, spades,
and axes to open the way for rations and the Rough Riders'
sorely needed dynamite gun, as Wheeler reshuffled his line.

Before moving on four miles the morning of the twenty-
sixth, the cavalrymen received ninety pounds of bacon,
twenty-five pounds of hard bread, three cans of tomatoes,
eight pounds of coffee, and twelve pounds of sugar. They
pitched their second camp on the banks of a large creek,
and there Colonel A. L. Wagner questioned a new prisoner.
A brigade swung past. Later in the day, four thousand
Cubans, threshing closer to Santiago, smiled upon the
Americanos. Captain John H. Parker's Gatling Battery
rattled along. Around two or three blockhouses on a high
hill to the North, Brown saw men looking down upon his
own position.

Early next morning, he saluted Colonel Evan Miles as
he passed with his brigade. Miles, the unrestrained captain
who had thrown back Paiutes and Bannocks in the Blue
Mountains of Oregon, no longer displayed the dashing carriage of his youth. But he possessed the same determina-

tion. Before the close of day, additional rations came, also three batteries. And the Spaniards forsook El Pozo Hill, near the trail.

On the twenty-eighth, Brown and Lieutenant E. Anderson, Seventh Cavalry, cut through the ragged tangle to the foot of the hill. They detected little but sour-mash smell in and around a gaping sugar mill. They climbed to the matted summit and observed, two miles distant, barracks and trenches teeming with the enemy. A Cuban officer joined the two Americans, directing their eyes to El Caney, Ducoureau House, San Juan Hill, and Kettle Hill. Brown got out pencil and notebook. When he returned to camp in the evening, drenched by a slanting rain, he handed a clearly defined sketch to General Young.

Another day brought another battery, and news sifted in that six hundred Spaniards clung to El Caney though none remained in Ducoureau House. Swarms of the Americans kept slashing at and ironing out the roads. In the twilight, they sloshed about a camp hit unmercifully by a blinding downpour.

Shafter, now ashore, made the best of a precarious situation. The big guns had not been landed. A storm might swing stores-carrying craft beyond reach. General Pando, with eight thousand men from Manzanillo, could be expected to increase armed opposition. But more implacable foes—diseases of the wet season—could not be driven back by bullets. So came action.

Brown welcomed wholeheartedly a move on the last day of the month. Alert to the need for wire nippers as well as other articles, he sent Lieutenant Osborne back to the *Leona* for them. Lieutenant Rivers and Corporal Lindley left with other sick men for Siboney. General Young, too, was ill, but the "General" sounded in mid-afternoon. Soon Brown gazed upward in envy—at a balloon, high and dry. The men, feet soaked from wading small streams, camped in position of support to the batteries at El Pozo six hours later. Lawton stood before El Caney. Brigadier General Henry M. Duffield's newly landed Michigan Volunteers, in reserve at Siboney, comprised a threat to Spanish forces on the left.

More pride would have come to these liberators of Cuba had they known that, on that day, Dewey, after biding his time at Cavite, was welcoming General Anderson's 2,491 men of the First California, Second Oregon, and Fourteenth Infantry. This spearhead of land troops, before reaching Manila Bay, had without opposition captured Guam. Now they made ready Camp Dewey while awaiting the arrival of Greene's brigade.

The firing upon El Caney from Lawton's batteries and infantry started at five-thirty in the morning of July 1. The engagement of San Juan, Captain Brown called his first "real battle." But his fighting against Indians stood him in good stead in the bushwacking assault against stoutly opposing Spaniards in scattered blockhouses and behind natural and invented obstacles. The First Cavalrymen hunched closely in a "line of masses" behind Grimes' battery, almost atop El Pozo. The field lay before them "like a map." Parenthetically, Brown would later describe the impetuosity of uninitiated soldiers:

Many officers and men whose curiosity was now aroused to the highest pitch were unable to resist their intense desire to "see the show" and deliberately left ranks for the El Pozo view-point. Soon afterwards Grimes' battery opened up and the enemy replied at once, getting the range quite accurately and killing and wounding several men. It was amusing to note how soon these "rubber necks" lost their curiosity, and how quickly they seemed to remember that their proper places were with their troops which they rejoined with commendable alacrity.

Shortly, Lieutenant Colonel Edward J. McClernand dashed up, asking immediate help for Lawton's left flank. A stream had to be crossed. Before reaching it, the cavalrymen engaged the enemy—pecking away at the balloon—for the first time. Now led by Colonel Wood, the brigade, of which Brown's Troop E was a panting unit, rushed northward. They discarded packs, waded the stream and, in compliance with orders, sprawled in the high grass.

An hour later, they filled their canteens with creek water and advanced against the "iron pots" on Kettle Hill. Sprayed by a withering fire, they charged upward. Colonel Henry Carroll spoke crisply to the leader of Troop E: "Take as many men as possible and hold the hill."

Then the Colonel fell, shot by an enemy to whom he had exposed himself.

It had taken Lawton until midafternoon to form his firing line within a thousand yards of the enemy at El Caney. And though Sumner and Kent pushed their regular infantry divisions to San Juan, they did so in spite of the dilatory tactics of the well-meaning but amateurish Seventy-first New York, who had not been sufficiently trained for the puzzling operations. Too, five thousand more Spanish troops had outsmarted the Cubans, to gain entrance to Santiago.

As the day waned, Brown reported to Viele on the ridge beyond Kettle Hill, and learned that Sumner had directed the cavalrymen to establish support for any recoil of advanced lines. Darkness silenced the shooting. Wearily, Brown and his comrades returned to pick up blanket rolls and haversacks. And before he entrenched his troop on San Juan's slopes, the Captain walked slowly, sadly to a fresh mound on a scarred hill. In the stillness, he bowed his head. Memories of Major Forse, forever at rest, thrust aside all other thoughts. Those days in Idaho and Oregon were so near—yet, too, so far away.

Intense firing began at dawn for the men holding the steep ridge below Forse's grave. It did not diminish during the entire day. Small groups of regulars, including those of the colored regiment, and Rough Riders seasoned by rich experience akin to the task at hand, struggled upward. They stood in tall grass and fired volleys at the sheltered enemy. Occasionally, in the rear, an alert supporter also took aim. Then a Spanish sniper tumbled from a tree.

At the first opportunity, members of Troop E helped themselves to a bit of food and gulped coffee. When evening brought heavy rain, they gave up ponchos and shelter halves for a dozen wounded men. Others dug graves for those who would not answer the morrow's roll call.

This done, Brown counted out twenty rounds of extra ammunition for each of his men. With others likewise provided for, they advanced to the aid of Galbraith, holding tenaciously to a fretful position. Lashed by the rain, they labored with pick and shovel. Firing had fallen off, but it blazed forth again near the midnight hour. Up and down the line the Americans answered, adding to the shocking toll they had already exacted. General Chaffee, inspecting the lines, reminded Viele that his trenches fell short of the crest.

Trench-building went on the third day, as did the fighting. In the boilery of the attack, Brown waved his hand to Captain W. O. Clark. The meeting of former classmates was marked by the vomiting of the artillery and the tempest of rifle fire as the Americans neared the summit. At last the enemy fled from the main blockhouse, dodging deadly fire from the Tenth Cavalry and those under Wood. At midday, Dorst carried a flag of truce to the Spaniards, demanding their surrender. Firing ceased.

The attackers, also possessing El Caney, now faced delay as well as repetitive swamping rains. They lent ear to conflicting rumors of full victory on land and on sea. True, Sampson had smashed the Spanish fleet in its effort to flee, and Hobson had become a national hero and a captive in the bottling attempt. But Toral, the Spanish commander, though willing to let Shafter march into Santiago, wanted to go with his men, unarmed, to Holguin. Such terms could meet only cool reception in Washington. Encircling trenches were lengthened and manned while the truce dragged out.

With nothing but the wet ground to sleep upon, and muddy trenches to guard, the victors at San Juan lacked the spirit to celebrate the Fourth of July. Yet deep satisfaction ran through the Second Squadron when it was given a new commander—Captain Wainwright, a man whose service denoted a thoroughgoing cavalryman of proved competency.

Brown scribbled sparingly: "Too busy and tired to write up journal." Next morning, he moved his men to a new camp immediately north of the pit for the dynamite gun.

The Spaniards' exchange of Hobson on the afternoon of the sixth provided something to shout about, and the band-playing lifted frayed spirits. Brown celebrated by taking a bath. For the first time in a week, he pulled his shoes off his swollen feet. Then orders came that the truce was to end at 5:00 P. M. A heavy battery with Coehorn mortars wheeled into position near by at suppertime.

With misgivings, Brown, brigade officer of the day on the seventh, watched the grumbling men eat a short-rationed breakfast without coffee to wash it down. He dispatched a written complaint that the troopers "were being charged for tobacco, and that they should have twelve pounds coffee to 100 rations." In the emergency, each ration also required a half ounce of tobacco and two ounces of coffee. Instead, mail came that night, the first the cavalrymen received in Cuba.

The complaint, however, harvested results the next day, for the ration issue "consisted of hard bread, full ration; meat, full ration; coffee, two-third ration; sugar, about one-half ration; tomatoes, about one-half; beans, a hatful for the troop."

And it did not rain! Brown got permission to tear down the house on Kettle Hill and he used the material

for a splinter-proof shelter. Troop E also worked day and
night on the trenches and completed loopholes atop the
parapet. In a hot sun that scorched their backs, they heard
cheering in the camp of the Rough Riders. Wood had been
made a brigadier general! And Brown wrote: "Proposition
on the part of Spaniards to evacuate this province and
march out with the honors of war submitted to Washington." Meanwhile, Brigadier General Wallace Randolph
was landing with troops from Ohio, Illinois, and the District of Columbia.

The Captain, on the tenth, watched vigilantly in the
trenches from midnight until 8:00 A. M. A reply came
from Washington in the afternoon. If the city did not
surrender unconditionally by 3:00 P. M., a bombardment
would commence an hour later. Toral remained obdurate.
Between four-thirty and seven that evening, the Spaniards
dodged fire from land and sea. Troop E sent over its quota
in platoon volleys, and the dynamite gun once more barked
angrily. But the enemy answered. Captain Charles W.
Rowell, Second Infantry, hit by a Spanish shell, fell dead.

Bombardment commenced again at daylight, continued
until an hour after noon. Then followed another truce
while the Spaniards buried their dead and negotiated for
terms of surrender. General Miles had come from Washington, accompanied by Massachusetts troops and units
from Illinois under Brigadier General G. V. Henry. In the
trenches, Brown, though shaken by an attack of malaria,
kept his troop on guard.

All-day and all-night rains cheated the troopers of
sleep, spoiled their food, and imperiled the sick. On the
thirteenth, their leader found time to write:

Troop in trenches from 10:00 A. M. to 2:00 P. M. Lieutenant Edw.
Anderson, 7th Cavalry, came around about noon and we made some
estimates of distances to Spanish trenches. Generals Miles and Shafter
are said to have gone to the lines this A. M. to see General Linares. Later
Miles and Shafter went to right of line, which Anderson says now

touches the bay, completing the investment. River last night deep enough to swim a horse. Heavy rain at noon today and everything got wet again. The issue of rice to the regiment was three cups. *Chicago Record* of the 30th ultimo received. Rough Riders have now taken post on our right. General Randolph has landed with forty guns and is supposed to be getting into position. Twenty-six cases yellow fever reported at Siboney and the houses there were burned last night. Large flocks of buzzards hovering over Spanish entrenchments. Private Zipfel became suddenly delirious, hysterical and violent at 8:40 P. M.

In unrelenting rain, Zipfel went to the hospital the next morning. Troop E now had only forty men out of sixty-six fit for duty. From their trenches they heard vociferous yelling among cavalrymen to the south. A passer-by bore the news that Santiago had surrendered.

Early in the afternoon, Brown jotted, "McKitrick, General Shafter's son-in-law, came around and announced at each camp that the Spanish General surrendered 12,000 men in the city and 8,000 to the east of here, all of which are to be sent back to Spain as soon as possible. Refugees from Santiago to be allowed to return. No officer or enlisted men allowed in front of our lines. No cheering allowed. Rain P. M."

On the fifteenth, the capitulation became a reality. American soldiers on Cuban soil had good reason to cheer, even if it were prohibited. They stood ready to slash their way through barbed wire and over barricades, but the surrender had saved thousands of lives. Added to hundreds of casualties already incurred in battle was the mounting list of yellow fever victims. Dirty and hungry, yet with happy bantering, members of Troop E welcomed a weighty mail of papers. Brown put aside his *Army and Navy Journal,* dated two weeks back, to note the delivery of half a sack of potatoes and a handful of onions.

Next day, one without rain, the Captain watched the refugees straggling toward Santiago. They were going home. Where, he mused, was he to go? General Miles was making ready to depart for Puerto Rico, and rumor had it

that he wanted the cavalrymen to go with him. Would
they go? They would not, for the expedition that was to
accompany Miles could not be drawn from units invaded
by disease.

So the men who had come to fight, and had fought, congratulated one another in silent complacency when time
came to show courtesy to the defeated. But strains of
"The Star-Spangled Banner" stirred pent-up emotions
which no longer could be suppressed. Of the formal surrender, no picture would prove of more permanent worth
than that which Captain Brown inserted in his penciled
diary:

July 17. Went over on the Rough Rider road this A. M. to see
refugees come in. Command formed at 9:45 A. M. on the trenches to
see the surrender, or rather to be under arms at that time. Spanish
troops could be seen passing out of city and trenches. At noon all troops
formed on line of trenches and twenty-one guns fired by Capron's
battery, when Stars and Stripes were run up on Governor's Palace.
The Star Spangled Banner was played and all troops cheered. (This was
one of the most thrilling scenes which I ever witnessed.

Due to lack of proper food, with no shelter except "dog tents,"
exposed by turns to the debilitating effects of torrential rains and a
tropical sun, and from sleeping in the mud, about thirty per cent of our
men were ill, but on this occasion every man who could possibly
stagger to his feet hobbled to the line of trenches which for miles
encompassed the city of Santiago.

As they stood there in their tattered and mud begrimed blue uniforms
with wan, sallow and drawn faces, covered with a straggling three
weeks' growth of beard, they little looked like the splendid corps which
had sailed from Tampa a short month previously.

At exactly noon the signal was given, and as cheer after cheer went
up from thousands of lusty throats along mile after mile of trenches,
there was left no doubt in the minds of those present that the partici-
pants fully realized that they were taking part in an important event
in the history of the Western Hemisphere.

Spain's power and intolerable, tyrannical rule in islands just south of
us had been broken, and that, too, by Shafter's little corps of 800
officers and 16,000 men; while with the raising of the Stars and Stripes
over the Governor's Palace at Santiago, a new epoch in Cuba had begun.)

It was a fighting soldier's picture. It was the picture of a soldier serving as he was expected to serve, not asking why, when, where, or how, before winning through in the struggle.

With victory achieved, however, he could, with the impartial historian, ponder over many things. He might, in due course, arrive at the conclusion that there had not been sufficient cause for the war.

Of one thing he was immediately and positively certain: the army had to find its own way out of a perilous predicament into which it had been thrown with so little foresight.

CHAPTER XIX

Escape from Pestilence

ON THE second day of renascence, Brown hurriedly shifted his men to castrametation a mile and a half west of El Caney. But tormenting rains, wretched shelter and food, and the spread of the odious yellow fever exacted a heavy toll among soldiers who had fought their battles. They now wished to return home. Even the higher ground in the hills afforded few choice camp sites. The doctors, believing cleanliness would eradicate the cause of the fever, labored heroically.

Officers grabbled when chance came to buy a dozen small cans of salmon. The *Leona* had been unloaded and, on the twenty-first, Osborne procured five wagons to haul sorely needed equipment for the regiment. The Captain, slapped down by malaria, sought refuge from the rain in a comrade's shelter tent, the first overhead protection he had had since his landing in Cuba. Shafter still was trying to unravel transportation about the city and camps. In the evening, Major Allen Smith brought word that Manila had fallen. Greene was settling down at Camp Dewey, ready to welcome Generals Merritt and Arthur MacArthur to the Philippines.

No letters had come to the men in Cuba for six weeks, but on the twenty-second came a bit of chin-lifting. Brown wrote shakily:

Two wagons arrived & in "E" troop we got our camp kettles, a new paulin & my bedding roll which gives me a shelter tent, cot & change of underclothing. Had fever all last night. Galbraith started for camp with a lot of fresh beef & took the wrong road & got stuck with his load but beef arrived so we had some for supper & will have two meals tomorrow. This is the first fresh meat which the men have had since June 6th. Got my mattress & a conical wall tent for the men. Maj. Smith brought in word of a 10 days armistice & that Gen. Miles had before the official word could reach him taken 2000 men & a war ship & sailed for Porto Rico. Sleep under a tent tonight for the first time since we landed as my bedding roll is wrapped in shelter tent.

Slowly, painfully, supply conditions improved. Three days later, Troop E laid hands on full rations of potatoes and onions, along with a chunk of tainted beef. Nine men fell ill. From fifteen wagonloads of mail, troopers seized eagerly anything addressed to them. In a Chicago paper, Brown read news of the annexation of Hawaii by the United States. To come later would be word of Miles's gaining a foothold on the south coast of Puerto Rico. It was a move that would permit him to send four columns fingering across the island to greet the fleet at San Juan and announce conquest by mid-August.

On July 29, a ray of hope shone through cloudy Cuban skies. An order, to be published to the men, had it that they would sail for Long Island whenever the fever diminished enough to permit the journey.

In an all-morning rain the next day, mail was distributed around the camp. Captain Will read leisurely two-weeks-old letters from Helen. But his mind turned quickly to the ugly sights on all sides. "Dorst," he jotted, "agrees with me that conditions here are going to get worse." The ground beneath the tents oozed and slickened. The general court-martial, to which he was detailed for a few days, was one of gloom.

Colonel Roosevelt took command of the Second Cavalry Brigade the first day of August. To Wood fell the task of purging Santiago of its filth and rehabilitating natives who lacked proper food, clothing, shelter, and civic responsibility. As soldier sick rolls lengthened, men prayed for the hasty arrival of transports. Brown bought and gave to his troop two dozen cans each of apricots and peaches, a can of pears, and a can of soup. The fever, he heard with burning ears, had claimed the lives of two men in Sumner's Brigade the day before. Yet with undisguised pride he pointed to *Harper's Weekly* of July 16, carrying "a very complimentary reference to 'that splendid trio, the 1st & 10th Regulars & the Rough Riders.'"

The Captain, on the third, penciled a lengthier entry than usual:

The last of the men's bedding distributed this A. M. Got the troop filter in working order. Heavy rain this P. M. Meeting of Division and Brigade Commanders in town to discuss the condition of affairs. Two propositions had been sent from Washington on recommendation of the Surgeon General: first, to change our camp every two days and keep us here; second, to send us to San Luis about forty miles north of here on the railroad. The Generals at first prepared a "To whom it may concern," but subsequently changed the form to a joint letter to General Shafter, stating that we should leave at once, and that if our departure were longer delayed those ordering it would be responsible for the loss of thousands of lives, etc. Colonel Roosevelt also wired the Secretary of War and Senator Lodge, and secured moreover authority to give the Associated Press an important letter which he, Roosevelt, wrote to Shafter urging in the strongest terms our removal. The letter of the Generals went to the Associated Press.

Of Roosevelt's going against army discipline with his plea for saving the lives of men stricken, or about to be stricken, Brown learned more after the meeting of the general court-martial the next day. Summoned by the future President and given trivial orders for policing the camp, the leader of Troop E was halted as he turned to go. Parenthetically, his revised diary told why:

"Sit down and I'll tell you what we did yesterday at the meeting of General Officers and Brigade Commanders." He [Roosevelt] said in effect that it came out at their conference that the Surgeon General opposed our return to the United States through fear of bringing yellow fever with us; that it was proposed that our camp be moved up into the hills so as to be on higher ground. The Colonel said that he had climbed those hills and no suitable camp ground was to be found there; and moreover the rains were heavier and more frequent in the hills, the problem of supply would be more difficult, and we had hardly the strength to move there anyhow.

The War Department authorities he said might pigeonhole the official views of the division and brigade commanders, but if he could get a statement of the situation in the newspapers he was confident that such pressure would be brought on the administration that they would be obliged to bring us North. He realized fully the gravity of the step being taken, but laughlingly added that he did not fear any danger of being court martialed for it.

Rumors of an early departure sifted into the tents with the rain. And before noon, moving orders were received. On the fifth, Brown heard that the Third and Sixth Cavalry were to leave on the morrow. After reporting twelve men sick, he strolled over the ground where battle had been waged the first three days of July. Aching and sweating, he worked long hours at payrolls and muster rolls. Ships for the expeditionary forces slipped in silently.

Troop E folded its tentage August 7, destroyed high piles of clothing to thwart infection, rode a train into Santiago, and those who were able marched aboard the transport *Matteawan*. Stricken men were carried to the hospital in the stern of the ship. Strong ones worked far into the night handling baggage. Cavalrymen mingled with artillerymen. Dorst, Garlington, and others of the division staff were going to the States with them. At 2:00 A. M., Brown, "with a high fever," went to bed.

At noon, the *Matteawan* eased out of its berth to follow in the wake of other transports. Brown's fever had broken, but his legs sagged as he stopped on deck to chat with Dorst. The two officers mulled over their successes and failures. The Major, wrote the diarist, felt it to be "unfortunate for us that we had that old man (Gen. Wheeler) to command the Cavy. Division."

The pebbled shores of Cuba receded. Cuba—where lurked the unseen yet stabbing enemy after guns were silent. Cuba—where medical officers groped to conquer the antagonist which at first they called "filth," only to discover later that its name was the Stegomyia mosquito. One of Brown's messmates, Walter Reed, along with Finlay, Lazear, Carroll, and Agramonte, would solve the puzzle. And Gorgas, son of a Confederate soldier, would rise eminently to achieve practical results in the light of the lantern of Science.

A strong eastern breeze tossed the ocean into hissing foam on the tenth as the ship swept past San Salvador Island. Sixteen men of Troop E fell ill. Next day, though the sea was less agitated, four of them were in the hospital. Other soldiers, shadows of former ruggedness, were carried aft. At suppertime, a stoker, raving as he raced to the deck rail, leaped overboard. The sea claimed his body.

Delirium seized more of the sick, though they were given constant attention. From the steward, Brown bought them milk, tea, pears, rice, and prunes. By the thirteenth, the wind had spent itself. Sultriness followed. The sea turned glassy. When night came, an artilleryman escaped from the choking air of the hospital to plunge blindly to death in unruffled waters.

Before another daybreak, a cooling, wind-driven rain conveyed relief. Yet it took all morning for Brown to dry out clothes shaken from his soaked valise.

At noon of the fifteenth, dry-throated men sighted Shinnecock Lighthouse and, seven hours later, the *Matteawan* anchored off Long Island. For the returning troops, the first official news of peace-treaty terms came from a naval craft. Scattered in front of his ship, Brown could see yellow flags fluttering atop the *La Grande Duchesse, St. Louis, Gate City, Miami, Vigilancia,* and *St. Paul.* Then, with eyes fixed upon the shore, he thought of the man in Troop D who had just died, a man who had wanted to live only to see his native land again.

Next morning, the Supervisor of Health of the Port of

New York climbed aboard the *Matteawan* with a trio of medical officers. After inspection, the ship was permitted to prepare for disembarkation. A few officers were the first to leave, at noon of the seventeenth. Two hours later, a lighter took on the baggage and stricken soldiers, accompanied by ten men from each troop. Two more lighters came alongside in the afternoon, one for the remaining soldiers and the other for their horses.

That night, Brown made it of record that "the Red Cross people were on hand with a nice, fresh ham sandwich for each man when we landed. Had just got in camp when a terrific storm of wind & rain burst down upon us."

Three days were spent in the detention camp. Brown sent off a letter to Denver, the need for his fountain pen underscored. When he could, he procured fresh bread for all of his troop and commissaries for the sick. Fresh vegetables were scarce, but he tracked them down in an effort to balance the diet. When he moved his men to the more permanent quarters of Camp Wykoff, he obtained some bed sacks, straw, and blankets. Still stalked by malaria, he tumbled into bed with a chill, only to rise a few hours later to care for others.

A violent thunderstorm raged the night of the twenty-fourth. Lightning struck down a tent. Amid the roar and flashing, Osborne, still battling, died. And trooper Desch also succumbed. The Captain's jaw set firmer. He rode a horse to the station, pleaded for needed supplies—and got "enough to get along on."

Troop E received drawers, blue flannel shirts, leggings, and a few hats. The Red Cross provided the sick with tea and cream to augment soup and oranges furnished by the commissary. After visiting the hospital, the leader sent off Osborne's bedding roll and trunk. To Desch's mother in Chicago, he dispatched a telegram worded with sympathy and understanding, with prideful mention of a Rough Rider's gallantry.

As the days passed, camp and hospital conditions improved. Once more Troop E greeted favorite mounts, brought from Lakeland. Brown, happy in unpacking saddles, ordered the grain allowance increased. The animals showed lack of proper feeding. Newly arrived recruits listened cockily to hard-boiled admonitions of veterans granted furloughs.

On September 5, the Captain went over to discuss grazing privileges with Roosevelt. The Colonel asked him to prepare a report explaining the advantages the troops would have enjoyed if emergency rations had been available as previously urged. Still without his fountain pen, Brown completed a pencil copy of the report the next day. In another year army men would be reminded of the ration again, and again there would be faltering.

In spite of eleven out of thirty old men marked up on sick report, Troop E found cause to be cheered. Lumber arrived for tent floors, the mounts got in a bit of grazing, and July pay at last was drawn. More men left on furlough. Thirty recruits drifted in while rumors predicted an early move to a permanent post. New ordnance came, and the Captain felt favored enough to forget the creeping fog, cold rain, touches of fever, and disapproval of an immediate leave for himself.

A week's travel rations for the troop were drawn on the twenty-seventh. The men wasted no moments in loading their train and bidding good-by to America's largest city. Bound for Fort Washakie, Wyoming, they faced westward joyfully. When, two days later, the train paused in Cleveland, pale Captain Brown met two old friends. Major and Mrs. Armstrong had come to greet him.

The troopers sped on through Chicago to Omaha, toward the Rockies. At nightfall of October 2, Cheyenne was reached.

There, the fighting Captain fell into the embrace of his

two sisters. For Helen and Grace, the reunion was too brief. They insisted on proceeding to Rawlins where camp was provided for the repair of transportation to the post. For almost a week, the sisters ministered to their yielding brother before returning to Denver.

It was a five-day march in blusterous weather and eddying snow before the cavalrymen saw Frémont Peak. Twenty-two miles more lay before them on the last day. The citizens of Lander stood ready to greet the tired troopers many hours before they reached the outskirts of the frontier town. In a halt that lengthened to a stay of two hours, the soldiers ate unhesitatingly the food offered by housewives and the few girls who had no husbands. And, the Captain noticed—but not too closely—more than one chilled trooper found a genial host with a warming draught.

An hour before retreat, Brown led his men into the fort of which he assumed command. Escape from pestilence had ended. It was good to be a part of the West again.

Some time would elapse before the Captain would receive his silver star, earned in the Santiago Campaign.

CHAPTER XX

Finding a Way to the Philippines

AFTER the Americans had been able to raise their flag over Manila in mid-August, there were conditions to be remedied in the Philippines as well as in Cuba and Puerto Rico. Peace negotiations with the Spaniards were under way, but far from accomplishment. Emilio Aguinaldo, leader of the Filipino insurgents, had made Greene's victory easier, but bowing to control by the United States was another matter. There was cause for alarm among regular forces when the American Government ordered one hundred thousand of its volunteers to be discharged before the termination of their contracts. They also wondered when they would get khaki to replace sweat-saturated flannel and wool clothing.

Aguinaldo, establishing an independent government, had, in October, forty thousand willful followers close to Manila. Most of the Americans in that city were volunteers. The ranks of regulars had been thinned by disease and by battle. Yet they buckled down to their diverse tasks while wondering when Congress would replace men departing amidst rumblings of grave portent.

The name Aguinaldo, meaning "Christmas box," also denoted a fighting package. Though he realized the people needed an older, more properly educated leader for future guidance, he bowed to the wishes of his idolizers. His reputation as a fighter against the Spaniards made him President of the self-willed revolutionary government.

General Merritt, after he went to Paris, labored as hard for a satisfactory peace as he had fought upon many fields of battle. On December 10 came the signing of the treaty. And Merritt returned to his soldiering, soon to learn that peace was not what erstwhile allies wanted.

At Fort Washakie, Captain Brown shook off chills, while the last of the Indian uprisings was put down—in his native state. From Fort Snelling, men of the Third Infantry marched to Leech Lake Agency to pacify indignant Pillager Chippewas. By the end of October, the soldiers and men of the Fourteenth Minnesota, at points along the Great Northern Railway, had closed the last chapter in the country's long record of strife with the red men.

Brown spent Christmas with his men, and the next day he rode out of the post. Granted a twenty-day leave, he entrained for Denver and the East. Visits were paid relatives and friends in Ohio and New York. He had time to drop in at the offices of the manufacturers of his tent shields. They paid him a 10 per cent royalty on army sales and a slight increase on civilian purchases.

During the first week of the new year, 1899, he made contact with friends in Washington who helped to pave his way out of stagnation. President McKinley extended a welcoming hand to the commander of Fort Washakie, and, Brown wrote in his diary, directed Adjutant General Henry C. Corbin "to bring attention to my case when army is increased." Influential friends from the Buckeye state introduced him to Senator Marcus Hanna, political Titan of the Capitol. And there followed conversations in regard to the Regular Army's welfare with Corbin and Inspector General J. C. Breckenridge.

Recurrent chills and fever, however, attacked the Westerner in his rounds. When he returned to Denver on January 12, he was granted another week for rest. Yet on the journey back to his command, he became "sea sick" and suffered a "bilious attack on stage & laid over at Lander." He completed the trip heavily bundled in a buckboard.

From routine, in February, he again turned to a study of the emergency ration. His essay on the subject for the Officers' Lyceum drew the attention of Brigadier General H. C. Merriam, commander of the Department of the Colorado. The essayist received a letter stating, in part:

> The Department Commander deems it of such value to the service that he would like your permission to forward it [the essay] to the Adjutant General of the Army for the dissemination of the valuable information and suggestion contained therein.

The message was written on the thirteenth, two days before West Point was to graduate its Class of '99. These men, going out to meet the urgent demand for new officers, witnessed an act that would impart a thrill to all their successors on the banks of the Hudson. The athletic corps adopted black, gray, and gold as its official colors.

Meanwhile, General Otis had assumed command at Manila. While the peace treaty was awaiting ratification, he found it difficult to pursue McKinley's policy of "benevolent assimilation" of the peoples lately freed from Spanish throttling. Of the 20,870 American soldiers in the Philippines, only a fourth of them were regulars, and 1,650 of them had served their full enlistment terms. The volunteers elected to remain and aid in the work just begun. Astute leaders of recalcitrant natives had whipped up rash evidence of open hostility to civilized methods of administration.

In the first week of February, forty thousand Tagalogs attempted, after undercover preparations, to wrest Manila from the placating Americans. The attackers, hurled back into screened lairs, with three thousand of their number lost, welded their organizations as they planned stubbornly against forces found not so weak as they had imagined. Congress, rubbing its eyes, again decided its Regular Army needed more efficiency and strength.

By March 2 Congress had acted. The President was empowered to build the regular forces up to sixty-five thousand men and to organize thirty-five thousand volunteers into twenty-seven regiments of infantry and two of cavalry. The latter, however, would be entitled to discharge by July 1, 1901. The appointment of volunteer officers by states was discontinued, they being given federal commissions by the President. Aside from the staff, the regular officers with volunteer units could continue in the same duties. No finer group of volunteers and seasoned officers had ever before been made available for the country's fighting forces.

While awaiting reinforcements, the troops in the Philippines had chiefly to defend themselves, but Generals MacArthur, Wheaton, Marcus P. Miller, and Alfred T. Smith grabbed islands and inland points from *insurrectos* in sudden clashings. Brown, isolated in Wyoming, felt as detached from the stirring events as if he had been sent to the Yukon. He got overly impatient. Through channels, on March 18, he sent a feeler to General Otis. Briefly, he begged: "When opportunity offers would like detail Philippines."

Opportunity did not knock. Not even after Otis enlarged his operations upon receiving more regulars. Not even after MacArthur and Lawton, by mid-May, claimed the country north of Manila, forcing Aguinaldo and his cabinet to flee the city of San Isidro for more northerly parts. Not even after swarms of blue-pants soldiers were stricken down by disease or wounds, and offensive thrusts called for the holding of plucked areas peopled with natives bent on destruction.

Generals Funston and Irving Hale, in June and July, were aiding MacArthur, cracking attacks or pushing outward. But while guerrilla warfare grew apace, Otis saw many of his regulars, discharges in hand, depart for the United States. And eight thousand volunteers left for home. Surely Otis, now compelled to reorganize, to place new recruits soon to come, would need officers who had the experience of San Juan and Kettle Hills blazed into their records.

So thought Brown as he filed away his Sharpshooter's Certificate for 1899. He fretted a while longer. Yet there was some consolation in reading the live-wire articles in the *Journal* of the United States Cavalry Association. The new editor, Charles Dudley Rhodes, graduate of the Point a decade back, was an officer who would go far with command as well as with the pen.

On August 14, the sharpshooter sat down and wrote to a friend who could understand his desire for action. The friend was Roosevelt, and he occupied the Executive Chamber at Albany, New York. A telegram from the A. G. O. at Washington, handed to Fort Washakie's commander on the nineteenth, started him strutting. For he read:

YOU HAVE BEEN APPOINTED MAJOR, 39th INFANTRY VOLUNTEERS. WIRE ACCEPTANCE TO THIS OFFICE.

Accept? What had he been waiting for? At Albany the following day, the man who loved to cut red tape sent off two letters a fighting cavalryman could understand. The first was good.

My dear Captain Brown:—
   Replying to yours of the 14th instant would say there is no man who I back more heartily than I do you. I will write to Secretary Root at once, forwarding him your papers, and enclose you copy of my papers.   Faithfully yours,
                              Theodore Roosevelt

The second, to Elihu Root, was better:

My dear Mr. Secretary:—
   I should have included in my recommendations the name of Captain W. C. Brown, now on duty at Fort Washakie Wyo. In fact, I think Captain Brown and Captain Stevens were almost the two best among the many good men whom I last recommended to you. Captain Brown

is a peculiarly thoughtful man, excellent in the field, and at the same time excellent for headwork. He would make an invaluable field officer for a fighting regiment, or possibly even better in the Inspector General's or Adjutant General's departments. You see that the fine fellow asks that if he cannot get a promotion he wants merely a leave of absence to enable him to go on active duty. He would be a credit to the army and I back him up heartily.

I enclose his papers.   Faithfully yours,
                                                THEODORE ROOSEVELT

Once on his way, the Captain had but a few hours to say farewell to tearful but proud sisters in Denver. At forty-five years of age, and getting bald, the wearer of the gold oak leaf marched buoyantly again. Six days after wiring acceptance of his appointment, he reported at Fort Snelling.

Until September 15 he happily served as adjutant to his old friend, beaming Colonel Dorst. Then, transferred to the Forty-second United States Infantry, within three days he saluted at Fort Niagara, New York, the regimental commander, Lieutenant Colonel J. H. Beacom. There was much to do in the role of range officer during the brief period allotted for target practice. When a telegram conveyed the news that Grace had been severely injured in an accident, brother Will made a hurried trip to her bedside. He provided all needed care, and returned within the week.

Upon completion of its organization, and with Brown assigned to the command of the First Battalion, the regiment entrained October 30 for the presidio of San Francisco. Armed and equipped for field service, each man carried 200 rounds of ammunition. Mounted officers were permitted to take their horses.

He arrived at the post on the bluffs overlooking the Golden Gate on November 6. The causes of the earlier confusion in shuttling troops to and from overseas service had been erased, and more khaki was being found. On the last day of the month, Brown, with the First Battalion and

Companies E and F of the Forty-second Infantry under his leadership, stepped aboard the United States transport *Dalny Vostok*.

Fresh organizations with eager and fit men had preceded them or were to follow. *Insurrectos* already had caused greater losses among American troops than had been sustained from the first to the last day of the war against Spain. Seated at Tarlac, in the plain of central Luzon, the dictatorial Aguinaldo schemed, surrounded by his cabinet. By the last of September, troops under MacArthur and the younger Wheeler had seized Porac. Then a three-prong advance swung the gates inward against the country ruled by Aguinaldo—Lawton by way of San Isidro to mesh with Wheaton's water-borne forces, Young and his cavalry thrusting boldly to the west, while MacArthur was to follow the railway after leaving Angeles. Elsewhere other troops were shaking the teeth of harassers.

As impatient to draw near the enemy as when he left for Cuba, Major Brown nevertheless knew there would be stiffer and longer resistance. In the month it took to cross the Pacific, it dawned upon the men that they needed fortitude. The first day of December was rough. Nearly all fell sick. Soon they became accustomed to the throbbing of the engines and to the whipping winds. Officers attended lectures. Noncoms and enlisted soldiers received instructions in signaling, first aid, and other essentials. And the doctors vaccinated them.

On the seventh day of the voyage, khaki uniforms were unpacked and issued. No more itching—for a while at least. The cosmopolite crew was rounded up by the doctors, Brown writing: "Part of crew vaccinated, to which the Chinese objected, & only submitted to when they saw that they would be forced." When on the eighth the diarist sighted the palm-fringed shores of the Hawaiian Islands, he donned his khaki. For two days, sea-tossed soldiers rustled through Honolulu, gleeful to feel land beneath their feet. The Major and his fellow officers had less worry when the ship weighed anchor.

In the morning of December's last day, the transport nosed around rocky Corregidor Island and came to rest in Manila Bay. Within a few hours Brown presented himself to General Otis. The one-time head of Leavenworth's school threw aside the usual reserve to welcome his former instructor. What a long way both had come! And how much there was to be accomplished in the crossing of paths!

Brown refrained from confessing that he agreed in part with an absent high-ranking general that it would take "several generations" by "slow process" for the majority of the Filipinos to achieve proper self-government. Instead, the Major asked how soon debarkation of his regiment might take place.

"You may start preparing tomorrow. You will march ashore the second."

Brown returned to his ship. He was ready for action again. On the second day of 1900, he and his men walked down the gangplank, to take station at La Loma Church.

Meanwhile, Aguinaldo had barely escaped capture when MacArthur plunged through Tarlac, and had slipped away from Young's incisive troopers far up in the Tangandan Mountains. But General Pilar, right-hand man of the insurgent leader, had been captured. His government dismembered, Aguinaldo sought a deeper recess for safety. The direction of aggressive bands, however, continued. The *insurrectos* by no means accepted routs as defeats.

Shifted from the north to head a slicing expedition in the south, Lawton was held up by unrelenting rains at the Mariquina. While trying to effect a crossing of the swollen, angry river at San Mateo he had defied death once too often. When his body later was borne through the streets of Manila, sorrow seamed alike the faces of Americans and

Filipinos. And few knew of a plot to bomb the funeral procession.

At the close of 1899, American troops in the Philippines, ever marching, ever fighting, realized they had paid a stiff price. About one thousand of them had died of diseases, half that number had been killed, and the wounded totaled 2,223.

At the year's end, a force of 51,167 officers and men, many of them sick, faced torridity and wetness, steaming jungles and rasping mountains, sharp hunger, and ceaseless watchfulness, while beating back the tricky and leering enemy.

CHAPTER XXI

The Major Shoots Straight

THE arrival of brisk, unfaded regiments in the Philippines permitted wider movements and deeper thrusts
against the treacherous enemy. General John C. Bates,
taking over Lawton's command of the First Division of the
Eighth Corps, gave the *insurrectos* little time to count their
trophies. Within a few weeks Generals Wheaton and
Theodore Schwan, stinging fast and often, cleared Bacoor
and Laguna de Bay before advancing hundreds of miles
farther. General William A. Kobbé took the Forty-third
and Forty-seventh Volunteer Infantry and a battery of the
Third Artillery to isolated isles. At Legaspi, in the latter
part of January, he cracked a hard shell when Paua,
Chinese leader, fell into his hands.

Brown, after stamping around La Loma Church for a
week, moved to the Pumping Station. As sultry days came
and went, he again started to wilt. Spells of fever and chills
flagged him. He made trips into the city, sitting on court,
obtaining quinine, phenacetin, and bromide. He read
eagerly news from the fighting fronts, but his diary mentioned only his physical condition. Had he come this far
only to meet disappointment? He had—for at least a few
weeks.

On February 8, the doctor discovered the real trouble.
A corporal was called in to wait upon the sick man. Next
day, Major Brown, victim of smallpox, entered the hospital
at Manila. He was not to rejoin his First Battalion until
spring of the next year. Of more immediate regret, how-

ever, was the necessity of burning personal articles to prevent the spread of smallpox.

> 1 cot, 1 mattress, 1 chair, 1 khaki riding trousers, 7 towels, 2 pair socks, 3 handkerchiefs, 1 night shirt, 1 white shirt (outing), 3 suits underwear, 1 pair spectacles, 1 Austrian coat tent (half), 1 shaving brush, 1 razor, 2 blue flannel shirts, 1 helmet, 1 abdominal bandage, 1 mosquito bar, 1 blanket, 1 hairbrush, 1 wall pocket, 1 pair slippers.

Even the fountain pen went up in flames. This was the last diary entry until the doctor informed the victim his day of liberty drew near.

Brown left the hospital on the twenty-seventh. He did "a lot of shopping" in the city to replenish his wardrobe. The next day he rode a launch to Pasig and reported at Regimental Headquarters. Much was to be done in equipping certain companies, for there were "many men actually barefooted or in stocking feet."

On March 7 the Major assumed command at Taguig, garrisoned by Company M. The civil populace, numbering seven thousand, and on the increase, required steady vigilance on the part of the police and military. Occasional plunderers had to be dealt with sternly.

During the last ten days of the month, Brown inspected field stations in the vicinity of Manila, reporting on units of General Robert M. Hall's Brigade of the First Division. The inspector, upon finishing his report, accepted an invitation to lunch with Assistant Adjutant General Wagner and other staff members. It gave Wagner a chance to inform the Major that he was pulling for him, for the action in the field he craved. But there also was some pinch-hitting to do.

Brown, reporting to Wheaton at Calamba, April 2, learned that some things needed sharper attention at Paete. Insurgents had become overbold, their activity leading to urgent scouting by and clashes with the American soldiery. Within twenty-four hours Paete had a new commander.

Somehow, he got ragged men new supplies and reorganized the system of scouting so that natives might feel assured when they went to sleep that their huts would not become torches before daylight. Sundry buildings were searched for contraband. Carrier routes, no matter where they led, came under strict scrutiny. Brown himself set the pace for the detachments he sent forth. His diary entry for April 8 limned adventuring:

All broke camp about 5:20 A. M. . . . . I took trail up valley & thence up the mountain to where we were on the 6th. When near the top the advance guard caught sight of some 6 to 10 natives running up the mountain in frantic efforts to get away from a hut on which a white flag was flying. About 12 shots were fired at them but so far as known none hit. Our men charged on up the trail & when 150 y[ar]ds from hut a man (who proved to be Musician Henry Vance 37 Inf) dressed in insurgent's uniform jumped up and yelled "don't shoot. I'm an American." Two other prisoners were taken at same place where they were concealed in grass.

I went back & searched & burned hut & we subsequently captured another native who came to see the house burn. Vance said it was an insurrecto hut & there was an outpost above on the mountain where we found several bolos, bows & arrows, spears & a few cartridges.

Two miles further on we captured on a stream 3 natives, one dressed in red trousers & blue coat. We then struck toward the . . . . valley . . . . and about 5:20 P. M. started for Paete, arriving at 7 P. M.

Communication with Manila was carried on chiefly by gunboat, and by this means Brown journeyed past Santa Cruz on the twelfth. He was on his way to take an examination with some thirty other captains of the line for appointment to the Adjutant General's and Inspector General's Departments. In an overnight stop at a river town he slept fitfully. More than a dozen *insurrectos* swooped down with blazing rifles upon the corral. Defenders, splattering streets and by-paths with bullets, repulsed them.

Before returning to Paete, the traveler had another pleasant chat with Wagner. And he marveled at the strategical knowledge imparted by his brilliant yet unassuming host.

At Paete, as elsewhere, the water supply demanded continual filtering and analyzation. Most of it came from a spring. Cases of malaria increased in spite of precautions. Before April was out, Brown was carried on a stretcher from a boat to the Division Base Hospital at Calamba. But he soon went back to face marauding insurgents.

In May, the weather grew warmer, then hot and sultry. There were few comfortable sleeping hours, no matter how tired the soldiers were from the gathering of supplies, policing, flag-raisings, shepherding children to school, or seeking out and burning insurgent quarters in rugged and densely wooded areas threaded only with prickly trails.

However, tortuously and slowly, the Philippines were being lifted out of age-old lethargy and recalcitrance. Insurgent leadership was crumbling. Garcia had surrendered to Bates in Mindanao where volunteer infantrymen were erecting garrisons as they shoved back opposition. In a northerly push by Major Peyton C. March and Colonel Luther R. Hare, Aguinaldo again slipped through stretched fingers, but a chieftain fell to rise no more.

As leader of the Philippine forces and governor general, Otis had taken lank strides. Now he was succeeded by MacArthur, another tireless fighter and colonizer, with commanders in the various regions who proved adaptable to shifting scenes. And back in Washington Congress gave the army men something to talk about. The office of lieutenant general was revived for the Army's senior commanding chief. And, to provide all branches of service with a school that would give the ultimate in strategy and pertinent studies, the establishment of an Army War College in the Capital was authorized.

All this had transpired by the time Brown stood ready to move out of Paete to Malabon the first week in June. Boats carried the men and their paraphernalia to Pasig on the fifth. There they bivouacked during a rainy night, sleeping on cots set up along the twiggy shore. The deluge compelled the Major, when he halted at Manila, to seek medical aid for his rising fever. Upon reporting to Wheaton, the General gave him "positive orders as to boiling water" for drinking. And again there was a short stay in a hospital.

Conditions at Malabon taxed all resources. The upper portion, because of flood waters, was submerged. Roadbeds had to be lifted and bridges built. Cisterns became polluted and men, failing to boil water before drinking it, paid the penalty. Brown, in quick stride, procured distilled water from the sugar refinery. And when he went into Manila to speed the sending out of acutely needed material and to get measured for a new khaki suit, he was confronted by fellow officers astir over developments far removed from Malabon.

The Boxers in China were gnashing their teeth at foreigners. Again Civilization was to swing its military scythe: within a month General Chaffee leading an American force to the new theater of war to assist soldiers of European powers. . . . . MacArthur sending in advance Colonel Emerson H. Liscum at the head of the Ninth Infantry. . . . . Americans, French, British, and Japanese seizing walled Tien Tsin by mid-July. . . . . Liscum meeting death in the attack. . . . . Arrival of reinforcements and Chaffee. . . . . The painful march across the baked earth of North China to the gates of Tartar walls enclosing Pekin and the British Compound. . . . . And, before the end of blazing August, relief for the legations and Christian Chinese, an end to misery and fear.

Brown, while this problem was being resolved, had to thwart the plans of attackers to disarm his patrols and disrupt the teamwork in local and regional administration. He went back to Pasig at the close of June, to command that station for several weeks. On the Fourth of July, the native populace joined in the celebration of American independence. The Major filled a new fountain pen.

Had flag raising and presentation of flag to the Presidente at noon. At 2 P. M. to 5 P. M. soldiers' sports. At 5 P. M. the Presidente, 2 padres & ladies called on the comdg Officer. After which the Filipino band gave us a serenade. One musician got his band instrument broken in the teamster's shack.

During the days that followed, the commander and the *presidente,* mayor or council head, teamed well, even if they differed over the taxation of saloons and cockpits. Frequent inspection of schools revealed earnest progress. On the twenty-first, the commander received word that he had been appointed Acting Inspector General of the Fourth District, Department of Northern Luzon. The department was commanded by Funston, and the District Head-quarters was at San Isidro, Province of Nueva Ecija.

Three days later Brown appeared in Manila for instructions. He talked with General Bell. The energy and efficiency of the West Point graduate of '78 was reflected in the conservation. The man of the Class of '77 felt more assured of the triumphs that were to come. When he reached San Isidro on the twenty-ninth and became a full-fledged Inspector General the next day, it marked an upsurge in force not easily battened down.

During the nine months the Major was to be in his new role, the insurgents' guerrilla fights, one or two a week, lent constant excitement to the American Army's tasks. Funston, who had wrought wonders with the Twentieth Kansas and First Montana Regiments before they returned home, soon whipped up a not-to-be-outdashed spirit among other volunteers and regulars. He relied no little on organizations of discerning Ilocanos and the Macabebe unit. The Macabebes comprised the Squadron Philippine Cavalry though, Funston conceded, it "was really a battalion of infantry, as I never saw one of its members on a horse."

Panteleon Garcia, the captured local chieftain, was succeeded by José Alejandrino as commander of central Luzon. In his treatment of prisoners Alejandrino neglected to show the quality of mercy with which Aguinaldo and Lacuna, a favored subordinate, were endowed. The fear of falling into the hands of sub-leader Tagunton, the heartless ex-bandit, cowed many natives. The boldest and quickest sallies, however, came from the ever-stirring Lacuna. Like a hornet, he buzzed, stung, and buzzed off again.

On the second day of August, three wounded men limped into San Isidro carrying a note from Lacuna to Funston. Brown questioned them, learned that they had survived an attack made on their group while eating lunch in high grass. Lacuna, boastingly, provided the information that a Negro deserter from the Twenty-fourth Infantry was doing a splendid service as an insurgent lieutenant. In time, a six-hundred-dollar reward for the Negro, David Fagan, dead or alive, was to result in his losing his head to a Tagalog schemer.

Brown's task of checking and reporting on troops, property, transportation, money accounts and multitudinous problems spelled no end of labor. The Inspector, more often than not, rode out with a small escort. Stations usually lay far apart. Branch-laced trails were rough and unprotected, and the cart or wagon roads were not much better. Sometimes a trip was by water, as the journeying to and from Baler on the east coast. Rafts came in handy when swollen streams swept away bridges. In mid-August Brown was forced to bed with a chill—in a bed Aguinaldo had once prided himself in owning.

In Manila on October 7, the Inspector heard reports which sent him to bed beaming. At last somebody knew what field troops needed, for, he wrote, "5,000 aluminum equipments have been ordered from States for use over here." But there was other good news. In addition to thousands of other American troops diverted from their reinforcing of victorious forces at Pekin, Chaffee had begun withdrawing most of his men from China to Manila. Days of insurrection in the Philippines surely were numbered.

On the night of the tenth, after return to San Isidro, Brown joined in an elaborate celebration at the post staged by the Municipal Council in reciprocation for a social function sponsored by Funston the same week. The better class of townspeople sat down to a "super" supper with the officers. There was trumping for the *baile* later in the evening, but the Americans kept their arms within reach—on racks outside the ballroom. In spite of mutual courtesies, it paid to be on guard against sudden forays by perfidious bands. They lurked not far away.

Two nights later, Funston planned a quick raid. When he started out at five o'clock the next morning, he was bolstered principally by mounted scouts under Lieutenant Richard C. Day, and Troop A of the Fourth Cavalry under Lieutenant John Morrison, Jr. Accompanying them were Lieutenant Burton J. Mitchell, Funston's first cousin and aide, and Medical Officer Frank D. Pease.

Brown, sharp-set to go along "for the excitement," was granted his desire. He sprang to his horse and the party trotted south to the barrio of Santa Cruz. He wrote of the episode which followed:

At the foot bridge over the swamp we surprised the insurgent outpost & exchanged a few shots with them, driving them in. Leaving our horses we crossed the bridge & proceeded about ½ mile when we got a strong fire from the front & our left flank from 30 to 60 insurgents at ranges varying from 100 to 400 yds. They put up a good fight for about 30 minutes & then disappeared to the east. Pvt. Robinson of the headquarters detachment was one of the 3 men on the point & [was] wounded at almost the first fire.

We killed one of the insurgents & wounded two.

Week after week reports of clashes dribbled in. Insurgents jumped American soldiers, shot down people of their own blood who incurred disfavor. MacArthur had to get tougher, and he did. Sterner measures than the disarming and freeing captives must be employed. His men, given the green light, struck more boldly and deeply. Townsmen, held for communicating with Lacuna or other leaders, chafed under restraint. Patrols were doubled and troopers slept with their clothes on. Yet *insurrectos* kept striking and breezing away with alarming quantities of firearms and ammunition.

Because of routine duties, Brown waited long days for another fight, but he practiced diligently for the first opportunity. He procured one of the newly invented Colt automatic pistols, a few of which had been sent to the Philippines for trial in the field. From mounted and dismounted positions he found the weapon effective in his hand. His laudable reports on it were to be proved unexaggerated.

The Inspector received news of McKinley's re-election and the election of Roosevelt as Vice-President while he checked over the arrival of 205 stores-laden bull carts at a station on November 7. The carabao, at the rate of two miles an hour, could pack two hundred pounds in a day's travel of twenty miles.

Worries melted at San Isidro on Christmas. Soldiers and natives alike fared well on the holiday. The "Presidente & Council," Brown set down, "called at Gen. Funston's office to pay respects." And the firecrackers kept popping "all day long." Those unlucky enough to be in San Isidro's prison got a bit extra at the table. The average daily cost of feeding them came to seven and one half cents in gold.

On the night the nineteenth century vanished, officers and four ladies of the garrison held a peculiar watch. Assembled at District Headquarters, they took turns keeping the phonograph rotating. When midnight came, the bugler sounded "Taps" and, on the first minute of 1901, he blew "Reveille"!

In the first month of the new year, some fifty leading insurgents went to the island of Guam without their consent. The deportation had a goodly effect, but resistance still flared whenever a hive of the enemy was stirred. Lieutenant Morrison died in a fight against too strong opposition.

At intervals, Funston rushed out of San Isidro to strike at the enemy, only to return in plain disgust. Between January 15 and 22 he conducted a luckless scout in the mountains to the east. On the twenty-fifth, however, his persistency was rewarded. Early in the morning, the General started southward with thirty mounted men of the Twenty-second Infantry, Lieutenants Mitchell and Raymond Sheldon, and Dr. W. P. Chamberlain. Brown, yearning to try out his new pistol, went along.

They set fire to some of the bush country, and shot down four fleeing insurgents. In the afternoon something bigger—something that Funston was to make well known in his writings—was flushed. But Brown kept his version of the story buried in the pages of his diary:

.... After lunch we started down the right bank of the Malimba River & after a couple of miles crossed to the left bank to reconnoiter the Canadaba Swamp & a mile farther we discovered men on the other bank trying to dodge out of observation. Gen. Funston yelled at the men to get that man, shoot him, &c, & about that time a man in blue uniform mounted a pony & started at full speed to escape. I fired at him with my Colt Automatic & got in 7 well directed but rapidly fired shots at about 75 yds when the man rolled off the left side of his horse on to the ground. To flank these fellows out I then galloped across the creek by a ford 100 yds above and as soon as we were out of the tall grass in relatively open ground a man fired at us from the open at 150 yds. I emptied my other pistol clip at him. Before this I had twice noticed that when on the South side of the creek we were being fired at with Mausers from a clump of bamboo. We advanced west [,] our man retreating[,] & after retreating 200 yds or more being continually fired at by our men he fell shot through the body & I think also the left wrist. We left him in an apparently dying condition & by that time there being no further firing. We found about 6 small shelters which had been used about a week. More or less rice & cooking utensils about. We then looked for the man shot from the pony who proved to be Lt. Col. Tomas Tagunton who under Lacuna's orders did all the recent burning of barrios about here. He was dressed in full uniform with straw hat on which was his insignia of rank—gilt star on red disk. Cutting open his left breast [there] was found near the surface one of my Colt Automatic bullets which had passed through the base of the heart. Tagunton's pony had to be shot to get him with papers &c. on him. Lt. Sheldon remained in ambuscade at Tagunton's camp overnight.

All the Americans had come through unscathed. From San Isidro that evening, Funston wired the good news to the Adjutant General at Manila. The "monster" Tagunton, he explained, had been "the author of nearly all the assassinations that have taken place near here and is the man who has attempted several times to burn San Isidro. . . . . He was assigned as successor to Natividad in command of the Guerrilla Band of this region. He was much feared and his death will have a very beneficial effect."

Next day, four of Tagunton's men, preferring the protection of the garrison, asked to be given the oath of allegiance. Moreover, they reported that a dozen of their seventy fellow insurgents wished to forsake the hills and make amends.

Brown had picked up a bolo at the scene of the skirmish. It was an ugly weapon, but it was a *genuine* souvenir, and he sent it home. In time, he would have a watch-chain charm made of the calibre .38 rimless-smokeless bullet which ended Tagunton's splurges. The pistol, to be kept until his own death, would, according to his wish, go to "Fred. K. Funston (son of Gen. Funston), ... San Francisco."

On the stock of a weapon Tagunton must have seen all too briefly his slayer polished the inscription:

1 9 0 0
I T T

CHAPTER XXII

Aguinaldo Is Ensnared

THE time drew near for mustering out the volunteers. Congress, to maintain defense strength in far-flung places, in the first week of February nodded approval to building an army of 100,000 officers and men. The law gave birth to the Philippine Scouts and the Puerto Rican regiment, with 12,000 natives to be formed into units wherein regular officers would be captains and majors. Service was confined to the islands.

Brown and his fellow officers digested the new legislation. It was to cause many promotions, changes in methods and commands, extension of training, and instruction in schools as well as camps. Problems of transportation and organization, however, brought slow relief to MacArthur. In six months, 30,000 of his 70,000 men were to depart. Ponderous-moving legislative wheels made it necessary to procure every available regular to replace volunteers. Luckily, events in the field started the tumbling of the last strongholds of the *insurrectos*.

Brown stood in the wings of the stage when the drama reached its climax. Of the capture of Aguinaldo he wrote a first-hand account. Only a short summary of it was to be printed in the *Infantry Journal* in 1925. Withheld details now define more sharply an event long since pictured by the pens of the principal actors as well as by writers with world-wide audiences.

On February 10, a windy and dusty day, Brown scanned the mail and reports which had accumulated at San Isidro during his late stay in Manila. Funston, pecking at his headquarters, opened a telegram from Lieutenant J. D. Taylor, Jr., commanding a company of the Twenty-fourth Infantry at Pantabangan. The message from this small town in the northeastern corner of the Province of Nueva Ecija, at the edge of Luzon's vast central plain, revealed the whereabouts of Aguinaldo.

The answer to a baffling question asked for more than a year had come. Taylor wrote that one Cecilio Segismundo had come to him as a courier tired of war's demands. He carried dispatches from Aguinaldo to a cousin of the chief and to other leaders in the insurrectionist cause.

Aguinaldo, the courier asserted, was at Palanan, on Luzon's east coast, about fifty miles north of Casiguran. The hideout could be reached only by rough trails or footpaths. The leader had about a hundred armed insurgents and, to keep Americans mystified, he was performing under the name of Teniente Abandanero.

With timely speed and accompanied by the paymaster and an escort of soldiers, the messenger arrived at San Isidro on the eleventh. Funston found him to be an Ilocano of high intellect, loosing his information in fluent Spanish. Palanan, about six miles from the sea, was being well guarded against any surprise approach. The town, its houses of bamboo and nipa-thatched, claimed two or three hundred residents, with twice that number in its valley. Insurgent soldiers had quarters in a convent. Across the street from them, living in more private style, were Aguinaldo and his staff: Dr. (or Colonel) Santiago Barcelona, treasurer; Colonel Simeon Villa, chief of staff; and Commandante Nasario Alhambra, in charge of the local troops.

As Aguinaldo later revealed, he first sought refuge in Palanan in September, 1900. The villagers had received him enthusiastically and warm-heartedly. He listened to band concerts on Saturday and Sunday afternoons in the plaza in front of his house, and enjoyed an occasional dance at the parish house until the latter part of November.

Tranquillity was shattered for a time by receipt of news that fifty Americans were in the near-by mountains. The insurgent leaders hid out for a few days, until the Americans left. In a short time, Major Alhambra had forty more men on hand to insure greater protection.

The cipher letters of the message which Segismundo turned over kept Funston and his staff in an all-night sweat. The General relied chiefly on his able secret service employee and former adjutant of the Insurgent Army— Lazaro Segovia, a youth of twenty-three years. Born in Madrid, Spain, Segovia received his A.B. degree when he was fifteen years old. He enlisted in a garrison regiment of the Capital, and studied in a private college. When troubles rose in Cuba, he was recalled to full-time military duty. He later went to Manila by transfer, to be attached to a regiment of natives in 1895.

Segovia, fighting in the first revolution which began in 1896, seven times received the Red Cross for "gallant conduct." When hostilities flared up between Spain and the United States, he surrendered with his comrades in Manila on August 13, 1898. The fighter did not desire to return to Spain when more adventure was near. He took up arms with the Filipinos but, in May, 1900, gave himself up to General Funston. The American commander thereafter employed the Spaniard on many missions, always finding him clever, alert, and trustworthy.

At the break of a new day, Segovia pointed out the cipher's key word, in Tagalo, which he also knew. Brown, nursing a bothersome "cold," came in to watch the red-eyed, hair-scratching men decode the important communications. They learned: that Aguinaldo, in offering brigadier ranks to Colonels Lacuna and Sandico, urged the latter to come to the vicinity of Palanan with four hundred men; that Aguinaldo wondered if his fellows felt "despondent" over "Emperor" McKinley's re-election; that Aguinaldo signed the majority of his letters as "Magdalo" and was often referred to as El Dictator.

Translation ordeals over, Funston tried to sleep, but he arose in a few hours. His head whirled with plans. He and the courier Segismundo talked long and earnestly how best to ensnare the vulpine Aguinaldo. Finally, they decided upon a bold and ingenious plot. A party, Brown unfolded,

.... was to land at Casiguran Bay at night with about 80 Macabebe scouts dressed in insurgent uniforms, armed with Mausers, Remingtons and a few Krags and thoroughly disguised in every way as insurgent troops. The officers—General Funston, his aide Lieut. Burton J. Mitchell, 40th Inf., Capt. R. T. Hazzard and Lieut. O. P. M. Hazzard, 11th Cavalry, U. S. V., and Capt. H. W. Newton, 34th Inf., U. S. V., were to accompany the command, being passed off as American prisoners.

As it turned out:

The expedition was nominally commanded by Hilario Talplacido [Tal Placido], an ex-insurgent Captain from Jaen, Nueva Ecija. The real head, however, was Lazaro Segovia, who acted as Hilario's lieutenant. Other Tagalos who acted as Officers and Non-Commissioned Officers of the expedition were Gregorio Cadhit, ex-lieutenant of the insurgent army, and Dionicio Bato, ex-Sergeant of the insurgent army.

On February 16th General Funston went to Manila under telegraphic orders and the entire plan was discussed by Generals MacArthur and Wheaton, the former being quite hopeful, but the latter rather doubtful as to the result. Lacuna at this time having from information received shown a disposition to come in and surrender, General Funston returned on February 24th to San Isidro to effect this, but later was recalled, and on March 2nd returned to Manila where [the] U. S. S. Vicksburg, Captain E. B. Barry commanding, was secured from the Navy to transport and land the Expedition near Casiguran on the Eastern Coast.

Lacuna's signature was cleverly forged on papers having his stamp and purporting to be signed by him. These, substantially as follows, were prepared to be forwarded by the Presidente of Casiguran, known to be an insurgent, on whom the expedition was to be passed off as insurgent reinforcements for Aguinaldo. Both letters purported to have been written by Lacuna in the Bulac mountains east of Penaranda, Nueva Ecija.

In the first, dated February 24th, Lacuna acknowledged receipt of

Aguinaldo's letters, thanks him for his promotion to the grade of Brigadier General, and also narrates some of the insurgent success in Nueva Ecija as well as informing him of the death of Lt. Colonel Tomas Tagunton and the fact that Lt. Colonel Natividad had surrendered to the Americans. In the second letter, written four days later, Lacuna states that he has just received orders from the Commanding General at Central Luzon directing him to send one of his best companies to El Dictator, Aguinaldo. This company the letter stated was under the command of Lazaro Segovia as Captain, with Lieut. Colonel Hilario Talplacido in Chief Command. The latter, so it was stated, which was true, was formerly an insurgent officer but since his capture by the Americans had been living quietly at Jaen, Nueva Ecija.

These letters, Lacuna is made to say, were sent by the east coast to avoid capture by Americans stationed at Bongabong, Pantabangan and Carranglan.

Secrecy in all respects was essential. As the expedition made ready for departure from Manila Harbor aboard the gunboat *Vicksburg*, duplicates of the dispatches carried by the first courier fell into the hands of American infantrymen. They indicated, Brown learned, "that Aguinaldo was making every effort to secure the desired reinforcements." Success for Funston's plot depended in the main upon the fully trusted Macabebes, who spoke the language of the Tagalogs, their hereditary foes.

Meanwhile, Brown had helped the people of San Isidro to celebrate George Washington's birthday anniversary with a colorful parade, sports, the bucking of horses, and a *baile*. On March 3, Funston ordered him to report to Manila before proceeding to Baler to make a field inspection of that coastal station.

The Inspector joined Funston and his secret expedition aboard the *Vicksburg* when it lifted anchor on the sixth. Brown, Captain H. C. Hodges of the Twenty-second Infantry, and Surgeon W. E. McPherson were going as an examining board to Baler. The two line officers also had in hand an imprisonment sentence of ninety-nine years for Lieutenant Colonel Novicio, insurgent. The Filipino had been tried by a military commission, for he had captured and buried alive one of a group of prisoners taken near Baler. The prisoners had been with a party under Lieutenant J. C. Gillmore of the United States Navy, formerly an aide to Shafter.

Of the officers and crew of the ship, none but Captain Barry knew the real aim of the venture until Manila faded from view and no contact could be had with parties ashore. Safely through San Bernardino Straits, the vessel tussled with rebellious seas, and on the ninth anchored in Antimonan harbor. Segismundo had warned that the gunboat should not approach shore points from which tidings could be carried to Aguinaldo. Funston, therefore, wanted native sailing boats, or *bancas,* for deception and to reduce laborious marching to a minimum. Lieutenant Mitchell tried to obtain some of the craft at Antimonan. He failed.

The *Vicksburg* cast anchor at Polillo Island in another attempt to procure boats. Three were bought, along with a supply of chickens, coconuts, and sacks of rice. When the ship steamed toward the northwest on the twelfth, a few men rode the newly purchased *bancas* at the end of towlines. Combing waves reduced the speed to six knots. But this did not suffice. One by one, the small boats slushed full. The doused occupants grabbed ropes and at last took to a boat lowered from the deck.

Though the misfortune brought regrets and fears to Funston and his men, the General harbored no thought of delaying his landing. At once he finished drafting the contents of the two invented letters from Lacuna to El Dictator. Segovia rewrote them in proper and flawless style.

At the same time, thousands of miles away, infusive Vice-President Roosevelt, wishing to gain more reward for his comrade, late of the First Cavalry, sent a letter to the Secretary of War.

Let me respectfully call your attention to the case of Captain William C. Brown, of the Regular Service, who has just distinguished himself by a particularly neat surprise of the bandit chief Lieutenant Colonel Tomas Tagunton. He not only possesses exceptional gallantry and energy, but he has made a study of his profession in matters of equipment, commissariat and the like which really fit him to render the utmost possible service to the Army. He served with, and afterwards under me at Santiago. He was an exceptionally fine officer.

Brown was not to know until years later that the letter was filed with his efficiency reports at the War Department.

Through clinging haze, pelting rain, and hammering seas, the *Vicksburg* knifed its way past Baler Point. In the first hour of the fourteenth, it anchored 400 yards from shore, twenty miles south of Casiguran. All lights hooded, the ship's boats dropped into an inky blackout. Eighty-nine men, including Funston, who now wore the uniform of a private, went ashore on the gloomy sound. Their boats snailed back to the ghostly vessel.

At 2:00 A. M., the *Vicksburg* swung around and, by noon, cast itself into Baler Bay. Only officers communicated with the shore. That Brown and Hodges had been sent to perform designated duties was an acceptable excuse for the presence of the gunboat. In the event that Funston, his officers, and Macabebes should realize success, arrangements had been made to have the *Vicksburg* appear off Palanan on March 25 to meet them and their prisoners.

The Major made a formal inspection of Baler's garrison and hospital. With Captain Barry, he sought out the mounds of the four men Gillmore had lost. Thoughtfully, the visitors returned to the ship to carry out preconceived plans. Brown wrote:

To deceive the natives further, the *Vicksburg* proceeded to Casiguran bay on March 18 (remaining until the 24th) to make inquiries concerning the five American prisoners who, according to the story concocted, had been carried off by insurgents and who, we knew the president of Casiguran would be told, were being carried off to the north. The town was a compactly built little village of about 120 houses, but deserted by its inhabitants, who had fled to the mountains when the *Vicksburg* had entered the harbor. The extreme timidity of the natives was such that it was only after the most persevering efforts and energetic display of white flags that we got in touch with them.

We finally succeeded, however, and by liberal presents of hard bread, accentuated by the strong curiosity of the native, in prevailing on three of them to come aboard where their inquisitiveness was the source of no little amusement. They were questioned closely by us to ascertain whether a company of insurgents with American prisoners had been seen, but they lied so cleverly that although we found subsequently that the expedition had for two days been guests of the town, no reply or hint that they let drop gave us the slightest information on that score.

Funston's land party, on the fifteenth, proceeded to Casiguran where, Brown was to learn, the town's vice-presidente "was called upon for a courier to precede the expedition up the coast and to announce to Aguinaldo the coming of the desired reinforcements, and to advise him that five American soldier prisoners captured on the Pantabangan-Baler trail would be brought along." Two days later, after the procurement of supplies and a dozen native packers and guides, the march to Palanan was resumed.

The plodders carried four days' rations—rice, corn, sweet potatoes, and a few pieces of carabao meat. A ninety-mile course at the edge of the sea and through a choking wilderness called for herculean efforts. "The trail, if such it could be called," averred Brown, "led for the most part along the beach alternately through soft sand and beds of boulders, the latter varying in size from a man's head to a house." The men defied slapping rains daily and they were forever fording streams. One they waded across seventy-four times. Mess kettles were unslung to do their bubbling twice a day, and the natives gathered devilfish, octopi, snails, crabs, and other foods to fill out the menu.

On the twenty-second, the expedition halted eight miles south of Palanan. Word was sent to Aguinaldo that rations had run out. In camp, the American officers, stripped of insignia, and giving the appearance of truly disheveled prisoners, made last-minute plans. So far they had played their part well, but doubts arose. Would someone sell them out at the final ditch? Would Aguinaldo catch on to the deception?

Brown chalked out the history-making events on the Palanan River.

The rations came the following morning together with instructions from Aguinaldo that the American prisoners should be left back at camp under guard and that the main party should proceed to Palanan. His idea in doing this was to avoid the possibility of recognition by the Americans and consequent disclosure of his whereabouts. To do this was to deprive the Macabebes of the leadership of the American officers (something to which they strenuously objected) at the most critical moment, and it was accordingly decided that they would follow a short distance in rear of the column.

When approaching the river, south of Palanan, eleven armed insurgents appeared stating that they had been sent to take charge of the American prisoners and thus permit the entire command to proceed to Palanan. Here Segovia showed his skill and quick wit by halting, getting them in conversation, treating them to cigarettes and asking questions about trails, etc. while a Macabebe sergeant and private slipped from the column and running at full speed back on the trail got the "prisoners" off in the jungle, from which place of concealment they had the satisfaction of seeing Aguinaldo's guard proceed past down the trail to the now deserted camp.

This danger past the "prisoners" hurried on after the main column. "Colonel" Hilario, his leiutenant Segovia, and the courier Cecilio and the other Tagalos preceded the column and on arrival were ushered into the presence of Aguinaldo and his staff (seven in all) in his office where they were cordially welcomed.

Meanwhile the main column crossed the river and as they arrived in town some 30 or 40 of the insurgent troops were drawn up in line to honor them with a salute.

To Segovia was entrusted the duty of giving the signal for attack and although engaged in conversation for only about twenty minutes, recounting real and imaginary insurgent successes, it seemed to Segovia an age. Finally, seeing that his men were practically all up, he excused himself on the plea of dismissing his company as it was much fatigued from marching. He gave the signal and Gregorio yelled, "All right, Macabebes, now's your time!" at which our people astounded the insurgents by pouring a hot volley at a range of about 25 yards into the command drawn up to receive them. Hilario at the first shot seized Aguinaldo about the waist, claiming him as a prisoner. The former at first thought the whole thing a joke. He was soon undeceived by noticing that his own troops were firing back.

Some of the Macabebes took charge of Colonel Santiago Barcelona, Aguinaldo's Treasurer, who being a remarkably bright and clever man is thought to be one of his chief advisers. Major Alhambra, shot in the face, bolted through a window and ran for the river; as he was not seen after jumping in it was thought that he was drowned.

Col. Simeon Villa, shot through the shoulder and finger by Segovia, rushed out of the room and down a trail pursued by the Macabebes who brought him back. Two insurgents were killed, the rest broke and ran, firing a few shots back at the Macabebes[,] eighteen of them throwing away their arms in their flight and abandoning 1000 rounds of ammunition. A native bandsman, who came in the line of fire, was hit five times and was brought by our people to Manila for surgical treatment. The only casualty on our side was a slight wound in the forehead received by one of the scouts.

The Macabebes in their excitement then opened fire on the office, and Hilario and Cecilio were obliged to hurry out to stop it, leaving Aguinaldo alone in the house.

As the firing commenced the officers, who were crossing the creek, hastened up and were able to get into the final part of the melee. General Funston found two Macabebes punching up the Treasurer with the muzzles of their Remingtons, yelling, "Are you Aguinaldo?" which Barcelona strenuously denied, pointing to the real owner of the name.

The Macabebes were wild with excitement and fairly hugged the officers in their joy over the successful outcome of weeks of labor, hardship and danger.

Valuable papers and about 1000 pesos in insurgent funds were captured in the office at Insurgent Headquarters.

Upon conversation later with Aguinaldo he wanted to know how Lacuna's signature had been secured, and when told it was forged and the letters made up to suit the conditions, Aguinaldo, who is ordinarily undemonstrative, threw up his hands in amazement, saying, "What can't you Americans do?" He not improperly considers himself somewhat of an expert in the strategems of war, but he had been beaten at his own game!

Order was soon restored, the Filipino flags over office and barracks hauled down, and a heavy guard—including one officer continually present—placed over the prisoners.

Natives, who had deserted the town when the fight blazed startlingly, soon drifted back to their habitations. On Monday morning, the twenty-fifth, they watched covertly the departure of Funston's party with the trio of distinguished prisoners and wounded bandsman. Palanan slipped back into its primitive niche.

The late guests came to the beach at noon. Elated Americans built two signal fires, then raised a bedsheet carried away from the village. Attached to a ten-foot pole, the sheet flapped back and forth.

Aguinaldo, lifting binoculars to his eyes, saw a ship on the horizon. El Dictator, grim and bewildered, waited silently.

Away from Turbulency

AN HOUR after noon Captain Barry rushed to the *Vicksburg's* cabin. Stridently, he elbowed Inspector Brown. He could discern a signal in the shape of a pillar of smoke rising from the beach, fifteen miles away. The personnel in the cabin hurriedly gained the bridge. Lieutenant A. T. Long, navigator—later an admiral—peered through the vessel's telescope. Brown raised his "16-power" binoculars to his sharply speculative eyes but he espied nothing unusual.

For a few moments he stood in puzzled anxiety,

. . . . and we were about to conclude that we were going in to the shore too soon and would "flush the game." Subsequently we learned that the column of smoke at first went up satisfactorily, but almost immediately a strong wind spread the smoke along the beach, making it invisible to us. Presently, however, I detected a small white patch on the beach and a moment later noticed that it moved, so I announced that some kind of signal could be seen.

We were slowly moving in toward the shore and one of the ship's signal men soon made out the message, "We have him," being wigwagged from shore, a bedsheet being used for a signal flag. The wild shouting and cheering with which this news was greeted and which rang through the gunboat from quarter deck to fo'castle, relieving the tense situation, can well be imagined, for we all realized that it presaged an early cessation of the guerrilla warfare which through mountains, swamps and rice paddies had waged for over a year and which was gradually filling both hospitals and cemeteries.

The anchor of the *Vicksburg* sank. Five small boats hit the water with a splash. Senior officers of the ship, Captain Barry in the lead, struck for shore to pick up the victors and the vanquished. Drenched by a pounding surf, plucky Aguinaldo, with Lieutenant Mitchell as his guard, came out in the first dinghy. Brown, ranking officer aboard the gunboat, jumped to the head of the gangway to welcome them. A camera in the hands of Captain Hodges clicked.

A picture given later to the Major showed the Filipino commander in a half-step, right hand raised to a light banded helmet, in the salute of an American soldier. From a wan face pitted by smallpox, dark eyes looked straight ahead and lips sealed themselves hermetically. A uniform of light material, hanging loosely and dripping, draped the slim, short figure. A white cloth or handkerchief protruded from a lower pocket on the right side of the sagging blouse. Binoculars hung from a strap which angled across the chest and over the right shoulder. Baggy trousers telescoped into knee-length leggings.

Lieutenant Mitchell, the brim of his campaign hat folded upward by a stiff breeze, presented the noted insurgent. The crew uncorked bottled emotion. There rose "cheers from lusty throats," Brown divulged, "doubtless contributing to the prisoner's discomfiture, for at that instant he appeared to me a somewhat 'scared hombre,' . . . . he probably had visions of joining some fifty or more of his subordinates then in exile at Guam, a fate which the average Filipino seemed to fear more than death itself."

As other dinghies scraped the crustaceous hull, all kodaks on the gunboat snapped. Aguinaldo recovered his composure when Assistant Paymaster Rogers conducted him to the cabin. He accepted dry clothes, puckering his lips at the mention of an early family reunion in Manila. His two companions fared well at the hands of the wardroom mess.

At five o'clock, the ship slid toward the open sea. Brown, thrilled with the events of the day, did not, however, record them in his diary. Instead, he became a seeker of autographs. Entered in the diary with pen and ink were two rippling signatures:

EMILIO AGUINALDO

SANTIAGO BARCELONA

Simeon Villa, ostensibly, still had a painful shoulder and finger. From Segovia and other members of the joyous expedition, Brown obtained the detailed acocunt of their exploits. Aguinaldo, he found, spoke Spanish hesitantly. His diary next day stated:

> Weather very windy & rough sea last night. Gen. Funston & Aguinaldo rather the worse for sea sickness. Many of the Maccabebes sea sick but generally through the day all have been on deck & resting, the sea being relatively smoothe in the afternoon.

On the return voyage, Brown wrote later, Aguinaldo "was assigned to the captain's mess with General Funston, Captain Hodges and myself, and at our second meal he laid aside his knife and fork in the midst of the repast and made a neat address, expressing his appreciation for the courteous treatment which had been accorded him by his captors. His quiet, dignified and courteous demeaner kept him on good terms with all of us."

A listless sea and warm breezes dissipated all sickness on the second day. The captives, basking on the sun-bathed deck hour after hour, smilingly faced the kodaks. Brown spent the entire day writing his account of Aguinaldo's capture. In the evening, Funston read it and, after additions, gave the story his approval.

The *Vicksburg*, at three o'clock in the morning of the twenty-eighth, dropped anchor in the northern part of Manila Bay. Ports were closed and lights extinguished. The vessel shunned other craft. It became desirable to postpone for several hours the breaking of the good news to the public.

At dawn, Funston, Mitchell, Lieutenant Glennon, ex-

executive officer of the gunboat, and Aguinaldo boarded the ship's steam launch.

Segovia gazed upon Aguinaldo for the last time. The Spaniard, a leading figure in Funston's expedition, was the next year to dedicate his book treating of the episode to the American commander. A few years later, Brown would receive an autographed copy from the author. Segovia's loyalty to the United States stood the test until his assassination in 1910 by long-hating enemies.

The launch, after leaving the *Vicksburg,* chugged up the Pasig River to Malacañan Palace, residence of the Governor General. MacArthur and his aides, awaiting breakfast, greeted Funston and his party in sunny cordiality. Mac-Arthur could not disguise his rippling pleasure in the meeting. He invited all to sit down and get on with the meal. Tactfully, and gradually, he chipped the granitic reserve of the insurgent leader who fidgeted in his chair and seemed to lack appetite. The Tagalog's face flashed a quick smile when he received assurance that his family soon would be invited to greet him.

Breakfast over, MacArthur sent off an official dispatch. It soon gave headlines to newspapers thousands of miles away. And, in spite of guarded secrecy, word that Aguinaldo was in the city spread like fire through the streets and paths of Manila.

Though more deaths would come in the rounding up of Filipinos reluctant to surrender, the citizenry and the armed forces celebrated in joy. The top figures in resistance had been dethroned. Safety from waste and death itself was in the offing. Shortly, Aguinaldo would be swearing his allegiance to the American government and asking, by proclamation, that his fellow countrymen follow only the path of peace and security. To himself came no humiliation.

In midafternoon, Funston returned to the *Vicksburg.* Her men had held target practice, and her captain had paid

an official visit to Admiral Remey of the Flagship *Brooklyn*.
Villa and Barcelona followed Aguinaldo to Malacañan. The
Macabebes and their leaders went ashore.

Then Funston and his fellow officers quit the vessel for
Manila. Brown, buying one of the screaming newspaper
extras, felt cheated in the purchase. The printed accounts
of Aguinaldo's capture, he decried, were "almost entirely
wrong as to details."

Next day he had his own account off a typewriter. But
it was not for publication. In due course it would be in the
mail on the desk of a man in high office in Washington.
In letters to his sisters and friends, the Inspector was more
reticent.

He called upon General Wheaton, and again picked up
the thread of routine, of drawing up reports and inspecting
commands. Meanwhile, rewards came to those who had
disturbed the peace of Palanan. Funston, thirty-six years
old, received appointment as a brigadier general in the
Regular Army, and commissions in the Regulars went to
the officers who accompanied him. Segovia accepted $1,500
in gold. Smaller amounts of money fell into the hands of
the loyal Tagalos and Macabebes.

Upon his own request, Brown was relieved from inspection duty April 20. He wished to rejoin his regiment, preparing to sail for home. San Isidro and its days of alarm
were left behind. The Major put his horse, Dick, and his
baggage aboard a car at San Fernando and rode to Manila.
A few days later he assumed the role of assistant mustering
officer of the Forty-second Infantry. The soldiers, awaiting transportation to San Francisco, fretted at Camp
Wallace but, their officers noted, they did a good job of
parading in line of masses. When General MacArthur reviewed the brigade and addressed it, responsive pride bubbled to the surface.

The day came when Dick was turned over to a new
owner for $150 in gold. His saddle went for eight dollars

more. Brown marked time and applied for a month's leave with permission to visit Japan. He would join his regiment when it arrived at Nagasaki. MacArthur and Wheaton approved. Before leaving Manila the Major made some friendly calls. He found Aguinaldo living happily with his family and his memories. He called on Captain O. J. Brown, with whom the days at West Point and on the Oregon trails were revived.

On the warm night of May 9, Brown set sail for Japan, one of the light-hearted travelers. In cool weather off Formosa he donned his blue clothes. After the five-day voyage to Nagasaki, there were rides on trains and by ricksha to and about the leading cities of the Nipponese. Shinto and Buddhist temples, curio shops, factories and salesrooms, main streets that were "really a succession of bazaars," industrial exhibitions, waterworks, acrobatic performances and wrestlings, botanical gardens and schools— all these the soldier from Denver saw and wrote about to two waiting sisters.

A soldier on a holiday, however, had to notice other things. On a parade ground in Tokyo, he eyed smart-drilling infantrymen and engineers. On an excursion out of Kobe, he paid heed to the marksmanship of naval vessels hurling shells at floating targets.

On June 2, he took quarters on the U. S. transport *Thomas* at Nagasaki and did some comparing. In spite of Oriental efficiency in factories and with guns, other efforts failed to smack of modernity. While a quartet of divers scraped the ship's bottom, a lengthy string of men and boys, women and girls coaled the ship in a drizzling rain. The transport required eighty-one tons of coal for each day of sailing. Not until the evening of the fourth, and after a visit to Japanese military barracks—"all very clean & neat"—did the Major and 1,911 other persons aboard the *Thomas* leave the harbor and its brood of foreign men-of-war.

Unaware that Brown was following in the wake of his regiment bound for San Francisco, the happy Vice-President sent from his home in Oyster Bay, on June 6, a letter which failed to catch the addressee at Camp Wallace.

I am in receipt of your letter of April 27th, and you are very good to have sent me that exceedingly interesting account of Aguinaldo's capture. I heartily wish you could have been with Funston, for it surely was an interesting experience. It was as good a bit of service as has been rendered of recent years.

In a day or two I hope to have Colonel Howze up here for the night and also Major General Young, and then I will know a little of the Philippines at first hand. I have seen two or three returned officers who formerly served under or with me. When you get back to the United States I very much wish I could see you.

With warm regards,
Faithfully yours,
THEODORE ROOSEVELT

The *Thomas* put in at Yokohama for more coal before plunging into the nineteen-day voyage across the Pacific. In the still hour of one o'clock in the morning of the twenty-sixth, Brown stepped onto the dock of the presidio. The Forty-second Infantry had arrived five days earlier and was to be mustered out on the morrow.

It was the end of the regimental trail. The Major of Volunteers again became Captain Brown of the Regular Army. He aided in mustering out the other units as orders came for him to join his First Cavalry troop at Fort Washakie. Before proceeding to Wyoming, however, the deserving officer was granted a two-months' leave.

The chief task of the army in the Philippines had been accomplished. The Islands were prepared to accept the guidance of a civil governor, William H. Taft. General Chaffee as military governor had fewer burdens than General MacArthur who, after having planted hundreds of posts and stations, returned to the United States and peace.

Helen and Grace had their brother with them two weeks

before he journeyed eastward, to Chicago, to Cleveland, and to the Nation's Capital. At the Army and Navy Club in Washington, he encountered active and inactive officers thirsting for more news about the Philippines. They pried in relays.

The Captain longed to see West Point. Colonel Albert L. Mills, Superintendent since '98, urged him to pay the visit. Fellow members of the Association of Graduates, grown mightier since its fathering by Robert Anderson in 1870, were carrying out vital principles. The Class of 1901, headed by the brilliant Douglas MacArthur, had graduated on February 18. On that day, too, Peter Smith Michie had been buried. The third of the three strong pillars—Thayer, Mahan, and Michie—had fallen to the ground.

Alumnus Brown arrived at the Academy on August 3. Once more he went to parade, to mess, to drill, and to the cadet hop. Though hazing had been wiped out that year, the Cadet Corps did not suffer for lack of virility. The dare-and-do atmosphere was not dank. Through Cullum Memorial Hall, almost new, the visitor sauntered for the first time. And he saw Professor Charles W. Larned, in his twenty-fifth year as head of the Drawing Department. Larned had, with colleagues, recommended the Academy's coat of arms, which had been adopted while the Spaniards quit Cuba.

Three days on the banks of the Hudson sufficed for the "old grad." He now yearned once more for the breezes smelling of Minnesota's verdant prairies. When he arrived in St. Peter, he yielded himself to the friends of by-gone years. The friends produced a horse and buggy, took the pilgrim down to the old Traverse place.

New tenants had settled down, but the memories which came flooding back over old trails were as fresh as the wind which swayed the grasses in the cemetery plot. The yesterdays were good, their peoples the same, their children the same. It was reward enough to be one of them—

the stuff of which America was made. Here the turbulent tide turned and flowed back.

Denver was reached again in mid-August. Two weeks more of rest in the shadow of the Rockies, then the soldier relinquished the remaining ten days of his leave. He felt ready for duty, lonesome for the throatiness of a bugle.

CHAPTER XXIV

Around the World

CAPTAIN BROWN again saluted Troop E, First Cavalry, at Fort Washakie on September 2. Four days later, words from the press and the telegraph shocked every hamlet in the country. President McKinley, while attending the Pan-American Exposition at Buffalo, New York, had been twice wounded with bullets fired by Leon Czolgosz, anarchist. When the citizen from Canton, Ohio, died on the fourteenth, the former commander of the Rough Riders became Commander-in-Chief of the nation's armed forces.

For the next decade and a half, there would be little need for Brown and his cavalrymen to keep bright the sword for battle. The Regular Army, nevertheless, was not to sink back into the pit of complacency that had been dug before the penetrating ray of a new century. Roosevelt, Secretary of War Root, and the men near them saw to that. Science, the Army and Government marched faster as the world moved faster. Old lands, close to or far from the shores of America, awoke to startling changes. Isolation was in retreat.

The Regular Army had more tasks to perform, more problems to solve. The training and the performance broadened. In the broadening, Brown endeavored to contribute his share toward obliterating the treadmill of garrison and the creaking of tactics. And there was always a chance of improving the soldier's equipment.

For several years, the troop leader had been trying out spur attachments for leggings. Letters patent had been granted him. In October, 1901, the Office of the Chief of Ordnance notified the inventor it was interested in the possibilities of manufacturing leggings with spurs permanently sewed on them. The Chief, however, emphatically did "not approve of the *detachable* spur." Cavalrymen— Brown notwithstanding—continued to wear spurs attached to their boots in the grand old manner.

With winter's clamps upon Fort Washakie, the Captain submitted his application to take the War College course. The indorsement by Major General Otis, Headquarters Department of the Lakes, at Chicago, dated December 23, was heartening.

> I was in charge of the Fort Leavenworth school during four years ending with 1884 while the school there was organized and developed. Captain Brown . . . . was a zealous and indefatigable worker, with quick mental perception, retentive memory and power to impart instruction, and hence became not only a student of high standing but an assistant instructor of ability. . . . .

It took a deal of time, however, to get the college in active operation. Early in the new year, the Second Squadron of the First Cavalry was advised to prepare for service in the Division of the Philippines. Transfer to Troop L at Taal, Province of Batangas, came on June 23 for Captain Brown, but he was to wait two more months before leaving Wyoming.

The army still faced stiff tasks in the Philippines in spite of the overthrow of dictatorial opposition. The whittling of insurgents went on in the provinces of Samar and Batangas. In April, Generals Bell and Frederick D. Grant had seized two perfidious leaders. The fanatically brave and wary Mohammedan Moros of Sulu maintained tougher and longer resistance. Upon their bulwarks dents were deepened by troops under the veteran Colonel Frank Baldwin and the younger, but equally audacious, Captain John J. Pershing. A stunning blow dealt at Byian, Minda-

nao, brought Baldwin the star of a brigadier general on
June 9.

Moros defied tamers, but President Roosevelt added cause
for celebrating July Fourth by declaring the insurrection
at an end. Filipinos rejoiced upon being pardoned and
given amnesty. A military governor was now unnecessary,
but the Medical Corps was sorely needed. In almost three
thousand fights the army had lost 330 officers. Enlisted men
killed, dead, or wounded numbered 6,746. Yet against
these casualties were to be set the thousands upon thousands of lives in the populace claimed by inundations of
Asiatic cholera. The Medical Corps, aided by other service
branches, had a huge hygienic task to perform.

While marking time at Fort Washakie, Brown entertained his sisters. Their school days, topped off with a trip
to Europe, were ended. Now they were women. Helen
was betrothed to Myron Jones of Denver. Brother Will
arranged for the wedding at the post July 23. On that day
he gave her in marriage and saw the happy couple depart
on their honeymoon. Grace, separated for the first time
from her sister, and not fully recovered from the accident
of three years before, broke into tears. Will prevailed upon
her to stay at his side. He promised to take her with him
to the Philippines.

Yet return to the isles of the Pacific, now that the smoke
of battle no longer hovered over latticed trails, did not
please the man who preferred to add to his knowledge that
which was offered the army at home. He was foregoing
the chance to participate in planned service schooling, the
maneuvers and demonstrations in field trials. And the
cavalry was to receive a new drill regulation that would be
followed in most part for decades ahead. Formed in single
rank, the troop became divided into platoons and squads,
tall men in the center and the shorter men on the flanks.
The major became drill leader of the squadron of four
troops.

Troop E left Fort Washakie for San Francisco on the last day of July and two weeks later sailed away. On August 20, Grace departed for Denver to prepare for the overseas tour. Brother Will did not relinquish command of the post until the twenty-fifth. Four days later, he walked with Grace, in San Francisco, on a shopping tour of the stores.

The date of that reunion marked a break-off in the Captain's diary-keeping. He surrendered the task, for many months, to his sister. She did not fail him. Her day-by-day entries teemed with satisfaction or dissatisfaction in that which was unfolded. The trip of 7000 miles across the Pacific, by way of Guam, was to be made aboard the *Sheridan,* one of four large transports.

The *Sheridan,* forsaking its dock September 1, halted at the Golden Gate in a fog too thick for safety. Of the hesitant start and days that followed Grace wrote more frankly than her brother might have advised:

. . . . Will being the ranking Capt. has the C. O.'s room. It is fine. . . . . I have a small stateroom to myself, ... I am on the upper deck with all the *Army* people, so am blessed, and am next to the toilet room. . . . .

SEPT. 2—We left at 4 A. M. and were over the "Bar" before I got up. Some of the passengers were sick this A. M., others went to the table but concluded that they didn't want any more breakfast. So far Will and I are all O. K. I am very glad that I have some warm clothing as it is very cold and cloudy. Will went to bed at 8 P. M. in order to get warm altho he had on his winter flannels. . . . .

SEPT. 3RD—. . . . Cloudy but sun is trying to shine. 286 miles today. I am so sorry that we are going north of Honolulu and won't stop there. . . . . There are 6 ladies on board who are going out to Manila to be married. They had to let it be known in order to get transportation. . . . .

SEPT. 5—Much warmer . . . . Oh I do wish that Helen was here. *Two* of the would-be brides are at our table. Have been helping Will get his reports out. . . . .

SEPT. 6—There was a card party on board but we didn't go. Will didn't want to. . . . . All unvaccinated people were vaccinated this A. M. I was exempt. . . . . The entertainment for tonight was boxing matches by several of the ship's hands, also a hospital steward used hypnotism on several men. . . . .

SEPT. 11—. . . . We went all around down in the hold. Saw where the cooking was done—kneeding the bread by machinery—bunks for the men, the hospital, cold storage room, storage room for canned goods, boxed goods, men's dining room, men's wash room &c, rooms of the ship's men, trunk room &c. . . . . Tomorrow we will skip Friday Sept. 12 and call the day Saturday the 13th. At 8:30 P. M. we crossed the date line and oh the blowing and screaching of the ship's whistle. It sounded like all the demons were turned loose at once. It screached & howled, then the searchlight was turned on. Then all of us who had never crossed the date line were called on the lower deck to do our stunt. . . . .

SEPT. 13—. . . . Will is getting discouraged about my learning Spanish. He says that I don't remember much of it and he is right. This evening we had a dance on Will's side of the ship. We invited some of the dancers to rest in his room between dances. We had a very pleasant time. Will danced twice. Then he wanted to go down to supper and I had to go down too. He seems to be having a very pleasant time visiting the officers. . . . .

SEPT. 17—. . . . Crossed the Tropic last night so are in the *Torrid* zone. . . . . We are so bothered with the ants on the beds and every place except on the table. . . . .

SEPT. 18—. . . . We expect to be in Guam on Saturday. I wore my blue & white dimity down to dinner tonight, the first time that I have been in a summer dress for dinner since we started. The other ladies didn't so I couldn't. . . . .

SEPT. 19—It is just 3 years ago today that I was hurt. . . . . Some one says that our corsets will mildew on us if we don't change twice a day and dry them out. . . . .

SEPT. 20—. . . . At 10 A. M. Guam was sighted but we have to go nearly around the island before we can land on account of the reefs. . . . . We expect to go [ashore] tomorrow. . . . .

SEPT. 21—. . . . We left the Sheridan . . . . went over in a native boat and with native oarsmen. Some of them were very pretty native boys. We were rowed over but they put up the sail to bring us back. . . . . Later we took on the Filipino prisoners, about 36 of them. Will took some pictures as they came aboard . . . . a woman came over with the Filipino men. The Justin, an American supply ship, is anchored near us & there is also a small Japanese ship near. Our coming is the event of the month. . . . . We took up the anchor at 6:15 P. M. and all seemed glad to be out in the open sea again. . . . .

SEPT. 24—. . . . We have the Filipino on board who had the bomb that they were going to throw at Gen. Lawton's funeral procession. He is one of the prisoners. Had a farewell dance at night. . . . .

SEPT. 26—. . . . Arrived in Manila all O. K. . . . . came over to the

Hotel Oriente. Run by an American. The rooms are great barns of things but we were very comfortable..... One of the waiters in the dining room looks like one of the World's Fair mummies in a nightgown. .... There are 3 waiters for every two people .... we are well waited on.....

SEPT. 27— .... Yesterday it rained very hard & a spout from the house opposite my window poured water on the sidewalk & men came there to take a bath. Just threw hat aside & washed as if they had no clothes on & rubbed themselves where they wanted themselves washed. Face, hair, arms & on down. It was all very funny. [A man] pulled out his trouser's front & rear & let the water run down inside..... Can hear the trumpet calls from my window in the hotel if there was not so much noise..... So much from chickens, men, women, children, carts &c.....

SEPT. 28— .... Saw the Market, it is the Filipino department store. .... Children with just a slip on like the Roman kids wore. One little boy's was open down the front, not fastened at all so showed the nude figure..... Wooden shoes on so many of the people, but most of the Filipinos go barefooted. A few wear hats. The more aristocratic ones dress in white suits, hats, shoes &c and look very clean..... The walls of the fences look so old & are moss covered. .... Swamps in the middle of the city.....

On October 1, when the farewell reception for General Chaffee was held, Captain Brown received appointment as regimental quartermaster, First Cavalry. He was to report at Batangas, in the province of the same name, relieving his old friend Captain Galbraith. Four days of stuffy riding on a small steamer brought Will and Grace to the town of 12,000 people. In the problem of finding a house and servants, Captain-Adjutant S. B. Arnold and his wife lent a helping hand.

They rented a dusty structure and called upon soldiers to repair and clean it. They took their time. Day-by-day troubles increased Grace's desire to return home. All day long she was "wringing wet." She fought ants and mosquitos. As she lay on her bunk at night she watched lizards dart after flies on the walls and ceiling. Now and then a lizard missed its aim and fell to the floor. Sterilized water was essential for washing and cooking, and the water had to be boiled for drinking. Dry-goods boxes served as dresser and wash stand. Walls were whitewashed.

Like others of the community, Grace fought off dengue or breakbone fever. Her nerves failed her for a time. She recovered, and prayed that the stay in the islands might be brief.

Will lent encouragement to her paramount desire, but duties crowded him. Troops occupied buildings in the town and more permanent quarters were necessary for the garrison. As commandant for a period, he bargained with natives to procure a site for the new post of Camp Mc-Grath. Accompanied by General Bell, commander of the Third Brigade, he had made an inspection of needed ground.

With the ushering in of the year 1903, Will broke the cheerful news to his homesick sister: soon they would be returning to the States, after a trip through Russia. Grace took heart and awaited Washington's pleasure. She took pride in the review of troops so efficiently staged by her brother when Governor General and Mrs. Taft paid a visit on January 20. General Jesse M. Lee also was there. Two days later he convened a board, with Brown as a member, to examine the site of the post and to pass upon the location of the buildings which were to care for regimental head-quarters and six troops of cavalry.

As week after week went by, Grace bowed less to pensive meditation. Inexplicably, she too was becoming a Regular. There were rides on lantern-lit bamboo rafts pulled by the carabao, the novelty of Filipino weddings and funerals, fiestas, religious processions and observances. Worries evaporated before the banter of people at the flag-bedecked Filipino theater where bamboo poles served as perches, tiered like chicken roosts. Will was elected a member of the fun-hatching Military Order of the Carabao of the Philippines, and that led to more balls and conviviality.

With the coming of June, the First Cavalry's tour of

the islands neared its ends. In the spirit of the troopers, Grace was ready to move on. She was certain not a word of *The General* would ever escape her, but she entered the bugle call in her diary.

> Don't you hear the General say,
> Strike your tents and march away?
> Don't you hear the General blow?
> Strike those tents and off we go.
> Strike tents! Strike tents!
> Pack 'em up, pack 'em up, pack 'em up.
> Strike tents! Strike tents!
> Strike tents!

Captain Brown still insisted that Grace be the chief diarist when on June 13 they left Manila as vacationists.

After two days of smooth sailing, their ship glided past a sea speckled with fishing junks and came to rest in the harbor of Hong Kong. Women and children paddled or steered the sampans for taking off baggage or freight. The streets of the city, where all distances were measured from the clock tower, boasted only a few horses. There were no cars. Coolies with chairs and jinrikishas shuttled incessantly.

The Browns procured rooms at the Waverly Hotel, and for the next nine days, Canton, Macao, and other intriguing places beckoned. Muzzle-loading cannon on junks gave a hint of defense against common piracy. At the British military establishment at Kowloon, the Captain found the Indians to be "tall & spare & fine looking fellows. Officers say they are very brave & make fine soldiers."

The couple went on to spend a day in Shanghai. Handsome slatted carriages with driver and footman vied with humble "rickshaw" and wheelbarrow. Along Nanking and Bubbling Well roads cavalryman Will noted that the singly driven Chinese ponies were larger than the Filipino ponies.

Yokohama was reached July 5. A tour of Japan, ancient empire whose people forever gazed upon mountains or sea, was compressed into two weeks. Seven more months of peace lay ahead of the Nipponese before war with Russia would begin, but behind a screen of normalcy forces were being polished for the struggle. From Nagasaki the Captain went out to Omura and visited the Forty-sixth Regiment of Japanese Infantry. He decided to write a note:

.... Regtl ordnance storeroom with supply of extra stores as arms, intrenching spades, pack saddles &c. Kept scrupulously neat & orderly. Have regtl Tailor & Shoe Shops where men detailed make their own clothes & shoes; men under arms marching simply at command look toward the officer saluted. Battalion marched past us at parade order & in fine shape. Kitchens not very neat. Barracks clean & neat, mattresses filled with straw which is changed monthly. Officers mess rather plain but with a good reception room. Men quartered by squads in large 2 story barracks—2 cos to the barrack. 1 Regt=12 cos=1500 men & 50 officers. Only 2 prisoners in guard house. Fish & rice seems to be about all men get—cooked in large kettles & sent to barracks to be eaten in dormitories.

The travelers steamed through the fog-shrouded Yellow Sea and burst out at Dalny, seaport of South Manchuria, on the twentieth. From the city to become known as Dairen they started the train ride of 5,810 miles to St. Petersburg. At frequent intervals they passed strings of box cars flying green and white guidons and crammed with Russian soldiers. Fifteen thousand of them were shifting eastward in spite of the fact that Czaristic circles had let it be widely thought that evacuation of Manchuria was at hand.

Barracks of stone rose at various points along the line. In Kharbine, inhabited by 6,000 Chinese, houses were being built for 46,000 people, ostensibly the Czar's. The Captain felt more deeply impressed by Russia's colossal strides when he visited a strong military station near Irkutsk. The garrison, extending warm courtesies, boasted six regiments, one of which was cavalry.

Once past forested and mountainous regions, the passengers glided through a land of oil wells and grain fields unconfined by fences. Few harvesters had as yet replaced

scythe, sickle, and cradle. Grace, irked by the inconveniences of the train and the difficulties of the language, had
become tired. Will, she wrote, scolded her for objecting to
"those things & said that I ought not to have come on the
trip if I didn't want to put up with these things." The
army veteran was chastising the recruit.

Fifteen days after leaving Dalny, they viewed the Krem-
lin in Moscow. They halted briefly at St. Petersburg. More
pastoral was the trip in August through the Scandinavian
countries, Germany, France, England, and Scotland.

In the land of the Scots, their forbears, the touring
Browns absorbed that which Edinburgh prized. Grace
thrilled to a ride in an automobile, stopping at the house of
Knox, at the place where Scott was born, and at the steps
of the house where Burns had lived. History lay open at its
brightest pages. Then a scanning of Glasgow and the
Americans wished to return to a land that was new.

On the evening of September 6, when they landed in
New York City, Grace had only one thought: *"Must see
Helen,"* she underscored. Next day Will bought her ticket
to Denver. He helped her aboard a sleeper of the East Shore
Railroad, reminded her that she would be passing West
Point within the hour.

A farewell kiss, and the soldier was one with the Army
again.

CHAPTER XXV

Field Maneuvers and Rifle Range

BEFORE departing for Washington to report to the Adjutant General, Captain Brown received an invitation from Oyster Bay. Signed by the White House Secretary, William Loeb, Jr., the telegraphic message stated:

THE PRESIDENT WOULD BE GLAD TO HAVE YOU TAKE LUNCH WITH HIM ON SATURDAY SEPT NINETEENTH AT ONE O'CLOCK TAKE TRAIN LEAVING LONG ISLAND CITY ELEVEN ARRIVING HERE TWELVE TWENTY

Roosevelt, thirsty for information on the Russo-Jap crisis, listened to a firsthand report of the military situation in Manchuria and Siberia as seen through the eyes of his guest. For the benefit of the casual tourist, a description of the journey appeared in the November issue of Cook's *Traveler's Gazette.*

In the War Department at Washington, Brown witnessed the happy results of hypodermics and the applications which the military had received. The Dick Bill, in spite of weaknesses, had swung the militia of the States toward training of a National Guard that would find closer kinship and responsibility with the Regular Army. Belated attention was being paid to the writings of Upton. Thanks to Secretary Root, the former West Point cadet could read the published *Military Policy of the United States* as penned by his former commandant. A cornerstone had been set for the War College building. General S. M. B. Young was serving as its first chief of staff. A chief of artillery had been added to the General Staff.

The first national rifle contest, at Sea Girt, New Jersey, had uncovered surprises. The New York National Guard's team took first prize, the army placed fifth, and the marines won the last, or sixth, prize. Intensive practice on the firing range gave impetus to arms improvement. Regular Army officers, detailed at militia camps, obtained hearty co-operation in instruction.

War Department orders having been issued for field maneuvers at West Point, Kentucky, and Fort Riley, Kansas, the returned cavalryman requested that he be placed on duty status and permitted to attend them. The Chief of Staff approved. On September 24, Brown reported to Brigadier General Kobbé, in command of Headquarters First Brigade, Maneuver Division, in Kentucky. The Captain became the brigade's Adjutant General.

When Kobbé commanded the division of four brigades for several days, his adjutant was obliged to prepare and superintend the formation of the division for review. Thousands of soldiers, paying heed only to commands of small unit leaders, grasped little of complex exercises. A division in review spelled color and precision of movement. Watches timed accurately, brigades formed on the ground at five-minute intervals. The orders, in part, read:

II. Brigades will form in order of their numbers from right to left; Divisional Artillery and Cavalry in second line, left of the Artillery in rear of left of 2nd Brigade. Cavalry on left of Artillery, right in rear of right of 3rd Brigade.

IV. The line will be formed and so reported to the Commanding General of the Review Division, after which orders for passing in review will be sent to the Commanding Officer of the 1st Brigade only, the other Brigades conforming successively to the movements.

V. Bands in each Brigade may be consolidated. Only the band on the right of each Brigade will play as the reviewing officer approaches and passes along its front.

In passing in review only the band at the head of the Brigade will play and wheel out of line. In passing in review as the head of each Brigade arrives at 100 yards from the reviewing stand the band at its head will again begin playing if not already playing and the band or bands of the next succeeding brigade cease playing.

The spectacle went off well. Kobbé commended the beaming adjutant for his all-round efficiency and "indispensable value."

Brown moved on to Fort Riley, and after mid-October joined the headquarters staff of the Fourth (Kansas) Brigade, Maneuver Division. He served as Acting Inspector General. From Brigadier General J. W. T. Hughes, Kansas National Guard, he won praise for "extreme patience," "exceeding good judgment," and "gentlemanly conduct."

The Captain soon was to gain more substantial reward in the replacement of his two bars with the oak leaf of gold. On his way to take station at Fort Clark, Texas, he stopped at Fort Sam Houston to be examined as to qualifications for promotion.

He reported for duty at the headquarters of the First Cavalry at Fort Clark, Colonel Martin B. Hughes commanding, November 23. To be prepared for elevation, the Captain was assigned to Troop M.

In conformity with a general order of January 26, 1904, issued by General Chaffee, who in the second week of the new year had succeeded Young as Chief of Staff, arrangements were made for testing out the improved Springfield rifle, Model 1903, at Fort Clark. An experimental range or camp was established for firing the new magazine rifle which was to replace the Krag. It was thought best, emphasized Brown, "to have it thoroughly tested at all ranges from 100 to 2,000 yards by a series of experimental firings to obtain desired exterior ballistic data, particularly drift up to 2,000 yards and the variation due to a mile of wind normal to the plane of fire."

Captain Clarence C. Williams, on recommendation of Major General William Crozier, Chief of Ordnance, was sent to oversee the range. Williams, summoned elsewhere late in February, left Captain Brown in complete charge of the task. A coterie of the Army's best riflemen assisted him. No books set forth methods to be pursued. Brown's ingenuity must be the guiding factor.

As rifles barked on the Texas plain, the Army followed intensely the course of the Russo-Japanese War which had begun February 6. In its all-out endeavor to push Russia back over the Amur River in northern Manchuria, Japan was revealing its strength as a first-rate military and naval power. In the Philippines, American forces had dwindled to about fifteen thousand, many of them still doggedly at the heels of Moros. Money was allotted for the permanent defense of the islands.

To improve and provide instructors for the Army War College, officers were being sent to the Army Staff College at Fort Leavenworth. A major general was put in charge of each of five grand territorial divisions, with brigadier generals heading the departments. A military secretary took over the office of Adjutant General. Across the country regulars and militia joined successfully in maneuvers. Elements of battle invoked realism.

Brown's advancement to the rank of Major, Third Cavalry, came on July 28. Not until August 11 did he announce completion of the firing tests and abandonment of the camp at the experimental range. He had secured important ballistic data. On his recommendation, two improvements in the rear sight were made: the intervals of range on the leaf of the rear sight were subdivided to indicate twenty-five yards; notches previously used on the sight leaf were replaced by more definite serrations.

The Chief of Ordnance, pleased with the results obtained, concluded that the firings "showed that the barrel of the new rifle is, as was anticipated, more rapidly eroded and worn than those of any previous model.

"The erosion of the bore, which occurs principally at the seat of the bullet, is due to the chemical and mechanical action of the gases emerging from the cartridge shell at a high temperature and under a pressure of about 49,000 pounds per square inch. Experiments are being made for the purpose of obtaining, if possible, a barrel steel which will more effectively resist this action of the powder gases. Experience so far shows that erosion increases with the percentage of carbon contained in the steel, and also in the case of nickel steel, with the percentage of nickel. The erosion in barrels made of nickel steel is greater than in those of simple carbon steel."

Gradually, improvements were to evolve for the rifle of bolt action, demanding uniform smokeless powder for its ammunition. Increased power, accuracy, speed, and ease of handling guaranteed the weapon's effectiveness.

Experimentation ended, Major Brown accepted leave and journeyed to the country's Capital. General Chaffee directed him to proceed to Manassas, Virginia, there to report to General Corbin for assignment to duty in maneuvers. At the end of August, detailed as observer of damages, he was issued a horse and given a permanent tent. Day after day, heat notwithstanding, the Major rode out upon the terrain where the second battle of Bull Run had been fought. Tensely, he watched 5,000 regulars and 21,-000 national guardsmen tackle the problems that would be met in actual combat.

Generals of the future learned the hard way. First Lieutenant Ben Lear was laying a puissant foundation for a notable career as Adjutant of the Fifteenth Cavalry.

The small army stepped lively despite the need of an increase in pay. Living on pay boosted little since the latter years of the 1860's did not entice men from civil life. The army had fallen off to half the strength authorized. Yet "fours right" was forgotten. New drill regulation made "squads right" familiar in a company split into two platoons.

The cavalryman gave up his horse and returned to Washington. With leave in September, he left for New York.

He visited the Springfield Armory before turning westward to join the crowds at the St. Louis Exposition. Then he set out for his new regiment, the Third Cavalry, at Fort Assiniboine.

He reached the northern Montana post in the closing days of November, and did not need to be told that winters there had not lost their bite. After an absence of thirteen years he noted that more people had come to the Treasure State to defy ice and snow, to cut shorter the distance between ranches and hamlets and cities. Men who relied on irrigation ditches vied with men who counted their sheep or horses or cattle by thousands.

No longer did wether bands of from five thousand to seventy-five hundred drift as a cloud on a grazing front which had to be ten to forty miles in width. Drivers had forsaken the broad trails when the new century had come, when Montana had more than six million sheep. Men who had painstakingly planned sheep drives welcomed the double-decked railroad cars. Fewer were the worries—and losses.

Aside from practice marches, the usual garrison duty prevailed at the fort. News of unusual interest stirred the command in January, 1905. On the second day of the new year, Port Arthur had been surrendered to the Japanese.

Brown had prepared a professional article on the experimental work done with the Springfield rifle. Proofs for revision had been sent him, and these he sent with a letter, asking suggestions, to Captain T. C. Dickson, Office of Chief of Ordnance. Another letter, also requesting criticism, went to the Springfield Armory.

Dickson, who had adapted the rear sight to the service rifle with some minor modifications, in his answer of February 1, held the opinion that the article was the best "that has yet been written on the new arm and I congratulate you most heartily upon it." In supplying fresh information he asserted that "the adoption of the new rifle decreases the load carried by the infantryman 1½ pounds." The cylindrical ramrod type of bayonet had been carried on rifles in the war against Spain. Revealing was the half of Dickson's letter explaining how the bayonet matter had developed importance:

In regard to the ramrod bayonet all work on the manufacture of the present design has been suspended; several experimental designs have been prepared and submitted to the General Staff, which body, it is understood, will determine what, if any, changes in the present design should be made. I am inclined to believe that some form of knife bayonet will be adopted, and I am decidedly of the opinion that no matter what action is taken many officers will continue to express dissatisfaction with it. Personally I believe that the present bayonet should be strengthened and made slightly longer which, in my opinion, would prove entirely satisfactory under all conditions of service in which our Army is liable to be engaged. It appears that some of the officers who witnessed the operations between the Japanese and Russians in Manchuria are strongly of the opinion that the bayonet will hereafter be one of the most important weapons of the soldier. That is hard to believe in the face of the increased rate of fire of magazine rifles, machine guns and all kinds of field artillery. Perhaps these officers are correct and perhaps the Army is to again suffer from snap judgment.

A sufficient number of the new rifles to equip all troops in the Philippines, China and Alaska were on board cars when the agitation in regard to the bayonet was renewed and all issues of the new arm have been suspended until the bayonet question is settled. This action is to be very much regretted and will probably delay equipping of the Army until next Fall.

Among helpful hints in the answer from the Springfield Armory was the pertinent paragraph reading:

It is contrary to the practice of the Ordnance Department to refer to the present models of rifle and carbine as the "Krag." They are known officially as the U. S. Magazine Rifle, Model of 1898 and the U. S. Carbine, Model of 1899.

The article, as revised by Major Brown, appeared in the May-June issue of the *Journal of Military Service Institu-*

tion. The attention it attracted in military circles was not confined to those of the Western Hemisphere.

On June 17, the small arms expert and the army lost a loyal friend and tireless worker. Colonel Wagner, towering strategist, died at Asheville, North Carolina, while efforts were put forth to appoint him a brigadier general. The body was taken to Washington, then escorted to Arlington by troopers of the Thirteenth Cavalry. The fruits of Wagner's labors did not cease to be gathered. Before the summer waned, the Army Signal School, for instruction of officers, took its first steps at Fort Leavenworth.

At Portsmouth, New Hampshire, Russia and Japan signed their peace treaty on September 5. And while the ink was drying, the idea that the Orient should be for the use of Orientals to the exclusion of Occidentals set itself more deeply in the minds of the striding Nipponese. Meanwhile, Moros who would one day hurl themselves against invading Japanese, continued to prick the side of American soldiers, Filipino scouts, and constabulary.

Except for the thrill of watching spouting geysers when assigned to court-martial duty at Fort Yellowstone, Wyoming, Brown encountered little excitement in the West. A taste of fire-fighting in near-by mountains and occasional field exercises provided the only breaks in routine. Again he had bored into a study of emergency rations and the October *Infantry Journal* carried his article, "A Plea for the Emergency Ration."

The regiment of cavalry then was ordered to the Philippines. Before its departure, the Major procured a leave for November. On his itinerary, in and out of Denver, were the familiar visits across country to the Atlantic. When he faced westward he traveled to Chicago with General Bell. The folks in Denver saw him for a few days before he went on to San Francisco. He dined with General Funston and his family, and they thought of a "Yuletide package"—Aguinaldo.

Ten days before Christmas, ten troops of the Third Cavalry slipped outward on the transport *Buford*. Major Brown once more looked forward eagerly to sunsets in other climes.

Four months hence, San Francisco, as he had come to know it, would totter before earthquake and fire. To Funston would fall the task of leadership. To the presidio and Fort Mason would stream homeless thousands seeking refuge and care.

CHAPTER XXVI

To Australasia for Remounts

THE *Buford* dropped anchor inside the Manila break-water on January 15, 1906. Next day the regiment, led by Colonel Dorst, established itself at Camp Stotsenburg, Pampanga. The cavalrymen fraternized readily with news-devouring troopers. Major Brown chatted often with a young officer, some day to be met in France on Pershing's staff. He was Captain George Van Horn Moseley, Fifth Cavalry, adjutant to General Lee at camp headquarters.

In due course the Major noted the beneficial changes wrought in the islands and the people. The days which Taft had spent in governorship had lent greater understanding in his role as Secretary of War for the past two years. To the command of the Philippines Division had come Major General Wood, anxious to sweep aside the obstacles which the new Chief of Staff, General Bates, had found to be all too plaguing.

The Filipino rejoiced in making known his pro-American sentiments. For Americans liked to solve problems.

The Third Cavalry faced an acute need for remounts. Colonel Dorst, looking to Australia as the most convenient market, consulted Brown. At the end of July, the Major wrote the division commander:

Inviting attention to the recent letter from the Commanding Officer, 3rd Cavalry, setting forth the necessity for supplying the regiment with several hundred new horses, and suggesting Australia as a possible market where they could be obtained cheaper than in the United States, I have the honor to state that I should like to visit Australia and some of the East Indian Islands to the north of there and should be glad to undertake to investigate the subject of the feasibility of securing horses from that quarter.

The contemplated journey to be made at my own expense and to entail no claim for mileage. I request however that my status while absent be that of duty[,] the journey being regarded as being "for the convenience of the Government" and so ordered. . . . .

Late in August, General Wood forwarded the letter, with his indorsement, to the Military Secretary of the War Department. It received the favorable attention of Major General Bell, who had begun a four-year term as Chief of Staff. A cable authorizing the visit was received at Manila October 5. Wood allowed Brown three months—yet needing an extension of some weeks—to complete the duty.

The Major left Manila on the twenty-first, on a steamer of 1,400 tons, with space for fifty head of stock on her deck. A week later, the ship hesitated at Port Darwin, northern Australian town boasting 200 whites, a sprinkling of Chinese and aborigines, a cable station, and botanical gardens. During sultry days and nights, the journey continued across the Gulf of Carpentaria, past Thursday Island, into the Coral Sea. Townsville, Queensland, dotted with fruit-laden mango trees, was reached the third day in November.

The cavalryman who "knew his horses" began to pry into the horse market from all angles. Sales and auctions, horse ranches and breeding stations demanded attendance. Interviews with agents, dealers, and buyers as to the cost of horses had to be gained. Steamship agents were to be queried about transportation rates. When Brown left Townsville to proceed westward 368 miles to Winton, he had reason: " . . . . After looking over their very fair cab horses which they regard very highly I doubt whether they have many horses about here such as we want."

The vast and arid interior offered remounts and more. Wild turkeys raced through the land of sheep, cattle, and horses. Ranchers used a sort of horse collar canteen for carrying water. Coolers of coarse flax kept the water at about seventy-five degrees when the thermometer read forty degrees higher. Thirsty "boss" horses dug deeply in the ground to get a first drink of water, then others came to take their turn.

After swinging into action with his camera, the Major boarded a stage for Longreach. Thousands of horses and many fine stallions had gone to the Japanese. The Yankee spoke for horses a year ahead. Back to the coast by rail, he obtained figures on shipping them to Manila from Rockhampton and Brisbane. At Toowoomba and Sydney, hundreds of horses were being sold at auction. Few of them, the observer quipped, "I would consider fit for our service."

At the end of November, the Major sailed for New Zealand to comb both islands. At Auckland he learned why the country had neither strikes nor beggars. Prosperity reigned. The traveler went south to Wellington, then to Christchurch, attending a full-blooming exposition and a contest in field firing staged by New Zealand troops. "Can get horses here," he noted, "but it will take time as they have to be picked up 1 to 5 on a farm."

Further search led to Dunedin, Invercargill, and Bluff. A steamer was taken to Hobart, Tasmania. Men of war rested in the bay. On the streets, three days before Christmas, the cavalryman fought for room to walk among sailors and jostling purchasers of gifts. He journeyed on to Launceston. There, as at Christchurch, he sought out a target range, the homemade sliding targets of iron evoking his admiration and envy. The firing methods were ahead of those of his own army. Especially did he ponder the merits of the Barr and Stroud self-contained base range-finder.

After a landing at Melbourne and a glimpse of the Victoria Racing Club course, he hurried to Sydney. Horse flesh was the lure. On New Year's Day, 1907, excitement ruled at the sixteen-hurdle steeplechase race. Crammed into two more weeks was a deeper investigation of the remount prospects. Then the visitor sailed for Manila. His steamer, *Orange Branch*, plowed the seas sluggishly, gorged with 500 tons of frozen meats and 15,000 railroad ties for the Philippines.

Chronic boiler and engine troubles made the ship a frequent victim of strong currents. While the captain, his three mates, chief engineer, and Japanese carpenter fretted with multiple worries, the complacent Chinese sailors gleefully hooked and hauled in flying fish and shark. Opposite the southern tip of Mindanao the second week in February, Brown thought it wise to sketch in his diary the ship's route and drift. Howling winds, backlash of a typhoon, had swooped down!

The next week all hands gained a short rest in the harbor of Cebu. Brown did some cabling. Not until the twenty-third did the *Orange Branch* reach Manila. The cost of keeping the 500 tons of beef refrigerated totaled forty dollars a day.

At last the Major reported in person to General Wood and handed him his report. He also addressed himself to an adjutant general again. The title of Military Secretary had vanished from the army. Further discussions were held with staff officers at Fort McKinley. The report explained in detail that suitable remounts could be had for $125, delivered on ship, and that $35 more would defray the cost of transportation, feed, and attendance. Highly descriptive was Brown's professional article, "Australian Horses for the Philippines," soon appearing in the *Cavalry Journal*.

After reporting to Colonel Dorst, the cavalryman went with his Third Squadron some twenty miles north of Camp Stotsenburg for thorough drill and instruction in field work. Observations gained in New Zealand and Tasmania were put into practice. Though novel, they proved worthwhile. Troopers learned new tricks in how to span creeks and rivers. A dam built across the Bangot River provided a swimming hole at a sun-pierced camp.

On his return to regimental headquarters, rivalry in firing advanced keenly, the Major himself showing what could be done with his telescopic sight on the Springfield rifle. He tried it out at night, at a range of 1,000 yards, with a candle placed at center of the bull's-eye. Cross hairs of the sight illuminated by a lighted string, the firing was done from a stand with a muzzle rest. A telling score of thirty-three out of forty shots resulted.

The army, however, did not swallow all of Brown. He kept in contact with friends and kin, among them being a cousin of New York, rising to prominence in educational circles. The cousin's name crept into the diary entry of April 29: "Sent P. O. Money Order No. 7146 for $25 to Dr. Sam'l McCune Lindsay for Life Membership in Child Labor Prevention Society."

The Major's report on the novel features introduced in the field work, when submitted to the division commander, elicited an encouraging reply from the aide:

> General Wood read with much pleasure your report, herewith inclosed, and says he would be very glad to have an extra copy for file, which can be used as a basis for experiments further to be made throughout the Division.
>
> He is glad to see you take the initiative in this matter and render such interesting reports on the results.
>
> He used your telescopic sight with much pleasure and great success on the range this A. M.

In his "Appliances for Crossing Streams," published shortly in the *Cavalry Journal*, Brown gave new ideas to replace the old.

The division commander summoned him to Manila in mid-July to disclose that, authority having been received to buy 300 horses in Australia, he desired the Major to accept the detail. Brown had no inclination to refuse. Veterinarian C. D. McMurdo, Tenth Cavalry, and a clerk selected from the Quartermaster's Department at large were to accompany him. The sum of $50,000 was provided, in a hampering manner, a deposit to Brown's credit with the Assistant Treasurer of the United States, New York. Fortunately, the Australian bankers did not quibble.

General Wood wanted horses averaging 15.3 hands high. Any under that would have to be "good." Preference was for geldings, mares to fill in no more than a fourth of the number.

Brown arrived at Brisbane on August 14 and opened an office. He found the American custom of advertising and the buying in of mounts on contracts let to the lowest bidder somewhat of an obstacle. "The Australians," he wrote, "were so desirous of establishing commercial relations with us that, although strenuously objecting to our business methods, a bid was received for 50 remounts far out in the 'bush' at 23 pounds sterling each. What practically amounted to open market purchases or informal contracts were from that time on resorted to."

Brown picked his horses carefully, few being under three years of age, none over seven. They were capable of trotting briskly and steadily. Most of them were in the age bracket of four to six years, and brown, black, bay, or sorrel in color. A sound chestnut was passable. Light-colored horses, not blending with terrain, the cavalry had learned to spurn.

The Descriptive Card of Public Animals Form proved unsatisfactory. It provided no front view of the horse, though on no other part of the body would a greater variety and more certain identifying marks appear than on a horse's face. Brown had a suitable cut made and used it to print the front view on the blanks issued by the War Department. The addition, adopted hastily by the Department, was retained in years following.

The purchasing of remounts, the Major discovered, presented not half the problem as the task of keeping his clerk sober. In and out of the hospital, week after week, went the clerk. His work and debts had to be assumed by the officer, and patience ran out in September. The irresponsible fellow was shipped home, third class. He left his watch with the "boss," who was out of pocket $170. From his few dependable clerks in Manila, the quartermaster sent out a replacement with a greater degree of stability.

The first lot of horses was shipped early in October. A few weeks later Brown learned that the remounts were highly acceptable in Manila. He received a cable advising him to buy 300 more than originally authorized. At the close of the year, he had bought and shipped half the total asked. Queensland provided all but twenty-five of the animals.

On the first day of 1908, an additional fund of $49,000 came to complete the dealings. The work on the range, from sunrise to sunset, proved a difficult chore. On a hot day, 400 horses were rounded up and sorted, yet Brown obtained only thirty-five "possibles."

The Yankee cavalryman had covered much of Australia when his beating of the bush and the hunt for a few trained polo ponies came to an end. The last 125 of 600 horses were loaded on steamer at Townsville. Well provided with compressed forage, they had Brown's attendance upon starting for Manila on April 3. Aided by a following breeze and fair weather, the ship *Gulf of Venice* took only twelve days to propel itself to glistening Manila Bay.

The Third Cavalry had returned to the States. Pershing, wearing a star, commanded the Department of Luzon. His predecessor, the long-serving Major General John F. Weston, moved into Division Headquarters to replace Wood.

Tests for physical fitness were being conducted for all field officers, and Brown proved himself still a tough horseman. The quickened pace which the army now demanded of its officers and men, however, was accompanied by an encouraging readjustment of pay. Brown's yearly salary, boosted to $3,000, came to half that paid a brigadier general.

In the swiftly rising, inflexible Pershing the veteran
Major noted qualities of tested steel as he spent a few
weeks settling accounts and writing reports. Trade relations with Australia had been accelerated by the cavalryman with a keen eye for bartering. The remounts were
purchased at an average price of $100 each. Freight,
food, and attendance cost $36 a head additional. The 600
were $20,000 cheaper than a like number bought in and
shipped from the United States.

The British and Dutch obtained a large number of their
horses in Australia. Brown, wishing to learn how the animals were handled before being placed in the ranks, procured a two-months' leave to visit Java and India. Then
he could return to his regiment in Texas by way of Europe.
The trip, for the convenience of the government, also
would permit observation of changes introduced by Lord
Kitchener in the instruction and training of the active
army, native troops, and equipment.

Hurriedly, Brown wound up his affairs in Manila. After
intermittent haggling with the inebriated clerk sent back
from Australia, the man's debt was canceled in exchange
for $100. On May 12 began the journey, with a stop at
Singapore. In Batavia, the eye rested on "well-metaled
streets, steam-train system, canals running lengthwise
through the town which furnish bathing, washing & boating facilities for the natives." Everyone had "a deep front
porch."

The United States consul arranged for a call on the
commanding general, leading to inspection of a squadron
and a veterinary hospital. Arresting was the custom of
native troops, privileged to have "soldiers' women" living
in their barracks. More agreeable to the bachelor-cavalry-
man was the mounting of running horses at the remount
depot at Padalarang. Side trips gave views of highly cultivated rice terraces.

Presentation to His Excellency the Governor General of

Java at his summer residence at Buitenzorg brought more extended courtesies to the American. At Djokjakarta he went through the barracks of native troops and "married (?) men's quarters." A better lure was "a white guard (mounted) of about 50 men on excellent horses" in the grounds of a swarthy sultan who also boasted one wife and forty concubines, pits for cock fighting, and a school for the children. Well-groomed and sleek Australian horses were inspected at the cavalry garrison in Salatiga, where three squadrons displayed the pride of Java.

On June 8, Brown was back at Singapore for a day, then on to Panang and to Colombo, Ceylon. On the sixteenth, a night boat landed him at Tuticorin, India, in the land teeming with sects, castes, and tribes. The tourist on the train had his electric fan, shower bath, diner, and compartment bed—if he carried his own bedding—but he gauged the speed of the masses by the large and high-cover two-wheel cattle carts. He measured their prosperity by spindle-legged men, coolies naked except for a "G" string, women and children working on a rock pile.

At Madras, Calcutta, and Darjeeling, the soldier out of America's West stopped to listen to the heavy breathing of Mother India. At Benares he did more than that. He watched the Eighteenth Native Infantry at drill, and, in their equipment, noted the up-to-date aluminum cooking kit alongside an experimental lantern for night marching made from an old oil can.

Lucknow and its military atmosphere held him for a week. Royal Dragoons, native lancers and infantrymen, and medical officers unfolded surprises for the visitor. He found tablets for sterilizing water, while discovering that regimental commanders of cavalry had an allowance of money to forage their troops! Furthermore, wrote the guest, "These people study Henderson's Stonewall Jackson assiduously."

Agra and Delhi, with their musty forts, sheep of mon-

strous tail, and burden-bearing camels, were quickly left
behind for full days at the busy remount depots of Sahar-
anpur and Abmednagar. At the latter place Brown met "a
Mr. Churchill." More Australian horses were found in
cavalry stables at Bombay, but another breed of animals
compelled the special attention of the diarist. He looked
long and wrote briefly.

> Went out to the Arab Stables & saw about 100 Arab stallions. The
> characteristic of the Arab is gentle, clean limbs, square rump, small trim
> hoofs & an inclination to be dish faced. Height 13.3.

In mid-July the Major boarded the steamer *Castalia* and
sailed for Suez. Ten days later, in the Red Sea, came his
turn to entertain fellow passengers. He should have related
a first-hand hair-raising experience of his colorful career.
Instead, he talked more than an hour on how Funston captured Aguinaldo.

When Suez and the fertile Valley of the Nile had been
surveyed, the travel-worn officer journeyed to Naples.
There he toiled up the slopes of Vesuvius and lingered to
study the half-uncovered city of Pompeii. Hastily, he
passed on to Rome, to Paris, to London, to Liverpool.

Aboard the *Lusitania* in the mean of August, the absentee
of the United States Army sailed for home. His luggage
bulged with reports on horses, canteens, and whatnot—a
miscellany Lord Kitchener's lancers could not easily have
deflated.

CHAPTER XXVII

War College and South America

IN WASHINGTON, August 23, Major Brown was directed to spend the next few weeks on duty assigned by Chief of Staff Bell. Reports of the ventures in Java and India were prepared for publication in the *Cavalry Journal*. Brown's fondness for humor met rebuff when the part relating to concubines in Java succumbed to blue penciling.

Bell, nevertheless, stood ready to recommend the writer for the War College. A friendship was cemented with General William W. Wotherspoon in the College, as various offices were visited in the divulging of recently acquired information. Especially persuasive were arguments on the feasibility of a canteen for insertion in an aluminum cup.

Out at Fort Myer, the Wright brothers, aided by army officers, tested their biplane. Short flights proved successful, but no money came from Congress to buy one of the machines. After having had a look at the new invention, Brown commuted frequently to the Virginia field. His diary recorded his enthusiasm:

September 5— .... Went out to Myer to see the Wright Aeroplane fly but it failed to start.
September 7— .... Went out .... to see Mr. Orville Wright fly his aeroplane. He was successful & flew about one minute.
September 9— .... Went out to Ft. Myer & saw Mr. Orville Wright fly for 1 hour & 2 minutes.
September 12— .... Went out .... to see the Aeroplane make a record of 1¼ hours. ....

A few years more and airplanes would become the winged terror of the sky. Few were those who had the vision in 1908.

When Brown left Washington to join his regiment, his interest in aluminum compelled him to stop at Pittsburgh for an interview with officials of the Aluminum Company of America. A week in Denver yielded satisfaction and pride in a recently purchased large brick house at 875 Marion Street. There, in a quiet, abundantly shaded residential section, sister Grace would henceforth welcome the soldier-brother whenever he sought homey comfort.

At the end of September, the Major greeted Colonel Dorst at Fort Sam Houston and took charge of his Third Squadron. In November, detail in the Pay Department was offered by Paymaster General Whipple. The man who had just given a two-hundred-dollar check for a sleek mount while vowing to stick with the cavalry answered with "most emphatically no."

The horse, however, turned out to be fractious. At the conclusion of a riding drill in December, Brown was thrown violently to the earth, the injuries placing him on sick report for two weeks. The day after Christmas, he entrained with Troops I and M, Third Cavalry, for Fort Wingate, in northwestern New Mexico. Two days before the new year, 1909, he assumed command of the post where the Sierra Madre or Zuni Mountains ran southeast in a zigzag bulwark to abut the parched Plains of San Augustine.

In the next few months of placidity, while the Army of Cuban Pacification was welcomed home, opportunities arose to study steps taken for the cohesion of the National Guard and Regular Army. Since the previous summer, the superintendency of organized and unorganized militia had rested in the newly created Division of Military Affairs of the General Staff. Orders from Headquarters of the Department of the Colorado named Brown inspector of the National Guard of New Mexico. In the annual inspection, in April, he pointed out a deal of laxity. He suggested remedies. At the conclusion, the Territory's adjutant general, R. A. Ford, wrote Department Headquarters, in part:

Major Brown was very thorough and strict in his interpretation of the orders governing the inspection, and his criticisms were, without a single exception, well grounded. In making his criticisms and comments Major Brown displayed a sympathetic knowledge of the circumstances under which Company commanders of the militia have to work, and his tact and evident interest in the welfare of the organization made even his most severe criticisms very acceptable.

When Colonel Dorst procured a leave, Brown commanded the Third Cavalry from April 23 to June 24. The needs of the army were being emphasized vigorously by Secretary of War Jacob M. Dickinson, who had succeeded Secretary Luke E. Wright in March. Half a million dollars should be spent for airplanes. An increase in officers was imperative. Though improvements had come to West Point, more were required in the contemplated enlargement of the Cadet Corps. Superintendent Hugh L. Scott, lately major of the Fourteenth Cavalry, nurtured jealously the undying spirit of the Corps.

On May 12, Captain Joseph S. Herron, Second Cavalry, adjutant at the Military Academy, informed Brown of certain embellishment.

The new Headquarters building is about to be completed and occupied and after discussing with the Superintendent, Carson, Rivers and Coe, I have decided that the Adjutant's office in the new building, which is a commodious and stately room on the second floor, overlooking the Hudson River, will need some appropriate adornment on its walls, and I can think of nothing more useful and interesting than the photographs of the thirty Adjutants of the Military Academy. I now have some of them and am making an effort to secure all of them, and I will be extremely obliged if you will send me one of yourself with your autograph—7 x 9½ inches outside measurement of mat. It is my intention to arrange these photographs as a frieze in hard wood around the room to match the trimming of the room.

The former adjutant procured the services of a careful photographer. Upon being relieved of regimental duties, he visited Eastern cities. He returned in July to command the cavalry at Fort Wingate.

A telegram advised him that if he desired detail as a member of the year's class at the Army War College, he should submit an application therefor at once. Brown ruminated, but only for a moment. At the end of the formal application, which he mailed to the Adjutant General, was a reminder of patient hoping.

"Nearly nine years ago I submitted a similar application (see copy enclosed) which has evidently also been lost, mislaid or overlooked."

At last, on August 8, after shipping his horse, the cavalryman left his post for Washington. In Chicago he spent a full day hunting for the shunted car which contained his mount. When found in a suburban switchyard, the animal received kind attention.

The next week Brown entered the War College. The routine of instruction, however, did not restrain him from evincing a healthy interest in the remedy long overdue in the system of regimental promotion. Officers, whose services dated back to before October, 1890, and who were victims of stagnation in a particular regiment, had seen many men with briefer service climb to higher ranks because of flexibility in transfer and reorganizations. After the division of field and coast artillery into separate and stronger branches in 1907, veteran officers of cavalry and infantry found themselves ofttimes hurdled in rank by young artillerymen.

At the College, Lieutenant Colonel C. St. J. Chubb, Second Infantry, consulted Brown on a proposed bill to correct the unsatisfactory situation. The Major invited the attention of Superintendent Scott to the provisions. The bill, asserted Brown, "although somewhat lengthy and somewhat complicated was well thought out, and by an addition of not to exceed 28 additional officers, those who had been overslaughed were to be reinstated in rank as far as this could be done and not prejudice the claims of those who had gained by regimental promotion."

In October, Chubb, Brown, and Major Eben Swift held a conference on the subject with Chief of Staff Bell. The General was sympathetic. He encouraged Brown during the months it took to pave the way for the introduction of the bill by a member of Congress.

The War College did most of its fighting on paper, while winter held forth along the Potomac. Helen came from Denver to tidy up her brother's apartment and share the Capital's celebration of New Year's Day, 1910. After she had left, the officer put into form his ideas for a shelf attachment for tents, and resumed frequent walks to the Army and Navy Club or bracing horseback rides. Too, he aided the veteran Major Charles B. Hardin in the writing of an article on the Sheepeater Campaign of 1879.

On April 4, the bill for readjustment of rank was introduced in the Sixty-first Congress. Two weeks later, Brown, accompanied by Lieutenant General Bates, argued favorably before the House Military Affairs Committee. Then mumps made a prisoner of the Major, a patient for Helen. At the month's close, Major General Tasker H. Bliss, Acting Chief of Staff, and Secretary Dickinson gave Brown audience on the bill.

Before the convening of the next session of Congress General Wood, the new Chief of Staff, found himself deeply interested in another bill for the procurement of extra officers. In the meantime, Congress had authorized the number of West Point cadets to be increased by one-fouth, appointments to be made every three years by the congressmen.

The battlefields of Virginia, green and flower clad, beckoned to officers of the College in May. Brown rode and camped with the staff in a study of past and present, a revivification of Chancellorsville, and the planning of an engagement, the name of which only the future could reveal.

As summer progressed, military tournaments, emphasizing adroitness in physical competition rather than in tactics, were staged in widely separated centers. On June 30, the College class reported at the camp for instruction at Gettysburg. Brown, as inspector and instructor of the National Guard Cavalry, did a wholesome job with troops from Maryland, Pennsylvania, and New Jersey. On them, by the last of July, he had left the imprint of bristling experience.

The class returned to Washington to delve further into studies while, ring-necked, they battled waves of heat. In mid-August, Brown sought relief in a brief trip up the Hudson to West Point. Genially, Colonel Scott pointed out the liberal shade. A month later, Scott returned the visit. He brought with him the Sultan of Sulu. The Moro leader, bending and appreciative without stint, voiced new desires for his as yet untamed archipelago.

As work at the College neared completion, the Major's thoughts turned to the value that would ensue from collecting military information in a tour of South America. He procured a leave for three months. In the fading days of October, he sailed from New York aboard the steamer *Alliance*.

A two-days' visit to the Panama Canal was crammed with interviews and sight-seeing. The project which the United States had taken over from the discouraged French in 1904 still had four years to go before traffic would flow between the Caribbean Sea and the Gulf of Panama. Nevertheless, triumphs had been wrung steadily from distressing obstacles.

John F. Stevens, of Marias Pass fame, as chief engineer, had built a huge organization with broad plans, had gathered together the major portion of mechanical supplies and labor forces, and had started actual construction. This done, he had resigned in 1906. He felt satisfied in having paved the way.

President Roosevelt thereupon had appointed Colonel George W. Goethals, of the Army Corps of Engineers, to guide to a successful conclusion the building of the canal. In spite of highly deserved recognition, Goethals, in his later years, was to give the greater portion of the credit to Roosevelt and Stevens.

He believed his predecessor to be "one of the greatest engineers that ever lived," the Panama Canal being Stevens' "greatest monument." The man "was a wonderful organizer and a remarkable judge of men. He had unerring insight in the selection of his assistants and I found when I went to Panama that his organization was about as perfect as anyone could make it. The result was that more than one half of the work was done for me in advance."

From the beginning Colonel W. C. Gorgas of the Medical Corps fought yellow fever, and achieved wonders in sanitation. Other army officers with West Point training labored mightily and without prejudice with civilian engineers and gangs of the toughest fiber.

Brown, awakened by a bugle at four-thirty in the morning, found that the builders brooked no delay. Railroad officials handed him a ticket. He rode a dirt train through the eight-mile gash that was Culebra Cut. After dining at the Commission Hotel, he called on Goethals. In the dynamic administrator was discovered the zeal and determination from which sprang the energy he had seen surging onward from Colon. Talk was not only of mucky slides, shattered machinery, or triple steps in the Gatun Locks. No "if" was uttered by tightened lips. The isthmus would be traversed. Did the Major see the canal as it was to be? What about its type of defense?

Next day Brown went down to Gatun, to the office of Colonel William L. Sibert. The engineer, with 10,000 men toiling under him, took his guest on a motor-car tour of the locks. The man who had thrust a railroad through the Philippines did not like "to prognosticate." He expressed the belief, however, that in fifteen months his cement work should be completed. Here again, there was little doubt.

That evening the Major dined with Goethals and, with a party, accompanied him to a dance given by the American Institute of Mining Engineers at the Tivoli Hotel. Dancing ended before midnight, for reveille accepted excuses from none.

After crossing to the Bay of Panama, Brown sailed southward on the steamer *Guatemala*, "a clean boat with large staterooms," yet with drawbacks. "Passengers on this line," read the diary, "have to keep their doors locked on account of thieving of the crew." Off the rugged coast of Ecuador a tourist missed his new panama hat. Brown guarded his own more closely.

First visitation in South America was paid the Peruvian military establishment at Lima. The city itself, though hampered by narrow sidewalks and cobblestone streets, dipped into modernity with electric cars and electric lights. French instructors held forth at the military school. Skill in gymnastics was exhibited. Troops, ever ready to thwart revolution, carried Mausers. When Brown reboarded the *Guatemala*, he eyed ponies of mounted infantrymen being loaded on a Peruvian transport for service in the North.

Headed for Valparaiso, the American let nothing escape his attention whenever the ship dropped anchor. Sugar and cotton came out of Cerro Azul. Back of the fifty adobe huts at Lomas sloped a country barren and sandy. The ship's captain had to go ashore and awake the people of Atico though the night was young. More life stirred behind the breakwater at Mollendo with a railroad probing the interior. Arica also had a railroad boom.

Past Pisagua, the deep channel curved close to precipitous banks, then to Iquique, a city of 40,000 persons and boasting annual exports of nitrate worth $13,000,000. Stored in tiered white-topped tanks was its water supply, brought overland ninety miles. Mules provided motive power for a street-car line.

Antofagasta had more room to spread itself between the sea and abruptly rising hills. In its two-company garrison the American found things "thoroughly up to date," from the storeroom with Maxim guns to an inviting officers' mess. Chañaral procured its water from the sea and distilled it. Caldera, on the fringe of flat lands, was the first port in Chile to possess a sandy beach for bathing. Hills covered with green bushes and small trees, along with cultivated plots, offered an innovation at Coquimbo. A group of robust soldiers caught the visitor's gaze. In a stock car were horses and packed saddles, coats on the pommels and German cooking utensils carried to the left.

On November 27, Brown bade farewell to the *Guatemala* at Valparaíso. An Australian cabman drove him out to the race course, to the station of two squadrons of lancers. At near-by Vina del Mar he inspected a full regiment of the lancers. Most of their horses were from Chile, a few from Argentina. They had their own method of disciplining the unruly: numerous solitary cells in which the prisoner found only enough room to stand erect.

A call at the Chilean Naval Academy revealed an immaculate and modern institution, including swimming pools and workshops. There was electrical equipment, and German aluminum blackened cooking utensils were used.

At Santiago, a military attaché became more than affable. Between visits to the Military School of Chile, a regiment of Cuirassiers, the cavalry school, veterinary and horseshoeing classes, the Major attended German opera and watched mounted drill in a city park. Chilean cavalrymen galloped too slowly, but they had a neat way of halting from the gallop, like the shifting of gears.

From Chile's towns of sidewalks paved with egg-sized

pebbles and a flag pole leaning from every house front, Brown faced toward Buenos Aires. On the cog railroad he climbed up and over the towering, chilling, scene-enthralling Andes. His diary for December 7 recorded a startling change.

Travelling all day in a flat country with herd upon herd of cattle in sight. Great fields of alfalfa. Some wheat and barley. Corn about 2 [feet] high. Strawberries in season. Have never before travelled in so flat a country, nor seen continuously so many cattle or alfalfa fields. .... *Very* dusty and warm. Cars are not calculated to exclude dust.....

In the Capital of Argentina, Brown sat down to a meal in the Jockey Club, surprising in its magnificence and in the fact that it kept itself up on 10 per cent of the proceeds of the betting at horse races. Out in the street the Major saw all arms of troops pass by in full dress, part of the funeral procession of a former high government official. The coffin was carried, as a mark of honor, between two hearses. The second hearse contained the many floral tributes.

When he inspected the First Argentine Cavalry and interviewed courteous officials, Brown set down notes the reading of which could only have surprised his fellows at home. The military library had "the most modern works. .... The Argentine 2 93/100 Rapid Fire Field Gun is of later model than that in the German Army..... There are over 15 stallions in Argentina that have cost more than $75,000.00..... Soldiers sing on the march.'.... Large kites used as targets for balloon target practice..... Last year 185 wealthy Argentinians gave 1 to 3 horses each to the army."

And the price of a mount ranged from $66 for an ordinary cavalryman to $440 for one that would make a general smile!

The next lap was to Montevideo, Capital of Uruguay. The smallest republic in South America had ten regiments of cavalry, 300 men in each regiment. Of interest were the facts that Uruguay's chilled beef could be laid down in New York or Liverpool at six cents a pound, and that hides, such as sheepskins, went to Canada and then down into the United States to evade duty.

Brown spent a pleasant day with United States Minister Edwin V. Morgan, and the host expressed the desire to have a report from the viewpoint of "a military man" on the new railroad running to Rio de Janeiro. The Major, willing to make the trip, had the minister's secretary as companion and aide. They stopped to inspect troops at Rivera, where a strip of neutral ground 100 yards wide separated Uruguay from Brazil.

The train zigzagged slowly through jumbled hills. When it reached a snug little village on Christmas Day, it did not move at all. Church bells rang out and there was a lively discharge of skyrockets and bombs. Under way once more, the passengers rode across a high plateau, through thick forests, then emerged into an immense arc of cleared meadowlands.

All along the way, Brown met people bubbling over with hospitality. Sometimes they refused money for meals or lodging. Often they gave him a big lunch for the next day. The American's back became well thumped, for the method of shaking hands in Brazil included vigorous patting.

From Sao Paulo, a side trip was made through the rich region of coffee trees to Santos "to see the wonderful engineering work on that road." When, on the second day of January, 1911, Brown arrived at Rio de Janeiro, he had become the first American to make the trip through by rail from Montevideo.

A hasty glimpse of a cavalry squadron, and the Major sailed for New York aboard the ship *Tennyson*. In going out of Brazil's busiest harbor he noted well the modern fortifications, stern turret guns mounted on low cement-covered emplacements at strategical points. A halt in the picturesque little harbor of Victoria presented a reminder of Nagasaki in Japan.

As the ship put out to sea again, a fellow passenger bemoaned to the cavalry officer the tale of a missing overcoat. He had ordered it, at a cost of twenty-five dollars, from the United States. On its arrival in Brazil the customs charges were thirty-one dollars. The fellow though realizing he was headed for a much colder clime, left the coat with the customs officers.

After nine days of travel, the *Tennyson* dropped anchor at the island of Barbadoes to replenish the supply of coal. Brown stepped ashore. It was Sunday and he rode about the British-ruled town. The island of 200,000 population, mostly Negroes, he discovered to be one of cleanliness and order.

On the outer fringe of the Caribbean, the ship cleaved its way over a smoothly rolling sea. Far north of the Windward Islands the white caps tossed high and recklessly, and cold winds swept over the salted deck. A snow storm compelled anchorage at Sandy Hook before a Brooklyn dock was butted the same day.

It was January 22. Brown, casting sympathetic glances at a man racing to buy another overcoat, shuffled down the gangplank.

CHAPTER XXVIII

Shifting About

WHEN he reached Washington, Brown had his reports on the South American military establishments well in hand. Portions of the writing were accepted by the *Army and Navy Journal*, and a description from the viewpoint of a tourist went off to be published in Cook's *Travelers' Gazette*.

To Chief of Ordnance Crozier was shown a photo of a storeroom in Brazil which contained tiers of aluminum canteens, "Made in Germany." It revealed that a country usually regarded as a third- or fourth-rate military power possessed canteens far superior to those in the United States Army. Most of the troops still carried the old tin vessel of the type used in the Civil War.

Inquiry about the readjustment bill brought the answer that it was "dead." The War Department, seemingly, did not want anything advocated that might impede the chances of its so-called "612 extra officers' bill." But Brown had hopes that by abridgment of his measure it could become a part of the proffered legislation. On January 24, he conferred with Captain Johnson Hagood.

Hagood, wrote Brown later, drafted "a substitute of a single paragraph which comprised all the main features of the measure to be attached to the Army Appropriation Bill. Colonel Scott and Major Brown conferred with General Wood the following morning and the latter consented to efforts being made on the measure as soon as the extra officers' bill should be reported out from the House Military Committee. It was reported out that afternoon and both these officers then worked for the passage of the bill, Colonel Scott's wide acquaintance with congressmen making his efforts an important factor. Both the former and present Judge Advocate General were consulted as to the effect of the proposed legislation and both Colonel Scott and Major Brown given a hearing before the House Military Committee January 31, 1911, on the measure, which though changed in conference . . . . so that something like forty extra officers resulted, it finally became a law in the last paragraph of the Army Appropriation Bill approved March 3, 1911."

The whole army, including deserving officers long overlooked, was benefited. It now took strides that had no match in the past. Efficiency overrode slothfulness through the reawakening of all service branches. Enlisted men, as well as candidates for commissions, met rigid tests. No one must have reason to accuse the soldier of not working. The evolvement of new instruction and practice, along with expansion, demanded strict application to jobs.

Brown, reassigned to the Third Squadron, Third Cavalry, in the field near Fort Huachuca, Arizona, left War College friends on February 6. His horse, shipped from Fort Myer, followed him.

Brigadier General Walter S. Schuyler, commanding the Department of the Colorado, was confronted with Mexican border troubles. One Jose Maria Maytorena, from below the Rio Grande, proved particularly bothersome. Brown scarcely had time to report at Fort Huachuca when he received orders to proceed to Nogales, there to assume command of United States troops. The units stationed at the border city—Troop B, First Cavalry, Company I, Signal Corps, and a detachment of the Eighteenth Infantry— faced the task of enforcing neutrality in that vicinity and westward to Arivaca.

The crumbling of the rule of Porfirio Diaz meant the end of twenty-six years of prosperity. There had been too much exploitation of Mexican resources by American capitalists, said the enemies of the man. A feeling spread among the people that the friendship between Diaz and the capitalists had deprived Mexico of much of her heritage.

Factions in Mexico disturbed not only their own people, they also annoyed American officials. Brown and his soldiers rode fast and often to thwart the smuggling of guns and ammunition across the line. Snow and rain chilled them to the bone. When dry, the powderlike sand swirled into their tents. There were times, however, when friendly Mexican citizens invited the American officers over for a ball or fiesta.

On March 2, orders came to submit a requisition for field cots. That meant a long stay. On the same day, Brown received word that letters patent had been granted on February 21 for his shelf attachment for tents. Triangular in shape for fitting into a corner, tapered from inner to outer ends, it was constructed of stout fabric and held in place by ropes or cords. It occupied little space and could be quickly detached or folded with the tent. Free use of the invention was granted the Regular Army.

Warfare between Mexico's Federal and insurgent troops blazed openly and heatedly early in March. Francisco I. Madero, revolutionist, pressed forward as the strong man. The entire length of the irregular border demanded increasing numbers of United States troops. The heaviest concentration was effected in the newly created Dpartment of Texas, under Major General William H. Carter.

On March 11, Brown received promotion to Lieutenant Colonel of Cavalry and, on the same day, left for Fort Huachuca. Upon reaching it, he was ordered to proceed to San Antonio, Texas, and report to his regimental commander. Soon he had gained needful information from Generals Carter and George Bell, Dorst, Colonel Stephen C. Mills of the General Staff, and others. Ordered to Galveston were three regiments of coast artillery under Brigadier General Albert L. Mills.

The organization of a maneuver division for intensive field training accounted for the presence of 14,000 regular troops at Fort Sam Houston. Handicaps prevented full mobilization, but the largest body of troops assembled in a single camp for many years seized opportunities for varied experiments. Brown reported to Colonel James Parker, Eleventh Cavalry, for duty with a provisional cavalry regiment organized as stated in a letter from Adjutant General Henry P. McCain of the War Department to General Carter, March 18:

For the purpose in studying in a practical way the problem of reorganization of our cavalry, the Secretary of War directs that the 11th Cavalry, which has been brought to full strength for this purpose, be temporarily organized into two provisional regiments.

The first regiment will be composed of two squadrons consisting of three troops each, and one Machine Gun Platoon. The second regiment will consist of three squadrons of two troops each and one Machine Gun Platoon. In addition to the commissioned personnel of the 11th Cavalry, a number of additional field officers of Cavalry will be ordered to report to you for temporary assignment to these experimental regiments. You will proceed with the provisional organization of these regiments without awaiting the arrival of additional field officers or machine guns.

Brown, wearing the leaf of silver, took command of the Second Provisional Organization (half of the parent regiment of 1,200 men) on April 5. There followed intensive instruction in regimental drills, field exercises, battle tactics, target practice, and marches to Leon Springs to test equipment and means of transportation.

When an expedition was detached from wagons, the cavalryman learned to to carry only essential things on his mount. A saddle blanket took the place of a bed blanket. Rain slickers and shelter tents without poles were in rolls. An extra pair of horseshoes, emergency rations, ammunition, tin cup, meat can, knife, fork and spoon were carried in the saddle pockets. Oats for the horse went on the saddle if a pack train was lacking. Weight allowance had to be made for saber, revolver and holster, or rifle and scabbard.

When San Antonio's flower parade swept by the Alamo, the soldiers exchanged wool for khaki. Texans saw Uncle Sam's aviators, the army's prideful few, pass in review.

Then, on the cool and windy morning of May 10, payday for the cavalrymen, disaster visited the camp. Lieutenant George E. M. Kelly, a native of England and member of the Thirtieth Infantry, took to the air with a repaired Curtiss biplane.

He flew above the tents of Division Headquarters and made a normal descent, watched by General Carter and his staff. When the plane, like a winged tricycle, touched the ground, the seat fork near the axle of the front wheel snapped. The steering gear tube jabbed into the ground and the engine-controlling wire was pinched at the foot rest. The cylinders, at the rear, opened to full capacity, sent the plane jumping into the air at seventy-five miles an hour.

Kelly, heedless of his own immediate safety, fretfully guided the machine away from the tents of the Eleventh Infantry. The bucking plane, after hurling the pilot from between its bamboo struts, crashed 150 yards from the point of first contact. It spun with a churning spiral of dust, then settled in a mass of splinters and twanging wires.

Comrades rushed forward, picked up the crunched pilot and rushed him to the post's hospital. He died within the hour. The man whose name Texas and the nation would not forget was the first to be killed in a Curtiss machine, the second American soldier to give his life for aviation.

Five days later, the band of the Twenty-second Infantry led the funeral procession to the National Cemetery at San Antonio. Brown's squadron of troopers escorted the flag-draped casket borne on a caisson, followed by the

firing party, a company of the Twenty-second Infantry.
Mourning comrades covered the grave with floral tributes,
among them a large wheel and propeller, and the emblems
of the infantry companies.

Diaz resigned the presidency on May 25, and the press
extolled the democratic ideals of Madero, his successor.
General Carter recommended the breaking up of the provisional regiments, but Washington demurred.

Expenses kept mounting, however, and sanitation required large sums of money. On June 14, the Secretary of
War ordered the cessation of the experiment with provisional cavalry organizations. That same day, in the same
camp, Brown reported to Colonel John F. Guilfoyle, commanding the Ninth Cavalry, for temporary duty. The
Ninth and Tenth Cavalry dated their beginning back to
July, 1866, when authorization had been made for two
mounted regiments to be composed of colored men.

Despite the lack of reserve supplies and delays in rail
transportation, maneuvering troops acquired knowledge.
The establishment of a School of Fire for Field Artillery
at Fort Sill, Oklahoma, and the issuance of a revamped
Infantry Drill Regulations spelled closer affinity to actual
combat principles. As troops left Texas for scattered stations, Brown stayed on with the men who traveled only
between drill field and stables. A Denver firm, manufacturing the canvas shelf for civilians, gave him a royalty of
fifteen cents on each shelf.

Reassigned to the Third Cavalry on August 7, the Lieutenant Colonel accompanied the troops on test marches
with new equipment. After annoying delays, he received
two of the expensive Barr & Stroud range finders. Day and
night he instructed officers and noncoms in their use. Gradually, he elaborated on the experiments in firing, proved
the efficiency of the instrument that had first won his
admiration in Tasmania. His description of the trials, and
another article, "Necessity for a Pocket Range Finder,"

appeared in the *Cavalry Journal*. The army recognized the
modern necessity of being prepared to prevent the night-
time selection and occupation of positions by attacking
troops.

Until the first of October Brown could hardly be weaned
away from the range finders and target shooting. A brief
period of court-martial duty at Fort Sill gave him opportunity to see the new buildings of the post, the system of
flash targets, the German targets of reduced and canvas life
size, and the Fort Reno Remount Depot with its thousand
horses.

There was a short leave in Denver, the electrical display
on the streets at night drawing the soldier from his fireside.
He had wired the Adjutant General requesting detail as
observer on either side of the Italian-Turkish War. The
request, however, was "not favorably considered" and by
mid-October the action-craving man was back at San
Antonio facing a fare of garrison tasks for months to come.
Little wonder the diary suffered for want of highlights except for peevish complaint over change of quarters, occasional hunting on the prairies, or the blowing of a "norther"
from out the Panhandle. Christmas fell on a Monday, and
it was a blue one. The ruled page for that day carried no
entry.

As the year 1912 got on its way, so did most of the soldier
guests of Texas. Their absence encouraged an increase in
the depredations by Mexican forces trying to unseat Madero. The successor to Diaz was not proving to be the
champion of pure democracy as had been painted. President Taft and American ranchers near the border breathed
easier after the sending of the Ninth Cavalry to Douglas,
Arizona, and the Thirteenth Cavalry to El Paso.

Brown, still stomping the walks of Fort Sam Houston, in
February, let it be known formally and informally that he
was willing to take the field officers' course at the Mounted
Service School at Fort Riley, Kansas. On March 30, he

arrived at Fort Riley, reported to General Schuyler, and settled himself in comfortable quarters.

For the next two months, the newcomer kept up with, sometimes ahead of, the younger officers in the classroom and on the field. He had passed his fifty-eighth birthday, had lost more hair from his head while gaining a little weight at midriff, but proved his agility beyond question. On a picked mount he cleared the four-foot fence with daylight to spare. Then he changed horses, to lead his class on a two-mile cross-country run at more than twenty miles an hour.

The last day on horseback at Fort Riley consisted in riding to the hounds and taking the jumps in "Magazine Canyon" for photos.

A leave for the month of June Brown used to good advantage. Sandwiched between visits to Denver and the Atlantic coast were trips to army supply factories and depots. In Philadelphia, the unique method of embroidering the eagle and coat of arms on regimental colors fascinated the veteran no end. What a contrast to the trooper's clumsy handling of his "housewife," or sewing kit!

The rounds in Washington came as a matter of course. New trends were illuminated in lunches and chats with Judge Advocate General Enoch H. Crowder, Chief of Ordnance Crozier, the future Quartermaster General Henry G. Sharpe, the veteran General Anson Mills, the former Alaskan explorer, Henry T. Allen, General Wood, the rising Frank R. McCoy, Liggett, and Moseley. All expressed satisfaction in the main with the efforts of the new Secretary of War, Henry L. Stimson, to organize and equip a force of mobile troops and coast artillery that would be able to meet dire emergencies. In case of war there would be less confusion and expense.

Wings in the sky were not overlooked. Other countries, even those in South America, had their planes with which to experiment. For aviation in the United States Army,

Congress soon became generous enough to appropriate $100,000.

His holiday ended, Brown drifted back to the Third Cavalry at Fort Sam Houston. Early in August he received a telegram from Adjutant General McCain.

Advise this office by telegraph whether or not you desire detail as attache to legation at Buenos Aires American minister having required that new attache be officer of considerable rank and experienced Both state and war departments consider this detail of much importance in connection with diplomatic and military work in South America By order secretary war.

The detail was declined. The cavalryman preferred to stay in the saddle. All was not yet serene along the border.

In another month special orders detailed him as Acting Inspector General in the Eastern Division, effective October 1. For a week before his departure, he commanded the Third Cavalry while Colonel Scott went off to Corpus Christi, Brownsville, and elsewhere to ascertain if a new revolution might be hatching.

Headquarters of the Eastern Division was at Governors Island, New York City, headed by Major General Thomas H. Barry, relieved as superintendent at West Point by Colonel Clarence P. Townsley. Brown reported to Barry on September 23 and began taking trips.

On November 5, he stood on the sidewalks of New York and watched hilarious crowds celebrate Wilson's victory in the presidential election. The man who kept singularly free of politics had seen his Republican friends of highly divergent views, Taft and Roosevelt, go tumbling before a popular Democrat.

Next day Brown headed for the jubilant South. Eleven national cemeteries, including those as far west as Shiloh, Tennessee, and Corinth, Mississippi, were visited. Property and the accounts of recruiting offices and military establishments were scrutinized. At Augusta, Georgia, a handful of officers at an aviation school merited encouragement.

When mud holes sometimes ensnared his automobile, the cavalryman prayed for a horse.

It was to be noted, however, that the Army was fast climbing out of ruts. The virile Military Service Institution of the United States rendered no little aid. Brown, newly elected a member of the institution, on November 22 was appointed to its Publication Committee by Acting President Bliss, West Point graduate of '75.

The Inspector appeared in Philadelphia the last day of November, to cheer for the Army football team that tussled with the Navy. After a call on Uncle Will Brown, the namesake returned to New York City to entertain Helen, to prolong her visit. Five days before Christmas, he was relieved from attachment to the Third Cavalry. For many more months he must forego mount and saddle.

Helen left for Denver when the year 1913 got a start. Frigid gales swept the metropolis, making more dismal a period of inactivity for the brother. Then came orders which bespoke sunshine, warming breezes. He was to proceed to the posts of San Juan and Henry Barracks, Puerto Rico, to make inspections.

The third day out at sea, Brown encountered weather warm enough to permit the shedding of flannel underclothes. At San Juan he was met by the well-schooled soldier, Lieutenant Colonel Lewis M. Koehler. A call upon Governor Colston, energizing administrator, yielded a pleasing perspective of the 3,435 square miles of the fourth largest isle of the Greater Antilles. At a reception and dance given by the Koehlers, the cavalryman out of the West met the military officers and their families.

The officers were members of the "Porto Rico Regiment of Infantry," so named in 1908 when it doffed its provisional characteristics to effect resemblance to a Regular Army unit. It still had two more years to await incorporation into the regulars and the mixing of its officers with those of the list denoting length of service.

In a twenty-day inspection of the regiment, Brown found that in its annual cost of $427,000 there was little wasted on frills. The sun-bronzed soldiers, well drilled and exercised, took keen pride in the care of quarters and equipment. Hospital facilities and laundry machinery of the military set the pace for forward-looking civilians.

An automobile drive across the island to Ponce, in the south, revealed marked progress. An old and huge barrack built by the Spaniards had, because of its healthy location, been converted into a school. The inviting harbor of Ponce testified to its value as a port. Brown went around the west end of the isle by rail, and ten hours later walked up the streets of San Juan.

Tanned, but again in woolens, the Inspector returned to New York on February 9. Three days previously the mobile Army of the United States had been organized tactically into six geographical departments—Eastern, Central, Western, Southern, Philippines, and Hawaiian.

Again trouble flared along the Mexican border. General Victoriano Huerta, aided by General Felix Diaz, nephew of the former President Diaz, accomplished the downfall of Madero. Huerta was sworn in as President of Mexico on the nineteenth. Three nights later, assassins finished off Madero. Of course, Huerta also had his enemies, chiefly Venustiano Carranza, Francisco Villa, and Zepata.

So much of the fighting favored the border that United States troops moved there with surprising alacrity. General Carter concentrated his Second Division at Texas City and Galveston. The division's strength was only half the 22,565 men needed for a leap into war, but it exuded efficiency from every pore.

After Wilson moved into the White House in March, he let it be known that he considered the Huerta Government unconstitutional. Great Britain and other countries, one by one, recognized it as the de facto Government of Mexico. Wilson's adamantine policy, however, was to bruise Huerta's administration throughout the year and longer.

Yet it was a dull year for the American Army, a dull and, to some extent, hapless year for Brown. Out of New York City he pursued his inspecting. Late in February, he arrived at West Point to examine accounts and property. On March 5, he entered the Post Graduate Hospital, to be operated upon the next day.

Entries in his diary did not reveal the nature of his trouble, but did state:

Tube removed. . . . . Stitches cut. . . . . Sat up in bed & in wheeled chair. . . . . Wound still open & leaking. . . . . Wound evidently healed. . . . . Surgeon's bill—$300.

It was the thirteenth of April before the "thrown" cavalryman left the hospital. Once out, he resumed a heavy schedule. Inspection of the Eleventh Cavalry at Fort Oglethorpe, Georgia, and dinner with General Baldwin at Catoosa Springs provided genuine pleasure.

On the first of July, in New York City, he celebrated forty years of continuous army service. It seemed not to enter his mind that it might be enough. Stuffy recruiting offices, as well as airy up-to-date quarters, received dutiful attention.

In the fading days of September he haunted the camp of instruction for regular cavalry at Winchester, Virginia. There he observed the movements of the Tenth and Eleventh regiments and two squadrons of the Fifteenth. Secretary of War Lindley M. Garrison, Stimson's successor, came along, each trooper proving himself to be a vital cog in a well-greased wheel. The cautious Inspector, detecting a bit of rust here and there, took notes. The men were good. The faults were in equipment.

At other camps, college students, as well as National Guardsmen, plunged into courses of instruction. And the

Army Aviation Corps had the magnificent total of fifteen planes with which to do its flying.

At the year's end, Brown, in New York, awaited a visit from Grace and more traveling. He had just completed a gruelling trip of 1,938 miles.

Siege of Naco

AS Inspector Brown shifted from place to place during the winter and spring of 1914, he observed that the renascence of the Army did not want for sword sharpeners. True, there was a deal of bickering, but there was less red tape. A study of foreign military administration gave impetus to improvements at home. The new *Tables of Organization and Field Service Regulations* received close attention. Officers and men gained more freedom of action.

Constructive suggestions laid on the desk of Inspector General Ernest A. Garlington by his subordinates piled high. But all things—from horseshoe nails to blueprint of auto truck "with trail"—merited comment. In March, Brown heaped extra emphasis on his favorite hobby, the emergency ration. He wrote frankly in his diary.

> Gen. Garlington refers to my emergency ration skit as making me a target. Suggests I correct many little details of inspection verbally. Thinks we had best let prisoners have tobacco as we can't stop it anyhow.

On April 21, Wotherspoon became Chief of Staff. Peyton C. March was among officers who had their eyes on green lights for the advancing soldiery. Brown's chats with him became more frequent. Legislation encouraged the inclusion of volunteer forces with organized land militia and the Regular Army for emergencies that might have to be met. Volunteers and regulars were to have the same enlistment terms, but no officer above a colonel was to be appointed to the former. A proportion of regular officers could receive volunteer commissions, resulting in temporary advancement for officers in the regular forces. Increased funds for army aircraft spun more propellers.

The soldier from Traverse des Sioux, who long ago had bartered for a gun and ammunition, received his commission as Colonel of Cavalry on May 18, to date from April 26. Hard and devious had been the climb to the rank of regimental commander, but each mile of the route had opened upon new vistas. The pleased wearer of the silver eagle looked forward to action, not to the past.

There was a stir of no little significance in Mexico. An embargo on arms and ammunition to that country had been lifted in February. Early in April, a small party of United States naval men had been arrested on shore by Huerta's soldiers near Tampico, besieged on land by Carranza forces. Huerta offered apologies, but Admiral Mayo demanded that the Stars and Stripes be saluted. Huerta did not comply, and President Wilson backed up his Admiral.

A landing force from Admiral Fletcher's ships off Vera Cruz took over the Mexican city April 24. Soon Funston arrived with a leathery contingent of regular soldiers. On May 4, as Military Governor of Vera Cruz, he placed the adjacent territory under control of United States armed forces. The troops were to remain until November 23, six days after the promotion of Funston to the rank of Major General.

Delivery of war supplies to any Mexican party through Vera Cruz was forbidden. The Huertista Government suffered heavily in the loss of imports, and was thereby weakened. United States troops from the Southern and Western Departments patrolled the Mexican border. Villa grew more impetuous, his followers became better organized and equipped. Pride of the Mexican people in Huerta's stand against Wilson sustained him well for a period. But harrying economic and military forces, and factionalism, wore threadbare his cloak of power.

In June, Brown took time off to attend the graduating exercises at West Point. The ride, stunts, polo game, organ recital in the chapel, parade, and hop contributed to his nostalgia. As he swung through the South once more in mid-July, there came news of Huerta's resignation of the presidency. In a fashion, government by the Constitution was being restored in Mexico.

A month later, Carranza became the executive head of the Republic. His avarice soon portrayed itself in divers ways. He disliked foreigners, seemed to be suspicious of Washington. Lack of agreement among the Constitutionalists and Carranza's strident orders did not smooth out chaotic conditions. Villa, who had been Carranza's most helpful general and unselfish in his own patriotic zeal, drew away from the new President. Relief had not come to the masses.

The relief would not come until after the drenching of the conflagration in Europe. It would not appear until the day when Washington and Mexico City disregarded distance, and the American people learned to respect the valued culture which Mexico possessed. Happily, that day would arrive before all democracies faced the barbaric enemies of their hard-earned freedom.

In Washington on August 16, Brown dined with Hugh L. Scott. The Inspector had just received an order relieving him of duties in the East and assigning him to the Tenth Cavalry, to take effect September 2. A hernia handicapped him slightly and he was advised to undergo an operation. Consultation with surgeons at Walter Reed Hospital, however, disclosed the fact that if he were operated on it would be nine weeks before he could climb into the saddle.

General Bliss, at Fort Sam Houston, wired the Colonel that the Tenth Cavalry was "seriously in need of Commanding Officer but if Medical Officers say you must undergo operation you must be guided by them." In the first year of the so-called World War, much of the

American Army was busily restoring order in places of labor unrest, especially in the coal fields.

Brown postponed the trip to the hospital, paid $200 for a dependable horse, and had it shipped to Arizona. Then he boarded a westbound train. Villa was in the field fighting Carranza, lashing at Falstaffian errantry.

The cavalryman stopped in Texas for a brief talk with Bliss, then hurried on to Fort Huachuca. On September 8, he assumed command of the post and the regiment of Negro cavalrymen. During the next two weeks, the men buckled down to intensive training, while their leader dug up new supplies and kept an eye on repairs.

On the evening of the twenty-third, a telegram was received from the brigade commander to send two troops to Lochiel immediately. Three hours later the troops, each with two officers and forty-nine men, rode out by rail from Huachuca.

Mexican revolutionists, knowing how easily refuge could be found north of the border if the tide of battle went against them, preferred to do their fighting in areas close to border towns. No matter if bullets laid low an American now and then or peppered American buildings. Hotel owners made their hotels bullet proof to cater to guests who desired security. Emboldened insurrectionists could go too far, however, and United States troops found themselves hard put to enforce neutrality laws.

Early in October, General Hill led one faction of Mexican forces into Naco, Sonora. He decided to throw up entrenchments and hang on to the town, which had only a broad street dividing it from Naco, Arizona. The wily Maytorena opposed with a siege. Casualties from bullets and shells occurred on each side of the border. The two troops of the Tenth Cavalry were reinforced by most of the Ninth Cavalry, under Colonel Guilfoyle. But the crossfire increased in tempo.

At noon of the seventh, Brown received telegraphic

orders to report to Colonel Charles A. P. Hatfield at Naco
with four troops, including the machine gunners. Within
two hours they were on their way. Darkness engulfed them
for some time before they neared Naco. Brown, keeping
double entries, wrote of the first night:

> As we arrived within 4 miles of Naco sounds of firing could be heard
> which continued all night. Before our arrival a call to arms had been
> sounded at 9:30 P. M.
>
> About an hour after our arrival there was heavy firing and cheering
> on both sides.
>
> Slept alongside a hay stack with my saddle for a pillow & with a
> paulin & saddle blanket loaned me by a trooper.

Next day Brown stood with Guilfoyle atop the Opera
House and had the hostile lines pointed out. The Ninth
Cavalry took charge of the east section of the town, the
Tenth held sway over the western half. Brown went into
a store, bought a dozen flags. He placed them along his
boundary line. The Mexicans were supposed to hold their
fire parallel with the line, but a goodly assortment of lead
and shrapnel fell on American territory.

When the troopers of the Tenth marched over the
ground to be outposted at night, both warring sides suspended firing. One of the Americans forsook neutrality,
leaped into Maytorena's Yaqui trenches and fired a shot at
Hill's trench. Brown arrested him on the spot.

In a short time the Colonel had a map made of his
section and familiarized himself with every angle. He took
post in the railroad station, all too frequently perforated
or scraped by hostile bullets. The firing he pictured as
"being heavier by night than by day, and included fire
from small arms, three-inch shell, shrapnel, Hotchkiss re-
volving cannon, rockets, land mines, bombs, bugle calls
and epithets!"

Ammunition in large amounts, and firearms, were supplied the belligerents from United States sources. That for

Hill's men was unloaded at the railroad station on the Arizona side.

October 11 turned out to be rather a grim day. To the north of the line a Mexican woman was hit, a trooper received a bullet in the hand, an officer was struck over the left breast, three shots whistled through the station agent's house, and one of three shells wrecked a house. Twelve Yaquis met death in the stockyards, while fifteen of Hill's men lost their lives in the Mexican town and trenches.

The cavalrymen stood under arms all night. Horses and mules were taken out of the camp. Troopers not sheltered by bullet-proof barricades sought better protection than canvas afforded. They returned to their tents whenever the hail of lead subsided. In two days the hostiles expended 258,000 rounds of bullets. Next day Hill procured 100,000 rounds of Winchester ammunition. Quickly, Maytorena obtained 125,000 rounds.

On the twelfth, Brown established heliograph communication with his post for emergencies. After another bad night, Colonel Hatfield read to him a lengthy letter asking Bliss for reinforcements. He also suggested that the contestants be ordered, at one- to two-day intervals, to transplant their forces three miles to the south. It was more easily recommended than accomplished.

The early morning stillness of the fourteenth was shattered by a terrific dynamite explosion, followed by smacking bullets. Hill got 270 Winchester rifles and 127,000 cartridges. Forewarned, Brown ordered railroad ties to be placed against the south side of the railroad station. Another day saw a bullet-proof barricade of steel plates erected for the troop in reserve. The Mexican rail depot went up in flames. Sixteen men of Arizona were killed, and another Mexican woman wounded.

On the sixteenth, 200 more Winchesters, model of 1895, and 25,000 rounds of ammunition drifted over to Hill. A Mexican officer complained that some of Brown's flags fluttered on Mexican soil. The doughty Colonel held that a foot or two made little difference, but he was willing to call a truce to permit a survey. That quashed the matter.

The din of firing increased. The stage was illuminated the next night for a more lively struggle. Maytorena rigged up a large searchlight. Bullets sang a heated song until daylight. Three troopers were wounded by stray shots, one mortally. Several civilians and some army animals were hit. Washington wanted to know if Hill and Maytorena would obey orders for an armistice. Hill was willing, but being on the defensive he could not falter when the enemy chose to keep attacking.

Brown ordered 40,000 rounds of ball cartridges from Fort Huachuca. One hundred and twenty-five of Hill's wounded men were assisted across the line and placed in the Opera House, then removed to Douglas.

For a few days only desultory shooting flared. With the arrival of a peace commission from Aguas Calientes, more rifles cracked in entrenchments. There came a declared truce on the twenty-third. Tattered men of both sides stood up on their trenches. Fear grew, however, that the Yaquis would not keep the faith. For the next four frosty nights, the Americans, though not leaving the inner camp, maintained a sleepless patrol. Maytorena's searchlight pierced the darkness.

On the twenty-sixth, for the first night since leaving Fort Huachuca, Brown slept with his clothes off—on a cot in the station. The days grew cold. The troopers burned up so many fence posts that they were restricted to an allowance of sixty two sticks a day for all purposes. Bombproof outposts rose in number.

While the American cavalry officers took obstacle rides, Maytorena procured artillery and recruits from Nogales, and Hill pounced upon artillery at Naco, Arizona. Two carloads of tentage came from Wingate for prospective Mexican refugees. As wintry winds blew stronger, troop commanders ordered stoves, and Brown had his tent floored with concrete. News from Mexico was unfavorable. Hill increased his supplies.

On November 8, Bliss, on a visit, declared that the United States policy remained the same. Officers were not to communicate with Mexicans, and fire was not to be returned unless a direct attack had to be repulsed. On the ninth, Maytorena, three or four miles distant, closed in for battle. That night the sizzling of rockets and a deafening mine explosion heralded the resumption of hostilities. All but the reserves of Brown's and Guilfoyle's cavalry again kept ceaseless vigil on the line.

The yelling and the scattered firing continued as before. Brown's diary for the fifteenth read:

> Firing pretty lively all day. Went out to the C Troop bomb proof near Monument 92 C where the Yaquis have 3 Colt machine guns. About 20 shells from Hill's Hotchkiss gun came past while I was there & some on our side of the line. A bullet struck the bomb proof while I was there. Gen. Bliss still here. . . . .

General Pershing, riding an auto truck from Fort Huachuca, dropped in for a day. Two days after he departed for the East, an unusually vigorous assault by Maytorena was staved off by the obstinate Hill. The immediate casualties of the defenders ran up to eighteen killed and fifty-one wounded. Some civilians again suffered injury and a woman did not survive her wound. Hill's total loss in wounded and killed came to 401. The series of attacks had cost Maytorena 115 men in wounded and slain.

On the nineteenth, Brown wrote: "Took day outposts about 7 A. M. Bullet struck our kitchen stove while we were at breakfast. Another hit the Sgt. Major's tent & another struck the ground at the tent cords of tent where Gen. Bliss & Guilfoyle were seated. . . . ." A three-inch shell, having no definite place to go, struck a full mile north of the line. General Bliss's stay was up that day. Reluctantly, he left for San Antonio.

The next day Brown could tell of his own narrow escape: "At 3:30 P. M. bullet struck my tent, passing over my head & a few minutes later about 7 or 8 bullets struck in the vicinity at the rate of about 1 per minute." It was only one of four times that the regimental commander's tent was punctured by hostile fire.

Ground for a new and safer camp had to be selected a mile north of the line. Orders forbade any more observation from the roof of the Opera House. Thirty-three casualties had been listed on the American side. Irate cavalrymen's fingers itched on triggers but they did not squeeze.

As November ended, it was reported that Maytorena had 1,500 more men coming from Agua Prieta. His attack did not sputter. Other soldiers, as well as civilians, died in Naco, Sonora. In the critical situation, Brown received an order to proceed without delay to Trinidad, Colorado, to appear as a witness before a general court-martial. A request for postponement was granted. Maytorena welcomed reinforcements but not enough for his needs.

When no more than the normal amount of battling threatened to upset the prolonged conditions, Brown went to Trinidad. Grace and Helen dropped down from Denver to see him. They conveyed the good news that war nearer home than Naco had been avoided. The coal strike was declared off in Colorado.

The Colonel returned to his regiment on December 12. General Bliss again was at hand, watching the cavalrymen move their camp back to a safer zone. He had ordered infantry and batteries to come to their support. Four days later, however, it became apparent that Maytorena was moving out some of his force. Spurts of firing grew weaker and farther apart.

A trainload of the Eighteenth Infantry, Lieutenant

Colonel Alfred Hasbrouck, Jr., commanding, arrived in a sheeting rain on the nineteenth. The downpour was one of Arizona's worst in years. Slushing churned the camp into a morass of mud, cheerless and cold. The infantrymen had to wait two days for their large tents.

General Scott, elevated to Chief of Staff in Washington on November 16, waded into the Naco camp on December 20. A yellow flood swept the scene before him. Two mules drowned in a raging stream, and six supply wagons stayed in the mud until waters subsided.

The sun blazed forth again two days before Christmas. In illumination of what had transpired in Washington regarding the Naco siege, Brown wrote in his diary when the sun had set:

> Gen. Scott called this A. M. & says his coming here was quite unexpected. Had taken some of my personal letters in to the Sec. of War. There were three methods proposed for handling the situation here:
>
> > 1st. Shell the Mexicans out. Sec. of War's plan.
> > 2. Put an embargo on am[munition] & close the port.
> > 3. Use moral suasion. Not Scott's plan.
>
> Scott says Sec. of War wanted to take measures long ago but the State Dept. would not consent; finally Scott sent in a mem[orandum] to the Sec. showing conditions intolerable at Naco. When Bliss asked for 3 regts. of Inf. & 3 more btries. Scott's opinion was asked & he approved on the ground that Bliss was on the ground.

Next morning Scott and Bliss held a tactful conference with Maytorena. On Christmas Day, Brown invited the officers to eat turkey with him. The turkey, a birthday gift for the Colonel, had come from Denver before the deluge had washed out wagon and rail roads between Naco and Fort Huachuca. In the dank evening, huge fires blazed in the Yaqui camp against a coppery mountain.

Maytorena, lacking reinforcement, had moved back the bedraggled remnants of his bands. Only an occasional shot ruptured the quietude of Naco, Sonora, as a splenetic Yaqui rear guard covered the withdrawal. On the twenty-eighth, Hill's men found 247 bodies of Yaquis on the outside of their trenches. Four women and a man were captured, but the man was not permitted to live.

Scott waited to hear from Maytorena. Brown, upon receiving an order to proceed to Columbus Barracks, Ohio, as a witness before another general court-martial, obtained permission from Bliss to go on to Washington for an operation.

Although there was a hitch in Scott's pacification, insurrectionists were scattering. On the twenty-ninth, four miles west of Naco, fourteen Yaquis chased two of Hill's men a thousand yards into Arizona. Pursuit by an American officer was frustrated when his horse sustained a broken neck.

The conduct of the Ninth and Tenth Cavalry won praise back in Washington. In his annual report for 1915, the Chief of Staff asserted:

During the siege of Naco, Sonora, which was carried on for two and one-half months, the American troops at Naco, Arizona, were constantly on duty day and night to prevent the use of the U. S. territory in violation of the neutrality law. These troops were constantly under fire and one was killed and 18 were wounded without a single case of return fire of retaliation. This is the hardest kind of service and only troops in the highest state of discipline would stand such a test.

Three months after the siege, Secretary of War Garrison wrote to Brown:

By direction of the President, I take great pleasure in expressing to the officers and enlisted men of the 10th Cavalry his appreciation of their splendid conduct and efficient service in the enforcement of the United States neutrality laws at Naco, Arizona, during November, December and January, last.

Early on the last day of 1914, the commander of the

regiment seated himself on a train. Shortly, the train made a portage around a break in the track. When the officer halted at Fort Huachuca, he issued an urgent order:

"Water six inches deep in my cellar. Remove all my household goods to south half of C. O.'s quarters so that they may be used by any one."

The Colonel, with wet feet, was like that.

CHAPTER XXX

Villistas, Carranzistas, and Spoliation

A TWO-MONTHS' leave after a brief appearance at Columbus Barracks gave Brown ample time to recover from the abdominal operation. He admired the efficiency of Walter Reed General Hospital and the beauty of Takoma Park, but he deplored the temporary loss of appetite. Under diary head of January 9, 1915, he scribbled:

Liquid diet. It has taken 24 hours to get all the ether out of my system.

On that day General Scott met Villa on the bridge spanning the Rio Grande River between El Paso and Juarez. Civil war was tearing asunder domestic life and the property of Americans in Mexico. Villa trusted the man whose word had been truth to Indians long before. In the belief that the United States would not interfere with his warring against the unrecognized Carranza, he was willing to give up huge sums of money that had fallen into his hands. He promised to try to prevent shooting across the border.

In Washington until February 10, Brown observed that his government seemed quite detached from the conflict that scorched Europe. Little money was in sight for a study abroad of methods employed in a new war. Poor were the prospects of an increase in the American Army. A lot of range finders came in, however, and the Colonel made every endeavor to send one on to the Tenth Cavalry.

On his way back to Arizona and wearing a new service uniform, he spent eight days in snow-banked Denver. The home-cooked meals restored his normal waistline. There was a day's visit with a few troopers at Naco. Calm had been regained. On February 24, he assumed command of his regiment and Fort Huachuca.

The next week he showed General Funston, who had come to Southern Department Headquarters, well-kept barracks and stables. Together they went to Douglas and Naco to inspect troops, including two of the Tenth Cavalry, along the international line. Throughout the spring and summer, considerable serenity prevailed along the adjacent territory while troubles brewed in the hinterland.

From the last of March until the exit of April, Helen brightened her brother's quarters. After the Colonel gave a garrison party for her, she dragged him off frequently to the theater and card parties and balls. Entertainments for the restless cavalrymen were provided in a large amusement hall. It narrowly escaped destruction when moving picture films valued at $600 went up in flames.

In good weather, emphasis was placed on field training. Constant practice with rifle and pistol on the target range developed expertness rapidly. Like the rest of the smallest army since 1865, watchers on the border were making the most of that which was provided. Secretary Garrison and the General Staff pleaded for more men and supplies. Aside from stationary troops, the mobile forces of the Regular Army numbered only 24,602 men.

France, upon entering the Great War, had 4,800 three-inch field guns, while the United States counted 700 in its field artillery units. France could boast of 500 airplanes and eleven dirigibles, and England possessed 250 airplanes and eight dirigibles. The United States, without a single dirigible, flew twenty-one military planes.*

The Panama Canal had become a reality. It needed protection, and several million dollars were provided for its armament. Colonel Goethals and Brigadier General Gorgas became major generals. Their chief assistants received de-

---

* W. A. Ganoe, *The History of the United States Army*, p. 452.

served advancement. Watchfulness at home rather than preparedness for stilling a tempest overseas was not, however, to be recognized later as wise economy.

President Wilson implored the Mexicans to unite and set up a constitutional government that would quench the fire of revolution. The willowy Carranza had not been recognized by the United States, for his forces as well as Villistas and other factions, had created turmoil and severe loss of life and property.

In a message on June 2, Wilson declared: "Mexico is starving and without a government."

At Fort Huachuca, Brown remained on the alert. Major Alonzo Gray, Inspector General of the Southern Department, after a visit to the post, issued commendation.

"The 10th Cavalry is in excellent condition as regards to training and equipment, but are short 309 horses, to mount all the men in the regiment."

On a leave late in June, Brown entered the Letterman Hospital at San Francisco to have a dental surgeon operate on an ulcerated tooth. The stay gave the cavalry leader a chance to send for Grace and escort her through the buildings and grounds of the Exposition. Displays of the latest inventions received wrapt attention. The enthusiasm of the veteran waxed warmest over the dictaphone and range finders. He found a relief map of Idaho in the Agriculture Building, and once again studied the terrain of his early explorations. After attending a concert by Schumann-Heinck in Los Angeles, the soldier entrained for his post.

Throughout the summer the affairs of the garrison on the piping-hot sands of southern Arizona ran smoothly. Yet some residents near the post, not in agreement with Brown's methods of maintaining discipline, petitioned the Government for his removal. An officer of the Inspector General's Department conducted a thorough investigation. His report that "all of the allegations in the petition are untrue and unfounded except in the cases of four persons who were excluded by the commanding officer for the public good in accordance with law" stilled the teapot tempest.

Brown saw little to write about. But at Plattsburg, New York, a camp of instruction was established which furnished a valuable pattern two years hence. General Wood, as commander of the Department of the East, gave business and professional men basic military training.

In September, Mexican raiders veered toward Texas. They crossed the border, descended on American towns and ranches, wrecked American trains, and made off with the booty. They were not averse to attacking or killing American citizens and soldiers in order to seize horses or equipment.

Soldiers of Carranza were among the bandits; nevertheless, appeasement gained headway. On October 15, the United States recognized the Carranza administration as Mexico's de facto government. Two months previously, General Scott had persuaded Villa to return to its rightful owners property worth a million dollars. Villa, in an attempt to replenish his war funds and increase his political stature, rode northward to seize Agua Prieta, the estimable port of entry opposite Douglas, Arizona.

To reinforce the Carranza garrison, Carranzista troops were permitted to use American railroad facilities on American soil. Yaquis, like mushrooms, popped up at Naco, Sonora. On October 27, Brown dispatched four troops under Lieutenant Colonel DeRosey C. Cabell to join the other two of his regiment at Naco. Seven wagons went with them, while heavy tentage was shipped by rail.

Brown took personal command of his six troops on the thirty-first. Early the next morning, many of the Yaquis drifted westward. Brown, finding few Mexicans in the trenches, reported over the telephone to Colonel H. J. Slocum, Thirteenth Cavalry, at Douglas, where Funston had taken command. Fighting at Agua Prieta commenced shortly after noon.

On November 2, Brown received every hour from Douglas, telegraphic bulletins on the bitter clash. In mid-afternoon, upon Funston's orders, he left with four troops for Douglas. After hastening along a dirt road, they pitched camp at Forest Station. The troopers obtained water from a trough fed by pipes from the railroad water tank. The Colonel, tired and dusty, slept that night in a hut built of railroad ties.

Reveille burst at daylight. A skimpy breakfast slid down precipitately, and the cavalrymen marched on to the Calumet and Arizona smelter, gaining it at nine o'clock. The Battle of Agua Prieta soon reached its climax. Brown squeezed it into two sentences:

> About 11 A. M. there was considerable heavy fighting & some exciting cavalry charging. This was to cover retreat of Villa's army which from noon till night was strung along the road to Aravachi Pass as shown by the dust.

In the afternoon, the superintendent of the smelter pointed out the international line to Brown. He marked it with flags. This done, officers and men washed chalky dust from their sweaty skins under pipe-line showers. General Funston sent for Brown. The diarist related: "I went in to see him at 8 P. M. Says he is sorry he sent me out on a Wild Goose chase."

That night, a Villista sergeant, suffering a dislocated shoulder, sought and received medical aid from an American officer at Douglas. Before being turned loose, he divulged the information that Villa had gone to Naco.

Early the next afternoon, Brown again talked with Funston. Major W. H. Hay, the General's chief of staff, came in stating that four Americans had been killed between the widening hostile lines. Brown was ordered to take his command to Naco at once. The return march of twenty-five miles ended for the dog-tired troopers at ten o'clock in the night.

Brown had something palatable for his diary on November 5:

> Went over in Naco & watched the crowd of Villistas in the street. Later Villa sent word he wanted to see me at the line. Got an interpreter & met him at the monument in town. He said he wanted return of two horses that had been taken from men who had got over the line by mistake, said he would do the square thing by the Americans tho they had recognized Carranza.
>
> Villa looked tired & worn out as tho from work & loss of sleep. . . . .
>
> Villa has asked that about 60 of his wounded be allowed to be sent to Juarez thru the U. S.

The Villista army continued to flock in on the sixth. Brown, drenched by a steady rain, stood on the roof of the Copper Queen Store to gain a sweeping view. In the Mexican town, Villa's leaders harangued a buzzing crowd. At scattered camps beyond muddy streets, large amounts of food were shoved into eager hands. Villistas had held up a mining concern at Cananea, a new railhead, making away with $20,000. Two doctors and two chauffeurs, captives for a while, crossed the line to safety.

Next morning, Villa left with 150 men for Cananea. For an hour in the afternoon Brown entertained Funston, Slocum, Hay, and Major James A. Ryan, Thirteenth Cavalry. After dark, Villa's collector of customs disappeared with $3,000.

When Funston had gone to Nogales, Brown forwarded a request for the removal of wounded Villistas. Funston replied that they could not be sent across United States territory. Brown sent a longer telegram explaining conditions: Carranza's consul was sending "all Villa deserters to their homes with Carranza funds. Suggest that Villa wounded who are quitting be allowed same privilege."

As the cars neared a slaughterhouse, Brown saw several hundred Villistas in trenches. A smaller group held forth on a hill five miles to the east. Lashed by a cold wind, fifty deserters reported in one day to Carranza's consul. Five others faced the firing squad. The American cavalrymen were kept busy at drill or horse exercise.

Brown made a further survey on the tenth. Four half-manned batteries were posted to the south. Villa had an estimated force of 4,000 in or near Naco and 3,000 at Villa Verde. They were only half-armed, each man having about 100 rounds of ammunition. On a westbound train rode General Obregon, field commander of the Carran-zistas. Little could be learned of Villa's plans from any source.

Within twenty-four hours Colonel Cardenas attacked Villa's troops seven miles southeast of Naco. While they were being driven toward Verde, the Villista Colonel Lopez left Naco and his provisions behind. The advance guard of Carranzistas, followed by 200 soldiers, entered the town.

On the morning of the fifteenth, Brown met Colonel Cardenas at the line. He informed him that his officers might come into the American business district for meals and shopping. When Obregon arrived in the afternoon with his staff, Brown greeted him smilingly. The Mexican General, with 5,000 troops at hand and more arriving, promised that his stay would be brief.

When Brown noticed several Carranza officers in the American town wearing sidearms, he lost his smile. Quick-ly, he obtained the co-operation of the Mexican staff in carrying out the prohibition of the weapons. The line of flags also was extended.

In the afternoon of the sixteenth, Cardenas led a strong force southward to pursue Villa. And after sunrise the next morning, Obregon's main body marched west around San Jose Mountain. Brown sent out observers to watch the guerrilla tactics of Villista groups. Wounded Mexicans crossed over to Arizona to go by automobile to Agua

Prieta as the American patrol to Crook Tunnel was withdrawn.

Nervousness at Naco ended with the occupation of Villa Verde and Cananea by the troops of Cardenas. Fresh supplies for Obregon, including three carloads of ammunition, were received at the American depot. By rail from Eagle Pass, Texas, came Carranza's reinforcements. As the Villistas fled west toward Nogales, the situation there became acute. Brown and his men again lost sleep, dozing when they could on beds of straw, with saddles for pillows.

Some troops had left for Fort Huachuca, and Brown went there on the twenty-fourth to check up on supplies. But again he was ordered to march out with six of his troops, this time to Nogales. The cavalry leader slept one night in a bed, and on the twenty-sixth reached Nogales by auto ahead of his command. Already a detached troop of the Tenth Cavalry, under Captain William S. Valentine, had joined Colonel William H. Sage's Twelfth Infantry in a fight against the incursion of the neutral zone by Villistas.

Colonel Brown ranked his classmate of 1877, but he assumed command nominally only, for Sage had made all the plans in anticipation of an attack. In the course of intermittent firing Villa deserters raced across the line, receiving the protection of a guard assembled by Brown. Men, waving hats, appeared on a hill southwest of the town. Sage sputtered, "I will attend to that." And Brown took the east end of the line.

The men swarmed onto a hill to the southeast. Brown saw red bands on their hats and ordered his men not to fire. The Carranzistas, led by Obregon, had arrived. With spurts of fire they soon had possession of the town.

Brown went to meet Obregon, Cardenas, and Calles at the border. Obregon asked, "Will you permit, please, that my officers go across to your Arizona?" Further, he desired that the Civil Governor, being held by the American soldiery, be surrendered.

The dusty leader of the Tenth Cavalry raised his chin, set it firmly, and replied politely. "There is cause for regret, but circumstances compel me to deny both of your requests."

Rigid discipline was essential that night. At least two execution parties were held for men guilty of looting and an attack upon a woman.

On the morning of the twenty-seventh, Brown turned over the command to the newly arrived General George Bell. Later in the day, General Funston appeared, replacing Bell. Brown, after giving a full report to Funston, laid before him a sketch map showing the places in the area that would need guarding. More than enough troops stood ready for the slight mischief that might arise. The cavalry was ordered to remain only two or three days, to see what move Villa would make. Obregon's men filled in at numerous outposts.

On the night of November 29, the citizens of Nogales gave a banquet, followed by a general reception, to the higher officers of the American troops and to prominent office-holders. Obregon and his chief of staff attended as guests of honor. Accompanied by one of his able officers, Captain O. C. Troxel, Brown conferred with Funston again the next day. The Colonel was advised to leave one troop at Nogales, taking the other four to Fort Huachuca.

He resumed command of the post on December 2. For another season he would have nothing more vexatious on his hands than a few drunken rowdies who fought off boredom.

At no time in the following months, however, was full pacification achieved in Mexico's northern states of Nuevo Leon, Coahuila, Chihuahua, and Sonora. Outlaws struck in these areas and in more southerly states. Villa had been severely lashed, deprived of followers and the means with which to fight, but he was certainly not an idle threat nor a man without appeal.

Recognition of Carranza, and the aid of the United States given his Mexican enemy at Agua Prieta, Naco, and Nogales, stung him to the quick. He held wormwood in his hand and revenge in his heart. Southward across the friendly desert, he drifted with those who had not been lost in battle or frightened into surrender. In the country around Rubio and Santa Ysabel, he pieced together a new force. They had to live by plunder, but in so doing they would the better learn lessons in how to strike at two enemies—Carranzistas and Americans.

Regulars of the American Army did more than watch and wait. They kept in trim. Colonel George A. Dodd, commanding the Second Cavalry Brigade, after a thorough inspection at Fort Huachuca in the latter part of December, reported in satisfaction: "This command seems to be in excellent working condition. The Commanding Officer (Colonel William C. Brown, Tenth Cavalry) and his officers are very active and much alive to the interest and efficiency of the regiment."

Early in the year of 1916, certain events lent poignancy to the discernment of what might be Villa's method of striking at those who opposed him. Eighty miles west of the city of Chihuahua, outlaws stripped property of the Cusi mining concern. The American Government, on January 3, asked that the recognized Mexican authorities send out troops to chastise the plunderers. No good result came from the request.

Carranza officials knew that Villa and about 200 men were dashing about in the troubled region. Yet they assured a party of Americans who set out by train from Chihuahua for the Cusi mines that there was not enough danger to warrant placing of a guard on the train. The Mexican Government issued papers for safe conduct.

On January 10, the train rolled along with the Americans trusting serenely in the papers they carried. Suddenly, Mexican bandits surrounded the train, forcing it to stop. All of the passengers stared into the barrels of guns in the hands of leering men. Clothing, stripped from eighteen Americans, blanketed the ground. Guns blazed, and the victims fell in heaps.

Urgent demand from the United States Government for the seizure of those responsible for the Santa Ysabel massacre stirred Mexican authorities into action. Lopez, Villista sub-chief, was said to have been the ringleader. It could not be learned, however, if any culprit faced the bar of justice for the crime.

Villa soon returned to the country about the Cusi mine. He and his men rode with the wind. And the wind bore northward and southward his threats to take American lives and smash American property.

Brown and his cavalrymen, as well as other wind-beaten, sand-sprayed soldiers, heard the rumors that time could not be wasted tracking them down. Yet sound judgment dictated the advantage of having arms within easy reach.

CHAPTER XXXI

Out to Capture Villa

GARRISON'S splendid record as Secretary of War ended on February 10, 1916. From the next day until March 8, Chief of Staff Scott served as Secretary *ad interim*. Newton D. Baker, from Cleveland, Ohio, took over the post on March 9, an eventful day. Wilson, seeking re-election to the presidency, promised to keep the United States out of war. Peace there would be for another year, but the slightly built Ohioan who became a cabinet member was to prove himself a giant in strife.

At the end of the first week in March, reports sifted across the Mexican border locating Villa and his men eight to sixty-five miles south or southwest of Columbus, New Mexico. It was heard that Villa, by making an attack on American territory, hoped to provoke the United States into intervening in Mexico. Increasing rumors strengthened the belief that the violent blow would fall on Columbus. But nothing was certain. Carranza men did not tell all they knew. And United States Army officials could not lawfully send scouts into Mexico.

Colonel Slocum, commanding at Columbus, three miles north of the Border Gate, prepared cautiously for eventualities. His Thirteenth Cavalry units, consisting of twenty-one officers and 532 enlisted men, normally guarded the border for a distance of sixty-five miles between Noria and Hermanas, New Mexico. In camp at Columbus he held Headquarters and Machine Gun Troops and four Rifle Troops, having 266 combatants.

Fourteen miles west, at Gibson's Line Ranch, Major

Elmer Lindsley watched with two troops of riflemen and a small garrison detachment. The Seventh Rifle Troop, under Captain Jens E. Stedje, took post at the Border Gate. All maintained necessary patrols night and day.

Columbus, on a wide mesquite-covered plain which sloped to the south, was small and with streets of shifting sand. Through it daily, east and west, ran the "Golden States" train of the El Paso & Southwestern Railway. The Commercial Hotel, near the railroad station and customs house, cared for all travelers. A few stores, with false fronts, and most of the scattered houses, built of mud bricks, or adobe, rose east of the wagon road which wound north from Guzman, Mexico, to Deming in New Mexico.

Like all pioneer citizens, those of Columbus had an empire to create out of the rough, and they seldom complained of inconveniences. Rattlesnakes sought the shade of cacti, but the people had to journey seventy-five miles to El Paso to find a tree with pleasing leafage. Yet cattlemen from Palomas, Mexico, and ranch folks from points more distant had many of their needs answered in the sprawling settlement of the four-year-old state.

No moon lent light to darkened Columbus on the night of March 8. People of the town, as well as soldiers of the camp in the southeast section, relied only on wicks and a small amount of kerosene. Soldiers, except those holding vigilance, slept in flimsy wooden barracks, their open stable sheds across a highway to the east. Only the mess shacks and hospital, of adobe, were impervious to bullets. Officers had quarters in various houses three to four hundred yards from the camp.

Midnight passed. Villista officers, wearing sombreros as black as the night, led small bands of plunderers across the boundary three miles west of the Border Gate.

When safely united into a force of 1,500, they approached from the northeast to within half a mile of the American camp. Then they split into twin columns. The first column attacked the stables from the southeast. From the second column, forking near the customs house, men leaped upon the camp from the west, while others dashed into the streets of the town. Telegraph wires had been cut.

Major Frank Tompkins, hard-biting cavalryman who had left his mark deep in the tropics, occupied a house on the western edge of Columbus. With him resided his wife and two other women. At four-fifteen in the morning of the ninth, they awakened to the cracking of rifles.

Cries of "Viva Mexico! Viva Villa!" rent the air.

The Major could not then join his troops, for Mexicans surrounded the house. The women's lives were in jeopardy.

Fury raged through Columbus. Some sentinels had been mortally wounded in the initial onslaught. But they had answered the fire of the attackers while their fellow troopers and officers rushed into the fray. Lieutenant James P. Castleman, officer of the day, hastily rallied his troop. He led them to a position on the main street where they could have a wider sweep.

Lieutenant John P. Lucas, after disheartening attempts that would have unnerved a man less brave, got his troop and machine guns into a strategical position close to Castleman. He also deployed thirty riflemen along the railroad track to bear down on the bandits, madmen who were looting, burning, and killing. Machine guns, after spouting a withering fire, jammed.

In the black night, the Mexicans fired thousands of shots at men they could not see. Ruin rained upon them when they set fire to the Commerical Hotel. Light from the flames made them easy targets for troopers protected by a curtain of darkness. Defensive positions held in the business artery, with the crossfire made effective by burning buildings, swung the invaders back to the west. More than threescore of their numbers had fallen.

Colonel Slocum, with his quarters northeast of the flame-devoured area, finally joined Castleman and Lucas. Then the red sun of dawn threw light into stubborn shadows. Eleven civilians and nine soldiers had met death. Many more suffered with wounds.

With the enemy in galloping retreat beyond his house, Major Tompkins rushed to Slocum. He obtained permission to make immediate pursuit with a mounted troop. Other troopers and officers caught up with Tompkins, inflicted punishment that cut deeply. For several hours they rode and skirmished across the border. And in the chase, between seventy and one hundred bandits fell into the dust.

Tompkins' feat was to bring him the Distinguished Service Cross. Villa, "The Lion of the North," became the hunted fox of the desert. The Carranza Government having proved dilatory in the protection of Americans or their property, the United States was forced to organize an expedition to run down the chief brigand, and render impotent his band or bands.

At Fort Huachuca, Colonel Brown and Adjutant Captain S. McP. Rutherford learned by telephone at noon of March 9 of the attack on Columbus. Half an hour later, they received expected word from Second Cavalry Brigade Headquarters at Douglas. Within four hours, the command, less the band and Troops L and M, set out for Douglas. Equipped for field service, they bade good-by to a station they would not see for a year. To the playing band, which halted mournfully at the post's limits, they waved and shouted.

Now that there was to be a punitive expedition to get Villa "dead or alive," its commander, pleasingly enough, became General Pershing. Coming from Fort Bliss, near El Paso, Pershing organized his provisional division at Columbus on the fourteenth. He chose Lieutenant Colonel Cabell as his chief of staff. Two columns were formed to enter Mexico at separate points and later converge.

The main column, based at Columbus, included the Eleventh and Thirteenth Cavalry, First Cavalry Brigade, under Colonel James Lockett; Sixth and Sixteenth Infantry, led by Colonel John H. Beacom; Battery C, Sixth Field Artillery; Companies E and H, Second Battalion Engineers, and two wagon companies. Attached were signal, ambulance, and hospital troops, and the First Aero Squadron.

Here was the first chance for the American Army to see how its aviation arm would behave in active field service. The squadron, commanded by Captain Benjamin D. Foulois, consisted of eight airplanes, an adjunct of the Signal Corps. Its chief duties were reconnaissance and the carrying of messages. The skill of pilots was to be pitted against wringing whirlwinds and crushing vertical currents of air. The Sierra Madre Mountains, rising to a height of more than 10,000 feet, challenged a crossing which engines lacked the power to achieve.

The second column, led by Colonel Dodd and composed of the Seventh and Tenth Cavalry, with Battery B of the Sixth Artillery attached, was to jump off some distance to the west. Rendezvous for the troops was at Culberson's Ranch, a short hike north of the border.

En route, Brown picked up Troops D and G and, after a hot, thirst-provoking march of 160 miles, arrived at the ranch the evening of the fourteenth. Joined by the Seventh Cavalry and the battery, the men spent two more days stripping themselves of equipment so they might head southward with little encumbrance.

Villa's trail was dimmer by a week. The quartermaster hurriedly dumped an abundance of ammunition into waiting supply wagons. When word had come that the fugitive had been seen south of Casas Grandes, Pershing decided to accompany Dodd and Brown on a swift, direct move. Wagons went to Columbus, to follow the eastern column already under way. Captain E. H. Yule had to take his battery on a less rough and longer route.

Valuable time had been lost before the American Government had obtained the Mexican government's pledge of co-operation for the chase. The expedition was not permitted to use Mexican railroads for the movement of troops and supplies. Ensuing events, warped by divers obstacles, revealed cool receptions. Many Carranzistas seemed to display more sympathy for the pursued than for the pursuers.

An auto accident delayed Pershing. The Second Brigade did not cross the border until one-fifteen in the morning of the sixteenth. The sky offered no moon, and the men shivered from the cold. It went into the record that "the road was choked with clouds of white alkali dust that obscured everything so that the pack train got lost in the darkness and did not rejoin the column until it had camped at Carriza Spring about 6 A. M., where a little water was found."

Men and horses rested until noon. At six-forty-five that evening, they pitched camp at Ojitos, fifty-eight miles from the jump-off into New Mexico. Brown, his face streaked like stick candy, recalled the long treks of 1878.

A march of fifty-two miles the next day ended at Colonia Dublan, on the Mexico North Western Railroad. Yule's battery, after making a record-breaking march for horse artillery, arrived at the same time. In a short move on the eighteenth to the Rio Casas Grandes, some supplies were procured from Mormon settlers. Villa had been there five days before, unfurling the Mexican national colors in deceptive intent. That night he was reported to be at the inland town of San Miguel.

Pershing decided to send out three separate columns of cavalry, paralleling each other, to put Villa in a vise. Grain had faded away, and the remainder of the bacon ration went to Colonel James B. Erwin and his Seventh Cavalry.

They proceeded southward on their horses before daylight of the nineteenth. Colonel Dodd was to join them as commander of operations two days later.

Troopers of the Tenth Cavalry, split into two detachments, were to see no more feeding by their Government until April 20. Their animals having undergone great strain, Pershing telegraphed El Paso and obtained a train from Juarez. For lack of space, Troops I and K lingered behind with weakened men and horses. It took time to build ramps, cut holes for ventilation, and get horses inside the cars.

Brown headed south with his ten troops in late afternoon. Patched-up box cars and flat cars, pulled by a wood-burning locomotive, comprised the "Mexican Express." A corral for which Uncle Sam would later pay $1,900 kept the fire roaring. Neither the conductor nor the engineer spoke "American." Officers and men rode in Mexican style, on top of the cars, sandwiched between bales of hay. Into the cactaceous interior they carried two days' rations.

The train groaned on its way. It made five stops in twice that many hours to replenish fuel and water. Troopers laid hold of anything that would produce fire and steam— old ties, lengths of telegraph poles, pieces of corrals, armloads of mesquite. Two miles from El Rucio, they saw a wrecked American plane near the tracks. Captain Robert H. Willis, Jr., after an unhappy landing, had been rescued by a fellow aviator.

Seventeen hours below Colonia Dublan, the train had progressed only twenty-seven miles. Brown was in a bigger hurry than that. He detrained with Major Charles Young's Second Squadron and Machine Gun Troop, fourteen officers and 258 men. Major Ellwood W. Evans's First squadron of eight officers and 204 men stuck with the train, proceeding to Las Varas. There they could reconnoiter south of Babicora plateau.

Brown watered and fed his stock. And the men ate dinner before starting out on what the commander knew would be a series of hardships. The American troops were to refrain from occupying towns. Captain Orlando Troxel, exceedingly adept at foraging and food-gathering, in a highly descriptive manner used his pen.

. . . . For this noon day meal, we ate the last of our Government rations except for perhaps some flour, and our pack train carried only oats. From this day on, we were to be "on the country." Each officer had a small amount of money. Personally, I had less than $10.00 but I had fortified myself with a check book which was to prove of no use as we were to strike only one place (Cusi) where money could be obtained for checks.

At first, we had not much trouble in getting a few supplies in exchange for receipts given by the Quartermaster, but as we went further south the natives became poorer and more reluctant to part with their supplies for a possible "scrap of paper," and one cannot blame them.

Considering all the varied circumstances of our being in Mexico, what should we do? To further embitter the Mexican people by taking away their last food and forage and not replace it with currency which they knew to be good and with which they could replace the stores taken, seemed to be the action to be taken as a last resort. It was then that Colonel Brown began giving his personal checks for supplies taken, and continued doing so until his totals aggregated something like $1680.00. We were so entirely dependent upon the country, especially as we had to depend each night on the supplies where we happened to be since we had no pack train, that I do not believe we would have continued south as we did had it not been for this assistance.

Brown camped in a canyon on Cunnivie Trail the night of the twentieth. At five-thirty the next morning, he led his troops over the rocky route, up and down hill, to San Miguel. Ten men with their families lamented the pillaging of the ranch. They declared Villa had left near-by El Valle two days before. The sun wheeled directly overhead, and good water was at hand, also some corn which could be bought. Sound judgment dictated a rest. Lieutenant C. B. Drake came in with a dispatch from Colonel Erwin telling of his position.

Over a good road that stretched southward through inviting country, the command next day marched twenty-seven miles to Chaves. They procured hay and corn for the animals. Drake had returned to Erwin advising movement to the south. A little farther on lay San Jose de Babicora, and from there in the evening, a Mr. Fox, civilian guide, conveyed worthwhile news to Brown.

To the southwest, at Namiquipa, Carranzistas under Colonel Cano had fought and routed Villa. Namiquipa, with a population of between 3,000 and 4,000, was supposed to lean more towards revolution than any other town in the length of Mexico.

Brown, thirsting for more information, got it the next day in a push to El Toro. He dropped in at San Jose de Babicora, the Hearst-owned hacienda that had been shaped by the hands of Jesuits in 1770. Several Carranza officers and ranch officials, employed by the prominent American, cordially offered assistance.

The chaser of Villa telegraphed Erwin, through Pershing, that Evans would join him on the morrow. Then he ate a hearty dinner, procured several sets of horse and mule shoes, and, with the promise that Mexican guides would be sent him, he rode off to rejoin his command. Colonel Cano's secretary called on him that night, paving the way for a conference with Cano.

The ill-clad cavalrymen now were in high, serrated country, whipped by a raw wind which spat snow and sleet. Fox entered camp before daylight with twenty Mexican guides. At nine o'clock, Colonel Cano and his staff rode out of the timber and went into conference at once. After a congenial parley, the Mexican soldiers departed for Namiquipa. A message relating position and plans was sent to Colonel Dodd. Brown was to follow Cano next morning, collecting corn, beans, flour, and other foods. Evans arrived in the afternoon. Disgruntled, he reported that the train had been wrecked, and sixteen of his troopers injured. Hiking was safer.

The strength of the two squadrons stood at 439 men and 526 animals. The scarcity of food compelled the tightening of belts. Only beef and frijoles (beans) could be obtained with any regularity. The beans were eaten for breakfast, when more time could be taken to cook them. The cooks battled high altitude, and the eaters battled indigestion. Each squadron possessed only three camp kettles, and kerosene cans were purchased to help relieve the worries of mess sergeants.

They could not find even a poor quality of corn meal or flour. Coarsely ground corn was mixed with water, patted into thick cakes and fried. The usual lack of lard and salt in the half-cooked cakes resulted in diarrhea and cramps for the men. Meat bones were carefully saved, for the scraped meat went into the making of ground-corn stew. It became a rare event when sugar, coffee, or any kind of fruit fell into the hands of the food gatherers. Parched corn, carried in a pocket, was to be nibbled on long marches, and it was boiled with water to make "coffee."

The dyed-in-the-wool cavalryman never thought of eating corn if his mount needed it. Oats could not be had, and wheat was fed to the animals only when necessary because of the resulting flatulency. Small amounts of fodder might be obtained, but grazing consisted mostly of dry grass, at which the horse stared or in which he lay down after a brief period of cropping. So corn, though ground up with the cob, the horses had to have.

Watering places lay far apart, while the drinking of alkali water met with taboo. At each halt the rider examined his horse's shoes. He must never postpone the tightening of a loose shoe. And the scarcity of horseshoes called for falling out of line to pick up any cast off from flying hoofs.

By the time Brown reached Namiquipa the morning of

the twenty-fifth, he felt like the old Indian fighter again, putting the needs of horses before the needs of men, sticking to the enemy trail no matter where it might lead. He knew the overzealous cavalrymen would be disappointed time after time. They were up against an outstanding problem: the sifting of the more trustworthy information from that which could be roguish or misleading. Each day Villa "seemed from reports to be only a couple of marches ahead."

Not until he had spent more than two hours collecting supplies did Brown confer with Colonel Cano. Then the Americans swung nine miles southward to Oso Canyon. With between two and three hundred men, Cano went northward to the Cervantes ranch. There lived the parents of Cervantes, second in command to Villa.

Brown, suspicious but not too impatient, wrote in his diary: "Cano sent out one scouting party to the east and came over in the evening and I told him that we could best cooperate by he locating Villa when I by a night march would attack him. He promised to do this for me and I stated that I would lay by here in Oso Cañon today and rest and wait for returns from scouting parties."

Meanwhile, a dispatch went to Colonel Dodd. Ice one-fourth of an inch thick formed on the mountain streams that night.

Searchers around the camp next day brought assorted loot out of a Villista cache—officers' clothing, a photo of Cervantes, two guns, wine glasses, and gold-banded chinaware. Brown received a message from Dodd, answered it, and sent a telegram to Pershing.

The Colonel rose early on the twenty-seventh and went to the Cervantes ranch to see Cano. Villa's trail had been found, said Cano. Asked to produce the scout who found it, the Mexican balked. Brown thereupon moved a dozen miles eastward to a good camp at Pilon Cillos. There he obtained 200 pounds of flour, some soap, and tobacco. A message came, revealing that Major Frank Tompkins was in Namiquipa.

For the next two days, the Tenth Cavalry had to be content with feeling out the territory while going southward to La Quemada ranch near Rubio. A captain and a group of men lent by Cano rendered various services. Temptation to leave the main trail became strong when it was learned that Lopez, one of Villa's leaders wounded at Columbus, had found refuge in a canyon near Pilon Cillos.

Brown tried to notify Dodd of the Villista's whereabouts and made inquiries at Rubio. He found a number of men who, forced to join Villa, had deserted. Four days previously Villa and eighty of his men had stopped at Rubio. Indications were that they had gone to San Diego del Monte. News came that Dodd had left for Guerrero, some distance to the southwest.

It was thirteen miles to San Diego del Monte. Brown and Evans arrived there on the thirtieth to learn that they lagged three days behind Villa. The man they wished to capture, they were told, had been badly injured in a fight with Carranzistas at Guerrero on the twenty-eighth. A leg broken below the knee had caused him to be carried on a stretcher. Brown sent a dispatch to Dodd at Guerrero. He hoped to learn something definite.

A weighty snow and a stiff gale buffeted animals and men. They had little luck seeking warmth in camp on the last day of March. Brown sent a small detail to the San Antonio railway station with a message to Pershing requesting advice on further movements.

Late in the night, Lieutenant J. F. Richmond returned to report that for four days no train had passed through San Antonio, and the telegraphic line was out of service. While the blizzard raged, Brown heated rocks to warm the earth on which he was to sleep. The Carranza guides had monopolized a room at the ranch.

While the Tenth Cavalry had been dogging the Villista

trail, troops of the Twentieth and Twenty-fourth Infantry had entered Mexico from Columbus. Other regulars had grouped along the border, and a new motor truck train wheeled southward. Pershing was preparing to move his headquarters to Namiquipa. There, 225 miles south of Columbus, he would have to weld strong links for the chain of supplies. Four other columns besides the Tenth Cavalry shared in the pursuit of Villa.

On the day that Brown rode into Rubio, Colonel Dodd, only four months from celebrating his sixty-fourth birthday and retirement for age, proved that a tough soldier never grew old. With 400 men he caught 500 of the Villista bandits off guard at Guerrero. In sharp clashes the Americans sustained only four wounded, while at least thirty of Villa's followers were killed, among them General Hernandez. Dodd's cavalrymen emerged from the skirmishes with a self-satisfying bonus of captured horses, saddles, arms, and two machine guns.

The wounded Villa was not in the fight. A lumbering wagon, stoutly escorted, bore him to a more remote place. His forces, lashed and frayed, would not again be able to assemble in strength enough for another battle with men from above the Rio Grande.

Yet the order—"Take Villa dead or alive"—still stood.

CHAPTER XXXII

Aguas Calientes to Parral

GENERAL PERSHING, in throwing out flying columns, performed near miracles in lending them support. He was never far behind, riding over bumpy
roads in an auto at speeds which approached factory tests.
Defiant of risks, he retained only small escorts. On March
30, at San Geronimo Ranch, about halfway between Namiquipa and Guerrero, he learned of Dodd's fight.

Although Villa's forces had been scattered, the elusive
leader must be tracked down. On the assumption that Villa
still fled southward, Pershing again ordered parallel columns to move in that direction. They were to converge
near the Durango line, restricting to Chihuahua, if possible,
the movements of the bandits.

The expedition's commander found Major Frank Tompkins a few miles south of San Geronimo and personally
ordered him to advance hastily along the middle route.
Tompkins, who had picked up Troops I and K of the
Tenth Cavalry, trimmed his detachment to two quick-
striking troops of the Thirteenth Cavalry.

Major Robert L. Howze, whose squadron of the Eleventh
Cavalry had passed Namiquipa, marched on the west, while
Colonel Brown was to proceed along the road farthest east.
Lieutenant Colonel Henry T. Allen, at the head of an-
other squadron of the Eleventh Cavalry, would leave Colo-
nia Dublan at once, marching southward by way of
Namiquipa.

Picked men comprised each of the hard-riding units,
and the sturdiest mules went into their pack trains. To

Colonel Dodd fell the task of watching the trails snaking into the mountains west of the communication lines.

Brown, without hearing from Dodd, got under way on April 1. He left Evans to guard the pass, quite unaware that the events of the next six weeks would keep the two squadrons from reuniting. On the way through the mountains, another horse, its strength sapped by cold nights and forced marching, fell dead. The rider removed all its equipment.

The enlisted cavalrymen did not have curb bits and sabers, yet the burden felt heavy enough. Attached to the ammunition belt was a Colt pistol, and diagonally across the man's body swung a bandoleer containing sixty rounds. Some troopers carried the rifles on their backs, some under their leg on the near side of the horse, others with the butt in a bucket.

The McClellan saddle and bags still had advantages over the newer saddle equipment in the carrying of more field rations. Too, the "McClellan" slipped less on grades of steep pitch than did the hinged type. The grain bag, when possible to fill it, lay strapped across the pommel. The few other articles were cut to a minimum.

Brown flashed a sympathetic smile as he looked over his troopers. Some of the hoods of the stirrups had disappeared. Men who frequently dismounted to lead fatigued and lame animals wore holes in the soles of their shoes, especially if the nights were moonless and the road rocky. So they tacked stirrup leather on as half soles. More than a few patched breeches resembled crazy quilts, pieces of shelter half vieing with coat lining. Occasionally there was not even a patch between the skin of a rider and the smooth saddle. The hats of many were just remnants of headgear, some replaced with cover fashioned from the linings from saddlebags.

An hour after noon, the Colonel's Negro horsemen approached the community and ranch of Aguas Calientes,

four miles northeast of the Mexico North Western Railroad. They saw 150 Villistas retreating from the squatty
village. As the main body turned south and to the left
around a low, blunt peak, the rear guard opened fire on
Troop E, advance guard of the Americans led by Captain
S. D. Smith.

Captain Valentine rushed his Troop F across the mountain's saddle to the extreme left in order to check the
scrappy stragglers. Major Young and Captain Troxel
dashed to the left of the village with Troop H, while Captain Albert E. Phillips gained a position for his machine
gunners at the ridge on the right. Brown held Troop G,
under Captain George B. Rodney, as momentary escort for
the pack train.

For the first time in United States Army history, overhead
machine-gun fire went into play. Captain Phillips and his
men laid down a barrage of bullets, while the other troopers
advanced to positions vacated by the Mexicans. When
Valentine encountered the chief resistance, Young and
Troxel swung over, their line of foragers advancing ob-
liquely to cover the front. They drew their pistols, but
their yelling was sufficient warning as they charged.

The remaining troops had only to march through the
village. Reinforcement by Troxel sent the Villistas scurry-
ing, their fire worsening in intensity and aim.

Troxel, reassembling his troop, sent word to Brown that
he was going after the main group, seen two miles ahead.
The troop leader, followed by Valentine, galloped onward
until the rifles of the pursued spat a clear warning. The
terrain and distance forbade dismounted tactics, and the
two troops, side by side, ran the enemy to the summit of a
semicircular ridge. There a stand was possible. Valentine's
men spurred to the right, and Troxel, with one platoon dismounted and the other galloping forward under protective
fire, reached a tip of the horseshoe-shaped elevation. They
faced few bullets.

Cautious riding in widening circles by the cavalrymen provoked no opposition. Finally they found a trail. It led them over the ridge and down its western slope to Mesteño Ranch. The hands of watches pointed to the numeral five. Messengers hastened back to Brown.

Three hours later, he rejoined his attackers for bivouac. They saw no more of the Villistas who, the ranch people revealed, were led by Beltran and had whirled by in clouds of dust. At least three of their number lay dead on the field, and they had lost some supplies and several ponies and mules.

Gleefully, Brown learned that not a single man of his command could show a wound. Only one of the horses was injured fatally, but a few weakened ones would soon drop by the way. The Colonel sent a dispatch back to Evans and found a rude cabin. Before a warming fireplace, he spread his blanket on the floor, to sleep soundly throughout the night.

Next day, flushed with its first attack, the column advanced south and east. Two trails, each yielding signs of fifty to a hundred men, were followed fifteen miles to Napavechi Ranch. Brown, convinced that the main trail crossed the railroad which ran eastward through San Antonio, marched into that town on April 3.

Local guides and messengers were not rendering the best of service, and camps shifted overnight. But a message went to Evans asking him to march to San Antonio. Brown betrayed no little annoyance when, in order to pay for a telegram sent to his commander, he sacrificed a $2.50 knife to a trooper for fifty cents. The diary entry was to the point:

.... Sent dispatch to Gen. Pershing. Find that authorities here will not take telegram collect and have wired Gen. Pershing so that he can arrange that wires can be sent collect. Also strongly urged that he arrange that we can get funds to pay for our supplies instead of giving receipts.

The time element involved in the sending of receipts and the return of duplicate vouchers did not make for patience. The attitude of a man who had supplies to sell indeed was not kindly to the "receipt method." He preferred cash on the barrel head, not checks on a merry-go-round.

Still, not all was dismal at San Antonio. The camp smelled clean, the water tasted good. Lieutenant Reynold F. Migdalski, quartermaster, obtained seven cords of wood at fifteen dollars a cord. In the absence of troop kettles, each man did his own cooking. That took lots of wood for individual fires.

By staying around two days, Brown got in communication with the Carranza General Jose Cavazos, who with 600 men had left "Cusi" (Cusihuiriachic) to chase Villa. The leader of the Tenth Cavalry desired co-operative campaigning. Cavazos, however, did not like the idea of Americans advancing at all, and he so replied.

Major Tompkins, astride his high-strung little Arab stallion and leading the two troops of the Thirteenth Cavalry, rode through on the second day. The Major and the Colonel came out of a huddle with many things clarified, the exchange of information to prove of greater benefit than either imagined. Brown had received orders from Division Headquarters to send back for supplies all but six mules of his pack train. Disabled men and horses also were to go to the rear.

On the fifth, the squadron marched into Cusihuiriachic on a pay-as-you-go basis. Captain Foulois, arriving by airplane, carried instructions from Pershing asking Brown for a report on his fight and general operations. The Colonel complied with his chief's wishes, accepted a map from Foulois, and looked up officials of the Cusi Mining Company. Courteously, they accepted his personal check in payment for food supplies, shoes, and underclothing. Of Mexican silver and mining company checks amounting to more than a thousand dollars gold, Brown generously placed $652 in the hands of Quartermaster Migdalski and lent each of his officers ten dollars.

Next day the command's march was twenty-two miles to Cieneguita, but its leader traveled more. At the start he had to find the occupants of a plane which had landed outside of Cusi. Lieutenants Ira A. Rader and Herbert A. Dargue delivered a message from Acting Chief of Staff J. A. Ryan. It revealed the positions of other columns, ordered a movement toward Parral to cut off Villa, and, regretting that Brown seemed tardy in sending back reports, stated that "the Commanding General directs that his orders on this subject be strictly complied with."

Brown replied at the earliest opportunity, but he, too, had a feeling of regret. His chasing around for aviators who could not readily contact him, plus twelve hours in the saddle, gave time for little else.

Parral was only a few miles north of the Durango line and 360 miles south of the international border, a third of the distance to Mexico City. On April 7, while Brown coaxed guides to stick with his column, the troopers put on a burst of speed. Seemingly irked that Tompkins had passed them, they caught up with and pushed ahead of the sweating Thirteenth Cavalrymen at Santa Rosalia. Before they ended the dung-blotting and rock-strewn stretch of thirty-four miles to La Joya, their guns relieved two horses of their misery. Another faithful animal was left in the vicinity, while buzzards circled the fly-infested flesh.

The men groped in darkness as they stretched lariat picket lines to permit their mounts to graze until dawn. For fifteen dollars enough wood was bought to cook the little food at hand. A strange youth came into the camp. Fifty bandits, he asserted, had recently departed from the village. Brown sent him home to change his clothes and serve as guide, but the informant failed to return.

Reveille next morning at five-thirty fell on half-deaf ears. The Colonel noted "officers and men showing signs of the hard work and loss of rest and are sluggish at times in obeying orders." They procured a Mexican blacksmith to shoe some of the animals, then rode for fourteen miles. They stopped at Satevo, which had been looted in turn by Villistas and Carranzistas.

The people appeared to be hostile. Brown met their judge, showed his coin, and all suspicion took wings. From one resident, Mexican silver pried loose two roomfuls of corn fodder. Hungry horses ate their fill. Hard money also procured more than enough chickens and eggs for the men.

In the approach to Tres Hermanos on April 9, Palm Sunday, the Americans ran into a large detachment of Carranza troops led by General Garza. The General and his staff gathered with Brown and his officers under a mesquite tree. They held a friendly conference and, en route to camp, Brown led his troops in review before the General. The size of the American horses evoked whispered "Ah's."

Accompanied by Captain Trevino of Garza's command, Brown rode seven miles on the tenth to the Carranza camp at La Manga Ranch. Several horses were offered for sale—at from two hundred to five hundred dollars. The Colonel gave one of Garza's men one hundred pesos for a horse which he wished to present to Major Young. About to ride away, he missed his saber scabbard. It was hastily restored.

A message sent back to Young brought the column forward. Soon they struck a trail over which Tompkins had passed the day before. On it four more of the Tenth Cavalry horses had to be shot by misty-eyed riders.

Brown set up camp at Sauz while the sun still blazed in a sky with little traffic of clouds. He then ordered all horseshoes turned into "a common pile for the common good of the command." Troxel later was to write:

This was heart rending to the men as well as to myself to give up our hoardings, but I was proud to see something like 35 shoes turned in by my troop of 43 men. One other troop turned in a similar quantity and one troop turned in one shoe. It is easy to determine which troop was the cause of the order and which one got the most shoes from the pile, but still it was the necessary thing to do. We had no forge and tools for fitting and shoeing, but could occasionally get some assistance from the very incomplete blacksmith shops at ranches. . . . . Undoubtedly a great deal of the fatigue experienced by our horses was due to their long hoof walls, none of which had been trimmed nor to which had shoes been properly fitted at least since March 16th—one month before.

At times the men held their horses standing in water to allow their feet to soak and to cool. The hoofs were saved from injuries induced by dryness.

Along the sun-baked road, which paralleled the Mexican National Railway many miles to the east, jogged the column on the eleventh. After eighteen miles in blistering heat, Brown ordered a halt at the edge of Valle de Zaragosa, traditionally Conchos. Here ran a crystalline stream. In a well-nurtured grove on its banks, the drooping cavalrymen sought another rest.

Crowds of curious and friendly villagers, unusually well dressed, swarmed around the camp. The arrival there the previous day of Major Tompkins had caused twenty Villistas to flee from the pleasure of raiding a cloth factory. One mule load of loot had been captured and returned to its owners.

Brown met a Captain Mesa, a friend of Parral's Presidente Herrera. Graciously, he was given valuable information and assistance in procuring a few supplies. Ninety Villistas had raided the town two nights before Tompkins appeared. They had killed seven Carranzistas, cut the telegraph and telephone lines, and had ridden away with bountiful supplies. Many residents chattered about an airplane they had seen cleaving the sky one day back.

At two o'clock in the morning of the twelfth, 300 of

Carranza's troops drifted into Conchos. Three hours later, the American camp stirred to life. Brown hired a ten-mule wagon from the Mexicans, loaded it high with supplies to relieve his shrunken pack train. Soon whips snapped and the wagon rolled into position behind the file of freshly groomed, even-gaited horses.

Again, as the sun rode high and lather splotched glistening rumps, shoulders and necks, the column halted. A trooper jerked a pistol from his holster and fired it at two reeling animals. A mule and a horse would suffer no more. Their deaths made a total of thirty which had been shot. A march of twenty-eight miles ended at Media Ranch, and a camp sprang up half a mile east of Sapien. Only a day's ride to the south lay Parral. Shortly, however, Brown was to learn that fate would bar his entrance into that small city.

At six-thirty in the evening, the campers saw in the distance a trio of Americans on horseback. They hailed them. The riders galloped toward the hallooing friends, the numerals on their collars disclosing them to be men of the Thirteenth Cavalry. In clipped sentences they reported that Major Tompkins, after having been attacked by Carranzistas at Parral, had been forced to fight back while conducting a cautious retreat. Now he was besieged at a ranch eight miles south of the Tenth Cavalrymen's bivouac.

That was all Brown needed to know.

"Have the bugler sound—" The command fell abruptly. The Colonel's orderly, quickly sensing his commander's gestures, already was on the run.

"Boots and Saddles!" Its trumpeting fanned fire.

There was a rattling of pans and cans, then a slapping of saddles against quivering horseflesh. Brown, face flushed, lips squeezed over his teeth, summoned Lieutenant Richmond.

"It is tough, I know, but you'll have to stay with the

pack train and weak horses. Someone has to stay. The rest of us must hurry. I'll send a detachment back to bring you on as soon as I can."

The old Indian fighter knew the agony of being left behind when there was action ahead. He remembered the fight at Oregon's Silver Creek that he had missed—and others. He shoved a foot into the stirrup, swung jauntily onto the back of his horse. His saber gleamed above his head, then fell, and the column raced forward.

The Colonel glanced at his big gold watch. It had ticked off only ten minutes since the shrill notes of the bugle had catapulted his men into action.

Easily the veteran rode across the earth. The thud of hoofs on sod was soothing music to his ears. How caressing the breeze!

Did he know that he was riding with the Old Cavalry against hostiles for the last time?

Rescue and Withdrawal

THE night of April 10 grew late. Encamped at Valle de Zaragosa, Tompkins entertained Captain Mesa, from the Carranza garrison at Parral. The affable Mexican promised to phone to Parral that the Americans were coming, and he would suggest arranging the proper courtesies.

Tompkins started to ride onward the next morning, and Captain Mesa decided to send a courier instead, for telephones were "dead." After stopping overnight at the hacienda of Santa Cruz de Villages, Tompkins left the irrigated and partially shaded haven for Parral.

The road into Parral, eighteen miles in length, made for easy travel and a mood for banter. The Major and his officers had been told that the town boasted 20,000 residents, a fine hotel with a hot bath and tempting food. Too, being on the railroad that curved southwesterly from the National's junction at Jiminez, transportation and other needs should be readily supplied.

The Thirteenth Cavalry spearhead of nearly one hundred men reached Parral at noon. There appeared no official host, however, and Tompkins marched with his advance guard to the guardhouse. He requested permission to enter the town. That was all right, and he followed a guide to the home and headquarters of General Lozano, the military chief.

Privately, the General ventured to tell some things. Villa doubtless was north, near Satevo. Why, therefore, had the American troops entered Parral? The surprised

Tompkins answered: "By your invitation extended through Captain Mesa."

"No message from El Capitan has been received," asserted the Mexican. "You Americans have erred in entering my town."

Coolly, Tompkins asked to be conducted to a camping spot outside the city. The request met with agreement. Tompkins also was introduced to a merchant. He promised to supply the cavalryman with a quantity of provisions.

An hour passed, however, before Lozano started to usher his guests through the streets.

From the plaza to the fringe of town a motley crowd tagged derisively at the heels of the column. They shouted, "Viva Villa! Viva Mexico!"

For a time Tompkins rode watchfully with the rear guard, under Lieutenant Clarence Lininger. As the Americans were led through a gap into a hill-enclosed hollow, the mob fired upon them. The Major rushed forward to tell Lozano. The General and his aides went back to prevent further shooting, but it dawned upon Tompkins that he had been led into a cul-de-sac.

A messenger then came from Lozano. He entreated Tompkins to withdraw in order to avoid a conflict with the rabble as well as uncontrollable soldiers. The Major explained his peaceful intentions, declared that he would march northward, but he wanted the provisions for which he had contracted. Instead of returning to Parral, the citizen joined growing numbers of Mexican troops on a hill seven hundred yards distant. To check a move of these troops to Tompkins's left flank, Captain Frederick G. Turner led his cavalrymen to a more commanding position.

Emboldened Carranzistas opened fire from the front and from the left flank. And they kept advancing. A bullet aimed at the erect Tompkins passed through the head of Sergeant Jay Richley, his body in a prone position.

At the instant the Sergeant met death, the Major, as a matter of self-preservation, felt compelled to return the fire of the attackers. He then saw his right flank, on the west, being heavily threatened. Escape had to be made from the hollow. Slowly, in good order, the troopers withdrew to the road which ran northward to Santa Cruz de Villegas. The opposition was not as dangerous with rifles as with pistols.

Still, fire from the Mexicans did not cease. Under a rain of bullets, Lieutenant Claude W. Cummings of the Medical Corps dressed unhesitantly the wound of Private Hobart Ledford, shot through a lung. Corporal Benjamin McGehee had been shot in the mouth, and both he and Ledford clung to their horses. Agonizing pain contorted the men's faces.

Tompkins, aware that Parral's garrison totaled more than five hundred men and that many civilians bore arms, had acted with the utmost discretion. Colonel Brown, he realized, was not far behind him. If necessity demanded taking a stand, it could be more ably made at Santa Cruz de Villegas. Contact with supporting bodies had been lost because of the deep penetration.

In column of twos, the cavalrymen retreated at a normal rate of march. They followed behind the pack train, with Captain Turner guarding the rear. On either side of the brown road billowed vast fields divided by thick stone walls as high as a man's shoulder. Mounted Mexicans, pecking from the flanks, encountered trouble in tearing down the gray walls. When they tried a closer approach the Americans dismounted and, taking steady aim from behind the rocks, felled enough to obtain brief respites.

Gradually, however, the pursuers increased in numbers and in boldness. Some cavalry horses were killed, others wounded. Tompkins, striving to halt a runaway horse, shuddered from a flesh wound burnt into his left breast and shoulder. Lieutenant Lininger, galloping awelessly to the rear, lifted a fallen corporal and dashed back with him to the column.

Ledford tumbled limply to the ground. Lieutenant James B. Ord, whose ear had been nipped by a Mauser bullet, picked up the exhausted man and seated him on his horse. They rejoined their comrades, and Tompkins fell back to offer water and to help urge onward the dying man's lagging mount. Courage impelled Ledford to request that the officers push on without him. Then another bullet crashed into his pain-racked body. He fell to the ground, dead.

Tompkins and Ord sped forward again.

Soon the Americans sighted the hacienda that meant refuge. Yet they must repulse a reckless charge of the Mexicans who were bent on keeping them out of the village. Turner deployed twenty men across the road. A keenly aimed volley, followed by blasts of rapid fire, emptied many Mexican saddles. The sharply stung attackers flew for safety.

Tompkins sent away three men to locate Colonel Brown.

Quietly, at four-fifteen, the Americans entered the village. Solemnly they provided care for six wounded men and sixteen injured horses. Soberly they heaved barricades into position, while expert riflemen climbed to the roofs of two buildings. On the ground stood the unruffled Tompkins, knowing how well he could count on his troop commanders, Turner and Captain Aubrey Lippincott. The Mexicans, half a mile away, started advancing again. But at eight-hundred-yard range Lippincott, adjusting the sights of his rifle with precision, spilled a rider.

That was accurate enough for the besiegers. They had already lost forty men.

A man bearing a flag of truce and a message approached Tompkins. Lozano, just arrived, prayed that the Americans retire "as soon as possible." If not so disposed, he would have to send "the greatest part" of his forces against them.

Tompkins wrote a brief note, explained how, though coming as a friend, he had "without any provocation" been fired upon and forced to defend himself. He concluded: "I am prepared to continue to the north if you can assure me that I will not be molested. If not I will remain here to await the arrival of other American forces.

"Awaiting your answer."

The writer hoped Lozano would puzzle long over the reply. A little more time and Brown surely would appear.

The spent sun dropped low in the heavens. Watches ticked off precious time. When their hands pointed to seven-fifty-five the outposts thought they heard the beat of hoofs. They flanged their ears to listen more intently.

Out of the darkness a trumpet sounded. It was—yes—it was "Attention!" A pause and the trumpet blew again. This time it was "Officers' Call." Trumpeters beside Tompkins answered. And Brown marched in without further ado.

On the hill to the south, the Mexicans puffed excitedly at their bugles. Their horses wheeled, and they were off to Parral.

Years after being wounded as a colonel of infantry in France, Tompkins was to write in his *Chasing Villa* that it was Brown's "prompt reinforcement on April 12th that turned back the Mexican attack and prevented a real battle, with the accompanying casualties, especially on the Mexican side. Had the Mexicans made a determined attack on my column at Santa Cruz de Villegas, their losses would have been heavy. This might have infuriated the people to such an extent that war would have been inevitable—a war that President Wilson was so determined to prevent. But Brown's prompt action on the evening of April 12th turned the Mexicans back and probably prevented war. To the best of my knowledge and belief his action on this occasion has never been adequately recognized."

Brown, as senior officer, took command at the hacienda.

First, he must send a platoon of forty men under Lieutenant Henry R. Adair to fulfill the promise made to Richmond. The detachment would be five hours getting back. Troops stood saddled and ready for relief.

Brown, probing the situation deeply, did not think of sleep. He sent the Mexican Captain Trevino to Parral with dispatches to be wired by Lozano. Notification of the serious predicament was to go to Pershing through the American consul at Chihuahua, as well as from Media Ranch through Conchos. Lozano also was invited to participate in a peaceful conference near the camp two hours before the next noon.

In mid-morning of the thirteenth, Brown and Major Young led a group of cavalrymen southward two miles. There a little white dog kept vigil at the side of its master. The body of Ledford, stripped of uniform and shoes, was lifted into a wagon and escorted back to the ranch. Faithfully, the dog followed.

Lozano did not appear. Instead, President Herrera and an interpreter came in the afternoon to discuss affairs with Brown and his officers. The civil official blamed citizens, too numerous for control by the military, for the attack. He upheld Lozano's previous argument.

Unperturbed, Brown explained how infinitesimal was the cause for a roaring fire which could so easily have been extinguished. The Americans would take down their flag and withdraw only when ordered to do so by their government. In the meantime, the Mexicans must deliver the body of Sergeant Richley to Santa Cruz, in a coffin. Messages, properly receipted, were to be wired from Parral. Too, urgently needed supplies, for which payment would be made, would have to be delivered.

Herrera departed, and the American garrison prepared the body of a fallen hero for burial. There was no coffin. An army blanket became a shroud. Slowly, all the men walked out to the cemetery of the ranch. The prayerful eyes of hardened cavalrymen shifted from the blood-red sphere that was the setting sun to the khaki-clad figures of Lieutenant Lininger, the trumpeter, and to the members of the firing squad. As acting chaplain, Lininger stood by the open grave. He paid tribute to one who had given his all to his country. Humbly, he consigned the mortal form to its resting place in Mexican soil.

The officer read after Psalmist David: ". . . . Surely goodness and mercy shall follow me all the days of my life: and I will dwell in the house of the Lord for ever." Captain Turner stepped forward and through his fingers sifted dust of the earth on the blanket.

Lininger led in the Lord's Prayer. The heads of listeners drooped lower. Lips, which at first faltered, caught on: ". . . . And forgive us our debts, as we forgive our debtors. . . . . For thine is the kingdom, and the power, and the glory, forever. Amen."

Thrice, then, volleys rang out. At last—"Taps."

In midafternoon of the fourteenth, guards admitted to the ranch a hearse bearing the body of Sergeant Richley in a coffin. Early in the evening, a ceremony similar to the one of the day before was held in the same cemetery. Dusk came on, pursued by darkness. And with darkness came twin dots of light afield—the headlights of automobiles.

Unknown to Brown and his men, an airplane had flown out of Chihuahua to drop at Pershing's field position a sketchy message telling of the ambuscade. Pershing had with him only forty men, five Dodge cars and a few trucks. The trucks were moved into a defensive square supported by entrenchments. The General then ordered two members of his staff, Captain William O. Reed and Lieutenant James L. Collins, to take four of the automobiles and twenty men and ascertain hastily the true state of affairs at the "front."

Floyd Gibbons, correspondent for the *Chicago Tribune*, one of five writers present, received permission to ac-

company the party out of Satevo, eighty-three miles north
of Santa Cruz de Villages. Gibbons never forgot that wild
ride. He was to tell the people of Denver about it in 1932.

"We rode over mule paths and mountain trails, pounced
into and climbed laboriously out of cañons and gullies. . . . .

"Well, it just happened that we hit a road which ran
straight into the hacienda where Colonel Brown . . . . had
performed his in-the-nick-of-time rescue.

"It was night when we arrived there. The moon was
spilling down over the parapets of those adobe tiers like
milk. There was a pool of water near a clump of cottonwood trees at the foot of the hill. And the camp fires were
flickering in the darkness.

"The challenge of that Negro sentry was one of the most
welcome sounds I ever heard.

"Those Negro cavalrymen were a grotesque sight. All
you could see of their faces was their eyes and white,
cracked corn dust sticking around their lips. They had no
food but cracked corn for five days."

Captain Reed disclosed to Brown that Pershing, who
had been led to believe that the Negro troops had been
fired upon, desired that he and the Colonel co-operate in
making all necessary arrangements. Unaware that Brown
had made repeated efforts to send him messages, Pershing
was disturbed over the lack of direct reports. Hopeful
of the Mexican Government's approval of partial use
of its railways by the Americans, Brown and Reed talked
of setting up a sub-base on the tracks between Santa Cruz
and Jiminez.

Discussion of critical matters ended, the men sat down
to partake of a skimpy meal. Gibbons, ever the persuasive
reporter, extracted from Tompkins a report of the fight.
The price was a fine slab of bacon.

Two hours before midnight, the visitors departed.
Brown dredged his diary from a pocket and wrote in part:
"I told Reed that I thought Gen. Pershing should come

here as the entire character of our operations had now changed. Reed thought the General would come."

At sunrise the next morning, Colonel Allen arrived with his troops, followed two hours later by the column under Major Howze which had clashed briefly but sharply with Villistas on the tenth. The units of the Eleventh Cavalry increased the command to thirty-four officers and 606 enlisted men, all needing rations. To feed their 702 horses and 149 mules they required six tons of hay and 9,000 pounds of grain daily.

Wagons came in with a few supplies from Parral, and Brown sent out foragers to search the countryside for beans and grains. His issuance of a personal check helped. The Tenth Cavalrymen fitted shoes and trimmed the feet of their horses with an outfit borrowed from the new-comers.

Hopes for a supply base on the railroad to the south were dashed when Mexican authorities forbade movements of American troops in that direction.

Brown, fretted by the circumstances, wrote to Pershing:

The greatest care has been taken to do no injustice to natives of the country. The chief difficulty from the outset has been to do this and still to secure the necessary supplies from a country which has been raided in turn by Villistas and Carrancistas. To maintain my command on this expedition I have already advanced the government over $1,453.00 of personal funds. Other officers have advanced several hundred dollars. How or when we will ever be reimbursed is problematical.

One thing, in my opinion, is certain, and that is that to seize supplies whether the owner is willing or not will sooner or later result in hostilities. Major Tompkins agrees with me most emphatically.

I hope it will not be taken amiss that I am putting this strongly, but I do so with a feeling that it is perhaps not thoroughly understood. The condition of this command at this date is such that if Villa were known to be within say thirty miles we could doubtless march there and defeat him, but to attempt any further marches without additional remounts may be regarded as impracticable.

When we left Casas Grandes March 19th everything pointed to our ability to capture Villa in about five (5) days, and the orders were such that we took no forage for the squadron and have but one saddler's kit for the command. From the commanding officer down, all baggage has been carried on our horses. I am so short even as to paper that it has been no little embarrassment, and I am writing this letter on paper given me by a native, and writing it fine to economize in material.

Upon questioning yesterday the presidente of Parral as to Villa's whereabouts I got but little satisfaction. He was thought to be in the Guerrero district they said—one report at Sta. Ana and another at Concepsion. They either do not know, or if they do give evasive replies. People who have recently been looted of horses and goods show the most discouraging apathy in trying to rid the country of this bandit.

From Parral, on April 18, two wagons loaded with supplies rolled in, bearing, among other things, badly needed civilian trousers. The molten sun had too long probed holes in the rags the men wore. Their fellow countrymen in the United States, meanwhile, were protesting strongly the attack by Carranza's soldiers. Pershing had written Brown:

. . . . Ascertain if possible whether attack was directed by the local military commander of the de facto government, demanding of him a disavowal of this base act. If the attack was directed by the local civil authorities demand the immediate arrest of the responsible parties. . . . .

The General was reinforced by 2,300 more regulars. Secure in his defensive position, the Colonel sent a dispatch in the nature of an ultimatum to the Presidente and a note to General Luis Herrera, chief of operations in the bandit-plagued area. The evasive General Herrera promised to come to the ranch for a conference on the twenty-first.

On the twentieth, men under Captains Rutherford and George B. Pritchard came into camp with a train of thirty-six pack mules, $2,300 in coin, and mail. The rations were the first received since leaving Colonia Dublan. Once more singing and laughter peeled forth among white and Negro troopers.

Next morning Brown and his field officers went into conference with four Mexican generals, including Herrera and Lozano. It was a brief meeting. Brown read and presented to Herrera a letter reviewing the Parral affair, and asked for "the most ample disavowal and apology." Ready to follow all other American troops northward, he desired a reply early on the morrow.

In the evening Colonel Cabell arrived in one of Pershing's automobiles. He brought orders directing that the troops withdraw by way of Satevo to Carretas, where hay could be more readily procured on the truck line.

Moreover, the aero squadron had ceased to function. Five airplanes had been wrecked, and one abandoned by pilots who had braved the hazards of deserts and mountains to reach succor afoot. The other two flying machines, worn by arduous service, faced a last trip—to the scrap heap. Among those on the border wrestling with aviation was Lieutenant Carl (Toughie) Spaatz, who would distinguish himself in the European War in 1918, who in 1942 would head the United States Army air forces hurled against Germany and Italy.

Allen and Howze departed at midnight. Dew sparkled on the grass when Cabell left the next morning, followed by the cavalrymen of Brown and Tompkins. Herrera had agreed to send the wounded troopers in railway cars to El Paso, but their comrades carried them in a little open wagon. Four miles out from the hacienda, a messenger overtook the marchers. He handed Herrera's reply to Brown.

At the end of the day's march at Conchos, the letter was copied and forwarded to Pershing. The Mexican General, still not willing to blame Lozano and his soldiers for the lamentable "accident," concluded "there is no room for apology."

Brown took solace in the fact that the people of Conchos were friendly towards his men. Corporal McGehee, death from his wound not far off, was having a tough time of it.

A girl, her black eyes swimming in deepest pity, tendered a bouquet of tame and wild flowers.

On the same day, Colonel Dodd set upon a stout band of Villistas in the old and mountain-cupped town of Tomochic, south of Guerrero. Candelaro Cervantes, with 200 men, had been trailed closely in spite of disheartening obstacles. Two more American soldiers tasted death, but the punishment dealt the bandits was severe enough to demoralize them. Dodd turned back toward Providencia.

Brown's command reached Satevo on the twenty-fifth. There it joined Troop M under Lieutenant Henry A. Myer, Jr., and the next day moved on to La Joya. Brown, again afflicted with a hernia, permitted an accompanying surgeon to examine him. Incidentally, he mentioned it to one of his captains. This, he noted, "caused me trouble later." The old campaigner had no desire to leave the field.

In obedience to new orders, the cavalrymen pushed on through Carretas to San Antonio, Chihuahua. In that town, on the first day of May, after having marched 657 miles since March 9, they met Pershing and went into camp with the Eleventh Cavalry and two battalions of the Sixth Infantry. On hand were pleasing supplies for men and horses. The troopers who had prepared their own doles over camp fires greeted with shouts of merriment the troop cooks and kitchens.

The Villistas being broken up into widely dispersed bands led by subchiefs, Pershing reorganized his troops and prepared to assign a patrolling regiment of cavalry to each of five created districts. The divisions were the Namiquipa, Guerrero, Bustillos, Satevo, and San Borja. Reliable information disclosed that Villa, pinch-faced by his ordeals, was recuperating in a mountainous retreat south of San Borja.

Refreshed by a night's sleep on a pile of hay, so different in a place of security, Brown greeted old comrades as they drifted into camp. All of the second day, after calling upon

Pershing, he saw to it that his men and animals procured their just share of rest and available supplies. When stars again blinked in the heavens, he sharpened his pencil and moved it across an unsoiled page of the pocket diary.

Reported to Gen. Pershing this A .M. & had Fox with me to explain the difficulty we had in securing messengers, guides & scout service, men &c & particularly why I did not leave Sta Cruz sooner for Satevo & said he regarded it as an error of judgment not to have left sooner from Sta Cruz for Satevo as he was *sure* the Mexicans would not allow supplies to come over the R R to us. Was informed that my demand for disavowal and apology and Gen. Herrera's reply did not go forward but was filed. Lockett arrived with his Hq and a squadron of the 11th Cavy.

Brown, however, was not glum. Pershing had, in spite of impotency dictated by the circumstances, given full and speedy support to his flying columns. Pershing, like all other fire-tested campaigners, had a warm spot in his heart for the man who, once finding an enemy's trail, stuck with it.

Out of the Saddle

THE SKY over Chihuahua was a sheen blue. The lilt of wild birds and the perfume of native flowers induced low humming from the tough-muscled Negro troopers as they fed oats, hay, and corn to horses whose ribs reminded them of washboards.

It was the third morning of May. Colonels Brown and Beacom arranged hurriedly for Colonel Wilbur E. Wilder's Headquarters and First Squadron of the Fifth Cavalry to go into camp immediately west of the Tenth Cavalry.

At nine o'clock, Brown exchanged greetings with Colonel Cabell at camp headquarters. It had been told him by some officer, said the Chief of Staff, that Brown had a hernia. To prevent further injury, the trouble would have to be remedied. A smile changed to a frown. The line officer protested that the matter was not at all serious, that such a report should have come only from himself. He walked slowly away, found the officer who had revealed the information, and learned that Pershing also had knowledge of the misfortune.

While the Colonel expressed his bitter disappointment, a messenger handed him a note from Cabell. It read: "Upon recommendation of the Surgeon 10th Cavalry, the Commanding General directs you to proceed to the Field Hospital at Namiquipa for observation and treatment,—reporting upon arrival to the Division Surgeon."

Brown went hastily to Pershing. Again he protested. Kindly, the General remonstrated, he did not care to go back of the surgeon's report. It was necessary that the order stand.

The day lost its brightness. The cavalryman out of the West now was out of the saddle.

At an hour before noon Brown sat dejectedly on the warm cushion of an automobile, his baggage piled around him and on the floor boards. The chauffeur started the motor and, followed by a lumbering truck, headed for Namiquipa, sixty-one miles away. Within a few minutes they met Colonels Wilder and Daniel L. Tate in funnels of dust at the head of their cavalrymen. When the motor-borne Colonel reached Lake Itascata, he looked over Major Lawrence J. Fleming's squadron of the Fifth Cavalry, and picked up Major Pritchard.

A few hours later, the car stopped at the Namiquipa camp close by the riffles of the cooling Santa Maria River. The unhorsed commander strode off to see Major-Adjutant John L. Hines and Major Jere B. Clayton, M.C., Surgeon. The warm welcome of the officers brought a smile back to the face of their guest.

Next day, between examinations in the hospital, Brown chatted with his regimental officer, Major Evans, the new commander of the Namiquipa District. In the evening, the Colonel received an order. He was to go to Fort Bliss Base Hospital for observation and treatment. Again, with the consent of the surgeon, he protested in a telegram to Pershing. But Pershing thought doctors knew best.

Brown continued his way northward in a truck train. He stopped for two days at bustling Colonia Dublan. Resourceful American infantrymen were constructing neat rows of adobe tents. He reached the raided town of Columbus the morning of the ninth. Friends gave him the chance to bathe and shave. He looked in a large mirror and he discovered why, doubtless, Pershing agreed with the surgeons. He turned to a scale and weighed himself. The needle pointed to 148 pounds, indicating that many pounds of good flesh had fallen away from a man who was showing his age.

At noon he took the "Golden State" train eastward. Off at El Paso, the Colonel gave the reason for his presence to General Funston in General Scott's private car. While Funston and Scott had been deliberating with Obregon and Trevino of Mexico, fifty Villa raiders had killed three soldiers and a boy at Glenn Springs, Texas. Also, Major Howze had lashed overzealous Villistas at Ojos Azules in Mexico. Negotiations were achieving nothing.

Funston took the hand of his old comrade in a firm grip and explained that he had been up most of the previous night. "Yesterday," he half whispered, "Scott and I simply threw up our hands."

Now, however, President Wilson was seeing the need of confronting the Government of Mexico with an increased force. All regular mobile troops were to go to the border. The National Guard units of Texas, Arizona, and New Mexico would turn out to aid the regulars.

"Obregon," the General emphasized huskily, "is ordering up big bodies of troops from the south by the trainload. Pershing is to fall back slowly to Colonia Dublan. It looks like big war."

The speaker smiled, placed a hand on the shoulder of the man who had fought while he was a stripling. "You need mending," he admonished. "Go out to the hospital—and rest."

Brown went. But the next day he called on Scott. It was another meeting mellowed by mutual service. In understatement Brown wrote in his diary that night: "Gen. Scott rather of the opinion that the Mexican situation can only be settled by one good fight."

Early the next morning the commander of the Tenth Cavalry submitted to an operation. He rallied strongly. Eight hours later he penned a letter to the sisters in Denver.

As days went by he grew tired of lying on his back. Yet

there were friends, many of them, who came to see him, to impart the latest news. General George Bell called. And Mrs. Frank Tompkins reported on the Major's whereabouts.

The bandages were removed on the twenty-first, the patient glad to have the act over with so he could read another letter from Scott. Ten days later he was permitted to sit up and admire the suitcase which would come in handy for the sick leave effective June 9. When he started to walk again, his weight was down to 137 pounds. Weight, however, was regained more rapidly than it had been lost.

On June 3, he hailed the passage by Congress of the vital National Defense or Reorganization Act. Battle units made for a peace force 170,000 strong. The country's army was to include regulars, guardsmen, volunteers, and reservists. To command new divisions and brigades, four major generals and nineteen brigadier generals were to be added, and the General Staff was increased in size. Among other provisions was the authorization for setting up training camps and, when needed, the power for executive drafting of the National Guard and its reserve into federal service with land forces. Army war strength of 287,846 men was permitted.

Brown harbored a more cheerful mood five days later when he boarded a train for Denver. At home, with impeccable Grace and Helen waiting on him, the Colonel got down to work again. The official report of his movements in Mexico, scarcely begun, had to be hurried along. The sisters helped finish the job. A few days of leisurely visiting passed, then dark news came into the cheery house on Marion Street. Valiant men of Brown's regiment—his boys—had joined the Nation's long list of heroes killed in action.

As American relations with the de facto government of Mexico became more strained, increased numbers of Mexican troops pressed Pershing's forces. Carranza officials, virtually opposing movements of American soldiers in any direction except north, made the situation precarious for restless forces and necessary scouting. Clashes occurred and causes were recondite.

On the morning of June 20, Troop C of the Tenth Cavalry, under Captain Charles T. Boyd, with Lieutenant Adair and thirty-nine enlisted men, left camp. They were to scout and gather information through the country toward Ahumada, where 10,000 Mexican troops had been reported assembling. A long ride across rugged terrain to the northeast brought them to San Domingo Ranch, in charge of an American. Boyd was joined there in the evening by Troop K of his regiment, led by Captain Lewis S. Morey, and employed on the same mission.

The next morning the two troops marched to the town of Carrizal, eight miles east of the ranch. Boyd contended orders necessitated his going through the place. Strongly superior numbers of Mexicans defended the town, and their commander vehemently opposed the passage of the Americans. Captain Boyd argued vainly, then formed his force of eighty men in a line of skirmishers. Mexican rifles spewed hot bullets as the cavalrymen dismounted on the edge of town.

Many natural obstacles and cleverly hidden Mexican guns entrapped Troop C when it resolved to leap forward. It dashed into a fateful fire. Boyd fell dead, Adair was hit. With only a blinding moment of life remaining, the young Oregonian gasped: "Go on, Sergeant."

Another surge, and upon the field lay the lifeless bodies of seven enlisted men. Troop K, farther out and better protected, lost contact with Boyd's command, yet it fought back as holes opened in the ranks. Captain Morey and several enlisted men sustained severe wounds. Twenty-three troopers became prisoners, and the troops, without officers, fell back to San Domingo Ranch. They were forced to scatter, to be rescued later by searching friends.

Nevertheless, the Mexicans had tasted bitter medicine. General Gomez, eleven other officers, and thirty-three men under them were killed. Fifty-three soldiers bore wounds.

Brown, distressed and yet proud, noted the far-reaching results of the fight. Its gravity was the climax to armed encounters. Pershing and his men yearned to strike back, but their government, foreseeing lightning from Europe striking across the Atlantic, was averse to carrying on war below the Rio Grande.

In addition to most of Pershing's army at Colonia Dublan, the Carranza Government faced on the border the National Guardsmen from the majority of the states. Upon demand, Mexico delivered immediately to American officials at El Paso the troopers captured at Carrizal. To iron out difficulties confronting them, Mexico and the United States each named three commissioners to confer at a chosen place and to agree upon recommendations of solubility.

By June 27 Colonel Brown was back in El Paso, ready for duty which others considered beyond his strength. Three days later, an order relieved him from assignment to the Tenth Cavalry, while Colonel Lockett severed connections with the Eleventh Cavalry. Brown dashed off a farewell message to his regiment, expressed his "sincere thanks" for its "hearty and loyal co-operation." The duties required of the Tenth Cavalry during the eighteen months of his leadership had been "unusual and exacting, calling for the exercise of the highest soldierly qualities." The manner of performance had elicited "in turn from the President of the United States, the Secretary of War and Chief of Staff, the highest commendation."

The disheartened Colonel packed up his household goods at Fort Huachuca. An order, which he feared, came all too soon. He was to report to a retiring board at Fort Sam Houston, along with three other colonels of cavalry,

Lockett, Galbraith, and George H. Sands, and Colonel
Charles W. Penrose, Twenty-fourth Infantry.

The board convened July 17. It went over the records of
the old fighters while they submitted to physical examinations. On the twenty-fourth, Brown appeared before the
board, listened dolefully to recommendation that he be
retired because his recent operation incapacitated him. Of
the group, only Lockett was to be retained on the active list.

The doughty officer, however, thought otherwise. His
sick leave did not expire until August. He hurried to Washington. With his career well outlined on paper, he started
protesting. The Acting Surgeon General examined him,
smiled and said: "The wound has healed over smoothly and
you are certainly all right just now."

The Colonel called on General Scott and wrote in his
diary:

> Gen. Scott said "Don't think for a minute that any one here is after
> you." Also said "If it is only hernia you have we can find plenty of
> work for you"—that I should have a fair hearing & could have my
> record placed before the Sec. of War & need not be in a hurry.

Brown, rallying quickly, went over to Baltimore. A
specialist examined him and gave him a favorable report
to deliver to Surgeon General Gorgas. The record of his
case was received in the Capital on August 7, and when it
was read at Walter Reed Hospital, he heard the cheerful
words: "Colonel, I think you have a pretty good case."

Two days later he appeared before General Scott. His
chief handed him a copy of a memorandum he had presented to Secretary of War Baker:

> This paper contains the proceedings of a retiring board in the case of
> Colonel W. C. Brown, U. S. Cavalry. The Board finds him incapacitated
> and recommends his retirement; this is concurred in by the Surgeon
> General. The circumstances are, however, that Colonel Brown made the
> long ride with Pershing, an unusually rapid and long forced march, and
> did not complain of any inability. The fact that he had a hernia was

mentioned to a brother officer, which coming to General Pershing's ear he was recommended to go before a retiring board. He was operated on at Fort Bliss for the hernia, and was on sick leave recuperating from the effects of the operations when he was ordered before the Board for examination. He does not desire to be retired; in fact is much averse to it, and points to his ability to do his duty as shown by his having done it without complaint under extremely hard circumstances in Mexico.

I recommend that he be not retired unless he shows real inability to perform his duties.

The Colonel, saved at last, soon appended a brief notation to his memorandum copy: "This paper which explains itself was approved by the Sec. of War." Brown was not giving up the army, and the army was not giving up Brown.

Yet duties became lighter for the soldier who had seen sixty-two years go by since the day he uttered his first weak plaint in a Western prairie home. Detailed temporarily in the Militia Bureau, he began on the fourteenth to compile a report on the recent mobilization of the National Guard. He served, too, on boards for retirement and for the examination of field officers in line of promotion. Copies of the mobilization report, completed December 19, were used by the Chief of Staff in his appearance before the Senate's subcommittee of the Committee on Military Affairs, on Universal Military Training. Brown himself gave personal testimony to the subcommittee.

In December, also, he witnessed the adoption of the drab moleskin fleece-lined overcoat for field service, the benefits of which he had strongly urged. Not as cumbersome as the long overcoat of cloth, it gave better protection in rainy or cold weather and withstood to a greater extent the wear and tear inevitable in the field. Officers took to the short but protective coat in an exhilarative manner.

At dinners with Chief of Staff Scott, Moseley, and other friends, the Colonel was wont to agree with them that it was high time the American troops in Mexico were brought home. Closer and closer approached the danger of involvement in the European struggle. On the last day of the year 1916, he sat in the Army and Navy Club with Colonel J. E. Kuhn, a friend of many years who would soon bear the title of Major General, National Army. They talked at length about Germany.

Relieved from duty with the Militia Bureau, Brown reported at Governors Island, New York, on January 8, 1917, to assist the Inspector of the Eastern Department. There was much to do.

Before the first month of the new year was ended, there came news that American soldiers were to quit Mexican soil. At New London, Connecticut, where they had first met in September, American and Mexican commissioners remained immersed in argumentation. And death laid its hands upon the shoulders of Funston.

Pershing's troops began their homeward trek on January 30. The Tenth Cavalry rode into Columbus, New Mexico, on February 5, and on the fourteenth it arrived at Fort Huachuca. It was home again. Although the National Guard had not seen service in Mexico, it had received invaluable training. From its sinews would come seventeen of forty-three divisions for compelling duty overseas.

Many American soldiers, twenty-five years hence, would look across the Rio Grande to see Mexican soldiers preparing against a common enemy. Obliterated would be the conditions which caused blindness, which gave rise to rending suspicions and scorn.

During the winter months Brown had little else to write about aside from a trip to Washington and the joviality at a dinner of the Order of Indian Wars. In April, it was different. At noon on the second, President Wilson read his war message to Congress. Resolutions for war against Germany were passed by the Senate and the House, and signed by Wilson on the sixth. On the morning of that day, Ger-

man ships in United States ports were seized. Three days
later came the break with Austria.

New types of warfare called forth all the ingenuity the
American Army could diffuse. The military machine had
to be overhauled, its momentum increased. New gears
demanded new cups of oil. Yet necessary adjustments
were made with as little delay as possible, this in spite of a
previous slackness in the efficient concentration of troops.
The new army was to have a million men, perhaps more.

When the President signed the Selective Draft Act in
May, steps already had been taken to care for the men to be
called, to give them intensive training. On May 16, Brown
began a five-day trip to Mount Jackson, Shenandoah Valley, Virginia, to examine a cavalry camp site offered for the
use of the Government.

From May 23 to July 23, the Colonel aided in the selection of suitable cantonment sites in the Eastern Department. Those chosen came to be known as Camps Meade,
Lee, Dix, and Upton. The last days of the month were
spent in visits to the camps at Plattsburg and Syracuse.

Pershing, as commander of the American Expeditionary
Forces, sailed for France. With him went fifty-three
officers and 146 enlisted men, the small ripple that preceded mounting waves. General Enoch H. Crowder,
named Provost Marshal General, prepared for registration
day on June 5, when the names of 10,000,000 were to be
signed in conformity with the draft law.

Brown refused to let age slow him down. His heart and
soul went into any work assigned him. He rode over to
Mineola, Long Island, and got into a Curtiss biplane with
a lieutenant of the Signal Corps as pilot. They ascended to
the dizzy height of 3,000 feet and traveled forty miles in
half an hour, "going above the clouds &c."

A week later, the Colonel invaded Hoboken. He spent
an entire day taking down the confession of a sugar thief

and an ex-alderman who acted as a "fence." Then he "nailed" an Italian grocer for buying the sugar.

While he watched fellow officers embark for France, the man who had participated in all of his country's wars since 1878 felt aggrieved that he might be left behind.

CHAPTER XXXV

In the Great War of Europe

ON A heat-burdened day at Governors Island, Colonel Brown sat down to read his daily paper. His eye caught a report: the War Department did not favor appointment of general officers who had passed their sixtieth birthday. He squinted at the thermometer, then sprang from his chair.

On August 4, he submitted to Adjutant General McCain a table showing how forty-six line officers of the army who were beyond sixty still were well qualified for promotion. The veteran made a special plea in behalf of himself, supported by a statement from his department commander, Major General J. Franklin Bell:

1. With more than ordinary sympathy I forward this appeal for recognition.
2. If single-minded devotion to one's profession and duty, even to the extent of having no other interest in life; if zeal far beyond the capacity of the average man to possess; if painstaking perseverance in and conscientious performance of useful work; and if willing, uncomplaining participation in disagreeable field service can merit recognition after more than forty years of exceptionally faithful service as an officer, Colonel Brown is certainly worthy of advancement in additional grade before retirement. His physical condition has always been and still is excellent.

Brown, with gratitude unveiled, addressed an informal letter to Bell:

Permit me to thank you from the bottom of my heart for your generous, cordial & vigorously expressed indorsement of my letter of this date.

We all want rank of course, but the impression made on me on reading what you had written was:—

What is rank anyhow compared to the estimation in which one is held by one's friends of forty years!

Encomiums such as you have given me are worth *more than rank,* much as we value the latter.

Let the star come or not, I'm not going to worry, but I shall treasure your written indorsement of my services with kindest pride and pleasure.

Cordially & gratefully yours,

W. C. B.

Other general officers gladly wrote letters approving his application for a brigadier generalship in the National Army.

In Washington, on the eighteenth, the Colonel called on Scott, whose efforts to take generals "right down the lineal list" met bristling opposition. Brown was advised to see Major General William A. Mann, Chief of the Militia Bureau, for Scott had spoken to Mann about his taking the old warrior overseas with him.

Mann approved and sent his caller to Colonel Douglas MacArthur, his chief of staff. The dynamic son of General MacArthur agreed unhesitatingly. But was it not an outrage that an officer of such capabilities should serve "this way"? Then, as his guest went out the door: "Keep on trying for one of the still existing places."

Encouraged, if not elated, Brown refused to call it a day until he bearded the Secretary of War. He gained access to Baker's office, and the busy man shoved papers aside to listen ten minutes to the soldier who was married only to the army. The Secretary compared his own small body with that of the rugged veteran. He chuckled.

"Well, you are about the best physical specimen I've seen around here. Have you your papers with you?"

"Yes, sir." The officer handed them over.

"I'll consider them."

After Brown had departed, Baker directed Scott to refer the papers to the Board of General Officers for report as to why it had passed by the man. Scott spoke up with ringing sincerity.

"And this man is as loyal as a dog."

A week passed and Brown opened a letter addressed to him by Secretary Baker.

After your call on me the other day, I took up with the committee which had charge of the making of recommendations for promotion the very earnest wish you expressed and went over with them the reasons which in their judgment had led them to withhold a recommendation in your case at present.

I am very happy to be able to tell you that your zeal, intelligence and character were all praised by every member of the board, and yet, for reasons which I feel it impossible to overrule, it was their judgment that the report as made ought to stand.

An unfavorable comment by a former commanding officer—and too many years behind him—had crushed the applicant's hopes. The hammering ranks of Mars demanded resiliency and hardness.

Brown, however, admitted no concavity when he was assigned to command an overseas casual camp at Fort Jay. This sort of "home work" was only placatory. Somehow a way must be found for egress from a noncombatant zone.

He requested of Scott that, if his appointment as a general officer in the National Army were not possible, he be allowed to accompany the Forty-second (Rainbow) Division to France. He would go in any capacity. He vowed to "make good."

The War Department became mellow, issued another order. On September 5, Brown reported for duty to Mann, head of the Forty-second Division, at Camp Albert L. Mills, Long Island, named for the officer whose death was still a fresh memory. The Colonel's immediate duties with the troops assembling from twenty-six states in the Union were as war diarist and inspector of the camps of the regiments.

Unknown to many rookies who took French leave—absence without permission—he made notes of their truancy. Later, in France, Major General Rhodes would become their commander. And he would have reason to call them all heroes.

General Bliss stepped into Scott's shoes on September 22. The next day, he and Baker reviewed the Rainbow Division, ate dinner with the officers at camp headquarters. Brown noted happily that commendation for the troops signified an early departure.

In the hope that there might be a chance to get into the saddle again in France, the cavalryman arranged to ship his horse, Gilderry. General Mann tried out Gilderry, pronounced him an excellent mount, and on October 1 ordered him to be sent to Newport News, Virginia, port of animal embarkation.

Cold, foggy, rainy days seemed endless. And while the Colonel waited impatiently, he partook of farewell dinners with the Lindsays and other New Yorkers. At last, on the sixteenth, all officers at headquarters sent their baggage to Hoboken. Brown passed down six items: trunk locker, small bed roll, black handbag, duffle bag, saddle trunk, and a box of official books.

At three o'clock of the dank morning of the eighteenth, a dimly lighted train with 1,200 men glided out of the camp for port. Others followed at intervals. The last pulled away at noon. The men from headquarters went aboard the *Covington,* once the *Cincinnati* of the Hamburg-American Line, and at eight o'clock that night the camouflaged ship eased away from the pier. At Tomkinsville, the flotilla of nine vessels, six transports, and three naval ships as convoy, was made up for the transatlantic venture.

Brown straightened his shoulders. He was off for France!

Next morning at three-fifteen, the guarded transports carrying 16,594 military passengers passed beyond the ghostly Quarantine Station, slipped out of American waters. Daylight was brief on the high sea. Darkness descended between four and five o'clock. Then metal screens were placed over the portholes so that no light beckoned to lurking, stabbing U-boats.

The third day out, there popped up the question of censoring the war diary which had been kept so painstakingly. Brown discussed the matter thoroughly with Mann and MacArthur and decided to pursue his own plans. He wrapped all his confidential papers in one package, tied a weight to it, and kept it with his life preserver. If the enemy boarded the vessel, the package would be cast into the sea.

The fear of raiders made the long dark nights, without even the chance to read, hang heavy on the soldiers. A night came when seven torpedo boats, painted grotesquely to render them visible only at a short distance, arrived as escort for the transports. The cruiser *Seattle* and the pair of destroyers turned back to the United States.

Afterwards, on the second daybreak, Brown and his warriors sighted through shifting mist the shores of war-torn France. The brood of torpedo boats had increased to eleven.

The tide and haze did not permit pushing into port until another day. Yet the *Covington* finally scraped its berth, shrouded in secrecy. Among officers eager to listen to news from the front, Brown left a blank in his diary for the name of the port.

The next morning, November 2, he stepped ashore in St. Nazaire at the mouth of the river Loire, exchanged some of his money for francs, bought a Sam Browne belt and a number of maps. To sister Grace went the laconic cablegram: "Safe. Well."

A week later the Yanks went on to Vaucouleurs. Brown spent a night in Paris and at Gondrecourt greeted General Sibert, who had arrived with the First Division in June.

The days were cloudy and the streets muddy as the men settled in their billets. They kept the shutters closed at night while German warplanes roared overhead.

More troops came from America. Brown turned over his war diary work to a lieutenant. MacArthur apprised him he should have a task befitting his rank. General George B. Duncan came in from a trip along the line and told how he had won his French ribbon. The first snow fell on the twenty-seventh, and on the last day of the month Brown rode an ambulance down to A. E. F. Headquarters at Chaumont. He had been assigned as assistant to the chief quartermaster, Major General H. L. Rogers.

After reporting to Rogers, the Colonel chatted with some of the leaders who were helping Pershing's forces gain momentum: Liggett, Moseley, Malin Craig, George C. Marshall, Frank R. McCoy, Bullard; Foulois, now a General; James G. Harbord, Chief of Staff; Adjutant General Benjamin Alvord, and William D. Connor, who, like MacArthur, would later serve as Superintendent of West Point. The hard-driving Summerall already had been boosting for the man he first encountered as adjutant at the Academy.

Brown wired for his mount Gilderry. But Rogers assigned him a car "permanently," and placed him in the newly created post of Inspector in the Quartermaster Corps. The designation was suggested by Brown himself, and of the situation he wrote:

The organization of the Inspection Service in the Quartermaster Corps arose from a desire on the part of the Chief Quartermaster to have his own inspectors who should investigate the needs of troops, the workings of various orders which put in motion the machinery by which they were to be supplied, and who should by phone, telegraph or letter keep him informed on all such matters.

There is no known law or even regulation covering such position. .... Reports made by Inspectors General and Acting Inspectors General have to go through too many channels before they reach the Chief Quartermaster to be of much use to him. This was a time of war, and delays, which in time of peace are of relatively little moment, are serious in their consequences—therefore regulations and precedents must be disregarded. . . . .

The necessity of doing away with accountability after supplies left the depot rendered it the more important that some officer or officers should be constantly observing, reporting and making recommendations looking to improvement in methods of supply as well as in the quality of articles furnished. Several conditions conspired to confine the duties of the Inspector in the earlier months to the prevention of accumulation of surplus supplies. Due to lack of system, probably for the most part unavoidable, troops arrived in their training areas weeks and even months in advance of their baggage, necessitating the requisitioning of supplies for immediate needs which, often slow in coming, frequently reached the troops at about the same time as their baggage. Having had so much difficulty in obtaining these articles, it was not unnatural that they should be loath to part with them even though no immediate need existed for what was now on hand. The duty of the Inspector in such cases was plain. Such supplies of necessity were ordered shipped back to depots in order that they might be available for issue elsewhere. . . . .

A division of the Great War was larger than had been the entire army twenty-five years previously, a period when only a brigadier and ten field officers had comprised the staff for inspection. In France, the massive and complicated Service of Supply, familiarly called the S. O. S., functioned with little friction. The Quartermaster Corps inspectors did not have as many activities demanding attention as did the Inspector General. They could perform their duties more thoroughly.

Brown paid his first inspection trips to the Forty-second, Twenty-sixth, Second, and First Divisions, the only fighting units in France from a total of forty-two organized divisions. Then he visited the First Separate Brigade, the Sixty-seventh and Fifty-first Field Artillery Brigades at Coetquidan, the Heavy Artillery Training Camp at Souge, and the Forty-first Division at La Courtine.

The repair, as well as new issues, of soldiers' clothing and shoes called for ingenuity and vigilance. The Inspector, because of the peculiarly all-round knowledge he gained, also became an instructor. Physical inspections of store-rooms, or other places where supplies might be kept, were made. Brown had his explanation.

Where shortages were found, report by telephone so that immediate steps could be taken to hurry supplies forward was usually resorted to. The hoarding of supplies was frequently the result of *wrong interpretation of orders;* as was instanced when the Inspector found that a Quartermaster, who was supplying several thousand men, had but five pairs of leggings in store, while one of the batteries dependent on the same Quartermaster had 150 pairs hoarded up for which it had no use. Or it might be *bad management,* as when a man was discovered in ranks stockingless, but whose Company Commander had an unopened box of 500 pairs of socks in his store room and had asked for 600 additional pairs for which he had no need.

It might be *poor distribution,* as when one regiment was found clamoring for more blankets while another only a few miles distant had on hand whole bales of surplus blankets. Such matters were usually adjusted by the Inspector on the spot.

The Colonel spent Christmas, a snowy one, at Chaumont. Through the hands of the new Adjutant General, Robert C. Davis, flowed a rising flood of typed directions. While soldiers labored to keep a large lot of vegetables from freezing, Brown added to his penciled notes: "Lack of hatred French vs. Germans. Marshall has seen more than any American officer." Indeed, Marshall wished to learn wherever learning might be had.

At the year's end, the Inspector ran into Gibbons, still reporting wars for the *Chicago Tribune.* They exchanged the latest news—and recalled a moonlit night in Old Mexico.

In the first days of 1918, Pershing insisted on the speedy and intensive training of the soldiers he would need in the spring. In America, the call was heeded. Faster and faster, the facilities shaped up for spanning the Atlantic with all that might be required.

Early in February, the Twenty-sixth Division, one of the first American divisions to enter the fighting zone as a unit, went on the line north of Soissons. Brown found it

necessary to go to the regulation station at Creil and near-
by points to observe the relation of troop movements to
the Quartermaster Corps. At Soissons he saw the cataclys-
mal effects of a new kind of war: bomb-gouged craters,
twisted and mucky trenches, rakish sortie ladders hanging
to ripped revetments, barbed-wire entanglements, crushed
and tottering masonry.

The Colonel made inquiries at the hospital four kilome-
ters south of Soissons. He jotted down the recommendation
of the Chief Surgeon of the French Army Corps "that we
should have a reserve of 2,000 uniforms & underclothes
complete for issue to men gassed with mustard gas with
which the Germans have recently made attacks here.
Men's clothes exposed to mustard gas must at once go
thru a disinfecting process as the gas clinging to the clothes
is very irritating to the skin."

On his way back to Chaumont to have the order filled,
he met and lunched with General Bell. The General had
kind words: "If I had to name a man for Inspector of
Q. M. C., I don't believe that I could name a better man
than you."

Between February 15 and 20, the Colonel inspected the
supplies of regiments behind the British front. One regiment quartered three miles back of firing bays possessed
$20,000 worth of clothing and supplies above its immediate
needs. The surplus went back to the depot. Within five
weeks the enemy launched a quick and powerful drive.
Saved from falling into its hands was the clothing Brown
had removed.

A few days later, luck was lagging when the officer set
out to inspect another regiment which, without warrant,
held an oversupply of material unprotected against fire.
The day before Brown appeared the storehouse burned. Its
loss amounted to $233,000.

Timely action by the Inspector, however, insured other
organizations from similar losses. In a three-day period

he saved enough equipment from seizure by the enemy, that more than offset the salaries paid the inspectors for the war's duration. As more Yanks stood alongside the Allies, he scanned everything from supplies in the rear to troop rations in the firing line. The occasional whine of a shell or the ps-zing of a bullet caused no distraction. And the man who had improved the sight on the army rifle learned time and again how often bullets were finding their mark.

When he dropped in on troops at the front near Badon-viller in April, he perceived the urgent necessity of supplying them with tinned emergency rations. He reported his conviction with vigor. In due course, a contract for 4,000,000 of the emergency rations was to be allowed. Only ten days before the cessation of hostilities, however, would the first consignment of the tinned food be unloaded in France. About 2,000,000 of the rations were to be delivered before the signing of the Armistice in Compiegne Forest where twenty-two years later would come a reversal of surrender.

In May, when 130,000 American soldiers set out for France, the Quartermaster General cabled a request that Brown's reports be mailed to him. Absence from General Headquarters averaged twenty-two days in the month. On the nineteenth, March, as Chief of Staff, took up the huge weight of the home front. Ever ready to make adjustments between Chaumont and Washington stood Baker, the mediator.

In an inspection of the gigantic supply depot at Gievres, Brown took steps which thereafter rescued material from weathering. By the first week of June he had called upon the American divisions behind the British front: the Second, Fourth, Twenty-seventh, Twenty-eighth, Thirtieth, Thirty-third, Thirty-fifth, Seventy-seventh, and Eighty second.

The arrival of 150,000 more well-trained troops from the United States in July increased immeasurably the duties of inspectors of supplies. Colonel B. Frank Cheatham became the inspector of divisions behind the British front. Brown was assigned the Toul group of five advanced divisions—the Second, Fifth, Twenty-ninth, Thirty-fifth, Seventy-seventh—and nine in the training areas to the east, consisting of the Sixth, Thirty-second, Thirty-seventh, Seventy-sixth, Seventy-ninth, Eighty-ninth, Ninetieth, Ninety-first, and Ninety-second.

Pershing now had James W. McAndrew as his Chief of Staff, with Harbord as dexterous head of the S. O. S. Moseley had succeeded Connor, named Chief of Staff for the Thirty-second Division. Other officers filled gaps where needed. At the front and in the rear, the A. E. F. struck the stride that was not to be checked by the stoutest adversary. The German retreat across the Marne which began July 19 meant more than could be imagined by doughboys caked with mud.

Brown, in his wide discretionary powers, kept his chauffeurs at the wheel. On August 2, he came upon Tompkins, commanding an infantry regiment eager for battle. Four days after, he saw President Poincare present Pershing with the Grand Cross of the Legion of Honor. On the thirteenth he called on General Foulois. And he made arrangements, satisfactory to General Mason M. Patrick, Chief of Air Service, to inspect various aero units.

A year had gone by since Congress had added $640,000,-000 to a first appropriation of $44,250,000 for obtaining 20,000 airplanes. To produce them, however, was another matter. With a force of fifty-odd obsolete planes at the outbreak of the war, the United States by the spring of 1918 had its pilots in France organized into only two observation squadrons and one for pursuit. They flew French planes. Before the summer was over, Foulois, Patrick, "Billy" Mitchell, and other riders of the clouds welcomed new flying strength, but never enough to outstrip the Jerries.

To Pershing, nevertheless, came sufficient ground troops. Against flailing Allied arguments he stuck by his decision to embody them in a strictly American Army. With stout hearts they began an attack on the St. Mihiel salient at 5:00 A. M. of September 12. At Tours, in the evening, Brown rejoiced over the break-through and capture of 8,000 prisoners. In three more days many more thousands of Germans surrendered, and the salient was wiped out.

Depleted and battered divisions of the Allies, girded anew, again drank from the cup of hope. They plunged into the Battle of the Meuse-Argonne on the twentieth. The Franco-American attack in the Argonne Forest started on the twenty-sixth. The next day the British ruptured the Hindenburg Line. Gradually, desperately, the Germans reeled backward, yielding long-held soil.

Greater became the area which Brown had to visit. Acute were the multitudinous problems. Devotion was rendered the dead and the wounded, those stricken with influenza, those who carried on. In a short time the Colonel would face retirement, but he still hoped for the star.

Younger officers in the line and on the staff had received merited promotion and many of them voiced approval of renewed pleadings by the oldest officer in the A. E. F., Inspector Brown. From Headquarters, S. O. S., to the Commander in Chief, A. E. F., went a written appeal accompanied by Harbord's letter of October 1:

1. Forwarded, approved and recommended.
2. Particular attention invited to the statements of Major General H. L. Rogers, under whom Colonel Brown is now serving, and to those of Major Generals J. F. Bell and J. E. Kuhn as quoted in Colonel Brown's letter. I do not think that at the close of his career the War Department can afford to deny a final promotion for retirement to a veteran colonel of over forty five years of faithful service; one of six survivors on the active list who have been brevetted for gallantry in action; one whose zeal and conscientiousness have never been questioned; and whose life has been one of single-hearted devotion to his profession.

In and out of Chaumont, to the quartermaster depot at Bordeaux, to troops on the verge of entering battle, journeyed the tireless inspector. He praised the tank school at Bourge, for there they let him squeeze into a baby tank for a pummeling ride.

After Bulgaria had surrendered, and United States troops had captured St. Etienne, his diary recorded multiplying rumors and official information. It was heard "that the Huns & Turks & Austrians have sent in a new peace proposition."

October 9: "Rumor tonight that the 4th German Army has laid down its arms." October 10: "Rumor that Kaiser has abdicated in favor of his third son."

November 1: "News today of Turkey's capitulation. Austria crumbling, losing 50,000 prisoners in one battle." November 3: "Papers say Kaiser has abdicated." November 7: "Got word after lunch that an armistice with Germany had been signed." November 8: "News of yesterday re armistice proved to be false. Our men reached Sedan today..... German delegation ask for immediate armistice which is denied & they are given 72 hours to decide whether or not they will accept the terms." November 10: "We hear that the Kaiser has abdicated & there is a big revolution on in Germany."

Then the war—the last war for Brown—did come to an end. On the eleventh, he waited at Issoudun for a car to take him back to Chaumont. The commanding officer of the Third Aviation Instruction Center disclosed the news that the armistice had been signed at 11:00 A. M. The Kaiser had fled to Holland. Revolution in Germany was in full swing.

When night came Brown watched quietly, pensively, the joyously celebrating throngs in the street where stood the Hotel de France. To him it was a time for meditation.

Almost 2,000,000 men had been sent to France to serve under Pershing. A few selected divisions made ready to occupy a portion of the Rhineland. The return to America of the others and demobilization pointed toward a gigantic task. The War Department adopted a policy, effective November 11, not to appoint or promote any United States Army officers during the period of emergency.

Brown felt uncertain about any chance of his ever being addressed as a brigadier general. At Chaumont on the fifteenth he wrote a full page in his diary:

. . . . Gen. Pershing stopped his car as I was going in to lunch at my billet & got out & said he had seen me a number of times but had not had a chance to shake hands; said he had heard from all sides good reports of the work I had done & wanted to say that it was appreciated.

I said that I would retire Dec. 19, 1918, & intended applying to be continued in active duty & hoped he would approve, to which he replied "I certainly shall." I also told him that I had an application in for appointment as B. G. before retirement. He said he understood that Washington would make no appointments till this affair was all over.

Colonel Brown had to wait while no exception was made in his case. Zealously he followed duty and drew up final reports, heartened by the appreciation of General Connor, who relieved the work-devouring Johnson Hagood as Chief of Staff of S. O. S. On his inspection tours in France, Brown had traveled some 16,000 miles by automobile and several thousand more miles by rail.

At Chaumont on the seventeenth of December, Moseley assembled his officers of Section Four, G. H. Q., and invited Brown. Moseley held back no words of regret as he addressed the gathering. Then he gave the veteran a chance to say good-by.

Erect, eyes smiling kindly at the men who were all his brothers, Brown went around the circle. Firmly he clasped each pair of hands. Huskily he uttered the words of farewell only soldiers could understand.

On the nineteenth he went to Tours, Headquarters of S. O. S. He had reached his sixty-fourth birthday. After forty-five years, five months, and nineteen days of active service in the United States Army, he had reason to put in capitals a word that crept into his diary entry. But there was no period after the word.

RETIRED

The next day he chatted with Generals Rogers and Connor, handed in his last report. Both officers, by word and letter, encouraged the departing Inspector to strive for the deserved star which doubtless would come through legislation.

Back at Chaumont for a few days, restless Brown read a letter addressed to him by Moseley, a man who did not forget:

Subject: Commendation.

1. Although very much your junior in the regular army, I cannot let the day of your retirement from active service pass without calling attention to your very unusual record. I first met you shortly after my entrance into the service and since that time we have served together at a number of places. During the last few months you have been on duty, which has been one of the greatest assistance to me in my work, although you are not directly a part of this office.

2. Graduating from the military Academy in 1877, you have during all these years devoted your entire life and energies to the service. Most of us have families to whom we give a part of our time, consideration and love, but in your case your whole life has been devoted to the Government. You have thought of nothing but its welfare and in your devotion to duty, to the exclusion of everything else you have set a most commendable example to us all.

3. It would be impossible for me to refer, except in the very briefest way to your record, ...

4. The service that you have rendered in connection with the operations of the Quartermaster Department in France have been of the greatest assistance, not only in the standardization of methods and issues, but in the protection of government property as well. General Rogers has repeatedly commended the work you have done.

5. As I look at you today, I cannot see that you have aged a bit in the last fifteen years and you certainly appear fully fit in every way for further active service in the field.

6. Please permit me to congratulate you for all you have done for

the service and I will consider it an honor if you will let this letter, bearing my signature, be placed on file with your record.

By order of the C. in C.

The "C. in C." was Pershing, already thinking of a citation for the receiver of the letter. Regulations, however, directed that "Col. William C. Brown, Cavalry, ... will proceed to his home."

Another Christmas with snow came to Chaumont, also a visit by President Wilson, fighting for permanent peace, and his compatriots. Brown attended the review of proudly stepping Yanks. Then he turned to his packing.

The last days of 1918 and the first of 1919 he spent in Paris, a Paris wearing a necklace restrung with two priceless pearls, Alsace and Lorraine.

Dressed conservatively in "cits," Brown, on January 4, went to Boulogne, then on to London. In another six days he reported for physical examination at the American Embarkation Camp, Knotty Ash, Liverpool. As he prepared to embark, word came that death had summoned General J. Franklin Bell. To Mrs. Bell the Colonel wrote a letter. It conveyed sympathy that came straight from the wounded heart of an officer-comrade and friend.

At noon of the eleventh, he went aboard the S. S. *Melita* and, with other officers, claimed a berth. At four-thirty in the afternoon, the ship eased out into a smooth sea. On the next day, anchorage was made off Brest to pick up more passengers and supplies.

Another night passed. Then ship and tide teamed together and the vessel moved on toward America.

Fanned by a light breeze, the old cavalryman stood on deck. His eyes were wells filled with memories, his jaw an immovable cornerstone. Now, he realized fully, he had "made good" in France. In his last war, as well as in all others gone before, he had upheld duty, honor, country.

CHAPTER XXXVI

At Ease

IT IS inspection day.

The hard-boiled but erubescent drill sergeant stands stiffly before his platoon of riflemen. His eyes flash. His voice thunders.

"Pla-toon—at-ten-shun!"

A clicking of heels. A straightening of the body, toe to head. Chin up. Chest thrown out. Rifles in a vertical position at the right leg of each man.

"Por-rt—ar-rms!"

A slapping of hands on rifles. Rifles hoisted to a diagonal placing across mid-body, butt over right hip, barrel above left shoulder.

"Ri-ight shoul-der—ar-rms!"

A leathery slapping of rifle slings on calloused shoulders.

"Por-rt—ar-rms!"

The slap-slap of rifles ported again.

"In-speck-shun—ar-rms!"

A metallic clicking of bolts thrust back. And the inspector walks down the line of men, two deep.

Guns grabbed. Eyes on polished wood and steel. Guns returned.

"Or-der—ar-rms!"

Rifles drop to the vertical position at the right side, butts thudding on the ground.

"Puh-rade—res-st!"

Rifles are held loosely in relaxed fingers. Left knees bend slightly and right feet are carried half a foot to the rear.

Butts or stocks are turned broadside against the toes of right feet. The men remain silent and motionless.

"At-ten-shun!"

Just to get rigid again.

"At ee-ease!"

Lessening of tension. Immobility erased. But formation and silence maintained. Ranks are not broken until the platoon is "dismissed."

How many times Brown had heard it all, through peace-time and wartime. It was part of him. Long past was the day when, as a cavalryman, the "order arms" had been barked; when he dropped his sword or saber to the front, the point on or near the ground. Long since had he sheathed the blade, or hung it by its knot.

What to do now? Surely, the man was still of the army though he was "retired." He was not dismissed. Certainly not. He was, he reminded himself over and over, "at ease." Yes, that was it—at ease. But not too much at ease.

The soldier, returning to Washington, did not rest on his well-earned laurels. He asked of those whose words kept rolling the ponderous wheels of the Quartermaster Corps that he be called to active duty. While the applicant awaited judgment, he prepared arguments for the intro-duction of a bill in Congress which would give him the rank of brigadier general. Congress was the court of last resort for the army man. Senator C. S. Thomas of Colo-rado and other influential friends made the initial moves in what was to become an oft side-tracked measure.

Frequent became the trips to New York and the ex-change of visits with Dr. and Mrs. Lindsay. They were among those awaiting the return of a son from an army camp. In March, General Rogers, who had replaced Quar-termaster General Sharpe, informed Brown that his request for active service could not, in the press of events, be met. His horse, Gilderry, had been returned, and a bill of sale

Courtesy of Colonel James Boyd, Denver, Colorado.

General William C. Brown, wearing his Sam Browne belt and some of his medals, shortly before his retirement from active service.

was made out for the mount the cavalryman no longer cared to ride.

The Colonel went to New York in time to be on hand for a talk and luncheon given by Assistant Secretary of the Navy Franklin Delano Roosevelt. There was more than the mere churning of salty waters behind the words of the young speaker, the man headed for the White House. After the annual dinner of graduates of the Military Academy, the journey homeward began. A pilgrimage to Minnesota revived that which had become dim. Then, in the first week of April, the wanderer greeted his sisters in Denver.

The weeks went by without diary entries. June 1 was an unusual day, described by one word, "Snow." Three weeks later came a document signed by General Pershing:

CITATION

Col. W. C. Brown, Cav.

For exceptionally meritorious and conspicuous services as Inspector, Quartermaster Corps, American Expeditionary Forces, in testimony thereof, and as an expression of appreciation of these services, I award him this Citation.

Awarded on April 19, 1919.

The summer past, Brown went back to his nation's capital city with nostalgia for its broad thoroughfares, innumerable circles, bronze statues, and marble temples. He wanted to work. Colonel W. R. Grove wrote the Quartermaster General that his services should be utilized in the Subsistence Branch, that "he does not consider it necessary to again be placed on the active list but simply use him in an advisory capacity."

General Rogers put Brown to work on October 6. The disposition of more than a million emergency rations, costing some $639,000, was the immediate problem. Under the rush of war, the rations had been packed improperly, and Brown advised that they be declared surplus and sold. There were buyers, the Polish Government taking half of the surplus. By the end of the year, Colonel W. H. Point, Chief of Subsistence Division, was pointing out that Brown's efforts "will no doubt result in a saving to the Government of something like $250,000.00."

The Colonel, working without pay, stayed on, trying to improve the reserve rations. On June 17, 1920, General Rogers informed General R. C. Davis that he had recommended his volunteer worker for the Distinguished Service Medal. The awarded citation he did not consider "exactly accurate," and asked: "Is there any way by which this citation could be amended to more completely express the character and extent of service performed by Colonel Brown?"

In addition to his research, Brown enjoyed valued sociabilities. He had membership in the West Point Mess, the First and Third United States Cavalry Clubs, Society of the Army of Santiago, United States Cavalry Association, Army and Navy Club of Washington, University and Explorers Club of New York City, and the Order of Indian Wars, of which his former troop leader, Bernard, had been the first president. With unwavering devotion, he attended the Presbyterian Church. He supported it consistently with financial beneficence.

In December, 1921, the reserve rations developed by him were tentatively approved for issue to the army in the event of an emergency. The meat component consisted of sliced bacon and corned beef. Pure sweetened chocolate comprised another constituent. The testing of the rations came in the next year. Adopted with the meat component, also including dried beef, "or other suitable cooked substitutes," were improved tin containers.

General Pershing had been Chief of Staff for more than a year when, on October 23, 1922, Colonel Brown was included in a list of men granted awards or citations. His previous citation was withdrawn, and the higher honor, Distinguished Service Medal, awarded:

For exceptionally meritorious and distinguished services. As Inspector, Quartermaster Corps, American Expeditionary Forces, from November, 1917, until December, 1918, throughout the zone of operations, he displayed the greatest zeal, utmost devotion to duty and indefatigable efforts. By his long experience, marked efficiency and tireless energy, he made highly intelligent inspections and recommendations, thereby enabling the Quartermaster Corps to improve the Services of Supply and the saving of a large quantity of important material.

Proud of his medal, happy over the completion of his labors resulting in the new reserve ration, the man switched his interest to duralumin and other developments. Early in February, 1923, Quartermaster General W. H. Hart, successor to Rogers, sent a letter to Adjutant General Davis extolling the servant who had no superior officer withholding praise.

Heavier became the weight of pleas before congressmen from whose hands must come the star of a brigadier.

Thinner became the ranks of old comrades. General Baldwin died in Denver on April 22. Brown, who accompanied the body to a grave in the green turf of National Cemetery at Arlington, gave tribute in the *Army and Navy Register*.

A dominant characteristic of Baldwin was that he was, first of all, a fighter. He had far more than his pro rata share of hazardous service, not simply because it was his luck, but because he sought it. . . . .

A generation ago his name was a household word all along the frontier between the 100th meridian and the Rocky Mountains. In the development of the Great West few names stand higher. . . . .

When Mrs. Baldwin set about writing the *Memoirs* of her late husband, Brown was among those who gave valuable assistance.

He returned to Denver in July, the summer of 1923 marking the beginning of a series of shifts each year for the next decade. Several months were to be spent at Denver or on historical itineraries in the West, others in Washington. He lent encouragement to military training in camps, colleges, and secondary schools. Endless became research labors in the history of the Pacific Northwest and the Indian wars, a first and last love. Historical organizations of various states received papers from his files. Impartially, he endeavored to correct misstatements of historical fact.

Among his fast comrades and co-workers stood Generals Scott, Miles, and Charles King, Colonels Frank Tompkins and E. A. Brininstool. Too, there were friends like Governor Julius C. Gunter of Colorado, John F. Stevens, the veteran engineer, and President Ralph Budd of the Great Northern Railway, who contributed unceasingly and heavily to the perpetuation of the glory in which the country from the Mississippi to the Pacific was bathed. Visits, whenever opportune, were exchanged. Frequent were neighborly chats with Major Charles B. Hardin, Retired, who could recall effulgently the wear and tear of the Sheepeater Campaign.

Honors from the War Department sometimes go forth slowly. On June 26, 1924, Brown received a letter from the Adjutant General. He had been cited "For gallantry in action against Spanish forces at Santiago, Cuba, July 1, 1898." Two weeks later, the silver star was delivered.

On May 15, 1925, the recently decorated veteran entered a street-car in Washington, a car which would take him to the Library of Congress. General Miles held a seat, and the two men fell into a conversation about early campaigns in the Southwest.

"General, Brininstool desires to have you present at the unveiling of the monument at the site of the Buffalo Wallow fight."

"When is it to be held?"

"In September."

"Colonel, I would like to study some of the maps of northern Texas and Oklahoma made in the Seventies, with just the old trails, cantonments, and so forth. I do not want a modern map."

The car neared the library, and Brown rose from his seat. "I will be glad to look them up in the Map Division, sir."

The maps concerning the operations of Miles's expedition in the Panhandle of Texas in 1874 were found, and Brown left a list of them at the Rochambeau, where the General resided. A few minutes later, the Colonel received a message. It stunned him. General Miles had dropped dead of heart attack.

Brown helped to arrange for the funeral, took his turn at watch over the casket. Scott and others arrived. In the afternoon of the nineteenth, while the nation's people grieved, the battle-scarred body of another of their heroes went to its resting place.

More often, now, the Colonel sought physical check ups, at the Fitzsimons General Hospital in Denver and in the Walter Reed Hospital. He wrote to or called upon friends who fell ill. To Takoma Park he went with Scott in March of 1926 to gladden Brigadier General Thomas Cruse who, after service at many outposts, had labored arduously in the ever-expanding Quartermaster Corps.

Apropos of the researcher's high resolve not to be idle, Brown had printed his abbreviated story of the capture of Aguinaldo. It was followed by his account of *Sheepeater Campaign in Idaho, 1879.*

Like all men who grow old thoughtfully, the Colonel remembered the place of his boyhood. He paid one of his occasional visits to Nicollet County, Minnesota, urging the St. Peter Association to gather and preserve in a printed volume all available material dealing with the vanished settlement of Traverse des Sioux. Authorship of the work was entrusted to Judge Thomas Hughes of Mankato. The visitor from Colorado became his hard-working assistant.

In the Newberry Library of Chicago, in 1926, he found the original sketches and diary of Mayer, the artist who had accompanied the Treaty Commission to Traverse des Sioux in 1851. Much of the material, along with diary notes and sketches of Nicollet, which Brown discovered in the Library of Congress, was printed for the first time.

In the files of the Minnesota Historical Society, he also uncovered bits of information. His findings, and those of fellow workers, comprised the ably documented *Old Traverse des Sioux* which was to come off the press of The Herald Publishing Company, St. Peter, in 1929.

He was digging at musty papers in Washington early in 1927 when he learned that he could replace the eagle with a star. The President was authorized by special law to advance to the next higher rank any officer who held a position on the retired list not above that of Colonel, and whose record was one of eminent military service. Promoted with Brown to the rank of Brigadier General February 28 were Colonels Wilber E. Wilder, William D. Beach, William J. Nicholson, Lloyd M. Brett, and Thomas B. Dugan.

Chief of Staff Summerall congratulated, happily and promptly, the man who long ago at West Point had lifted his depressed spirit. Months afterward, just to be of the army again, Brown took a fling with the aviators. At Langley and Bolling fields he soared and sped aloft in dirigible and plane. No new development dare escape his attention.

Stevens aided him in unraveling for Budd the long story of Marias Pass in Montana. A canyon then was named for Stevens, and the name of General Brown went on a Pullman car which glided along the Great Northern rails. There were meetings with General Charles King and Chris Madsen, the scout who had ridden in the Seventies with the Fifth Cavalry. They pointed out accurately, for marking by monuments, the spot where Buffalo Bill Cody had slain the Indian subchief Yellow Hair (or Hand) in single combat.

A trip to San Francisco afforded a pleasant visit with General and Mrs. Liggett and other friends. After conversations with Rowan, the man who had carried the message to Garcia, Brown prevailed upon him to document undisclosed details.

In Denver on July 26, 1930, the career of Brigadier General Irving Hale, prominent Colorado engineer, was concluded. Fellow citizens felt keenly the passing of the man who had been an honor graduate of West Point, a hero of the Spanish-American War, one of the founders of the Veterans of Foreign Wars of the United States, and a pillar in Denver's business life. The comrade who lived on labored earnestly to perpetuate the memory of him who had come to the end of the trail.

After he had seen the history of his birthplace put into permanent form, the unsaddled cavalryman had most of his days to spend in the capital city of Colorado, the city of brick or stone homes. Here the plainsman and the mountaineer met and lingered. Here they who raised cattle and sheep, and they who mined for gold, copper, silver, and coal pointed with pride to the pinnacle which the Centennial, or Silver, State had reached in striving for a towering position among the peoples of the Union.

The chosen flower of the Coloradoans, the columbine, was not of a species which could be easily overlooked. A genus of ranunculaceous plants, its gorgeous bloom, with spurred petals, vied strenuously with any other pompous growth Nature might create. The columbine partook of the white of snow-crowned peaks and the blue of the sky.

Here Brown kept young as he rubbed elbows with those who had built and still were building the West.

To the second story of his brick house he added a third, his own living quarters. He slept in his new apartment for the first time on the last day of 1930, slept thereafter—like any tough soldier—on a "regulation" quartermaster bed. There he studied, wrote, and sketched.

The den and workshop was of frame construction, two spacious rooms with large windows at both ends. Sandwiched between was a bathroom, also the narrow and winding stairway which led to the lower floors. In the center of the roof reposed a skylight, better to work under at a desk burdened with letter files. Tables, chairs, cabinets, bed, and a leather upholstered couch fell into convenient places. Shelves, breast-high and loaded with books, periodicals, and papers, extended along the sides of the rooms. Built-in shallow drawers contained maps and other flat documentary material.

A lone Indian rug of bright colors lay on the linoleum-covered and waxed floor. Only a man could decorate the walls with the nonchalant jarring of meticulosity. Tacked on or hanging to them were battle banners, troop pennons, a saber or two, large and small maps, colorful drawings of Indians and scouts, beaded work of the red peoples, portraits of famous army leaders and other notables, photos of comrades-in-arms who achieved greatness or who did not. Here and there a folded or unfolded note of historical or friendly worth hung limply.

In an inconspicuous corner was a miniature punctured target from the Philippines, with an open letter attached. Brown had shot the holes in the target, and Theodore Roosevelt had written the letter August 26, 1907, at Oyster Bay.

> I am greatly interested in that target. I have always kept the memory of the good shooting you and Stewart Edward White did when you were out here. I really do not understand how you could do such good shooting at night as this target shows.
>
> Let me know when you are back in the United States and in the vicinity of Washington.

A year after the house had been enlarged, Grace Brown lay ill, fighting off pneumonia. Dr. Harry C. Brown, faithful physician to the family, brought in Dr. J. N. Hall for consultation. They and nurses labored valiantly. The frail woman, however, entered the Beyond on the evening

of December 11. Christmas came with weighted memories
for the General and Helen, whose husband now was living
on borrowed hours. With decorations of greenery they
went out in their automobile, stood long and silently in the
plot at Riverside Cemetery.

In the fall of the next year, the General journeyed to
Washington. Assistance was given Colonel W. G. Ganoe in
the contemplated revision of *The History of the United
States Army*. He joined friends at the laying of the cornerstone of The National Archives, February 20, 1933, by
President Hoover. At last, priceless documents were to find
a secure refuge.

The return to Denver was on March 17. And on that
day General Charles King died at the age of eighty-nine
years. Few homes in America failed to remember the
author who had made vivid the days of campaigning in the
West. Brown's appreciation in the *Army and Navy Register* contributed a definite counterpart.

Thirst for research took the worker back to Washington
for the month of June. The last of many meetings with
General Scott at Princeton took place. Together they went
up to West Point to see another graduation, to hobnob once
more with rebounding alumni.

Fertile were the chats with Colonel Charles E. T. Lull,
then Chief of the Historical Section of the Army War
College. With Lull pointing the way, a small group of
officers at the College was launching the American Military
History Foundation. The Westerner signed up as a charter
member. The organization, later to evolve as the American
Military Institute, desired to inspire and advance historical
studies of many phases of military affairs.

At Colorado's capitol on August 13, the General ad-
dressed a gathering at the unveiling of a tablet to General
Hale. At home, he tackled the work that had no end. In
September, Dorothy Battle of the *Denver Post*, one of

many visiting correspondents, described well the workshop
and its occupant:

Although General Brown is 79, the hands with which he makes maps,
does printing and other work in the "den" on the top floor of his
home are steady. His blue eyes, unaided most of the time by glasses, are
as piercing under their shaggy, gray brows as when he fought in the
Indian campaign of the '70s. . . . .

In a drawer with souvenirs of the World War the retired officer keeps
samples of other inventions. There is a detachable spur for leggings,
lightweight horseshoes made of an aluminum alloy, a flexible stovepipe
ring, woven of asbestos, for tents.

Compact, folding equipment forms part of General Brown's collection. It is as amusing as watching rabbits spring from a hat to see a
comparatively flat disk of aluminum converted suddenly into a trio of
frying pan, water bottle and kettle, or to view a thin metal article
springing into a three-sided lantern, or to see some double-jointed bits
of aluminum straighten out into candleholders. . . . .

The modest and genial host, of course, did not divulge
the full story of the inventions. He might have explained
how, nearly every time he went through Pittsburgh, officials of the Aluminum Company of America honored him
with receptions. He could have mentioned the fact that
the United States Army was permitted to use certain of
his inventions freely.

Along with others, he had, in selfless motivation, made
the soldier's life more comfortable, assuredly less tiresome.

A Lone Survivor

NEAR the last day of January in Denver. A frigid, sawing wind drags out the first month of the year 1934. Naked branches scratch at the eaves. The trunks of thick trees are swathed in white raveling. Splotches of snow mix with soot blown from the yawning chimney onto the skylight. The den is comfortably warm, though immersed in shadows.

The General switches on the electric light at his desk. His pen, gliding back and forth, forms a skiagram on the sheet of paper. It does not take long, this letter to Sergeant Frederick Mayer of Highland Falls, New York, who had marched against the Nez Perce in 1877 and against the Bannocks and Paiutes the next year. Mayer, too, is getting old, in his seventy-ninth year. Retired in 1904, the General remembers, after serving the army actively for thirty years.

The writer dips his pen in the ink once more. Words of a soldier to a soldier:

John J. Neville, of our old Troop L, 1st Cavalry, died at Ager, California, on January 16. . . . . He enlisted May 8, 1875, and had participated in the Nez Perce War of 1877 and the Bannock War of 1878. . . . . So far as I know, you and I are the only survivors. . . . . General Frederick K. Ward, who also was in the campaign of 1878, died in Seattle a few months ago.

On February 10, Death knocked again at 875 Marion Street, taking Myron Jones. Winter gave way to spring. The bereaved Helen and brother Will motored to New Mexico, explored the wonders of Carlsbad Caverns. On April 30, a few days after their return to Denver, a messenger left a telegram. General Scott, he whose labors for the red men had buoyed him up in his last years, was dead. Brown responded liberally to requests for stories telling of the personal and public life of his close compatriot.

Then there were more talks with Madsen and trips to places where red men had fought white men. Spring stepped aside for summer. Brown, at home, opened a letter bearing the postmark of Highland Falls. On June 4, he read, Sergeant Mayer had passed away and had been buried in Peacedale Cemetery.

The General eased into his chair. Suddenly he felt old, in spite of his keen vision, clear mind, and a body not easily tired. Now he was the sole survivor. He was the only man left of that troop which had galloped forth from Fort Walla Walla to high and low roads of eastern Oregon and Idaho. It was to be remembered, though, that "good soldiers never die; they just go on living and living." Still that was not all. They must go on serving and serving.

Now and then Brown accepted an organization's invitation to meet, dine, and talk. At Denver's Adams Hotel he reminded his listeners that the country might forget too quickly the early Indian campaigns. It was worth remembering that the slowly promoted soldiers traveled one thousand to three thousand miles in the saddle in a single summer. Officers who had commanded thousands in the Civil War had led as duteously the skeletons of battalions on Western fringes. And it was worth remembering that there were good red men as well as good white men.

At home with guests, the veteran campaigner could be drawn out in a picturization of the frontier as it had been. Though he did not smoke, he kept tobacco at hand for those who indulged. If only with his sister, he would, at times, resurrect his brigadier flag and drape it on the mantel of the parlor's fireplace. Momentarily, the room became brigade headquarters. The sister was assigned to the staff. Orders were issued, explained, rescinded. Salute met salute.

After the bantering, each had many laughs. Will would leave the room and mount the stairs which led to his den. His flag would be purposely left behind. Helen then became the divisional commander. She removed the one-star banner of the brigade leader, folded it with soft caresses, and covertly tucked it away.

Meanwhile, the General busied himself in the writing and preservation of all phases of military history. But it was the colorful drama of the conquering of the West which received the greatest attention from him of faded ranks. Especially did he wish, in the few years which lay ahead, to bring out new details of the last Indian campaigns of the Pacific Northwest. In his desire to procure aid in marking the sites of several engagements of the Bannock War in Oregon, he contributed reminiscences to the *Blue Mountain Eagle* of Canyon City, in Grant County of feverish mining fame.

It was not a simple task to reawaken proper interest in events which to the layman seemed to be of such recent date yet concerning which little of accuracy had been recorded for public consumption. General Brown, however, saw many signs of a spirited growth in Western Americana. The faculties and students of universities, editors of newspapers and periodicals, and publishers of books, recognized the significant worth of presenting the story of the West in increasing variations.

The soldier and the scout, the roving Indian and his pony, the pioneer and his wagon, the crazed seeker of gold, even the cattle baron, all had marched across a stage of vast dimensions only to disappear overnight. Now it was for the individual writer or artist to frame in page or easel the tales that would never be relived. But above all, the picture must conform to actuality, truth must not be subservient to vibrancy or color.

The aging man, in his workshop and den, hastened his efforts to restore for posterity all that he might. Some days the rain spattered on the skylight over his head, some days the sun's rays poured through. And there would be other days when howling winds, driving snow from off the mighty peaks of the Rockies, would shunt aside the light of the steely disc.

The soldier who still considered himself "at ease" kept at his tasks. He studied and wrote of wars while hoping there would be no more wars. Yet, he reminded himself parenthetically, his country's frontiers had not been obliterated. They had merely shifted to the far corners of the earth. And they must always be defended tenaciously. The freedom and survival of Americans depended upon how much they battled for the survival of other freedom-loving peoples.

In September, Will rushed Helen about the "Progress" Fair at Chicago, saw her off for Denver, and went on to New York and Washington. Two things occupied most of his time: the going over of Scott's papers with Mrs. Scott and final attention to the story of the Mexican Punitive Expedition, now ready for the publisher. On October 23, he helped to carry the body of General Garlington to its place of repose. A week later, he walked in Denver.

In November, the veteran was asked for critical advice in the preparation of a case study of the Bannock war. He gave it. Then the author of the life of General Bernard, seeking helpful material from one who had known the colorful, robust cavalryman so intimately, was rewarded with valuable aid. Printed copies of Tompkins' *Chasing Villa* came before Christmas. Here, after no little toil, was the emblazoned record of American cavalrymen waging battle as they might never wage it again.

Another trip to West Point and Washington in the summer of 1935 engendered a deeper interest in the repository for rare documents. The National Archives, only one year along its way, displayed sure signs of the expert handling of records. By September, the story of Bernard came off the press in book form. Happily the man who had fought with the bearded captain thumbed his copies.

Winter gripped tightly the capital of Colorado early in February of 1936. The mercury sank to twenty-five degrees below zero. The General spent day after day in his den, and he was worried. Helen could not go about her regular duties. Dr. Brown came up the icy sidewalk more frequently, held consultation with a fellow physician and nurse. On the twenty-second, the mercury shot up to seventy-two. A week later, Helen came downstairs for a meal in the dining room.

Joyously relieved, Will left her in the care of the nurse, and at the beginning of March took a train for Washington. There was more research to be done, more help to be given active and inactive soldiers. A guide conducted him through the pristine marble corridors of The National Archives, its massive vaults ready to receive that from which the nation's life must be written.

At his room in the Army and Navy Club, he welcomed all calls, by person or by telephone. General Rhodes asked him for a certain sketch, got it before he thought a good start was possible. He did not know the Coloradoan had to make haste so that he might not fail to show a friend the cherry blossoms around the Basin.

An interstice landed Brown in New York City for a few days. The movie, "Message to Garcia," drew milling crowds to Rockefeller Center. Brown went, saw and, on a slip glued to a copy of the hero's booklet, wrote in part:

This story has been filmed & this year (1936) has been shown thru the country, but does not in the slightest degree represent the facts except as to title. Col. Rowan never *in person* took any part in representing himself in the film version, or even thought of it.

Dr. P. M. Hamer, Chief of the Division of Reference, The National Archives, gladly accepted the copy of Rowan's booklet. He and archivist Solon J. Buck found that the occasions when Brown could visit them spelled rich reminiscences and mellowly helpful criticism. They marveled at the alertness of mind exhibited by the campaigner who dexterously balanced the more than fourscore years on his shoulders. They prevailed upon him to send them other material.

Before April was out, Helen again had taken to her sick bed. She needed Will, and he was soon at her side. Doctors Brown and Philip Work guided the patient through paling weeks. Governor Gunter called and stayed to dine. In July, upon invitation, Mr. and Mrs. Ora McDaniel and their family came to live with the Browns. Their kind aid lifted oppressing gloom. The General, always appreciating a hearty meal, sat down regularly again to partake of food which, he made known emphatically, was not to be excelled.

And again in the den, after an obituary of Scott was finished, went on studies, the tracing of maps, the writing of letters. When September days arrived, arguments were shaped for the possible value of military instruction in the Civilian Conservation Corps.

Then Helen seemed "low." She gave Will a power of attorney. The first snow of the season fell. On October 10, the diary entry read: "Helen seems to sleep nearly all the time—even falls to sleep when talking. Dr. H. C. Brown came." And two days later: "President Roosevelt delivered an address at 11 A. M. to a large crowd at West entrance to Colorado Capitol."

December came. At two-thirty in the morning of the sixth, Dr. Brown was called. Helen, the steady hand of her devoted brother wrote, "seems to me to be unconscious—sleeps all the time. . . . . " She never again recognized those who grieved.

Brother Will, weary with sleeplessness, maintained a Spartan watch until ice-clad peaks glistened anew on the

morning of the eighth. Then the last thread connecting
the family ranks was severed.

It took all the man's courage to go on. The grief was
irreparable, but there still was work to do. And close by
stood loyal friends.

On his favorite stroll, Brown went out Marion Street a
short distance. Then he crossed to the west a few blocks
and, turning into tranquil Bannock Street, stopped at an
iron gate hung on a vine-covered wall. In the inviting
home set back in a recess of broadly branching trees, lived
the daughter of Dr. Brown. She had married Professor
James Boyd, the youthful and brilliant member of the
faculty of the Colorado School of Mines. In the second
World War, he would be serving in the Department of
War as Lieutenant Colonel of Engineers. From him the
General could draw out the latest information concerning
mineralogy, always one of his consuming hobbies. Refreshing chats, reciprocal pleasures—and reminiscences—now
meant everything.

Slower, much slower, grew the steps of the man who
looked forward to the sixtieth anniversary of his graduation
from the Point. On January 30, 1937, he mailed letters to
thirteen surviving classmates. Two weeks later, Governor
Hunter talked with him about the drafting of his will.
Shortly after, James Boyd was named executor.

Yet Brown had failed to accumulate personal wealth.
Never had he desired to place himself in any other position
than one of comfort and security. He had been liberally
compensated by his government, but much of his pay
flowed back in various channels. To invent was to give, to
investigate was to improve. The representatives of worthy
causes asked and received. Those in need had not been
turned away empty of hand.

The *Chicago Daily News* of April 1 carried an editorial
which did not go unnoticed.

The army and the navy, by rulings that make all inventions of their personnel the property of the government, have offered small stimulus to the improvements of their weapons. Such ideas as the rifle drift correction of Brig. Gen. W. C. Brown, the ammunition belt of Maj. Anson Mills, the Sibley tent and the Munson last shoe brought scant recognition and no reward to their inventors.

The munitions industry, despite much balderdash about its always dragging us into war—and into what war is not at all clear—has given to the army and navy of the United States the Browning machine gun, the Browning automatic rifle, the Colt's automatic pistol and the light tanks used by the mechanized cavalry. Light artillery has been borrowed from the French. The navy has almost a monopoly on the production of heavy guns, but the steel that makes them possible has been a commercial development.

The manufacture of arms and munitions in government armories should be encouraged. The navy should continue ship-building. But the best interests of national defense are served if this be done in competition with, and in cooperation with, private industry. In the past the interchange between private interests and government has given our defense forces the finest equipment in the world. There is real danger that government monopoly may result in stagnation.

There seems to be no reason why the possibilities for excessive profit in private contract cannot be as effectively controlled as can the possibilities for graft in government operation.

General Brown, after convincing himself that he had strength for one more long trip, in the last of May unpacked his baggage at the Army and Navy Club. There were talks again with General Rhodes and Dr. Hamer, talks relating to the disposition of historical papers. He went out to Arlington Cemetery "to see where H. L. Scott, H. L. Rogers and L. M. Brett are buried." On June 8, he breakfasted with General Moseley at the Pennsylvania Hotel in New York City. Moseley was wondering how long "F. D. R." would hold out with "Jno. L. Lewis." An evening with the Lindsays, then Brown went off to West Point.

Alumni Day was now the highlight for the grad of '77. Did he tell comrades it was his last? He "took a taxi & went to cemetery. My lot is slightly West of North of Chapel."

He met "many people" at the superintendent's reception. And, "Rested frequently during the day but by 9 P. M. was exhausted & went to bed."

The old soldier cut the graduating exercises, to go down the Hudson for an electric bath and massage. But "it did little good." Only a few more days were risked in Washington. On the train which carried the Westerner back home rode Admiral Hugh Rodman, and the salt of the sea and the dust of the plains mingled.

Denver offered surcease and unfailing hospitality in the months ahead. The final anchorage. A dinner at Governor Gunter's with John F. and Eugene Stevens provided more than mere food for a man who was "at home." On Sunday, October 3, the General became a member of Denver's Central Presbyterian Church, transferring from the Union Presbyterian Church of St. Peter, Minnesota. The congregation accepted him warmly, and obtained his promise to address them at a later date on national defense.

In mid-November he went to Fitzsimons Hospital for another checkup. Lieutenant Colonel John G. Knauer examined him thoroughly, gave an encouraging report, recommended easier going. While Dr. Brown also kept close watch, he visited his dentist and oculist. He who had been one of the army's best sharpshooters could not understand why, at times, he was "seeing double." This had to be overcome! More work lay ahead.

The General's interest in the preparation of the story of the Bannock War increased as it was gradually being pieced together. He continued to encourage its author. In Yuletide greetings, he wrote with a firm hand:

I shall look for that history of the Bannock Campaign (my first active service) with much interest. So far as I know it is the first real history of it written."

Age and the many years of hard, unrelenting service, however, inevitably exacted their toll. Before the winter

had been long on its way, the General was battling myas-
thenia and other complications. Mrs. Lindsay came to
Marion Street and tarried a few days. She conveyed cheer,
but went away knowing that soon another link in the
chain of kinship would be dropped.

Colonel Knauer lived with his family across the street
from the Brown home. A loyal friend as well as a physician,
he gave unstinted aid to the retired officer. A thoroughgoing student of history, he enjoyed the collection of his
patient, as did Dr. Brown. Then it was made possible, in
an endeavor to procure the best of attention, along with
baths and massages, to place the persevering sick man in the
Army and Navy General Hospital at Hot Springs,
Arkansas.

There, on the first day of May, 1938, the General rebuked himself for his laxity in correspondence. The date
of publication of the documentary study of the Bannock
War was approaching. In a long letter, containing lithe
reminiscences, he expressed his enthusiasm. But the sentences were short, some phrases clipped.

"Yours of the 25th," he began, "finds me here on 'Sick
Report.' Confined to my room & able to write only with
difficulty. . . . . " And, in conclusion, "Excuse scrawl as I
write sitting up in a chair."

Springtime resurrected many things. There was a burning desire to quit the hospital in the South, although he
often expressed a deep appreciation for the staff's constant
aid and encouragement of his fellow-patients. Buoyed up
with cherished hopes, the veteran returned to his home,
where he could look out once more upon the towering
peaks of the Rockies. In mountains he saw strength.
Courage plus an indomitable will kept his face turned to
the future as well as to the past.

Budd visited him in July, and noted how much depended
upon Dr. Brown and Colonel Knauer. In that month, also,
the still unbeaten warrior received his copy of the book

which related the story of the Bannock War. Once read, he forthrightly voiced his gratitude and pleasure to the author and to Dr. Hamer of The National Archives. He was, perhaps, "the sole surviving officer" who had ridden saddle throughout the entire campaign.

The letter told of his being confined to bed most of the time, "with a nurse in constant attendance."

Not all of his pent-up days were dull. Colonel Knauer entered the den one sunny day. He stopped to admire a huge and beautiful bouquet of flowers. Brown beamed pridefully.

"General, who sent you those lovely blooms?"

"One of the officers of the Aluminum Company of America remembers me all too graciously. Colonel, you know this man still thinks that my efforts resulted in the introduction of aluminum in our army."

"Well, aren't you guilty?"

"Only in a small way. I had to have the help of others." Brown made explanations. Colonel Knauer listened dutifully.

Then he stepped closer to the bouquet, the better to smell its fragrance. He turned back to his patient.

"General, corporations do have souls. I believe—that is, I wouldn't be surprised if the donor of that bouquet knows that what he claims is just about true. You should strive more for accuracy."

The General grinned like a schoolboy.

CHAPTER XXXVIII

Last Call

THREE days until August ended. Denver's citizens and
guests motored to and from Estes Park. They pressed
one another, for schoolrooms were calling students away
from the inspiring great outdoors. Once, the fighter on
Marion Street mused, he was of them. But envy did not
creep into his heart. This was as it should be; the old always
giving way to the young.

He entered Fitzsimons Hospital. On the second day of
September, the surgeons operated upon him. From their
examinations and diagnoses Colonels Knauer and Paul N.
Bowman knew that the strength that had been tapped,
tapped again and again, was not sufficient now. Rallying
was painfully slow. In four weeks there were four blood
transfusions.

On October 3, the three-story house received its master
again.

Through the days of autumn, with its smoky haze and
with its myriad of colors, the General read and heard of the
world's affairs. There could be no removal from his sick
bed in the homey den. It was the same when the old year
went out and the new came in. Of research he could do
little. And fewer letters. But now and then he had himself
propped up in the quartermaster bed so that he might
reply, shakily, to an inquiring friend. Into a new diary
went only a few brief entries.

Many prized possessions had been given away. To Colonel Knauer went, now, Tagunton's stamp for official
orders. Long ago Tagunton had ceased to give orders.

Far-away friends informed one another of the General's last-ditch fight. On January 17, 1939, General Moseley, in retirement at Atlanta, Georgia, wrote to a correspondent in reference to Brown:

"I have been devoted to him for many, many years and have served with him in the same regiment or at the same place on several occasions. . . . . When you see General Brown, please give him my affectionate best wishes. Tell him how I miss his letters."

By early February, the fingers of the feeble man were no longer able to use a pen, though he received dozens of letters from old, intimate, or casual well-wishers. Professor Boyd, heedful of every effort that drained the energy of the body of the patient, sent out the words, "The doctors tell me that he will not live more than a few weeks."

Doctors sometimes underestimate the will of the most willful patients. The General fought on.

The inventive mind remained alert. Neither Colonel Knauer nor Dr. Brown nor Mrs. McDaniel, nor others who came and went in their wholehearted ministration, should, the charge had decided, have to climb the stairs too often. At the right side of the bed stood a table supported by casters. Affixed to the edge of the top was a plain perforated board. The perforations varied in size so that any finger of the sick man's hand could twist the table with its papers, letters, and whatnot, to any desired angle.

Within reach of the left hand, on a wall cabinet, hung a large and heavy gold watch. Dangling from it was the chain with a bullet-charm attached, the bullet from Tagunton. Next to it projected a push button, wired to bells in rooms on the lower floors where Mrs. McDaniel or nurses might hear a buzzing command.

By the middle of March the commander seemed to be regaining lost ground. Once a day he was lifted from his bed and permitted to rest in his favorite chair. It was an heroic effort. Yet it was worthwhile. Spring was at hand, with life vibrating anew.

Colonel Knauer wanted the General to surrender the quartermaster bed. It should be supplanted with one which had a more comfortable mattress and springs which "gave" a bit. The man was obdurate. Colonel Knauer and Dr. Brown thought of a ruse, took Miss Grogan, registered nurse, and Miss Avers, practical nurse, into their confidence. They persuaded their patient that, by having a regular hospital bed, he could sit up in it without being moved to a chair. The ruse worked, and the new bed was ordered.

April came and went. Its floods of tears loosened the banks of snow on Colorado's greening hills, spilled into torrents which tore down bouldered pitches, raced into glazed canyons, and rolled, presumptuously, through flower-dotted meadowlands.

Like the snow, the General murmured to himself, he could not hold his position. Soon someone must take over for him. He gazed fondly into the adventurous past, glanced down the line of blue that guarded the frontier— and guarded it well. Thanks to Remington, to Charles Russell, to Paxson, to others, they of the frontier had been made immortal. He turned from yesterday as he found its life exhaled. He analyzed and compared.

Gone forever were the days when blue-coated troopers put spurs to their spirited mounts and thundered out from post and bivouac. But the cavalry could trot an average of eight miles an hour, hold an easy gallop of twelve miles an hour. . . . . Now dressed in khaki and olive drab, some cavalrymen still carried on with boots and spurs and horses. . . . .

Had not large numbers of cavalrymen, during the critical moments of Europe's Great War, marched seventy-five miles when called upon? And had they not reached the field of combat before the more readily informed infantry units, which consumed precious hours moving by truck and by rail? .... Had not the British, the French, and the Germans—and the Belgians and Russians, too—employed the cavalry at times to advance, to extend a flank, to turn the tide? Yes! .... Yes, it was all true. .....

Yet the troop pennon, once a challenging sign to war-crying red men, to other enemies, now is tacked upon a wall.

Many flags are furled. Dented bugles, bugles battered with usage, no longer sound the charge.

Armored demons, monsters of steel and of fabric, belchers of destruction, were bringing transfiguration to the most colorful and dashing branch of the army. There was a new word now—stream-lined. Thank God, the army looked ahead!

Here before him was the dressed-up official organ which Colonel Knauer had left, and which he must read and study again. Here was *The Command and General Staff School Quarterly,* replete with maps, diagrams, the latest index of periodicals on up-to-date strategy and equipment. It showed advancement. The army must advance!

What, ruminated the soldier of old, what would the next war be like? Would there have to be another war? Once there was a man and his horse—but now—but now. . . . .

Now the end was not far off. The last call.

There was no need of repeating the warning to those about him. And there was no longer reason to hesitate. Humbly, thankfully, he would meet his God. He had faith.

Two days before General Brown's summoning, Colonel Knauer wrote: "He had been talking fairly well at times, though more often in a whisper, and was oriented and rational. The day before death he was losing strength rapidly, though he managed a word or two now and then. He smiled often, and expressed his satisfaction, especially to his nurses whenever they made moves to rub his limbs or change his position in their efforts to make him more comfortable. His attitude during his last hours was like his attitude throughout life, one of unflinching courage, with courtesy to and great consideration of the efforts of all who surrounded him."

The sunny day of May 8 was the last. Mrs. McDaniel's cooking still tempted him, and he ate a hearty meal. The daily greetings were exchanged with Professor Boyd and his attentive wife. Colonel Knauer and Dr. Brown advised and encouraged their helpers, then went among other patients.

Twilight closed in, and the General was unconscious. For hours, the medical report reveals, he lay "in the same state, manifesting no outward evidence of discomfort with the exception of slowly increasing dyspnea." The two physicians, the nurses, Professor Boyd, and Mr. and Mrs. Mc-Daniel seated themselves in the den. Across their watchful faces crept shadows from the street light at the front of the house and from a screened lamp within.

Quietly, at ten-twenty-five, the cavalryman passed out of the West.

Funeral services were conducted in the Central Presbyterian Church by the pastor. Within a few days, all that remained mortal of General Brown, went back to West Point. With military honors, men of the United States Military Academy lowered the body into a grave which the alumnus of 1877 had long before chosen.

At Atlanta's Biltmore Hotel, early in May, still occupied with many duties, a retired army officer learned, belatedly, of General Brown's faint hope of living only a bit longer. On the eleventh he sat down to type, in the language of a perplexed soldier:

MY DEAR BROWN:
.... It is very difficult for me to realize that you have been immobilized..... I have been on many trips throughout the United States

working on the national situation to try to help. I have established an office here at this hotel. Sometimes when I am very tired, I rest in the morning.

Well do I remember that after your retirement, you established an office in your own home, and when you were late in the morning in going to work for Uncle Sam, the first thing you did was to write yourself an official letter of admonition.

I know of no member of the military establishment more fully devoted to the interests of his country than one, William C. Brown.

I hope this letter finds you in good spirits. Perhaps you can dictate a letter to me via your nurse. It is hard for me to picture you as being laid up even in the slightest degree, for throughout your whole service, I do not believe you lost a day.

My affectionate best wishes go out to you always.

Faithfully yours,
GEORGE VAN HORN MOSELEY

The letter was mailed promptly by the Major General. In Denver, the hour approached for the funeral of the man to whom it was addressed.

Sources

To offer even a partial list of sources for a definite biography of General Brown would add many printed pages to this book. As presented, the story itself reveals the versatility of the man and the need of gathering weighty material to support his writings. For some time Colonel Knauer has been painstakingly compiling his "Bibliography and References in Literature Concerning Brigadier General William Carey Brown, U. S. A.," to be presented with a volume of the Cavalryman's writings to the West Point Library. When completed, this list should serve student and scholar well.

The bulk of the large personal library archives of the General, including printed and unprinted documents of inestimable value, today reposes at the University of Colorado. Some important papers and books went, for safekeeping, to The National Archives and the Historical Section of the Army War College, while others were contributed to various historical societies.

The biographer had access to all these sources. He desired, in telling the story of the soldier and his times, to present as much new material as possible. Chief manuscript sources were: (1) diaries written by General Brown and his sisters; (2) orders and letters pertaining to the military record of General Brown; (3) personal correspondence to and from the General, his relatives, and friends. Few of the religiously kept diaries have been edited. That for the Bannock War of 1878 has been edited by the biographer for the Oregon Historical Society.

The General's lecture notes, his annotations and emendations on margins of maps, pamphlets, leaflets, newspaper and magazine clippings, and books, all filed meticulously, serve as invaluable guidance for the researcher.

Primary sources, rich as they may be, however, cannot give a full picture of the soldier and his relationship to army and country. Pursued over a broad field were the secondary, or printed, sources. Of these, governmental documents, Congressional Series, and other printed reports in the Library of Congress and elsewhere alone loom large.

Official service organs such as *The Cavalry Journal*, volumes of *The*

Army and Navy Journal, and of the *Journal of the Military Service Institution* (1880-1917) have been used extensively. *Military Affairs: Journal of the American Military Institute* offered consistently articles and notes of a scholarly nature on phases of war.

Authoritative historical quarterlies of national and regional scope provided up-to-the-minute studies by eminent researchers. Theses, published and unpublished, merited attention.

From newspapers as well as periodicals was gleaned much which threw light on the course of our nation's life and those responsible for our nation's destiny.

Technical works in the field of the military demanded patient scrutiny, for the science of war is ever changing. The number of these works is imposing, the new contrasting sharply with the old. Yet there are basic elements in tactics, strategy, discipline, administration, exercise, and instruction in weapons which weather all influences of time. Mechanization is not enough. The soldier still must be physically tough, highly trained, with indestructible morale. "Let us remember," says General Ben Lear, "that every effort by sea, by air and by ground is for one vital purpose—to advance the immortal foot soldier to take and hold the ground."

Thorough coverage of general histories and political works was imperative. America has cause for saluting more properly her historians who too often have been placed in rear ranks. Accounts of expeditions, wars, campaigns, and battles, whether treated objectively or subjectively, must all be weighed and balanced.

In biographies, autobiographies, memoirs, or reminiscences the researcher finds skeins as well as threads to weave his story with color and accuracy. Soldiers like General Brown do more than make history. They write it and preserve it.

From an overwhelming number of sources, a short "Selected Bibliography" of published accounts is given as representative of a wide survey. Emphasis is placed upon new works and writings of rare value.

Selected Bibliography

BOOKS

BAKER, JAMES H., and HAFEN, LEROY R., editors, *History of Colorado.* Vols. I-V. Linderman, Denver, 1927.

BALDWIN, ALICE BLACKWOOD, *Memoirs of Major General Frank D. Baldwin.* Wetzel Publishing Co., Inc., Los Angeles, 1929.

BRIMLOW, GEORGE F., *The Bannock Indian War of 1878.* The Caxton Printers, Ltd., Caldwell, Idaho, 1938.

BROSNAN, CORNELIUS J., *History of the State of Idaho.* Charles Scribner's Sons, New York, revised 1935.

CLARK, DAN E., *The West in American History.* Thomas Y. Crowell Co., New York, 1937.

CRUSE, THOMAS, *Apache Days and After.* The Caxton Printers, Ltd., Caldwell, Idaho, 1941.

CULLUM, GEORGE W., *Biographical Register of the Officers and Graduates of the U. S. Military Academy.* 7 vols. Originally published in 1868, now published every ten years.

DOWNEY, FAIRFAX, *Indian Fighting Army.* Charles Scribner's Sons, New York, 1941.

DUPUY, R. ERNEST, *Where They Have Trod: The West Point Tradition in American Life.* Frederick A. Stokes Co., New York, 1940.

DYER, JOHN P., *"Fightin' Joe" Wheeler,* "Southern Biography Series." Louisiana State University Press, 1941.

FEE, CHESTER A., *Chief Joseph: The Biography of a Great Indian.* Wilson-Erickson, Inc., New York, 1936.

FINERTY, JOHN F., *War-Path and Bivouac.* Press of Donohue & Henneberry, Chicago, 1890.

FOREMAN, GRANT, *A History of Oklahoma.* University of Oklahoma Press, Norman, Okla., 1942.

FRITZ, PERCY S., *Colorado, the Centennial State.* Prentice-Hall, New York, 1941.

FULLER, CLAUDE E., *The Breech-Loader in the Service.* Arms Reference Club of America, New York, 1933.

FUNSTON, FREDERICK, *Memories of Two Wars*. Charles Scribner's Sons, New York, 1911.

GANOE, WILLIAM A., *The History of the United States Army*. D. Appleton & Co., New York, 1924, revised 1942.

HEITMAN, FRANCIS B., *Historical Register and Dictionary of the U. S. Army*. Government Printing Office, Washington, 1903.

HICKS, JOHN D., *The American Nation: A History of the United States from 1865 to the Present*. Houghton Mifflin Co., Boston, 1941.

HUGHES, THOMAS, and BROWN, WILLIAM C., *Old Traverse des Sioux*. Herald Publishing Co., St. Peter, Minn., 1929.

KING, CAPTAIN CHARLES, *Campaigns with Crook and Stories of Army Life*. Harper & Bros., New York, 1905.

LOCKWOOD, FRANK C., *Pioneer Days in Arizona*. Macmillan Co., New York, 1932.

McWHORTER, LUCULLUS V., *Yellow Wolf: His Own Story*. The Caxton Printers, Ltd., Caldwell, Idaho, 1940.

MICHIE, PETER S., *Life and Letters of Emory Upton, Colonel of the 4th Regiment of Artillery, and Brevet Major-General, U. S. Army;* introduction by J. H. Wilson. D. Appleton & Co., New York, 1885.

MILES, NELSON A., *Recollections of General Nelson A. Miles*. The Werner Co., New York, Chicago, 1896.

PADELFORD, NORMAN J., *The Panama Canal in Peace and War*. Macmillan Co., New York, 1942.

PALMER, JOHN McAULEY, *America in Arms*. Yale University Press, New Haven, 1941.

PERSHING, JOHN J., *My Experiences in the World War*. 2 vols. Frederick A. Stokes Co., New York, 1931.

ROOSEVELT, THEODORE, *The Rough Riders*. Charles Scribner's Sons, New York, 1899.

RUSSELL, DON, *103 Fights and Scrimmages: The Story of General Reuben F. Bernard*. United States Cavalry Association, Washington, 1936.

SEGOVIA, L., *The Full Story of Aguinaldo's Capture, by L. Segovia of the Expeditionary Force;* translated from the original Spanish mss. by Frank de Thoma. Manila, P. I., 1902.

SEYMOUR, FLORA W., *Indian Agents of the Old Frontier*. D. Appleton-Century Co., New York, 1941.

SHINDLER, HENRY, *History of the Army Service Schools, Fort Leavenworth, Kansas*. Staff College Press, Fort Leavenworth, 1908.

THOMPSON, MARGARET, *High Trails of Glacier National Park*. The Caxton Printers, Ltd., Caldwell, Idaho, 1938.

TOMPKINS, FRANK, *Chasing Villa*. The Military Service Publishing Co., Harrisburg, Pa., 1934.

WILSON, RUFUS R., *Out of the West*. The Press of the Pioneers, New York, 1933.

WISSLER, CLARK, *Indians of the United States: Four Centuries of Their History and Culture*. "The American Museum of Natural History Science Series." Doubleday, Doran & Co., New York, 1940.

WYLLIE, ROBERT E., *Orders, Decorations and Insignia, Military and Civil*. Putnam, New York, 1941.

BOOKLETS AND PAMPHLETS

GATEWOOD, CHARLES B., JR., *Lieutenant Charles B. Gatewood, 6th U. S. Cavalry, and the Surrender of Geronimo*. Order of Indian Wars of the U. S., 1929.

KNAUER, JOHN G., "Death of Brigadier General William Carey Brown, Cav. Retired." Reprinted from *The Military Surgeon*, Vol. 85, No. 4, October, 1939.

MURRAY, GENEVIEVE, *Marias Pass*, "Studies in Northwest History, No. 12," Paul C. Phillips, general editor. State University of Montana, Missoula (no date).

ROWAN, ANDREW S., *How I Carried the Message to Garcia*. Walter D. Harney, San Francisco (no date).

TROXEL, O. C., and others, *Narrative of Service of the Tenth U. S. Cavalry in The Punitive Expedition*. Acme Printing Co., Tucson, Ariz., 1921.